Populism's Power

Populism's Power

Radical Grassroots Democracy in America

LAURA GRATTAN

OXFORD
UNIVERSITY PRESS

Oxford University Press is a department of the University of
Oxford. It furthers the University's objective of excellence in research,
scholarship, and education by publishing worldwide.

Oxford   New York
Auckland   Cape Town   Dar es Salaam   Hong Kong   Karachi
Kuala Lumpur   Madrid   Melbourne   Mexico City   Nairobi
New Delhi   Shanghai   Taipei   Toronto

With offices in
Argentina   Austria   Brazil   Chile   Czech Republic   France   Greece
Guatemala   Hungary   Italy   Japan   Poland   Portugal   Singapore
South Korea   Switzerland   Thailand   Turkey   Ukraine   Vietnam

Oxford is a registered trade mark of Oxford University Press
in the UK and certain other countries.

Published in the United States of America by
Oxford University Press
198 Madison Avenue, New York, NY 10016

Library of Congress Cataloging-in-Publication Data
Names: Grattan, Laura, author.
Title: Populism's power : radical grassroots democracy in America / Laura Grattan.
Description: New York, NY : Oxford University Press, 2016. | Includes bibliographical references and index.
Identifiers: LCCN 2015023497 | ISBN 9780190277628 (hardback : acid-free paper) | ISBN 9780190277635
(paperback : acid-free paper)
Subjects: LCSH: Democracy—United States—History. | Populism—United States—History. | Political
participation—United States—History. | Social movements—United States—History. | BISAC:
POLITICAL SCIENCE / Political Ideologies / General.
Classification: LCC JK1726 .G72 2016 | DDC 320.56/620973—dc23 LC record available
at http://lccn.loc.gov/2015023497

1 3 5 7 9 8 6 4 2
Printed in the United States of America
on acid-free paper

*For my parents, whose families worked on the railroads
in Kansas and in the auto factories in Detroit*

CONTENTS

ACKNOWLEDGMENTS

This book is an imperfect expression of the relationships and conversations that brought the ideas in these pages to life. First and foremost, I am grateful to Rom Coles and Peter Euben for their mentoring and friendship. In their years together at Duke, they created spaces for practicing political theory that refused to let it rest easily in its academic ruts. From Rom, I learned to see activism and theory as world-building practices that only ever thrive through their entwinements in each other. From Peter, I came to see political theory as a practice that we undertake in our everyday engagements with the cultural texts that shape social and political imagination. Peter's appreciation of the tragedy of political theory and Rom's shared love of Cohen's music also helped shape a central hope that animates this book: "There is a crack, a crack in everything / That's how the light gets in."

The light has also found its way to this book through the generous labor of colleagues who read the entire manuscript at one stage or another and some chapters more than once: Jason Frank, George Shulman, Mark Reinhardt, Roxanne Euben, Kevin Bruyneel, Ali Aslam, Lena Zuckerwise, Carol Daugherty, Joel Krieger, and three anonymous reviewers. Many others have provided irreplaceable feedback on various chapters: Harry Boyte (to whom I am grateful for years of conversation on populism), David McIvor (a good friend and colleague, who came through more than once with the intellect and savvy to help me navigate bumps along the road), Nora Hanagan, and colleagues at the Newhouse Center for Humanities who helped a political theorist write a cultural studies chapter on Chevrolet and Cohen (especially Eugenie Brinkema, Jessie Morgan-Owens, Patricia Melzer, Nikki Greene, Yasmine Ramadan, and David Olsen). At the risk of overlooking people whose shards of light have inflected this book, I am grateful to the array of colleagues whose comments and conversations about the book at one stage or another have helped me sharpen my ideas and changed my thinking on key issues: especially Susan Bickford, Tom Spragens, Kenan

Ferguson, Lawrie Balfour, Cristina Beltrán, P. J. Brendese, Joel Schlosser, Paul Apostolidis, Holloway Sparks, Jane Gordon, Craig Borowiak, Alisa Kessel, Stefan Dolgert, David Rice, Winter Brown, Christine Lee, Stephen White, Joel Olson, Joan Tronto, Kathy Ferguson, Jeffrey Becker, Vernon Johnson, Peggy Levitt, and Cathy Davidson.

Angela Chnapko has somehow made it feel easy to turn the fruits of these conversations into a book. I am grateful for her enthusiasm, steady voice of encouragement, and bottomless well of timely and sharp advice. Princess Ikatekit has also provided generous and seamless support during the production process. Finally, I am grateful to Favianna Rodriguez for stirring my imagination at the edges of art and activism and for designing the cover of this book!

A life of being a student and teacher brings with it many debts. My understanding of politics and life has been sharpened over the years by many people, not least of all my early mentors, Cathy Melanson, Joel Schwartz, Lisa Grimes, and John Dedrick. During my years at Duke, I was fortunate to work with political theory faculty who were not only outstanding scholars in their fields, but also provided an extraordinarily supportive environment. I am especially grateful for the opportunity to participate in two working groups with Ruth Grant at Duke's Kenan Institute for Ethics. Ruth's voice has remained with me and challenged my thinking over the years. Likewise, my graduate cohort remain sources of support and provocation. I am fortunate to continue to learn from them as they find ways to connect their academic and professional lives to their political aspirations and strivings. At Wellesley, I have found tremendous support from my colleagues in Political Science, especially Hahrie Han, Stacie Goddard, and Roxanne Euben. I am grateful for the friendship and intellectual energy of many other faculty on campus—especially those have been involved in the Project on Public Leadership and Action—and for students who truly push me to find better ways to do political theory.

I would not be a political theorist today, nor could I have written this book, if not for my engagements with two networks at the intersections of theory and practice. My time as a research assistant at the Kettering Foundation directly influenced my decision to pursue a career in academia by introducing me to faculty who are connecting scholarship with public life. During graduate school, I had the good fortune to deepen my exchanges with many of them through a working group on deliberative democracy and civic engagement in higher education. At that same time, seven years of community organizing with Durham CAN (Congregations, Associations, and Neighborhoods) and Duke Organizing was fundamental to my growth as a political theorist. Organizing helped me keep a part of myself "outside" the academy, as I worked with community activists, service employees, students, and faculty who were practicing political theory in their struggles to make Durham and Duke "livable wage" communities.

Their questions, anger, passions, and provocations run throughout the pages of this book.

I have several friends to thank for helping me figure out what it is I'm doing at the intersections of theory, practice, and life. Ali Aslam has been a constant in ordinary and extraordinary times: a patient ear for my everyday neuroses, a sounding board for my ideas (at their best and worst), and both counsel and cheerleader as life demands. P. J. Brendese has been a kindred spirit in lost times (which, to be clear, is most of the time), never failing to sharpen my sense of life's tragicomedies and its possibilities. In a few short years, Lena Zuckerwise has become one of my role models in political theory and life: I don't know how I made it through over three decades without her generous spirit, sharp wit, and wickedly keen perspective. I am thankful for the many years I have been able to rely on Jessica Levy's friendship and learn from her hard-won wisdom about resilience and laughter. Finally, I owe a special debt of gratitude to Enrique Urueta for reminding me about the stakes of populism in a moment of doubt.

Railroad companies and car manufacturers figure as villains in this story, but I come from a family of industrial producers in Kansas and Detroit. For my family still living in "the brave, the bold, the battered / heart of Chevrolet," the stakes of democracy's emancipatory promise have rarely been more urgent. I hope this project does some justice in conveying my debts to those who built Chevy's America, along with the hope I find in struggles—then and now—to transform it. On a more personal note, I am forever grateful to my parents, my brothers and their families (especially Matthew), and my Canadian family for being a steady source of love and support.

I am ever conscious of the ways in which I am the biggest exception to many of my claims in these pages. Fortunately, in politics and love, we don't act alone. Like me, this project would be less complete and far less ambitious were it not for Fiona Barnett, my tech support, creative director, and guide to the edges of my imagination. Thank you for encouraging me to take risks both small and impossible and for supporting me every imperfect step of the way.

Portions of this book appeared in different form as: "Pierre Bourdieu and Populism: The Everyday Politics of Outrageous Resistance," in *The Good Society*, Vol. 21, No. 2, 2012, pages 194–218. Copyright © 2012, The Pennsylvania State University Press. Used by permission of The Pennsylvania State University Press; "Populism and the Rebellious Cultures of Democracy," in *Radical Future Pasts: Untimely Political Theory*, ed. Romand Coles, Mark Reinhardt, and George Schulman (Lexington: The University Press of Kentucky, 2014). Reprinted with permission.

Populism's Power

Introduction

Populism and the Paradox of Democracy

On one side, then, we face the problem of peoples who do not aspire
to democratic freedom and, on the other, of democracies we do not
want—"free" peoples who bring to power theocracies, empires, terror
or hate-filled regimes of ethnic cleansing, gated communities, citizenship stratified by ethnicity or immigration status, aggressively neoliberal
postnational constellations, or technocracies promising to fix social ills
by circumventing democratic processes and institutions.
> —WENDY BROWN, *"We Are All Democrats Now"*

Like the American Dream itself, ever present and never fully realized,
populism lives too deeply in our fears and expectations to be trivialized
or replaced. We should not speak solely within its terms, but without it,
we are lost.
> —MICHAEL KAZIN, The Populist Persuasion

The twenty-first century has seen a resurgence of populist movements across the
world. *¡Ya basta!* echoed throughout Latin America at the outset of the century as
people joined massive popular uprisings against neoliberal policies. Antiausterity
protests and right-wing nationalist uprisings emerged as rival responses to the
global financial crisis that shook the Eurozone a decade into the new millennium. Student movements in Chile and Montreal were flashpoints for worldwide
student organizing to demand access to affordable higher education. In South
Africa, grassroots organizations formed the Poor People's Alliance to intensify
postapartheid struggles for land and housing. During the Arab Spring, streets
throughout the Middle East and North Africa rang with voices declaring, "The

people want to topple the regime." These enactments of people power resonated a few years later in Hong Kong, where mass assemblies wielded a rainbow of umbrellas against state violence in their struggle for democratic representation.

In the United States, a quick snapshot of grassroots populism in the twenty-first century reveals an offbeat cast: Christian fundamentalists, vigilante border patrollers, the Tea Party, Occupy Wall Street, broad-based community organizers, undocumented DREAMers, grassroots ecopopulists, and many more. Behind a cacophony of voices and styles of expression, populist actors promise to return democracy to its roots in the power of the people. Populist rhetoric and practice pit the people against the establishment in a struggle over the future of democracy. That struggle has been ongoing in American politics since the nation's revolutionary inception. Centuries later, people have not yet ceased to aspire to popular power when democratic politics strays from its roots. Populism's grassroots resurgence thus raises questions that are central to American democracy and to this book: Can twenty-first-century populist movements wrest meaningful power from elites and transform hegemonic structures and dynamics that threaten democracy? If populists can return power to the people, what kind of democracy will the people establish? Under what conditions, that is, can grassroots populism democratize power and politics today?

Mainstream media pundits routinely dismiss populist aspirations to power. Since the global financial meltdown hit the United States in 2008, for example, news headlines have charged populists with fomenting anger and instability. "Will Populist Rage Hurt Corporate America?" fretted *BusinessWeek*. A *National Review* columnist reproached those who called for a moratorium on foreclosures: "Populist Rage over Foreclosures Doesn't Justify a Breakdown in the Rule of Law."[1] Others depict populist "backlash" as relatively harmless, little more than a passing storm to be weathered. First the ominous forecast: "Populist Outrage Is Back—Ready?" Then the welcome news that "Today's Populism May Be Gone Tomorrow," and the nation's emotional barometer can return to its civil standard until the next high-pressure system hits.[2] A sign of today's individualized politics, some observers have even begun to treat populist anger as a mood we can now personalize in our digitally mediated lives. "Got Outrage? More Fodder to Feed Your Inner Populist," promised one cbs.com exposé on billions of dollars in executive bonuses at bailed-out banks. Not to be outdone, *Newsweek* headlined a review of a new iPhone videogame called "Squash the $treet": "Populist Outrage—There's an App for That."[3] When people do mobilize collectively for longer than a news cycle, analysts start looking for the puppet-master behind populism. "Who Will Be This Depression's Populist Demagogue?" a Gawker columnist asked once mainstream media finally admitted that the Tea Party wasn't going away. A couple of years later, CNN reassured a viewing public befuddled by Occupy Wall Street's apparent disorganization: "Occupy Wall Street Is Going Nowhere without Leadership."[4]

Decades of liberal scholarship have reinforced these views. Historians, political scientists, and scholars of constitutional law have engaged in an ongoing battle to discredit populism. Writing texts with titles like *Liberalism against Populism* and "Populism versus Democracy," liberal scholars charge populists with deifying the voice of the people. According to common liberal accounts, populists stir up faith in the impossible unity of popular will, which can only be enacted by transcending the mediating institutions of representative government—for example, individual rights, minority protections, deliberative procedures, and separation of powers. At their most sympathetic, liberal scholars characterize populism as apolitical and episodic, but acknowledge its periodic expressions of popular unrest as signals that some policy or procedure may be in need of reform. At their most fearful, liberal scholars warn that populism has serious antidemocratic consequences. Populists often foment reactionary backlash against elites and marginalized groups. To achieve their fantasies of unity, moreover, populists rely on antistatist tactics, for example, throwing a wrench in the operation of representative institutions and procedures or acclaiming autocratic leaders who circumvent them altogether. Liberalism's party line on populism thus treats it as an "empty" or "absurd" but potentially dangerous wish: that is, an illusion of popular democracy that, all too often, turns the people against democracy.[5]

Left critical theorists have added to the pessimism about populism. Pierre Bourdieu, for example, repeatedly evokes the "populist illusion" to dismiss the common "methodological voluntarism and optimism which define the populist vision of 'the people' as a site of subversion, or at least, resistance." According to Bourdieu's disciplinary account of social reproduction, people are habituated overwhelmingly to reinforce the status quo in our everyday speech and actions, and even in our acts of resistance.[6] Bourdieu's dim view of populism would, for example, support a common leftist critique of the 2008 election of Barack Obama: after he won the presidency, the mobilized grassroots base that had rallied around candidate Obama as a figure of "Hope" and "Change" went back to their private lives with the faith that President Obama would act as their political savior. Instead, he has ruled with the "soul of a technocrat," continued many of his predecessors' neoliberal economic policies, and expanded the executive prerogative carved out by the administration of George W. Bush.[7] If the project of democracy founders today because people living in capitalist, managerial states "do not aspire to democratic freedom," Wendy Brown adds, it is no less endangered by mobilized peoples who bolster "democracies we do not want."[8] Left theorists may depart from liberalism's party line against populism, then, but they too doubt that populism can be separated from its longtime equation with "democracies we do not want": for example, nationalism, racism, masculinism, demagoguery, and imperialism.

In the wake of American populism's "conservative capture" during the Nixon and Reagan eras, and given its ubiquity as a mainstream buzzword of politicians and pundits, it is understandable that democratic theorists and many activists have been eager to abandon populism to right-wing demagogues and mega-media spin doctors.[9] Indeed, before Occupy Wall Street captured public attention, populism's most visible and vociferous energies in the United States had seemed dedicated in recent decades to shoring up the boundaries of the body politic and reinforcing hegemonic forms of capitalist, state, and social power that narrow the horizons of democracy. After over half a decade on the political stage, moreover, the Tea Party remains influential: it celebrates neoliberal economic policies, while narrowing access to citizenship through border policing, voter suppression, and campaigns to scale back reproductive rights. In an era marked by the unprecedented movement of capital, commodities, and labor across borders, finally, it seems difficult to discount Richard Hofstadter's account of populism as a "paranoid style" of politics endemic to American political culture. Facing the inevitable vagaries of capitalism, Hofstadter argues, populists cling to the security of their cultural status to make up for their insecurity in the economic realm.[10] As capitalist dislocations intensify and nation-states find it harder to remain accountable to their citizens, populist rhetoric will undoubtedly remain a recurring tool to mobilize right-wing, reactionary backlash. At a time when democracy is increasingly antipopulist and successful populisms have largely been antidemocratic, perhaps it is misguided to turn to populism as a resource for radical democratic theory and practice.

I am not ready to draw that conclusion. In this book, I argue that grassroots populisms have a crucial role to play in democratizing power and politics in America. Radical democratic actors, from grassroots revolutionaries to insurgent farmers and laborers to agitators for the New Deal, Civil Rights, and the New Left, have historically drawn on the language and practices of populism. In doing so, they have cultivated people's rebellious aspirations not just to resist power, but to share in power, and to do so in pluralistic, egalitarian ways across social and geographic borders. These experiments in *democratizing populism* have enacted popular power in ways that open "the people" to contest and redefinition and create spaces for new visions and practices of democracy to emerge. Missing from academic and public discourse on populism, however, is an account of how populist actors enact popular power. Instead, discussions of populism focus on what observers see as the twin processes of resistance and identification, that is, how populist actors mobilize popular identification in opposition to a common enemy.[11] Without a systematic analysis of how populist movements develop the political capacities of grassroots actors and experiment with alternative institutions and practices of popular power, we can predict little about whether and how populism can democratize power and politics today.

The challenges to constituting popular power are steep and endemic. Trends toward de-democratization over the last few decades now threaten the lives and well-being of most people in the United States and on the planet. Central to these trends, the unchecked rise of global corporate and financial capitalism since the late 1970s has resulted in devastating economic inequalities.[12] In the United States, these conditions have been abetted by democratic institutions that appear more invested in capitalism's vitality than in citizens. Indeed, a neoliberal vision of politics has become pervasive since the Reagan era: market principles increasingly shape not only economic policy, but also decision making on myriad issues of public concern.[13] As neoliberal processes insulate politics from popular control, the resulting picture is grim: decimated social services; overcrowded and abandoned schools; shrinking access to higher education; gentrified cities; bloated and mismanaged prisons; open attacks on unions; slashed benefits and swollen pools of flexible labor; and environmental hazards that threaten the planet but first promise to wreak havoc on those with the fewest resources and least power.

Even as American political institutions harmonize their interests with the imperatives of the proverbial "free market," the global character of capitalist power has contributed to what Wendy Brown calls a "proliferation of walling" around and within nation-states anxious to mask their waning sovereignty.[14] Deregulation has accompanied and enabled vast circulations of capital, labor, resources, weapons, and communications technologies across nation-state borders. In response to recurrent threats (both real and manufactured), the US government *has* been willing to flex its muscle through perpetual war, intensified border securitization, and militarized policing.[15] State power in these areas is reinforced by the latest face of white supremacy: most notably, discourses of criminality and illegality aimed at blacks, Latinos, and immigrants in the United States and discourses of trafficking and terrorism aimed at enemies beyond its borders. Amid celebratory claims that America is fast on its way to becoming a postracial society, scholars have documented a "racialized state of precarity" in the United States. The undersides of today's security state, they show, have manifested with particular violence for those affected by American militarism in the Middle East and global South and by racial profiling, police brutality, mass incarceration, and immigrant detention at home.[16]

At a time when people in America face a heightened sense of insecurity, it is more difficult than ever to see political solutions to our problems. The privatization of politics obscures the complex sources of systemic wrongs and leaves political actors with few obvious levers of accountability to redress their grievances. Capitalist institutions and ideologies, moreover, have an unparalleled influence in shaping American political culture. Today, mainstream media and new social media combine to deliver dominant cultural messages to us anytime, anywhere. Neoliberal common sense—which celebrates the virtues of productivity, adaptability, competition, and freedom of choice—is thus deeply embedded in everyday life. It invests us in individualistic, passive modes of citizenship and reinforces socioeconomic divisions that forestall collective identification and action.[17] Today's individuals are burdened with the impossible fantasy of taking responsibility for bettering our own lives in the midst of conditions that, with significant variance, profoundly disempower most people. When that fails, it has proven easier to blame others or to grow cynical about the possibilities of politics than to question the free-market, consumer ideals that have framed the limits of our personal and political aspirations.[18] What we face today, then, is not only a grim forecast for our future, but also diminished democratic aspirations for changing it.

These de-democratizing trends are not inevitable. Dismissals of populism, however, reinforce the gnawing sense that they are. When liberal and left scholars roll out their litany of charges against populism, it often sounds as if they are really cautioning us to chasten our hopes and desires for democracy. Suspicious of populism's unruliness, its liberal critics insist that the institutions and procedures of constitutional government are sufficient to represent the will of the people—or they would be if we could implement this or that liberal scheme to perfect liberal democracy.[19] Such dismissals of populism have discursive power: they reinforce liberalism as the end of democracy. Left critical theorists have diagnosed the missteps in liberal theories of democracy. Liberal theorists assume that institutional proceduralism can rationalize contemporary forms of power that—in reality—not only defy, but also shape, liberal governments. Liberals also rely on the ideal of a rational citizenry, or at least one that sublimates collective energies to individual strivings for commodious living.[20] If these assumptions are erroneous, it leaves liberal theory ill-equipped to respond adequately to the conjoined threats of neoliberal dynamics that routinely disrupt people's everyday lives and reactionary populisms that recur periodically in response.

Left critical theorists, however, pen their own cautionary tales about the allure of democratic possibility. They provoke democratic theorists to wrestle with difficult questions about the viability of democracy as an emancipatory ideal in the twenty-first century. As Wendy Brown observes, "Democracy has historically unparalleled global popularity today yet has never been more conceptually footloose and substantively hollow."[21] Radical democrats who contest (neo)liberal perversions of democracy, adds Jodi Dean, must also contend with capitalist cultural dynamics that have captured the Left's rhetoric of pluralism, voice, expression, creativity, and transformation. When scholars and activists respond to the failures of democracy by calling for more democracy, Dean concludes, they mount scant resistance to structural divisions that preserve democracy for elites.

In the very same move, radical democrats sustain a flexible symbol of democracy "that can be filled in, substantialized, by fundamentalisms, nationalisms, populisms, and conservatisms diametrically opposed to social justice and economic equality."[22]

One senses a collective despair in the writings of radical democratic scholars, who have spent decades analyzing de-democratizing trends that have largely worsened. "What could be more of a fantasy," asks Wendy Brown, "than the notion of subordinating global capitalist economy, and its shaping of social, political, cultural, and ecological life, to democratic political rule, or for that matter, to any political rule?"[23] In a similar vein, Sheldon Wolin has come to conceptualize democracy as "fugitive." Contrary to popular opinion, he writes, "Contemporary democracy is not hegemonic but beleaguered and permanently in opposition to structures it cannot command." Wolin insists that democracy is not a characteristic of today's managerial, capitalist megastates, which evade modern limits on state power to seek a near total control over social life. It is, rather, an "ephemeral phenomenon" enacted by "those who have no means of redress other than to risk collectivizing their small bits of power."[24] He locates democracy's fugitive energies in episodic moments in which people come together to address common problems: primarily in local contexts, such as schools, community health centers, and community policing, but also in broader social movements, such as nineteenth-century Populism, the Civil Rights movement, and environmentalism.[25] If Wolin rescues democracy from hierarchical and uniform logics of rule, he concludes grimly that "what is truly at stake politically"—that is, the "heterogeneity, diversity, and multiple selves" that constitute popular power—are "no match" for contemporary modes of power.[26]

My own ambivalence about democracy is what returns me to populism. My engagements with populist culture and politics do not, in the final analysis, lead me to overcome that ambivalence. Instead, akin to Wolin, I find in populism resources that sustain a sharper disposition toward democratic hope amid conditions that daily threaten to reinforce despair. In this respect, I am at once more pessimistic and more optimistic than Wolin. I am more troubled than he is about the internal limits on every enactment of popular power. No democratic moment—including the ones Wolin identifies as exemplary of fugitive democracy—has succeeded in generating popular power without retaining investments in social hierarchies that reinforce institutionalized power and powerlessness. Rather than rescue democracy from logics of ruling and being ruled, then, I ask what forms democracy's fugitive energies must take. That is, what dispositions, practices, institutions, and discourses might cultivate pluralistic, egalitarian forms of popular power? In their struggles to enact popular power, moreover, what strategies should political actors adopt vis-à-vis institutions of capitalism and the state: when should democratic actors engage and disengage established institutions, and which institutions should they reinforce, disrupt, or reconstitute? In asking this last set of questions, I am more hopeful than Wolin that everyday actors can build on democracy's fugitive energies to democratize broader structures of power.

Democracy has long been a powerful fantasy guiding American politics. It has animated the desires and visions of white supremacists and black radicals, patriarchs and feminists, capitalists and socialists, nativists and immigrants. Cultivating the fantasy of democracy remains vital given conditions that attenuate our aspirations to see—let alone participate in—politics as a popular endeavor. By reclaiming populism as a resource for radical democracy, I aim to counter both the cynicism wrought by external challenges to democracy and the paralysis that takes hold of many on the left when they realize that every democratic act carries its own foreclosures.

DEFINITIONS AND PARADOXES

Populism has long been viewed as a barometer of democracy's health and future prospects. And yet it has been notoriously difficult to define. Few political actors call themselves populists, and there is no canon of populist writing by the hands of reformers or revolutionaries. It has instead been the work of scholars to spill ink over populism. They agree that populism is a recurring feature of modern politics, one that emerges in disparate geopolitical contexts, gives voice to competing ideological visions, and manifests in a variety of organizational forms. The earliest uses of the term are associated with agrarian radicalism in the late nineteenth century, most notably, Russian *narodnichestvo*, which celebrated the peasantry as the engine of socialist revolution, and the Populist movement in the United States, a mass insurgency of farmers and workers that sought alternatives to monopoly capitalism. The "canon" of populist case studies include the authoritarian populism of Latin America, embodied in the charismatic leadership of Argentina's Juan Perón; the rise of right-wing parties across Europe, exemplified by Jörg Haider's Freedom Party of Austria; popular resistance to apartheid in South Africa, mobilized by the coalitional politics of the United Democratic Front; the antigovernment rhetoric of the American Right, spurred by the white, working-class anxieties of George Wallace and the neoliberal ideology of the Reagan Revolution; and various grassroots social movements, ranging from the antisecular Christian Right to the multicultural New Left.

This range of precedents, however, has left scholars unable to reach any consensus on what delimits populism as a theoretical construct. They define populism, variably, as a flexible style of rhetoric, a strategy of electoral mobilization, a distinctive form of contentious politics, or more ineffably, as a political syndrome, a cultural ethos, or even a zeitgeist.[27] Populism's ideological flexibility and mal-leable form have driven many scholars to abstraction in search of unifying char-acteristics that define populism across all cases.[28] Some have recently converged around the claim that populism is a "thin-centered ideology," valorizing the peo-ple as a unified sovereign body in opposition to an identifiable, corrupt elite.[29] Or perhaps populism's people can be no more than an "empty signifier," as Ernesto Laclau has long insisted, resting populist politics not on a substantial popular will, but on the groundless ground of indeterminate demands.[30]

Populism may defy firm theoretical grasp. But it would be unthinkable with-out the widely held belief in popular sovereignty, the notion that the people are the fundamental source of authority in modern democratic politics.[31] Rather than raising the banner of populism, so-called populist actors speak the language of popular sovereignty—"Power to the people!" "The people have spoken." "Whose democracy? Our democracy!"—and often claim to be true democrats. Popular sovereignty is an endangered ideal today: it is assailed on one side by neoliberal rationalities that encourage passive citizenship and on the other by critics who worry that, in confusing popular power with sovereign power, modern democracy implicates exclusionary peoples in projects of mastery.[32] If popular sovereignty often veers toward one of these two poles, modern democ-racy's legitimating logic is nonetheless riddled with paradox. Populist moments emerge from and reveal an irresolvable tension at the heart of democracy: the fact that the people is indeterminate, that is, never at one with itself. Jason Frank characterizes this familiar paradox of democratic peoplehood by contending that the people are always "at once a constituent and a constituted power."[33] They are both constituted by an existing order—its laws, institutions, and discourses—and capable of emerging from the margins of recognized speech and action to withdraw their authority from that order or to authorize new rules of the game.

This democratic paradox, Bonnie Honig adds, is not contained to narratives of founding or times of extraordinary crisis in a body politic; it is the ordinary condition of democratic politics.[34] The daily activities of collective life—granting certificates of marriage and citizenship; making laws and policies regarding edu-cation, policing, reproductive health, or environmental protection; adjudicating issues from taxation to civil rights—are political sites that "(re)shape a multitude into a people, daily." The decisions made in these arenas routinely "recapture" or "reinterpellate" citizens into the "laws, norms, and expectations of [a] regime." They are also potential sites of contestation at which new democratic peoples and forms can emerge. What Honig calls the "vicious circularity" of the democratic paradox reminds us that we can never fully disentangle law from violence, or cre-ativity from destruction.[35] In other words, she insists on what Danielle Allen calls "imperfect democracy": every constituent moment, every democratic act has its "dissonant remainders," the "byproducts of political loss" that trouble the conceit of unity.[36]

Emerging from the paradox of popular sovereignty, populist moments raise two crucial questions for any theory and practice of democracy: Who are the people? And how should the people enact their power in politics?[37] The first question has to do with collective identity, that is, the boundaries establishing who belongs and who does not belong to a democratic polity, and the practices of social recognition and disavowal that contest the terms of inclusion and exclusion. Populism is widely characterized in both academic and public discourse by its symbolic and affectively charged practices of identification, which arouse the people on behalf of a common vision of collective identity and political life and either unsettle or shore up the borders of politics and democracy. It is less common to view populism in terms of its second, equally vital question: how do the people embody the ideal of popular sovereignty, that is, how do they enact their power collectively through institutions and practices of democratic self-governance? Modern democratic theory and practice have historically placed limits on the people's power, relying on constitutional norms and procedures to rationalize the unruly, conflicting interests of a multitude of particular individuals and to mediate between the people and government. It is against this backdrop that populist movements have emerged, time and again, not only to expose elite abuses of power, and often, institutionally embedded forms of social and political hierarchy, but also to experiment with alternative institutions and practices of popular power: from electoral strategies of referendums and recall, to cooperative economic and political institutions, to broad-based, coalitional forms of community organizing and social movement politics. Populist moments thus call us repeatedly to the work of interrogating which institutions and practices constrain the people's power and which shape people's political aspirations in ways that enable them to play a greater role in steering and, at times, transforming democratic politics.

I do not equate popular power with democracy. What I do argue is that America's grassroots populist tradition harbors a persistent democratizing aspiration. All populisms animate the ideal of popular sovereignty by mobilizing the aspirations of ordinary people to exercise power over their everyday lives and their collective fate. If elites and grassroots actors alike have used populist rhetoric and practices to regulate people's aspirations to power—for example, by turning them toward reactionary or assimilationist ends that fail to disrupt the status quo—I develop a theory of *aspirational democratic populism* in this book. Aspirational democratic populisms cultivate people's rebellious aspirations not only to share in power, but to do so in pluralistic, egalitarian ways across established horizons that restrict democracy. The concept of aspirational democratic populism allows me to emphasize three claims that are central to my arguments about populism and democracy. First, by aspirational populism, I indicate that populist politics has to do with the aspirations of actual people. In other words, populism—unlike, say, liberal proceduralism or technocracy—is openly premised on its ability to reach ordinary people. By studying how populist movements engage people in their everyday lives, I evaluate how populism not only animates but, in many cases, durably shapes people's aspirations to power. Second, by calling democracy aspirational, I mean to insist that democracy is not defined by the existing institutions and procedures of liberal, capitalist governance. If hegemonic powers have historically shaped visions of democracy, so have popular efforts to imagine and enact better forms of democracy beyond the status quo. Given that popular enactments of democracy reinforce many forms of power and powerlessness, democratization involves ongoing efforts to cultivate aspirations to popular power in emerging social groups. Finally, the central claim of this book is that populist politics can play a crucial role in democratizing power and politics today. For this to happen, scholars and activists will need to negotiate populism's dangers and distinguish which kinds of populist rhetoric and practice can democratize people's aspirations to enact popular power.

AMERICA'S POPULIST IMAGINARY

To say, with Michael Kazin, that populism "lives deeply in our fears and expectations" is to acknowledge America's ambivalence about populist rhetoric and practice—which arouse "the people" on behalf of projects that alternately create openings in or foreclose the horizons of democracy. Yet, Kazin is right in two senses that we—inheritors of America's contested populist tradition, as well as democratic theorists and actors in other contexts—are lost without ongoing efforts to evaluate populism's resources for democratization. First, populism's relationship to the paradox of popular sovereignty carries a political imperative. Democracy today faces severe threats of foreclosure, in part, because nominally democratic peoples, including many populisms, do reinforce the de-democratizing modes of power that constitute them. But in light of this ever-present danger, the inherent instability of the people enables, indeed demands, persistent efforts to narrate and enact more rebellious visions of populism, again and again, as part of radical democratic struggles to reconstitute the terms of collective identification and democratic politics.

In the United States, populism has been at the heart of iterated efforts to reconstitute the people and democracy from the Revolutionary period through today. If ruling classes and reactionaries have relied on populist rhetoric to shore up the nation's white, middle-class, masculine center, populism's history is also the story of radical democratic struggles to democratize power and politics. This is a second reason American democracy, in particular, cannot abandon populism. The remainders of populism's more rebellious moments live in the present, inspiriting, even as they are reworked by, democratic theorists and activists. We see this legacy in stubborn demands—for example, by Occupy Wall Street and the New Bottom Line coalition—to democratize wealth as part of efforts to democratize power and politics. We see it in efforts to preserve and innovate long-standing traditions of worker cooperatives and public work amid the relentless privatization of work and politics. We see it in the broad-based community organizing of groups such as the Industrial Areas Foundation and PICO National Network. In *America beyond Capitalism*, Gar Alperovitz calls these efforts examples of "twenty-first century populism," likening their visions of "pluralist commonwealth" to the cooperative commonwealth of the nineteenth-century Populist movement.[38] Populism's unwieldy past is thus embodied in the present, in some instances narrowing the horizons of democracy, but in many others acting as a reminder that democracy is not the proprietary right of any established social order, nor is it synonymous with any form or theory of political economy or government.

What I refer to in this book as America's *populist imaginary* has historically been a prominent countercurrent to the liberal, capitalist social imaginary that has been dominant in the United States. The concept of social imaginaries, as Charles Taylor describes it, points to the shared "ways in which people imagine their social existence, how they fit together with others, the expectations that are normally met, and the deeper normative notions and images that underlie these expectations."[39] Social imaginaries are not simply ideas. They are produced by and inhabit an array of technologies, institutions, and everyday practices; broad discourses and local idioms; high culture and low culture; media, music, sports, religion, and politics; and sundry emerging counterpublics. America's liberal, capitalist social imaginary, for example, contains ubiquitous norms, such as individual rights, contractual relationships, and social mobility, that underlie our daily actions and aspirations in areas as varied as marriage, consumption, work, education, welfare policy, and representative government. America's populist imaginary, I will argue, harbors a more robust notion of popular sovereignty, one that has historically been embodied in a motley tradition of social movements that have cultivated rhetorics and practices of enacting popular power. This alternative imaginary also resonates with people in their daily lives, for example, through voluntary cooperative efforts in neighborhoods and communities, religious practices that bear witness to radical equality, and political spin pitting the people against elites. If populist moments happen only periodically—and, often, episodically—America's populist imaginary is available to be picked up and reworked by disparate populist actors who hope to engage people in political efforts to contest the terms of collective identification and democracy.

I situate this study of populism in the United States, in part, because American scholars and activists have historically given voice to a unique tradition of radical democratic populism. Such storied traditions are missing in other national and regional contexts. Scholars of European populism, for example, primarily apply the term populism to right-wing nationalist social movements and political parties, while scholars of Latin American populism emphasize Perronist and socialist leaders who ride popular acclamation to authoritarian control.[40] In the United States, by contrast, the proper noun *Populism* refers to the People's Party of the late nineteenth century, a many-sided movement that, at its most rebellious, sought egalitarian alternatives to the rise of corporate capitalism and participatory spaces in a centralizing state. A small but persistent group of scholars have argued, moreover, that grassroots democratic populisms have helped radicalize American democracy from the revolutionary era to today.[41] Given my focus on the culturally specific context of America's populist imaginary, this is a book in American political thought. If critics of populism have largely shaped scholarly and public discourse on populism in America, I find common cause with scholars who locate in populism key resources for democratic politics.

Partly, however, contemporary US culture and politics exemplify the challenges of enacting popular power in nation-states that celebrate openness while pursuing strategies of governance that foreclose the people and democracy. Many of today's political buzzwords herald liberal democracy's success in surmounting horizons of law, territory, and imagination that have restricted democracy. Obama's election, in the eyes of many, proved that the United States is (or is fast becoming) a postracial society, and corporations now celebrate multiculturalism along with social mobility and free trade. Europe, meanwhile, boasts a common currency, cosmopolitan citizenship, and the ideal of postnational sovereignty in the European Union. As I have argued, however, the United States paces other states in facilitating de-democratizing trends, such as obscene concentrations of wealth, innovative forms of postracial racism, and militarization in domestic policing, border securitization, and international relations. Following suit, Eurozone policies favor technocracy and austerity over democratic participation and social egalitarianism. Many European states, moreover, have combined European integration with campaigns to tighten national borders to immigrants who embody the harm done by Europe's ongoing postcolonial legacies. In this larger context, this book is part of broader discussions in democratic theory and practice. I do not consider America the center of efforts to democratize populism; rather, I evaluate the perils and prospects of aspirational democratic populism in America as part of the scholarly response to this century's emergence of people's movements across the world.[42]

TOWARD A POPULIST POLITICAL THEORY

This book participates in a history of contested efforts to narrate populism, by reflecting on debates in contemporary democratic theories of populism and on the history and resurgence of populist politics in the United States. In evaluating the conditions under which aspirational democratic populisms might flourish today, my approach is both restorative and imaginative. Current conceptions of populism developed historically in tandem with the cultural and political events that shaped the dominant political order in America and with populisms that have both reinforced and contested the victor's version of the people and democracy. Therefore, I develop theoretical insights through engagements with democratic theory, popular culture, and historical and contemporary politics. I engage in a populist practice of political theory, by constructing a dialogue between the array of actors—past and present, academic and activist, elite and grassroots—that have contested the borders of populism and democracy in America.

My focus on cultural contexts and everyday practice differs from most liberal studies of populism. Liberal scholars typically focus on the narrow relationship between the people and government, hewing closely to liberalism's concerns with perfecting the institutional norms and procedures that enable individuals and minorities to flourish within the rule of law. I am interested in the broader processes of political culture that shape political subjects, and my normative and political concerns lead me to identify the rhetoric, practices, and institutions that cultivate people's aspirations to engage in collective action to change the rules of the game. In relation to liberal and left studies that do emphasize populist rhetoric or populist emotion, I add a focus on the everyday populist practices and institutional experiments that are crucial to the formation of subjects and political actors. More generally, populist political theory offers an alternative to conventional approaches to democratic theory. By broadening the spaces, practices, and actors relevant to producing democratic critique and vision, I emphasize the ways in which political practice can and should energize political theory. Cynicism least often takes hold, I want to suggest, and radical imagination most often emerges among those—scholars and activists alike—who engage in the political work of building alternative democratic futures.

This book imagines alternative futures for populism and democracy. I lay the groundwork in chapter 1 by evaluating prominent academic discourses on populism and developing my theory of aspirational democratic populism. Here, I take up liberal scholarship on populism in depth. Liberal dismissals of populism are based on a common assumption: they equate populism with theorists of democracy, notably Jean-Jacques Rousseau and Carl Schmitt, who believe popular sovereignty demands immediate identification between the people and law. Liberals thus accuse populists of erasing the difference and contestation that are central to politics and democracy. Too often, however, these scholars respond to populism by affirming liberal institutions and procedures that themselves limit the kinds of conflict that are proper to democracy. In doing so, they tame the paradox of popular sovereignty. By contrast, radical democratic scholars have reclaimed populism's rebellious excess to return the paradox of popular sovereignty to the center of politics and democracy. The most influential among these theorists is Ernesto Laclau, for whom populism's oppositional identification and action can rupture hegemonic orders and open spaces to reconstitute the rules of the game. If Laclau turns liberal fears into democracy's possibility, he too places collective identification at the center of populism. To situate my argument that populism is also crucially about constituting popular power, I highlight an oft-overlooked strain of American scholars, including Lawrence Goodwyn, Harry Boyte, and Elizabeth Sanders. These scholars recover an alternative tradition of radical democratic populism rooted in everyday politics and institutional experimentation. Cultivating rebellious aspirations, I argue, requires efforts to reunite the tactics that have come to divide radical democratic theory and practice: on the one hand, mobilizing the people against power; on the other, reconstituting popular power in everyday life. This requires engaging people in ongoing, unruly acts of constituting horizontal relations of power. Given the paradox of democracy—and the recognition that every constituent moment has remainders—the people must also engage in ongoing contests over the horizons of collective identity and democracy. This active concept of *horizontality* recognizes that popular power must be constituted both in our everyday experiences and at the structural borders that restrict political vision and action.

In chapter 2, I revisit populism's namesake in America, the nineteenth-century Populist revolt of farmers and laborers against the rise of corporate capitalism. Scholarly interpretations of that movement, including celebrated works by Richard Hofstadter and Lawrence Goodwyn, played a major role in shaping the discourses of populism's critics and admirers today. As I have suggested, liberal critics of Populism influenced what Walter Benjamin refers to as the victor's version of history. I return to Populism, then, to recover its rebellious aspirations to power. Populists coordinated mass resistance with everyday practices of generating grassroots power. The People's Party was the mouthpiece of Populist invective, mobilizing the outrage against the corporate revolution in America. The centralizing voice of the People's Party would have been disembodied and lifeless, however, without deep relations and looser affinities with decentered spaces of everyday practice. For decades prior to the People's Party, the movement relied on the energies of white farmers, black farmers, immigrant laborers, Marxist and Christian socialists, armies of the unemployed, suffragettes, temperance crusaders, and various middle-class reformers. These grassroots actors organized institutions and practices of political education, cooperative economy, and political mobilization that served as everyday incubators of Populist identification and power. Time and again, Populists confronted a central question that impacted the rebelliousness of their aspirations: could efforts to arouse collective identification and constitute horizontal popular power remain open to contests over the horizons of the people and democracy *within* Populism? Where Populism's everyday spaces thrived and crossed social divides, the movement succeeded in organizing people's aspirations to enact egalitarian, pluralistic forms of popular power. Where they did not, Populism failed to sustain its coalitional base, and its grassroots power reinforced hierarchies of white supremacy, nativism, and patriarchy.

In chapter 3, I take a "commercial break" from analyzing populist social movements and turn to ubiquitous cultural processes, such as advertising and music, that shape visions of the people and democracy. My premise is that populist movements that aim to contest the identity of the people and to reconstitute popular power do so not only in the narrow field of liberal institutions and procedures, but in a larger political culture that shapes people's ideas and aspirations related to democracy. Whereas scholars of populism have avoided the relationship between popular culture and populist politics, I argue that populism's ubiquity in popular culture is difficult to bypass when evaluating a style of politics that arouses collective identification and mobilizes aspirations to power. I turn to two cultural texts that elucidate competing strands of American populism that coexisted in the nineteenth-century Populist movement but have since defined themselves in opposition to each other: Chevrolet's ad "Our Country, Our Truck," which celebrates "the American people" rebuilding their nation amid crisis; and Leonard Cohen's song "Democracy," which envisions grassroots actors reviving democracy from the ruins of abandoned Chevrolet factories. Chevy's ad exemplifies what I call *regulated populism*. Invoking its target audience as a common people, the ad fuels reactionary aspirations to shore up familiar borders, such as nationalism, white supremacy, and patriarchy. At the same time, the ad's celebration of multiculturalism fosters unrealizable aspirations toward the ideal of limitless freedom promised by neoliberalism. By contrast, Cohen's song offers a vision and practice of *aspirational democratic populism* attuned to the paradoxes of democracy. The content and style of the song call listeners to imagine themselves in relation to a disparate array of actors who have enacted the promise "Democracy is coming to the U.S.A." That promise, never fully realizable, recognizes the paradox that new actors will always emerge to contest the structural hierarchies that limit democracy's horizons and to enact new forms of horizontal popular power. Drawing on my discussions of Chevy and Cohen, I develop an account of America's populist imaginary. The result of contests between regulated and aspirational democratic populisms,

America's populist imaginary both enables and constrains the rebellious aspirations of populist movements today.

In chapter 4, I analyze two populist uprisings that reflect the split in populist
ideology and aspirations since the nineteenth century and that both draw on
and revise America's populist imaginary for the twenty-first century. I evaluate the Tea Party and Occupy Wall Street as competing populist responses
to the global financial crisis that hit the United States in 2007. The Tea Party
reinforces America's regulated populist imaginary, updating the familiar narrative brought to us by Chevrolet—one in which "real Americans" must defend
unlimited individual freedom for a national people defined as white, male, and
Christian. Like nineteenth-century Populists, the Tea Party succeeded where
it combined grassroots efforts to generate popular power with the more centralized rhetorical invective of today's right-wing echo chamber. Unlike their
predecessors, however, the Tea Party's centralizing rhetoric and its decentered
spaces of everyday politics have combined overwhelmingly to reinforce hegemonic modes of capitalist, state, and cultural power. Emerging in the aftermath
of the same economic crisis, Occupy aroused collective identification to resist
rather than reinforce global capitalism. Occupy's rhetoric of "the 99 percent"
sought broad appeal across class, race, nationality, and national borders. In
many respects, Occupy replayed well-worn left divisions between resistance
and everyday politics. At its most promising, however, it cultivated rebellious
aspirations through experiments with horizontality that linked centralizing
resistance against "the 1 percent" with myriad experiments in enacting popular
power. In its ties with local and translocal organizing—for example, coalitions
with the local and national organizing of the New Bottom Line campaign and
affinities with populist movements outside the United States—Occupy's aspirational democratic populism enacted popular power at the horizons of the
people and democracy.

In the conclusion, I turn briefly to UndocuQueer, a movement led by queer,
immigrant youth who are contesting not only dominant discourses of citizenship, but also mainstream LGBTQ and immigrant rights movements. In doing so,
I examine populism from the extreme margins of today's social world, through
an emerging movement whose precarity in and across America's borders stems
from intersecting lines of legal, racial, gender, and sexual oppression. I treat
UndocuQueer as a limit case to stretch my account of aspirational democratic
populism and identify points at which the movement strains what any account of
populism can offer radical democratic politics. On the one end, I reiterate my central argument that radical democratic populisms have always emerged from the
margins of society to contest the terms of the people and democracy. Stretching
aspirational democratic populism, UndocuQueer intensifies the dynamic between

counterhegemonic resistance and decentered efforts to constitute popular power in "deviant" directions. On the other end, UndocuQueer's efforts to cultivate popular power across national, racial, gender, and sexual borders raises key challenges to pernicious constraints that have historically limited populism's democratizing promise. Recognizing the limits of populist identification, UndocuQueer activists shift their energies between populist visions and ones that are both illegible and insurgent vis-à-vis America's populist imaginary.

Aspirational Democratic Populism

Enacting Popular Power at the Horizons of Democracy

> It is clear that varied methods of social control fashioned in industrial societies have, over time, become sufficiently pervasive that a gradual erosion of democratic aspirations among whole populations has taken place.
>
> —Lawrence Goodwyn

Scholars debating the future of democracy are often quick to assign populism a fixed refrain. The term "populism" rolls off the tongue as a pejorative in both academic and public discourse, an almost instinctual refrain shaped by decades of liberal scholarship that deems populism apolitical and antidemocratic. At best, it encourages an "absurd" wish, the naive desire to express a unified popular will beyond the mediating institutions of constitutional, representative government; at worst, it betrays a "paranoid tendency," an explosive temperament prone to vilifying the enemies of the people and fomenting backlash against elites and marginalized social groups.[1] Whereas liberal democracy entails key norms and institutions, among them, individual rights, minority protections, deliberative procedures, and separation of powers, populism evokes reactionary, obstructionist masses and charismatic demagogues who usurp the people's power.

This party-line discourse discounts the myriad instances in which the people have emerged to redeem democracy not only from the hegemonic powers that undermine it, but also from the "gradual erosion of democratic aspirations" in late modern societies. This is the key insight of many radical democrats, who have forged a quieter but persistent counterrefrain on populism. As long as democracy remains indebted to the ideal of popular sovereignty, they insist, democratic theorists and activists must give an account of the people as collective actors, capable of enacting their power and authority in politics. Without such an account, democracy's future seems fixed by the preexisting rules and institutions of today's neoliberal, administrative states, not by the always shifting and emerging peoples who live within and across their borders.

Yet radical democrats have too often diminished populism's rebellious impulse by reinforcing a tired divide in democratic theory and practice. For some, populism's strength is its oppositional rhetoric, which mobilizes the demands of the people against the abuses and failures of established democratic orders. According to those who sing this tune, such energetic critique is crucial to mount resistance against the relentless drive of global capitalism, and its tightening grip on the economy, culture, and politics.[2] A second chorus insists that populist politics is most effective when it turns down its bullhorn of resistance and attends to the everyday work of cultivating viable alternatives to detached, top-down institutions and processes. In their view, populism's success in transforming democracy will depend on its ability to generate egalitarian, pluralistic relationships among the people, and to experiment with decentralized institutions and practices through which people can develop political capacities and learn how to wield power.[3]

The stakes of this missed connection are high. As I argued in the introduction and will elaborate below, democracy faces severe challenges in great part because broad structures and dynamics of capitalist and state power resonate in our everyday lives and diminish our aspirations to popular power. In response, populists cannot afford to shout with a disembodied voice, vocalizing the people's outrage at detached, dangerous configurations of power. All we may remember of populist uprisings is the image of a giant puppet head on a stick, unless protest movements also put in patient, sustained efforts to invest grassroots actors in cocreating alternative forms of democracy. At the same time, efforts to build civic capacities and institutions are bound to encounter resistance from unyielding market pressures at every turn, not to mention the layers upon layers of social and economic hierarchy that constitute our daily existence. The annals of history will record the minutes of very few church-basement meetings or city council negotiations, unless they find ways to connect the labor of local, immediate political organizing to more far-ranging mobilizations of radical critique and imagination.

In response to this impasse, I develop an account of *aspirational democratic populism*, which has historically cultivated people's rebellious aspirations to share in power, and to do so in more pluralistic, egalitarian ways, across established borders that restrict politics and democracy. Enacting aspirational democratic populism today will involve repertoires of populist practice aimed at disrupting the largely unconscious relays through which structural forces inhabit everyday life, but also initiating experiments in constituting popular power that link everyday politics with farther-ranging movements to transform culture and politics.

This requires not only building sustained resonances between everyday practice and outrageous resistance, but also reorienting both to include long-term strategies for reconstructing broad structures and dynamics.

POPULISM AS DEGENERATION OF DEMOCRACY: THE LIBERAL DEMOCRATIC REFRAIN

Democracy is threatened on all sides: from external forces of capitalist and state power that fracture political communities and diminish political lives and from internal paradoxes that reveal not only democracy's emancipatory promise, but also its avenues of popular foreclosure. Liberal democratic theorists have historically listed populism as one such "expression of a democracy permanently susceptible to turning against itself."[4] To justify their anxieties about populism, many liberal theorists turn to the paradox of popular sovereignty as posed by Jean-Jacques Rousseau: popular sovereignty demands both good citizens, who are able to enact and uphold public law, and good laws, which mold private, often egoistic citizens into public actors. But each presupposes the other. In contexts where both are lacking—whether the imaginary founding moment of Rousseau's social contract, or the social conditions in which first he and now we live—it is impossible to agree upon measures that can, without coercion and violence, organize a multitude of particular individuals into a well-ordered, egalitarian body politic.[5]

As Bonnie Honig has argued, Rousseau left the paradox of democracy insoluble. He "illustrates for us, time and again," she writes, "the mutual inhabitation of general and particular will, people and blind multitude, lawgiver and charlatan, properly durable institutions and institutions stabilized by force."[6] In the hands of liberal theorists, however, Rousseau represents populism's obsession with solving the democratic paradox. At best, populism is a "symptom" of the "pathology" of bad laws or institutions, a "malaise" hanging over a corrupted democratic state, remediable when populist uprisings lead to reforms in law or in the institutions and procedures of governance.[7] At worst, it is an expression of the people's "primitive" desire for organic unity, one that forecloses the democratic paradox once and for all, by erasing the distinctions between individuals and collapsing the boundaries between civil society and state.[8]

Indeed, in liberal imaginaries of populism, Rousseau often morphs into Carl Schmitt, perhaps the single greatest influence on critics and admirers of populism alike. Though Schmitt, himself, is not a theorist of populism, scholars rely explicitly or implicitly on his concepts of democracy and the political to offer a "populist interpretation of democracy."[9] Schmitt notably prunes democracy of its entwinement with parliamentarianism, which he views as ponderous, not to mention a "poor façade concealing the dominance of parties and economic interests."[10] To be true to the logic of popular sovereignty, he insists, democracy can rest on nothing but a "series of identities," for example, between the will of the majority and the will of all, between the people's will and law, between law and the state, between governing and governed. Schmitt admits that these identities are more symbolic than real. The end result is "not a matter of something actually equal, legally, politically, or sociologically, but rather of identifications." At stake for Schmitt is "the question of who has control over the means by which the will of the people is to be constructed."[11] Unlike the "artificial machinery" of parliamentarianism, with its cumbersome rules and divisive mediating institutions, groups or leaders who achieve symbolic identification with the will of the people embody the "direct *expression* of democratic substance and power."[12]

If the logic of identity commits democracy to horizontal relations of power within the people, and between people and elites, the appearance of such equality can only be sustained via the political line drawn between the people and its enemy. In other words, the equality implied by identity would be "meaningless" and politically "indifferent" without the presence of inequality, which, for Schmitt, cannot lie horizontally within the people, but must rest with an enemy at its borders. Democracy thus exemplifies, rather than escapes, Schmitt's influential logic of the political, which identifies the people with the cultural and territorial unit of the nation-state, and against both foreign and domestic enemies.[13] Contra liberal accounts of democracy, which assume "universal human equality" and thus open the door to both internal struggles for rights and external relations of cosmopolitanism, Schmittian democracy insists on the "substantial equality and homogeneity" of a bounded, sovereign people.[14]

Dressing populism in Schmittian garb binds it to dual fantasies about democracy, equal parts naive (in the face of the realities of life in complex, late modern societies) and dangerous to liberal democratic orders (established to secure popular sovereignty and protect individual rights): the one an aspiration toward popular unity, the other toward direct, unmediated popular control. If the former says something about how liberal scholars view populist identity, the other reveals their apprehensions about populist enactment, that is, how the people perform their power in—or, in many renderings, beyond—politics. The aspirations to popular unity and control often work together in liberal theories of populism, and in many of the "canonical" cases of populism that provoke concerns over populism's apolitical and antidemocratic tendencies. But it is worth separating them analytically to understand what fuels liberal anxieties about populism.

For many critics of populism, scholars and pundits alike, it is tempting to out-and-out dismiss populism's aspirations to a unified popular will. This is the impulse that led rational choice theorist William Riker to debunk "the grandiose (though intellectually absurd) claims of populism," which forget that the people is an incoherent mass, destined forever to "speak in meaningless tongues." In other words, individuals can barely be trusted to "amalgamate" their values accurately or fairly in what many liberals regard as the most basic democratic practice of voting, let alone claim any more robust status as a "corporate entity" possessing a unified will.[15] Moreover, what Koen Abts and Stefan Rummens refer to as the "phantasmal image of the organic unity" of the people reflects the common belief among liberal critics that populism conceives of the people not as a collection of individuals, whose wills must be mediated by interest aggregation, deliberation, or conflict resolution, but as a substantive body, bound together by ties of nature, history, or identity.[16] It is common for scholars and pundits to rely on an array of familiar tropes to undercut populist aspirations to unity. Populism's people have been charged with nostalgic yearnings for the virtuous harmonies, real or imagined, of a traditional or agrarian past.[17] They have been attributed romantic desires to overcome the alienation of modern society, with its industrialized economies and distant, bureaucratic governments, and to rediscover Rousseau's promise of mankind's natural moral unity.[18] They have been lent nationalist pretentions to tame the discordant pluralism of modern societies through visions of social integration, often associated with "heartland" cultural values, or more purely, *das Volk*. Indeed, in keeping with Schmitt's influence on prevailing accounts of populist democracy, most critics implicitly regard populism as a style of politics that equates the people with the nation, and many reduce the concept of populism further by narrowing its scope to the study of virulent nationalist groups.[19]

Rather than dismiss populist aspirations to unity as backward in relation to the vagaries of life in progressive, if necessarily alienating, modern societies, many scholars of populism treat it seriously as an antithesis to liberal standards of liberty and equality. Indeed, what Richard Hofstadter perhaps most influentially identified as the "paranoid style" of politics has become a regular feature of political life in advanced, Euro-American democracies.[20] According to Hofstadter, populists and other paranoid groups fan the flames of status anxiety, in reaction to feeling displaced by market fluctuations and changing racial and ethnic demographics in liberal, free-market societies. Central to populism's "political demonology" is its Manichaean rhetoric, which turns potentially political contests between adversarial interest groups into full-scale wars between good, in the figure of the people, and evil, in the costume of its enemy.[21] Given its reactive origins, populism's moralizing, Manichaean rhetoric defies political intervention and resolution. Instead, populist leaders and groups plant conspiratorial notions, which stir the people's anxieties against political or financial elites who plot to usurp their power from above. And they foment reactionary backlash, pitting the people against foreigners, immigrants, and racial others, who are charged with undermining the people's security or, in some renderings, their moral virtue, from below. Populism's political demonology thus mobilizes populist aspirations to unity through a kind of social catharsis, reassuring the people of its identity and power by scapegoating the dissenting views of individuals and marginalized groups. In this sense, populists "do not ask for political equality or equal recognition," clarifies Nadia Urbinati, "but for the political power of equals."[22] In other words, populists claim equality-for-us, while denying recognition to outsiders.

Populism's aspirations to popular control shift the analytical focus from contests over identity, that is, who belongs to the sovereign people, to struggles over political power, that is, how the sovereign people should enact its power in politics. When populists claim to embody the unmediated vox populi, they eschew the limits that constitutional, representative democracy places on popular sovereignty, and are often said to enact the people's power beyond politics.[23] In real terms, populists often prefer direct forms of participation, ranging from protests, worker cooperatives, community organizing, and social movements, to legislative and electoral strategies, such as initiative, referendums, and recall. While these forms of participation suggest a variety of strategies for engaging the state and other structures of power, populism is overwhelmingly defined as antistatist, "opposed to the establishment," "antisystem," "anti-institutional," "at odds with representation," "impatient with procedures," "hostile to deliberation," and in some cases, altogether unwilling to engage a corrupt, "ossified state."[24]

While scholars agree that populism is, at best, inherently ambivalent toward the state, they have reached little consensus on what this says about populism's relationship to politics and democracy. Some welcome populist movements, as a political referendum on unaccountable representatives, bad laws, or broken institutions, and at best, a provocation to reform liberal democracy from within. In such instances, populism restores equilibrium to liberal democratic regimes, resolving the periodic tensions that surface between its pillars of popular sovereignty and constitutionalism. For others, populism is no more than an apolitical symptom or pathology, an expression of popular unrest in the face of various maladies in established forms of constitutional democracy: for example, bad representatives or the impossibility of representation; an intellectual class that has receded from politics; political parties that have become managerial in their missions, shedding their role as mediators between the people and government; even fundamental inadequacies at the level of the constitutional rules of the game. Here populism may signal what is wrong with the establishment. But populist insurgencies cannot summon the power, for example, by devising political programs or other means-ends strategies, to change it.[25]

Populism's biggest critics regard it as a "degeneration of [the] democratic logic."[26] Nadia Urbinati puts the point best when she writes, "Despite its antagonism against the established order, populism has a deeply statist vocation. It is impatient with government by discussion, because it longs for limitless decisionism."[27] Here Urbinati captures dual anxieties about populism's aspirations to enact the people beyond politics. On the one hand, its antiestablishment stance obstructs and, at worst, diminishes key liberal democratic institutions and pro-cedures, such as constitutional rights, election by secret voting, and deliberative processes of decision-making. Together, these protect the "plurality of individu-als" as "concrete, particular others who need recognition as such," and they limit expressions of popular sovereignty that aim to suppress individual differences and minority rights.[28] On the other hand, the desire for immediate identification between the people and government needs an outlet. And it is often difficult for people living in today's mass societies to find that outlet in their harried, privately oriented lives. In many instances, then, populist desires for the direct, unmedi-ated expression of popular will are a cry for better leadership, not a demand for more participation.[29] Urbinati explains, "Populism as a modern phenomenon of mass mobilization has demagoguery as one of its main components." Unable to escape the slide into Caesarism, populist expressions of will are often displaced onto displays of plebiscitary acclamation that inaugurate or reinforce autocratic rule.[30]

Contra Schmitt, most liberal scholars accept as commonplace the democratic logic of Claude Lefort. Rather than define democracy by its living, breathing sub-stance, as the direct expression of the people's unitary will, Lefort argues that democracy can only live in modern times by sustaining an irresolvable tension. On the one hand, the symbolic legitimacy of democracy requires the "image of popular sovereignty." On the other, that image must always be "linked to the image of an empty place, impossible to occupy, such that those who exercise pub-lic authority can never claim to appropriate it."[31] To fill in the place of power, to enact "the People-As-One," steers democracy toward totalitarianism, which col-lapses all distinctions between the state and the social body, displacing internal divisions onto the figure of the "enemy Other." Cue liberal nightmares of populist democracy in Schmittian drag. But to empty the place of power entirely from its reliance on the image of the people, Lefort argues, goes too far in the other direc-tion. It disenchants democracy, inviting cynical corruption by bureaucrats acting in their own private interests.[32]

Populism's liberal critics thus turn to key institutions and procedures of consti-tutional democracy—for example, individual rights, minority protections, secret voting, deliberative processes, competitive parties, and separation of powers—to mediate conflicting interests and visions and to prevent any person or group from embodying the locus of democratic power. Here, populism's critics affirm differ-ent variants of liberalism. Riker, for example, defends a rational choice model, by which individuals aggregate their votes during periodic election cycles, exer-cising their authority only through the threat of "popular veto," not through the positive expression of popular will. The power of popular veto acts as a curb on governmental tyranny, and more constructively, it encourages officials to develop

platforms that appeal to the needs of both majority and minority interests.[33] By
contrast, Hofstadter and other centrist liberals in America and Europe envision a
more robust version of consensual politics. Looking to preserve a pluralist political center, in the face of both the class antagonisms of the Left and the paranoid
cultural politics of the Right, they appeal to representative institutions to mediate
conflicting interests and reach temporary compromises in the formation of public policy.[34] Deliberative democrats, taking their cues from Jürgen Habermas, go
to the greatest lengths to theorize popular sovereignty via positive processes of
collective, "institutionalized will-formation." They even assume that, over time, a
democratic citizenry can reach lasting consensus on cultural and policy issues, for
example, civil rights or redistributive principles. But for Habermas, popular sovereignty must nevertheless "become anonymous, retreat[ing] into democratic
procedures" that channel informal public opinion and influence into legislative
and administrative power.[35] By limiting popular sovereignty in these ways, liberal
democrats recognize that democratic processes at best generate partial "interpretations of the essentially open identity of the people."[36]

Yet liberal democracy can hardly avoid relying on the fiction of the people as
a collective actor. Liberal theorists are at times explicit about the need for cultural unity. Variants of liberal nationalism, for example, fashion political identity
around credal values, such as freedom, equal opportunity, pluralism, and inclusivity.[37] More often, however, the popular subject of liberalism remains underar-
ticulated, in theories that nevertheless defend the need for a "thin background
culture" to support the institutions and procedures of constitutional democracy,
or for dispositions toward reason, civility, and mutual respect to enable deliberative democratic practices.[38] As the work on modern social imaginaries reveals,
liberal subjects have in fact relied on a much thicker set of deep-seated images,
understandings, and expectations to "make possible common practices and a
widely shared sense of legitimacy."[39]

At the same time, constitutional and procedural accounts of liberalism remain
ill equipped to respond to the pervasive ways in which dominant cultural images
and norms shape the liberal subjects who engage in rational decision-making,
interest politics, and deliberation. By studying the interactions of individuals
and interest groups within preestablished institutional frameworks, these theories avoid interrogating how the same institutions are implicated in producing
and disciplining subjects, and in reinforcing cultural hierarchies along lines of
race, nation, gender, class, religion, and so on.[40] Indeed, state policies that contribute to the precarity of marginalized groups gain legitimacy by making symbolic enemies of (some part of) the people: for example, a "War on Poverty" that
has been drained of federal funding but manifests in the policing of homeless
people; a "War on Drugs" that has contributed to the occupation of black and
Latino neighborhoods by militarized police; a "War on Terror" that has justified

the surveillance of Muslim individuals and groups; and "Border Patrol" measures that have not only intensified violence at the US-Mexico border, but also created the daily insecurities of mass deportation. As Ta-Nehisi Coates writes of the growing movement against police brutality in America, "To challenge the police is to challenge the American people, and the problem with the police is not that they are fascist pigs but that we are majoritarian pigs."[41] If the norm of popular sovereignty legitimates state violence against marginalized actors, it is difficult to imagine solutions that do not entail oppositional contests over the boundaries of the people.

In their attempts to counter the troubling democratic scenario prophesied by Schmitt, liberal theorists have instead defended an undernourished vision of popular sovereignty. Few go as far as Seymour Martin Lipset, whose critique of populism justifies a technocratic form of democracy that relies on a healthy dose of apathy from the public.[42] Even liberal democracy, following Lefort's reasoning, cannot allow the image of popular sovereignty to be so emptied it becomes moribund—as it has, increasingly, in the wake of neoliberal forces that obscure the institutional sites of democratic accountability and reduce citizens to passive consumers of political life. But many liberal theories of democracy do require the ideal of popular sovereignty to remain dormant for long stretches, between periods of opinion polling, agenda setting, voting, legislative deliberation, and other formal procedures that govern the people's entry into the political process. Such procedures may play an important role in politics, but taken as prepolitical rules, rather than as political guideposts, they tend to tame the emancipatory power of popular sovereignty. As a result, quoting Canovan, popular sovereignty is now worshiped as a "patron saint inspiring and presiding over" a "proceduralized" democratic politics. To avoid democracy's disenchantment, the people need to "swallow" the ideal of popular sovereignty as a "democratic equivalent of Plato's 'noble lie,' whilst not believing it to the point that they attempt to act on it."[43]

By placing limits on popular sovereignty, populism's critics reinforce variants of liberalism as the best, or the only possible, form of politics and democracy in late modern times. Contra Schmitt, who places questions of power and antagonism at the center of political and democratic life, liberal scholars wager that constitutional norms and procedures can insulate political judgment and action from the most oppressive, destabilizing effects of social hierarchy and conflict. Many critics of populism concede, with Nadia Urbinati, that "it is reasonable and meaningful to claim that democracy does not only and simply entail a constitutional frame and rules of the game."[44] And yet few venture to explain how individuals often do generate collective identity and action beyond that frame, for example, beyond rational choice models of aggregating individual interests through voting, or deliberative norms and procedures governing intersubjective opinion and will formation. In other words, in foreclosing on populism, its liberal critics provide little insight into how the people come to embody and enact their power in politics, in ways that can disrupt and transform the rules of the game.[45] As we will see, a history of populist struggles reveal not only myriad ways of generating collective power, but also intense internal debates over whether and how to engage established regimes, how best to reform them, and how to build alternative institutions and practices that enable people to play a greater role in steering, and at times transforming, democratic politics. To reopen the question of populism's resources for democratization, then, is not to say that there should be no limits on popular sovereignty. It is to insist that the limits that constrain *and* enable popular power must remain open to ongoing contestation, as a central part of what it means to engage in democratic politics.

POPULIST RESISTANCE VERSUS EVERYDAY POPULISM: RADICAL DEMOCRACY'S SPLIT REFRAIN

Radical democratic scholars are often drawn to populism's "dangerous excess" beyond the rules of the game, and to its resources for reconstituting the terms of collective identity and political life.[46] They begin by locating populism's emergence in the more fundamental paradox of democratic peoplehood, recognizing that the people's undecidability presents "dilemmas of authorization" that trouble constitutional democracy more than its liberal admirers allow. Indeed, if the people are "at once a constituent and a constituted power," they are capable of emerging, at times from the margins of recognized speech and action, to withdraw their authority from the regime, or to authorize new rules of the game.[47] In this context, in which popular sovereignty is never fully realizable, populism raises inescapable questions for democratic theory and practice: Who are the people? And how should they enact their power in politics? By underscoring these questions, populism's radical democratic admirers awaken its rebellious potential, that is, its ability to engage marginalized and emerging political subjects in enacting alternatives to hegemonic forms of power. For radical democrats, politics and democracy are enlivened, even defined, by such struggles, which often generate more egalitarian, pluralizing social relations and forms of power. The trouble is that, so far, they remain divided over how populism can best constitute democratic peoples and enact popular power in ways that enhance radical democratic ends and means. In particular, they stake out narrow turf when it comes to raising populism's crucial questions for democratic theory and practice, with some focusing on populism's symbolic resistance, that is, its struggles over the terms of collective identity, and others shifting the emphasis to populism's affinities for grassroots politics, which cultivate more robust institutions and practices for enacting popular power. At stake in this division of energies, I will argue, is radical democracy's understanding of politics and what it means to democratize politics today.

Those invested in populist resistance join a growing movement of scholars on the left who hope to reanimate the antagonistic dimensions of politics.[48] These scholars worry that the mediating institutions of today's constitutional states support not pluralism and disagreement, but a "neoliberal consensus": one with variants in conservative and libertarian celebrations of free-market individualism, center-left appeals to "good governance" and "nonpartisan democracy," not to mention the deterioration of New Left social victories into claims that America is, or is on the way to becoming, a postracial, postfeminist society. Many scholars concerned with questions of pluralism, social justice, and economic equality identify a dual threat to democracy in this neoliberal vision of politics. First, by announcing the end of social group conflict, it masks ongoing structural divisions, such as those related to class, race, gender, and national belonging. And, it favors technocratic, managerial forms of governance that further depoliticize key issues, such as the roots of economic crisis or the borders of national identity, which properly reside at the center of political debate. Consensual politics thus swallows genuine dissent. Second, by effectively containing debate on crucial issues, it also limits the Left's ability to present people with alternative courses of action in times of widespread insecurity. This accelerates the moralizing turn in cultural and political discourse, and it leaves the door open for right-wing media and social movements to stoke reactionary sentiments and forms of protest.[49]

It is time for the Left, many scholars conclude, to develop viable counterstrategies in response. By inventing savvier forms of critique and resistance, they aim to expose ongoing wrongs at the heart of existing democratic orders and to reconstitute more egalitarian, pluralistic forms of democratic political community. Some scholars, most notably Ernesto Laclau, believe that populism has a vital role to play here.[50] Laclau argues that contemporary dismissals of populism are "dismissals of politics *tout court.*" This is not simply an analogical claim. The "anti-populist onslaught" takes part in "the discursive construction of a certain normality, of an ascetic political universe" that equates politics with administration, that is, with the management of the social body by established, institutional forms of power.[51] In other words, in a world where discourses carry "performative rationality," that is, the ability to construct social life in distinct ways, mainstream neoliberal dismissals of populism have contributed to dramatic reductions in the meaning and scope of popular sovereignty. Against this backdrop, populist discourse operates in distinctive ways to constitute "the people" as the proper subject of politics.

By pitting "the people" against "the establishment," populism offers a familiar, emotional script to mobilize the demands of disparate actors against a given order. But Laclau is clear that "purely differential identities" are only "equivalent to each other in their common rejection" of an enemy.[52] The negative category of the demand is thus central to populism's "logic of articulation." When an institutionalized system "can no longer absorb differential demands," the resulting multitude of frustrated demands share in common one source of solidarity: "the fact that their demands remain unsatisfied."[53] Laclau uses the metaphor of "equivalential chains" to characterize the process through which individual demands retain particularity, while also aggregating toward a larger set of social claims. Chains of equivalence have their source in the shared experience of lack, rather than in any positive substance or aspiration. Because of this, a collective popular subject can only emerge through the struggle for hegemony. That is, a popular subject takes shape through representation, when one demand comes to represent the voice of the whole. By the same logic, any given symbolic representation of popular identity must remain an "empty signifier," ensuring that the identity of "the people" is always unstable. The challenge for populist modes of representation, then, is to balance "extension," or breadth of inclusion, with "intension," or the depth of connection between populist symbols and particular demands.[54]

Laclau writes that populism is, "quite simply, a way of constructing the political."[55] Indeed, he often makes populism synonymous with the political, because it places social antagonism at the center of constructing political life.[56] The crucial point for Laclau, and for radical democratic scholars who have found much compelling in his theories of hegemony and populism, is that there is no fixed, a priori ground of politics beyond the play of identity and difference. This means, in particular, that politics cannot be contained within the established institutions and procedures of constitutional democracy. By constituting "the people" against "power," and conceiving of both as empty signifiers, that is, as placeholders for an ongoing struggle, populist discourse sustains what Benjamin Arditi calls the "internal periphery of democratic politics." Through its periodic mobilizations of the ideal of popular sovereignty, populism "functions as a paradoxical element that belongs to democracy." Reversing liberal arguments, Arditi argues that populism is an "internal element of the democratic system that reveals the limits of the system and *prevents its closures* in the presumed normality of institutional procedures."[57] In this sense, the identity of the people and the boundaries—or in Laclau's terms, the frontier—of politics remain an ever-contested "horizon and not a ground."[58]

Laclau's account of populism has clear debts and departures in relation to Carl Schmitt's theories of democracy and the political. Most notably, Laclau appropriates the political conflict between friend and enemy for radical democratic politics. He recognizes that populism is often captured by top-down, reactionary logics. Indeed, Laclau's earliest interests in populism stem from his efforts to distinguish the progressive authoritarian populisms of Latin America from the "popular interpellations" that also characterize the discourses of Nazism and Maoism.[59] By identifying "the people" and its "enemy" as unstable categories, however, Laclau leaves them open to internal contestation and redefinition. Thus, in Laclau's theory, populist discourse is able to reconstitute symbolic political community along lines that allow for deeper internal agonism and greater recognition of the impermanent edges of every expression of collective identity.[60]

By abandoning Schmitt's emphasis on the positive substance of populist identification, however, Laclau strips from populist discourse one of Schmitt's key insights: the antagonism between friend and enemy is "specially intense." Those who hope to mobilize a people must be able to charge political speech with an emotionally "polemical" quality that provokes immediate hostility in response to a threat that is "concrete and existential."[61] Laclau acknowledges that populism's formal "logic of articulation" is only realizable through the rhetorical and affective dimensions of populist discourse. In other words, populism's performativity, its ability to construct an actual political subject, depends on its ability to animate subjects to identify with the symbolic representation of popular power. And this depends on the quality of populist symbols and rhetorical devices (most notably, for Laclau, synecdoche, or the part representing the whole).[62] A number of studies have extended Laclau's formal theory to examine the social and political contexts, discursive traditions, and rhetorical and affective tactics of right-wing populist movements in Europe and the United States.[63] Similar studies of radical democratic populisms must ask how their rhetorical and affective tactics of collective identification can provoke intense outrage, while also generating emotional intensities that facilitate internal agonism.

At his most concrete, Laclau points to the antiglobalization movement as exemplary of populism's ability to generate radical democratic forms of collective identification across disparate social demands. For Laclau, global capitalism multiplies the experience of social dislocation, proliferating an unwieldy array of new antagonistic demands against existing orders. This, in turn, has opened the way for antiglobalization activists to introduce alternatives to modern institutions of representation, such as the party and the nation-state.[64] Laclau ventures briefly, here, beyond his insistence on populism's inherently negative "logic of articulation," always mobilizing "the people" against "power." Yet he declines to speculate on which positive institutions best reflect the counterhegemonic "new internationalism" he sees. Nor does he say much about how such institutions link wildly heterogeneous demands through "chains of equivalence" that are supple enough to build "extension" (or coalitional breadth), without sacrificing "intension" (or depth of representation). Chantal Mouffe (who, with Laclau, made hegemonic struggle a central category of radical democracy and has likewise, if less systematically, applied it to populism) offers a more enthusiastic account of the positive dimensions of a populist antiglobalization: "after a 'negative' phase limited to the critique of institutions like the IMF and the WTO, serious attempts are now being made to construct a positive alternative to the neoliberal order." Citing the World Social Forums, she recasts antiglobalization as alter-globalization, which "aims at a different world order, where inequalities would be drastically reduced, and where the concerns of the most exposed groups would be addressed—instead of an exclusive focus on the welfare of the middle classes."[65]

These concrete visions illuminate the key insights of a reinvigorated account of populist resistance, as well as its limits for theorizing radical democratic alternatives to hegemonic modes of power. On the one hand, doesn't populism need to mobilize outrageous resistance if it hopes to "shatter" the veneer of the neoliberal consensus? Populist resistance should aim to be outrageous, partly, in its willingness to identify and target persistent abuses of power and to steer popular anger toward these structural dynamics and those who benefit from them, rather than toward other vulnerable groups. To shrink back from mobilizing popular outrage is to let the neoliberal consensus set the terms of political discourse and participation. Partly, however, populism's outrageous resistance requires inventing extraordinary and unexpected practices of collective identification and action. As in the example of the alter-globalization movement, such practices need to build relationships across borders and scales of politics; they need to develop rhetoric that links economic, social, and political demands; they must listen and appeal to those who are outcasts in neoliberal society, and not only to its safe center; and they need to mingle the anger and urgency of outrageous resistance with more patient strategies aimed at constructing viable alternatives to neoliberal conceptions of the people and democracy.

On the other hand, in gesturing toward this more complex picture of populist resistance, Laclau and Mouffe raise more questions than their theory of adversarial democracy can answer. In particular, how can movements geared toward mobilizing resistance against hegemonic structures and dynamics also invest in the more patient, constructive work of training neoliberal subjects how to be radical democratic actors? In other words, beyond gesturing to promising examples, how can populists experiment with the positive work of building new, more resilient forms of democratic power and equipping actors to wield them? Without answers to these questions, theorists of populism fall into the same trap as liberal theorists who hang their hopes for democracy on liberal citizens—that is, reasonable, civil, and so on—who do not yet exist in reality. Moreover, in their efforts to "construct a positive alternative to the neoliberal order," how might insurgent populisms craft long-term strategies for engaging the institutions of capitalism and the state, in order to transform them? To construct "the people against power" absent an account of populist institutions and practices, that is, theorists of populist resistance leave too few resources to understand how the people enact their power as part of a transformative politics.

Questions of capacity building and sustainability preoccupy theorists of grassroots populism. In historical terms, theorists of this "new populism" gained prominence in the United States during the Reagan Revolution, marked both by the ascendance of neoliberal outlooks and policies and by the "conservative capture" of populist rhetoric.[66] Yet they did not advocate reclaiming populism's vociferous energies from the right, a tactic that would have been aimed at exposing that decade's dramatic expansions of corporate and state power.[67] Instead, they asked what it would take to "return power to the people," beginning with the more modest, behind-the-scenes work of developing civic capacities and rebuilding local institutions and spaces of democracy. Buoyed by Lawrence Goodwyn's *Democratic Promise*, a reinterpretation of nineteenth-century Populism, theorists of the "new populism" found inspiration in a historical and extant tradition of grassroots democratic practice: one that had emerged repeatedly throughout the nation's history to extend and deepen democracy, redistribute social and economic power, and enhance people's desires and capacities for freedom.[68] On Goodwyn's reading, agrarian Populism sustained one of the largest democratic mass movements in American history, largely due to its vibrant "movement culture," which cultivated people's civic aspirations and capacities through parallel institutions of cooperative economics and democratic education.[69] In the late 1970s and early 1980s, that tradition was seeing renewed strength and inventiveness in broad-based community organizing networks, such as the Industrial Areas Foundation (IAF) and the Pacific Institute for Community Organizations (now PICO National Network), along with a host of other local initiatives. These experiments in grassroots populism became incubators for radical democratic practice, radical in the sense that they were rooted in local communities and traditions and oriented toward the constructive work of transforming democratic cultures.[70]

Advocates of this "everyday populism" thus shift our focus from populism's symbolic contests over the boundaries of collective identity to the question of how democratic peoples should enact their power in politics. In light of this, they often have pragmatic reasons for downplaying the rhetoric of resistance. In the pedagogical language of broad-based organizing, tackling intractable "problems," for example, racism or militarism, promises to breed internal conflict and exhaust political energies before coalitions have time to grow. Instead, organizers focus on winnable "issues," which enable grassroots actors to develop their civic capacities and gain a sense of efficacy, while steadily building the relationships, resources, and institutions of grassroots democratic power. To appropriate Laclau's terms, everyday populists view the slow, relational work of "intensive" organizing as a prerequisite for "extending" their coalitional bases. On issues that are likely to raise conflicts of identity, for example, across race, class, or religion, they argue that intensive, relational organizing—aimed at perceiving common interests and building long-term trust—is the only way to sustain grassroots coalitional politics.[71]

For Harry Boyte, who has done more than anyone to develop a textured, theoretical account of grassroots populism, the "us versus them" stance of "red and blue populisms" poses a more existential threat to populist politics. Boyte detects a common formula in protest politics on the left and right: "Find a target or enemy to demonize, stir up emotion with inflammatory language using a script that defines the issue in good-versus-evil terms and shuts down critical thought, and convey the idea that those who champion the victims will come to the rescue." This rhetoric of grievance and blame, he worries, "lets us off the hook." And, it unintentionally fuels a neoliberal culture dead set on shrinking the status of citizenship. On the left, activists decry the daunting power of corporations, a growing security state, and market infiltrations of public institutions at all levels of society. The problem with these structural critiques is that they often reify institutions as static, unchanging entities, rather than seeing them as living, cultural relationships and practices that are imminently open to contestation and redirection. Failing to recognize the latter, the line between outrageous resistance and merely cynical outrage becomes thin. On the right, resistance against bureaucracy and the elite culture of latte-sipping liberals has its roots in reality: "Ordinary Americans have innumerable experiences of being made to feel powerless and stupid by liberal professionals." What is of real concern, however, is that right populisms have fueled a "know-nothing" culture in response: one that disparages not only expert knowledge, but also deliberative processes of public judgment, in favor of more immediate forms of knowledge based parochially in "community and personal experiences." While such personalistic knowledge may successfully fuel populist backlash, it does little to empower citizens to fashion durable responses to the most pressing challenges of the day.[72]

It is against this backdrop that Boyte defines populism's "essence: the idea that politics, owned by people, is the activity through which people of diverse views and backgrounds develop their power to shape the world."[73] Recalling the cooperative alliances that were, according to Goodwyn, the radical engines of nineteenth-century Populism, Boyte today emphasizes the democratic practices of "public work," an ideal of civic agency that "involves cooperative, egalitarian, practical labors 'across ranks' on public projects, with self-organized governance."[74] These labors take place anywhere citizens come together across lines of difference to solve common problems, whether this means, for example, organizing for local school reform, developing cooperative economic institutions to create jobs, or creating community infrastructure to support and protect immigrant communities. For Boyte, it is in the imminent practices of public work, as citizens engage each other in everyday processes of listening, deliberating, building relationships, and generating actions to meet common needs, that "the people" develop the cross-cutting civic agency they need to become "co-creators of the world."[75]

Far more than theorists of populist resistance, everyday populists appreciate that power is an embodied capacity, one that is patterned by our daily routines and habits. This was Sheldon Wolin's insight when he declared, "Populism is the culture of democracy."[76] He reminds us that the collective identity of a people is not solely a matter of symbolic or discursive identification. Instead, Wolin ties a people's collective identity to its "two bodies," the one referring to its state-level constitution, or the institutions that steer the social, economic, and governmental processes of the collectivity, the other referring to the people's cultural constitution, or its everyday practices, dispositions, and orientations toward politics. A people's collective identity is thus significantly determined by their "political constitution," that is, "the way a society is constituted to generate power." And this means not only formal structures and dynamics of power, but also the way power always depends on "accumulated dispositions" and "inscribed demands."[77] Wolin, who provides everyday populism's most probing critique of contemporary modes of power, recognizes that they do more than transform cultural and political institutions or rewrite political discourses; they condition our habits of perception and action, and our dispositions toward ourselves and the world.[78] In particular, everyday populists worry about dynamics that prevent us from perceiving common problems and uncommon political allies, and that dispose us toward stances of individualism, passivity, and even political fatalism.

But they also believe that grassroots actors can repattern their political dispositions and aspirations by inventing and engaging in alternative democratic practices. Populism is the "culture of democracy," for Wolin, because, amid the "creative destruction" of capitalism, "it is a culture that has not been defined by the urge to dominate and that has learned that existence is a cooperative venture over time."[79] Everyday populists recognize that developing grassroots power begins with sustained, cooperative efforts to reshape political culture, and in doing so, to build the capacities of emerging political subjects, who develop a heightened taste for political action. This often requires patient efforts to build relationships across deep lines of difference and hierarchy that have divided communities and reinforced cynicism about collective action. It also requires cultivating traditions that have been layered over by dominant cultural dynamics and reanimating them as resources for radicalism. We might point, for example, to local histories of civil rights, immigrant rights, and poor people's organizing that can remap imaginations of urban space and institutions and offer social hope to new generations of activists. Everyday populists also routinely draw on religious traditions and social movement narratives for their insurgent rhetoric and alternative visions of community. IAF Southwest regional coordinator Ernesto Cortés calls these local resources "the rich seeds that have been planted over the years by a lot of people."[80] Social movement scholar Craig Calhoun simply calls them "the roots of radicalism."[81] Such efforts to reshape political culture are the spatial, temporal, and relational practices of everyday populism. Whereas Laclau leads us to focus on the discursive logics of populist identification, and almost as an afterthought, on the rhetorical and affective practices of populist politics, everyday populists emphasize this broader range of practices, and a patient, sustainable timetable for democratic transformations of self and culture. In doing so, they shift our attention away from conceptions of politics and democracy that emphasize conflict, and toward practices of constituting the popular power that enables new peoples to emerge.

Yet do the best insights of everyday populists contain their own self-destructive logics, especially when we consider the allergic disposition that many of its proponents carry toward the politics of grievance and blame? In particular, if citizens are daily practiced in neoliberal common sense, how can public work avoid reproducing many of the greatest obstacles to democratic practice, even as it makes modest inroads into reconstructing other aspects of neoliberal culture and politics? These include not only external obstacles, such as those Wolin diagnoses in his most pessimistic accounts of "fugitive democracy."[82] They also include internal social hierarchies and divisions, *including* the "urge to dominate" marginalized groups, which everyday populists often gloss or obscure in their efforts to theorize the roots of cooperative commonwealth. Indeed, can grassroots actors avoid engaging in large-scale power analyses and placing blame if they hope to identify and craft long-term strategies to reconstruct the broader social structures and dynamics that relentlessly shape local institutions, discourses, practices?

While radical democratic theorists of populism talk past each other in these ways, they share with most liberal scholars an unwillingness to conceive of a populist politics that includes strategies for transforming large-scale economic, social, and governmental institutions.[83] But neither contests over the boundaries of popular identity nor local experiments in enacting new forms of popular power are likely to flourish in the absence of sustained efforts at broad structural reform. This dimension of populism gets its fullest articulation by Bayard Rustin, the lifelong civil rights strategist, advisor to Martin Luther King Jr. and the Southern Christian Leadership Council, and chief organizer of the 1963 March on Washington for Jobs and Freedom. Rustin was not a self-ascribed theorist of populism, but he was an architect of one of the most important populist movements in American history.[84] In his political writings and interviews, most famously his essay "From Protest to Politics: The Future of the Civil Rights Movement," he provides an indispensable voice articulating the need to engage—in order to revolutionize—broad structures and dynamics as a key part of any democratic populist politics.

Rustin calls Civil Rights activists beyond the direct action tactics that characterized the movement's center and fueled its most visible successes up to the Civil Rights Act of 1964. Sit-ins, boycotts, marches, and Freedom Rides had obstructed legal forms of segregation, most notably in schools and public accommodations. But these remained limited tactics in the face of more fundamental socioeconomic conditions, such as de facto segregation in schools, housing, and labor markets, that still severely constrained equality and freedom for most black Americans. To tackle these interrelated problems, deeply rooted in the nation's most important socioeconomic institutions, the Civil Rights movement would need not direct action, but political power. For Rustin, "political power" means "mobilizing people into power units capable of effecting social change" through engagements with large-scale, often national-level institutions. And this involves building sustainable "community institutions" and large, organized "power bases," as well as crafting long-term strategies to revolutionize broad social, economic, and governmental institutions. Exemplifying the movement's "political cutting edge," according to Rustin, was the Mississippi Freedom Democratic Party (MFDP), which built local and statewide coalitions in its campaign to displace Dixiecrat power and revolutionize the Democratic Party.[85]

While Rustin places institutionally oriented strategies at the center of politics, he does not confine political power within established institutions or channels of government. An enduring source of frustration for Rustin are liberal apologists, who "see the impossibility of racial progress in the context of present social and economic policies," but then "accept the context as fixed." Where moderates "admonish" blacks to "adjust to the status quo," Rustin insists that "envisioning radical political change" requires ongoing power analyses of social and economic forces that oppress black and working class peoples, *as well as* strategic efforts to negotiate paths in light of these.[86] This means, for example, not only working within the Democratic Party, but transforming it to meet the needs of black sharecroppers and laborers in Mississippi and beyond. And it means, as Rustin foresaw, that institutional reforms allowing for equal opportunity would be limited, in terms of improving the social and economic well-being of black Americans, "in the absence of radical programs for full employment, the abolition of slums, the reconstruction of our educational system, new definitions of work and leisure."[87] This is what Rustin meant, concretely, when he wrote that revolutionary politics "does not connote violence; it refers to the qualitative transformation of fundamental institutions, more or less rapidly, to the point where the social economic structure which they comprised can no longer be said to be the same."[88]

By the same token, Rustin criticized tactics within the larger black freedom movement that either called for wholesale disengagement from dominant cultural and political life or adopted a militant stance toward it. In different ways, the "self-help efforts" and "shock tactics" of the Nation of Islam (and later, in Rustin's estimation, of Black Power) prioritized moral regeneration, or the changing of hearts and minds, over positive strategies to generate political power. Rustin's response to such tactics has lasting relevance for theorists of both populist resistance and everyday populism: "It is institutions—social, political, and economic institutions—which are the ultimate molders of collective sentiments."[89] In other words, Rustin brings a kind of systemic political realism, or a concern for the broad, institutional contexts of political action, to radical democratic theories of populism.[90] To theorists of populist resistance, who celebrate populism as an "anti-institutional" political "rupture," he might query how it is possible to achieve massive, identitarian—and necessarily affective—realignments of power, without transforming institutions so that they facilitate, and sustain, new forms of symbolic identification and new political subjects. To everyday populists, who understand the interrelated tasks of transforming self and culture, he might ask how far self-help efforts and local revolutions can carry populist aspirations to power, in the absence of long-term strategies to engage people in changing the broad structures and dynamics that shape local political contexts.

Rustin's vision of politics is not without crucial oversights. Though he praises community power bases in Mississippi, he shows little appreciation for the subtler, everyday politics of the early Student Nonviolent Coordinating Committee, which played a leading role in organizing poor and working-class blacks to support the MFDP. Under the mentorship of Ella Baker and Bob Moses, SNCC organizers experimented with practices of receptive listening and local self-help, not primarily, as in Rustin's calculation, so that "those involved may find their appetites for change whetted . . . [and] move into the political arena," but to ensure that the movement's vision and strategies could develop, often in unexpected directions, through engagements with new political subjects emerging from the tenant houses and cotton fields of the South.[91] Likewise, while Rustin appreciated the "psychological factors" underpinning black militancy, stemming from a white social order that teaches—and only responds to—tactics of violence, he too often spoke and wrote of the youth movement as if he "understood them perfectly." Rustin attributed the riots of the 1960s to the "boxed-in feeling" of life in urban ghettos: "The constriction, the sense of no place to go, the lack of outlet, sharpen resentment and amplify every petty dislike into instant hate." This view, however, reinforces the belief that riots are spontaneous uprisings and discounts the savvy rhetoric of black activists—those Rustin does not count among "the more responsible Negro leaders" of the day—who tapped into people's everyday experiences to generate indignation and outrage.[92] If the MFDP's vocal challenge to the Democratic Party did finally "demonstrate beyond a doubt that politics and protest could be combined intelligently," Rustin consistently subsumed the outrage and uncompromising demands of the movement's radical voices to his own preference for strategies aimed at negotiating the constraints and possibilities afforded by dominant institutional configurations.[93]

But Rustin was right about the need for a "democratic constitutional revolution in the economic and social life" of America, one that does not shy away from engaging formal, large-scale structures and dynamics of power. Such a revolution is no less crucial today, though it is more daunting. As I will show in the next section, neoliberal constellations of economic, social, and state power are more nebulous than the industrial exploitation and open white supremacy of Rustin's day. Gar Alperowitz, one of today's lone voices for a structural approach to populism, insists that "a new and more militant twenty-first century populism" will require revolutions in not one, but both, of the people's two bodies. He chronicles a host of local experiments in public ownership taking place across America: around 8.8 million Americans participate in eleven thousand worker-owned firms or employee stock ownership plans; some 120 million Americans participate in forty-eight thousand cooperatives for workers, farmers, food, day care, housing, and more; innovative cities are prioritizing community development corporations, municipally owned real estate development, community land trusts, and publicly owned utilities ranging from Internet access to wind energy, solar energy, and electric power. If these experiments are Tocquevillian schoolhouses of pluralist commonwealth, "exploring new principles of ownership in everyday life," they also need to be scaled up to survive. Twenty-first-century populism must also include "challenges to corporations and elite concentrations of income and wealth," or in Alperowitz's prescient terms, the top "one percent." Alperovitz, echoing Rustin, thus calls for "strategic alliances to achieve power and momentum toward a thoroughgoing, elite-challenging paradigm."[94] The task for aspirational democratic populism, then, is to rearticulate the divided energies of radical democratic populism into a set of tensional relationships between outrageous resistance, everyday politics, and structural revolution—a set of relationships with resonance for radical democratic theory and practice in the face of emerging structures and dynamics of power.

EXPERIMENTS IN HORIZONTALITY: ASPIRATIONAL DEMOCRATIC POPULISM'S REBELLIOUS REFRAIN

Where liberal scholars have long exposed populism's temptation to foreclose democracy, whether through reactionary identitarian politics or by displacing the people's power onto charismatic leaders, radical democrats remind us that populist politics is rooted in the irresolvable paradoxes of popular sovereignty. Thus, populism also harbors a persistent democratizing aspiration, which exceeds not only familiar populist foreclosures on democracy, but also liberal efforts to correct for them via constitutional limits on popular sovereignty and democracy. In the remainder of this chapter, I develop an account of *aspirational democratic populism*, which has historically cultivated people's rebellious aspirations to share in power, and to do so in more pluralistic, egalitarian ways, across established borders that restrict politics and democracy. Aspirational democratic populism has crucial debts and resemblances in relation to existing radical democratic theories of populism. But it more faithfully tends populism's democratizing aspiration, by cultivating the tensional relationships between contests over collective identity and experiments with enacting popular power across a host of sites and scales.

Aspirational democratic populism has its source not only in the irresolvable paradoxes of popular sovereignty, but also in the ways this ideal has historically shaped the aspirations of actual people. Populism's "dangerous excess" begins with its ability to animate the usually dormant ideal of poplar sovereignty, by mobilizing the aspirations of ordinary people to exert a degree of power over their everyday lives and their collective fate. To aspire means to yearn for something that is out of reach. As Goodwyn reminds us, daily life in late modern societies is a hazard zone for democratic aspirations: they get narrowed by economic competition and social dislocation, distracted in mega-mediated public spheres, sublimated by the pleasures of commodious living, disciplined by social regulations and hierarchies, rendered cynical by distant, dysfunctional halls of power. People engaged in populist struggles often describe "waking up" to forces that have usurped their power and rendered them acquiescent.[95]

But activating the people's aspirations to power does not automatically steer populist excess toward rebelliousness. In many cases, the aspirations of neoliberal subjects are far too undernourished, not to mention unsupported by institutions and practices of power, to emerge as anything beyond the people's episodic appearance on the public stage. Populist moments often appear "episodic," "impatient," or "short-winded," not because populism is inherently apolitical, but because populist rhetoric lends itself to intense arousals of collective identification and affect, even in the absence of strategies for cultivating or sustaining people's emerging aspirations to power.[96] More troubling, populism's liberal critics are right to keep an eye on what I call populism's *reactionary aspirations*: those instances in which a perfect storm of economic insecurity and cultural status anxiety distort people's aspirations to power, breeding reactionary backlash and more virulent desires to dominate emerging social groups. This is a danger that everyday populists are rarely willing to countenance in their more celebratory renderings of populism. But liberal scholars raise a crucial concern when they caution that more participation, especially participation fueled by ressentiment, does not necessarily lead to more or better democracy. So too does the liberal refrain alert us to what, borrowing from Lauren Berlant, I call populism's *cruel aspirations*: its tendency to displace the people's aspirations to power, by acclaiming the rule of demagogues or, in the case of today's Tea Party, by placing people's faith in increasingly defiant forms of individualism. In cases such as these, when people surrender their aspirations to a strong leader, or to an impossible ideal of self-mastery, they may very well feel power vicariously, but they also end up reinforcing their own disempowerment.[97]

In speaking of populism's *rebellious aspirations*, I mean something different from an oppositional politics of resistance, whether it engages the people in reactionary backlash or in more productive struggles for hegemony. Unlike these modes of expression, rebellious activities do not exist for their own sake; they do not assume an already identified or articulated group, which claims power in relation to its enemy. Populism's rebellious aspirations are more incipient, emerging both to redress existing grievances and for the sake of possibilities yet to come. They begin in frustrated desires and cannot avoid naming a wrong or placing blame. Rebellious aspirations, for example, target sources of power that undermine people's capacities or exclude them from membership in the body politic or relegate them to chronic states of precarity. But if rebelliousness is oriented both against and beyond the status quo, it also requires the capacity to endure, at least long enough to open spaces for new democratic peoples and new kinds of democratic vision and practice to flourish. That is, populism's rebellious aspirations, though unruly, cannot survive absent the work of instituting new visions of politics (even as this entails deciding on matters of ruling and being ruled). Populism can only sustain people's rebellious aspirations, that is, by engaging them in experiments to build new practices, relationships, and institutions of power. Rebellious aspirations then take on a life of their own as people engage repeatedly in the disobedient activities of enacting alternatives to the status quo.

Populism's rebellious aspirations need to be cultivated. But efforts to do so will remain stunted, so long as radical democratic theorists and activists continue to divide the energetics of outrageous resistance and everyday politics. Stuck in this impasse, with neither oriented toward crafting long-term strategies to reconstruct large-scale economic, state, and social institutions, both camps mount scant responses to one of the fundamental characteristics of contemporary modes of power: that they operate via numerous relays between broad structures and dynamics, on the one hand, and everyday subjective practices and sensibilities, on the other. Unless populist movements become sensitized to these feedback loops, they will remain inadequate in the face of contemporary dynamics, most notably, megacirculations of power and hyperintense fields of resonance, which threaten to short-circuit populism's divided energetics: on the one side, wanting to rupture antidemocratic concentrations of power, and on the other, wanting to

root the more fragile beginnings of radical democratic power in grassroots institutions and practices.

Contrary to the conceptual tools of populist resistance and everyday populism, contemporary power increasingly accumulates via vast circulations of capital, finance, jobs, human beings, natural resources, weapons, communication,
and so on, that rupture and reconstitute material and cultural life. Such power
seeks totality in what Sheldon Wolin has termed "formless forms" of governance, most notably, endlessly innovative, multinational, corporate-state mergers, which fashion themselves as unfathomable, let alone unaccountable, to the
demands of popular discourse and representation. Moreover, where neoliberal
discourse celebrates continuous mobility, it conceals what are instead techniques
of "normalized agitation" and "perpetual demobilization," at least when considered from the vantage point of those whose everyday forms of work and community are uprooted and displaced.[98] The last decades of the twentieth century
witnessed Rust Belt factory towns abandoned at the whim of capital flight, labor
casualized through endless innovations in corporate restructuring, the power of
labor unions dismantled state by state, the life chances of marginalized youth outsourced to for-profit schools and, later, for-profit prisons, and immigrant dreams
traded between the welcome arms of corporate greed and the reactionary resentments of racialized border security. Staggering unemployment, gutted retirement
funds, and mass home foreclosures, all disproportionately affecting communities
of color, are the aftershocks of the first major financial crisis of the twenty-first
century, which finally brought the shadow dealings of the nation's deregulated
banking and credit industries into the public spotlight, only to leave them unpun-
ished, and even to crown them "too big to fail."[99] It is difficult to put faith in populisms that celebrate either the people's oppositional energies or their rootedness
in embodied democratic practice, when contemporary modes of power capital-
ize on the dynamics of rupture, at the expense of uprooting bodies, inherited
traditions and narratives, and many emergent communities of practice.

Coupled with these underregulated circulations of power, Bill Connolly
uses the term "resonance machine" to describe the intense "assemblages" of
ideology and affect that are made possible by rapidly changing communications technologies, which link corporate megamedia, new social media, and the
everyday spaces we inhabit, as we drive to work or school, relax in our family
rooms, wait to board a plane, gather for religious services, or spend our leisure
time at gun clubs, sporting events, or shopping malls. Resonant forces infiltrate,
pattern, and in key moments intensify our speech, perceptual habits, affective
responses, and dispositions toward the world. Connolly is most concerned with
today's "evangelical-capitalist resonance machine," a term he uses to describe
the "avenues of crossing and intensities of interinvolvement" between corporations, conservative think tanks, the Republican Party, evangelical churches, Fox

News, and its social media echo chamber. These parties amplify certain "affinities of sensibility," marked by dispositions of defiant individualism, extreme entitlement, ressentiment, bellicosity, and dogmatic fundamentalism, which reinforce both evangelical Christianity and unregulated, cowboy capitalism.[100] If the evangelical-capitalist resonance machine foments a militant spiritual defense behind right-wing visions of American politics, other forms of corporate-state mergers also rely on what Romand Coles calls "deceptive resonance machines." These name resonant assemblages that intensify our bodily attunement to the frequencies of media chatter and spin, while at the same time distracting or shutting down the dispositions that enable us to open toward the plurality and complexity of the world and toward those who are routinely made to disappear from public life.[101] Consider, for example, how easy it is to be lulled to sleep, and to have our edgier aspirations assimilated, by constant appeals from mainstream media, politicians, academic experts, and think tanks for "common-sense solutions" to issues as complex and as urgent to marginalized communities as gun control, immigration reform, and energy dependence.[102]

Contemporary American populisms face unprecedented dangers of fizzling out or sliding into reactionary and even fascistic modes, given their proximity to technologies of resonance that now saturate the feedback loops between neoliberal capitalist imperatives and everyday practice. At a minimum, people's aspirations to power risk being deflected or absorbed by contemporary fields of resonance, especially those that scramble the languages of capitalism and democracy. As Jodi Dean cautions, the flexibility of democratic rhetoric has created a demand for efficiency in governance, while pinning individual aspirations to capitalism's celebrated speed, hyperconnectivity, and abundance.[103] In the barely discernible sound waves of advertising, spin, and punditry, it is common enough to confuse revolution with the most up-to-date model iPhone or Chevy truck, while invoking technocratic pragmatism to brand real protest as mere reaction or wishful thinking.[104] In making sense of Occupy Wall Street's extraordinary eruption onto the public stage, for example, Americans can perhaps still hear the pedantic vibrations: "We know what Occupy Wall Street is against, but what are they for?" These anxieties return us to the doubts about the democratic ideal I raised in the introduction. Are our democratic aspirations now so flexible that they are fair play for both right-wing resonance machines and capitalism's resonant commodification of revolt? Are our democratic aspirations so fugitive that we cannot dream of revolutions that might transform these very structures and dynamics of power?

Amid these fields of circulation and resonance, aspirational democratic populisms can, and some do, cultivate rebellious aspirations to power by engaging people in *experiments with horizontality*. The concept of horizontality suggests, first and foremost, that populists seek to establish horizontal relations of power in a capitalist political culture that esteems technocrats, no longer obscures but still fails to punish the fraudulent activities of superelites, and makes competition and status-seeking ideological requisites not just for success, but for citizenship. The need to cultivate practices of and dispositions toward horizontal power sharing was Ella Baker's basic insight when she declared, "Strong people don't need strong leaders."[105] Contra neoliberal and many liberal visions of democracy, populists often experiment with grassroots, participatory forms of collective decision-making and action, for example, in consensus processes, cooperative economic activities, or community organizing. But Baker also organized youth, working-class people of color, and women to disrupt the bourgeois masculine social hierarchy within a more established Civil Rights movement. Indeed, as liberal theorists have cautioned, reactionary and assimilationist populisms demand equality-for-us, pitting the people not only against economic and political elites, but also, whether explicitly or through subtler forms of ignorance and exclusion, against new social groups clamoring for entry into the body politic.[106] In light of democracy's imperfection, even the most promising aspirational democratic populisms will reinforce some social hierarchies in their efforts to enact more horizontal relations of power.

For aspirational democratic populisms to enact the people's power beyond existing hierarchies, including those internal to any populism, they must also engage in ongoing contests over the *horizons* of collective identity and democracy. A horizon is both what is in front of us, the everyday limits of experience and perception that mark the borders of politics, and a sign of what is to come, the not yet imaginable political possibilities beyond the reach of sense and vision. In this sense, "horizon" acts as both a spatial and a temporal metaphor. It draws our attention to questions of inclusion and exclusion within "the people," for example, in terms of collective identity, territorial borders, legal recognition, or distribution of resources. It also reminds us that peoples emerge and take shape in part via contests over how to interpret the past, present, and future. As an active, contested concept, *horizon-tality* recognizes that the ground of horizontal power relations is always shifting, both in response to innovative forms of capitalist, state, and social hegemony that shape sense, perception, and vision, and in response to social groups and social ideas emerging from the margins of recognized speech and action.

Jacques Derrida helps us distill the meaning of horizontality, in this larger sense, when he argues that democracy is conditioned in the dissonant experience of being claimed by multiple "headings" at the same time.[107] He affirms that human social existence, insofar as it is linguistically mediated and historically finite, is bound to logics of cultural identity as one crucial component of ethics and politics. But he also argues that every cultural identity—in his example, European identity—is partially constituted by its "other heading," that is, its incompleteness in relation to whatever, inevitably, exceeds its grasp. Because of its conflicting horizons, democracy must always take "the structure of a promise," one that harbors "the memory of that which carries the future, the to-come, here and now."[108] As Derrida works the term *to-come*, it means something that has yet to emerge, even to be thought.[109] It can come from yesterday, today, or tomorrow, and from sites that are internal or external to the discourses, practices, and institutions by which a cultural identity gathers itself amid difference. It is carried not only by identifiable others, those socially and politically defined strangers who cross well-demarcated borders and trigger well-rehearsed postures and policies of closure. It emerges, all the more, with those indeterminate events that reveal previously unrecognized limits, whether to lay bare domination and exclusion within a people or to cast light on more just political relationships.[110]

Yet, given the continuous mobility and perpetual demobilization that define late capitalist political cultures, it is difficult to imagine how populists might turn moments of indeterminate rupture—for example, a financial crash or the uneven impacts of demographic shifts—into opportunities to cultivate popular power. Given radical democratic populism's divided energetics, it is even more difficult to see how populists can enact power in ways that break through the resonances that distract us and dull our senses in today's socially mediated lives. Horizontality's *promise* of democratization, then, demands an account of the energetics needed to contest the horizons of the people and democracy. The concept of horizontality actively sustains the tensions between the everyday experiences of embodied democratic practice and the oppositional energies that reveal what Laclau calls the frontiers, or the groundless grounds, of the people and democracy. Populism's democratizing aspirations are unlikely to flourish without the ever-recurrent promise, felt palpably in the "here and now," that the people's power can be enacted beyond any present configuration of material or aesthetic reality. Populism's outrageous rhetorics of resistance serve as iterated, vociferous reminders that the people have historically enacted themselves in concrete terms that move the boundary lines of power and powerlessness. And yet, the new horizons of possibility that dwell within what Martin Luther King Jr. called "the muffled groans and passionate yearnings" of emerging actors are never fully known at the moment a people begins to take shape in opposition to the status quo. It is by cultivating these more inchoate aspirations to power that populists can give shape to democracy "to come."

On the one hand, then, populism's rebellious aspirations must begin in people's everyday experiences, in the visceral sites of awakening to wrong, opening to hope, and recognizing allies and strangers who might join in the struggle for new and more horizontal relations of power. As everyday populists remind us, this requires engaging people in deep, patient work at the level of cultivating democratic dispositions and capacities, in order to provoke and sustain both resistance and radical transformations of power in the first place. This means inventing practices capable of dehabituating actors from being quite so responsive to the daily agitations, distractions, and affective vibrations of various neoliberal and right-wing resonance machines. And it means rehabituating them to adopt dispositions toward critique, public work, and collective action.

We might think, for example, of a long history of cooperative struggles, from agrarian cooperatives, to worker-owned factories, to today's solidarity economies.[111] These iterated experiments in cooperative economy pull individuals out of the isolated experiences of competitive capitalism, which condition people toward dispositions of deference and desperation in the face of so many commonplace explanatory justifications saturating workplaces and media: laziness, lack of skill, the need for efficiency, cost-benefit calculations, and the "right to work." And they disrupt these patterns and messages, in part, by introducing people to new practices and habits of deliberating over matters of governance, cooperating in the labor of production and sales, building coalitions with other industries and community institutions, and instituting alternatives to daily routines and hierarchies that had previously seemed inevitable. In this sense, the insights of everyday politics add a crucial, qualitative dimension for those who hope to mobilize populism's rebellious energies. It allows them to reframe populism's negative "logic of articulation," with its quantitative worries over balancing intension and extension to amass loud enough demands, and instead attend to the visceral and affective groundwork of rebellion, which determines qualities such as pluralism, relational trust, and buoyancy in grassroots movements.

On the other hand, to get stuck in the here and now risks parochialism, for example, by foreclosing the people in identitarian terms or limiting populism's constitutional struggles to questions about what is or is not allowed in the people's backyard. Populism's rebellious aspirations thus depend on its experiments with more disruptive repertoires of horizontality, which ensure that the borders of the people and democracy are never foreclosed once and for all, but always remain open to the emergence of new social groups and new ways of seeing and doing. This requires linking everyday politics to farther-ranging critique and positive vision.

The ideological and rhetorical tools of populist resistance enable people to perceive more clearly the ways in which deregulated capital, constitutional rules, state policies, and social hierarchies leave potentially rebellious peoples disempowered and divided. While it is important to create spaces to do politics under the radar of these structural dynamics, it is no less crucial to engage in broad power analyses, so as to negotiate paths in light of them, and even to transform them. Indeed, efforts to generate jobs and raise wages, or to counter predatory lending and home foreclosure, or to fashion sustainable local environmental policies will remain fragile and limited in scope, in the face of massive, unaccountable circulations of power, not to mention antidemocratic resonance machines that distract or breed resentment in many possible allies. Democratic theorists and activists should thus celebrate populism's flair for inventing counterhegemonic discourses, and they must find better ways to disseminate them via linkages between social media, alternative public media, and mainstream corporate media. Nor can populists overlook the need to develop the critical capacities of diverse actors and their dispositions toward outrage and rebellion, to counteract the soporific lull of deceptive resonance machines.

In calling people beyond the horizons of the here and now, aspirational democratic populism facilitates efforts by unlikely actors to engage each other across differences in their social identities, spaces, and times. As Connolly foresees, radical democratic "counter-resonance machines" must embody just such a "political assemblage composed of multiple constituencies whose diverse experiences resonate together, finding expression in churches, schools, factories, neighborhoods, the media, occupational groups, the electorate, a segment of the capitalist class, state policy, and cross-state movements."[112] To facilitate such resonance, finally, populisms cannot avoid crafting strategies to engage and transform large-scale structures and dynamics, for example, by reconstructing constitutional rules and state policies, seeking unlikely allies in state agencies and private businesses, appropriating media technologies, looking for openings to restructure viable markets of production and employment, and building coalitions with cross-state actors against international financial and governmental institutions.[113] Though these kinds of engagements risk assimilation, they are nonetheless indispensable to cultivating populism's rebellious aspirations, partly in resonance with, partly in the name of broadening the vision of, everyday, cocreative populism and giving form to the not-yet promised by populist resistance.

The concept of horizontality is no panacea for twenty-first-century anxieties about the democratic ideal. In business management and branding, the terms "horizontal" and "horizon" promise profit, not revolutionary change. Horizontal and vertical refer to business integration models that offer different avenues to monopoly. In journals such as *Business and Management Horizons*, readers might encounter start-up tips from Horizon Ventures, management advice from Horizons Business Solutions, investment strategies from Capital Horizons or Horizon Capital, and workforce training trends from New Horizons Computer Learning Centers. In today's cash-strapped public service arena, by contrast, the aspirations of nonprofit groups such as Horizons for Homeless Children and Horizons Anti-Poverty Program seem fugitive at best. In this context, it is easy to see why populists might want to hold fast to tried-and-true visions of how to arouse collective identification and constitute popular power. Protestors never seem to tire of the promise "The people united will never be defeated," and

I believe many still feel a sense of collective energy and purpose when we march through the streets chanting, "This is what democracy looks like!" Likewise, community organizers find familiar footing in IAF's "iron rule": "Never do for others what they can do for themselves."[114] Though I advocate new repertoires of populist rhetoric and practice—and crave a more resonant poetics of protest and everyday politics—I am not interested in abandoning what has worked. Recovering inherited traditions of populism will be crucial to cultivating populism's rebellious aspirations.

So will reconceiving the conditions and possibilities of populism and democracy today. Connecting populist identification and ongoing efforts to constitute pluralistic, egalitarian forms of popular power will require building resonances and relationships between things we typically keep separate in democratic theory and practice: ordinary practices and extraordinary spectacles; durability and disruption; the corporeal and affective qualities of politics and the symbolic and ideological politics of imagination. In developing the concept of horizontality, I see horizons as contact zones at which democratic theorists and activists might begin to think these dimensions of the political together in light of present dangers. Contact zones might be the intersections of social group difference, varying sites and scales of collective life, the presence of pasts that carry both dead weight and buoyancy, disciplined bodies whose routinized practices need disruption, but who cannot flourish without routes and practices that orient them toward better futures, and so much more. We contact alternative aspirations for democracy, that is, both at the hazy outer reaches of dreams we cannot yet bring into focus and in the immediate contexts and people we encounter in our struggles for change. My ambitions in democratizing populism stretch to those horizons that are not yet imaginable: democracy beyond capitalism, whiteness, nationalism, and other modes of domination and dehumanization. I do not think aspirational democratic populism will take us the whole distance. It does, however, offer crucial insights on how to connect the far horizons of our rebellious aspirations for democracy to the immediate horizons of the world we live in and the people we are today. Intensifying these connections is a crucial way theorists and activists can sharpen democratic language and imagination amid the flexibility of capitalist culture and cultivate fugitive aspirations that endure long enough to enact structural change.

"Fanning the Spark of Hope"

Populism's Rebellious Nineteenth-Century Commonwealth

For every image of the past that is not recognized by the present as one of its own concerns threatens to disappear irretrievably. . . . Only that historian will have the gift of fanning the spark of hope in the past who is firmly convinced that *even the dead* will not be safe from the enemy if he wins. And this enemy has not ceased to be victorious.

—WALTER BENJAMIN

The People's Party is more than the organized discontent of the people. It is the organized aspiration of the people for a fuller, nobler, richer, kindlier life for every man, woman, and child in the ranks of humanity.

—HENRY D. LLOYD

Populism's namesake in America—the late nineteenth-century Populist Party, or People's Party—emerged from decades of working-class and middle-class struggle against the banks, railroads, and manufacturing companies at the heart of America's first corporate revolution.[1] In the years leading up to the heyday of the People's Party in the 1890s, Populism's revolt of "the people" against the "money power" took shape in the insurgent activities of white and black agrarian rebels, urban immigrant laborers, agitators for women's rights, prohibitionists, greenbackers, single-tax advocates, saloon utopianists, Marxist and Christian socialists, armies of the unemployed, and other "cranks, tramps, and vagabonds."[2] Celebrated with a capital *P*, the original "Populism" was really many populisms at once.

This chapter evaluates the links Populism built between the centralizing politics of the People's Party, which mobilized mass resistance against the corporate revolution, and the decentered spaces of everyday practice that were the incubators of overlapping experiments in becoming a people. The disparate actors who formed Populism's unwieldy coalitions saw the People's Party as a chance to reassert horizontal popular power in opposition to unprecedented hierarchies of wealth and political influence during the Gilded Age. Launched at the St. Louis Industrial Conference in 1892, the People's Party codified its vision in the preamble to the Omaha Platform adopted later that year: "We seek to restore the government of the Republic to the hands of 'the plain people' with whose class it originated."[3] To organize one of the most massive and sustained social movements in America's history, however, Populists needed more than the rhetoric of unity in the face of a common foe. The centralizing voice of the People's Party would have been disembodied and lifeless without its deep relations and looser affinities with myriad, decentered spaces of everyday Populist practice: the public work of cooperative farming; the insurgent rituals of boycotts and strikes; the political education carried out in rural lecture circuits, immigrant social halls, and union reading rooms; the revivalism of prohibition; the cross-cutting fabric of women's social networks; the disruptive energies of suffrage; and the resilient efforts of black communities to build schools, promote economic independence, and secure civil and political rights. These were the spaces in which, for decades prior to the People's Party, grassroots Populists experimented with parallel institutions and practices of political economy and democracy. In doing so, they cultivated dispositions toward horizontal cooperation and spirited rebellion in people who had come to accept the inevitability of social division and hard times. Drawing on an array of organizing traditions, they mobilized the motley crew of actors whose experimental modes of becoming a people both produced and contested Populism.

Populism's namesake in America exemplifies both the promise and the persistent challenges of aspirational democratic populism. The Populist movement began in the experimental spaces of the agrarian and labor movements of the 1870s and 1880s, as farmers and laborers invented alternatives to the everyday rituals of domination that had for decades marked their horizons of economic and political possibility. These horizons had long constrained working people's abilities to imagine more egalitarian, pluralistic forms of collective identification and democratic life. Populists found ways to cultivate their rebellious aspirations by linking their multiform experiments in horizontal power to broader visions of resistance and structural change, first in the agrarian and labor movements and then through the People's Party. These links were often tenuous. Indeed, the effects of the corporate revolution were uneven, layering new inequalities over old ones, including hierarchies of race, ethnicity, class, and gender from which

Populism was not immune. Populism's move into the electoral arena, moreover, was a source of heated debate among agrarian and labor leaders, who worried that their movements could not withstand the friction of mobilizing broad-based identification behind the People's Party. Time and again, I argue, Populists confronted a central question that impacted the rebelliousness of their aspirations: could efforts to arouse collective identification and constitute horizontal popular power *against* the corporate revolution remain open to contests over the horizons of the people and democracy *within* Populism?

To speak of Populism's radical democratic aspirations is largely unthinkable in academic and public discourse today. This is because the movement, unsuccessful in its own day, is still not safe from liberal-capitalist forms of democracy that have "not ceased to be victorious." History is a practice of narrative montage: historical narratives gather biographies, events, and other images from the past in connection with present conceptual frameworks of recognition and disavowal. What Benjamin refers to as the victor's version of history still shapes which images are available to public memories of Populism. At best, public memory records Populism as an ill-fated, third-party reform movement. That movement foundered on the inability of white farmers to win the support of black farmers, immigrant laborers, and sundry radicals at the periphery of the People's Party, and it was ultimately co-opted by the Democratic Party of William Jennings Bryan. At worst, we remember Populism as a nostalgic backlash against capitalist modernization, as notable for its racist, nativist, and patriarchal rhetoric as for its economic grievances.[4] Populism's more rebellious images—evident, for example, in the everyday radicalism of its agrarian cooperative crusade, the autonomous organizing of black farmers and laborers, and the groundswell of women's rights activism in the movement—have smoldered in obscurity.

By "fanning the spark of hope" in such images of Populism, the narrative I tell in this chapter recovers unexpected resources to cultivate aspirational democratic populisms today. I argue that Populism was able to cultivate the rebellious aspirations of disparate actors where it succeeded in mobilizing broad-based resistance and identification in tandem with its multiform experiments in constituting horizontal power. Where this failed, Populists were unable to sustain the egalitarian, pluralistic forms of popular power needed to transform a democracy increasingly subject to corporate and state control and resurgent racism and nativism. Revisiting Populism, then, recovers crucial orientations toward populist vision and practice that have been layered over by liberal, capitalist history, but it also revives tensions that contemporary populists have largely avoided by splitting their energies between everyday politics and resistance. Rather than finding prescriptions in Populism, I argue that its practices of centering and decentering identification and power suggest a crucial dynamic for negotiating the horizons of democracy.

THE VICTOR'S VERSION
OF NINETEENTH-CENTURY POPULISM

Prominent histories of Populism, written in the latter half of the twentieth century, played a key role in shaping current scholarly dismissals of small-*p* populism. In turn, the consensus on small-*p* populism limits what we are able to learn from the Populist movement. We can trace much mainstream American discourse on populism to Richard Hofstadter's Pulitzer Prize–winning work, *The Age of Reform*.[5] Hofstadter characterizes the "agrarian revolt" of the 1890s as a reactionary response to the Industrial Revolution. The People's Party capitalized on "a kind of popular impulse that is endemic to American political culture," led in this case by farmers and small business owners who were anxious about their slipping status in a period of economic change and heightened immigration.[6] They responded to their anxieties by blaming immigrants and conspiratorial elites, and by seeking refuge in a return to the "golden age" of a more harmonious, self-sufficient, yeoman farm society.[7] For Hofstadter, Populism's blend of suspicion, nativism, and nostalgia is characteristic of an "old and recurrent" style of rhetoric and imagination in American political culture. From early anti-Masonry to the People's Party to Barry Goldwater, populists have fomented a "paranoid style" in American politics. Populist "fringe groups" fan the flames of "status anxiety," or in today's terms, "culture wars," in reaction to feeling displaced by market fluctuations and changing racial and ethnic demographics.[8] Joined by other Cold War–era liberal scholars, notably, Daniel Bell and Seymour Martin Lipset, Hofstadter helped shape the consensus view of American populism as an illiberal, irrational form of mob rule.[9] That such views still hold sway, even among those sympathetic to populism, is evident in Barack Obama's infamous 2008 campaign speech: "it's not surprising" that these groups "cling to guns or religion or antipathy to people who aren't like them or anti-immigrant sentiment," in order to shore up in cultural status what they lack in economic security.[10]

The liberal consensus on Populism has not gone unchallenged in scholarly circles. Historians such as Norman Pollack defend the People's Party against "the charge of double irrationality," that is, the accusation that Populists promoted "retrogressive" views in response to "nonexistent grievances." Pointing to Populism's egalitarian ideology, they conclude that the movement was a "progressive social force" seeking a viable alternative to the very real crises of capitalist modernization.[11] Lawrence Goodwyn's study of agrarian Populism in his book *Democratic Promise* remains one of the most influential attempts to recuperate the movement's radical democratic politics. Far from reactionary, Populism cultivated an "intensely democratic 'movement culture' of self-respect and aspiration." It was able to stem, for a time, the "gradual erosion of democratic aspirations" that would come to characterize late capitalist societies.[12] Why was the liberal view of Populism ill equipped to appreciate this? First, Populism's critics, and many of its admirers, had not yet studied Populism. Instead, they had analyzed its "shadow movement," that is, William Jennings Bryan and other opportunistic Democratic leaders who ultimately co-opted the People's Party. Second, liberal and capitalist theorists had few tools to analyze social movements outside the model of interest groups and electoral politics. Thus, they were primed to see as spontaneous and reactionary a movement that was, in reality, the result of decades of grassroots organizing and cultural change. Goodwyn also wrote to counter Marxist scholars, who saw American Populism as a "spontaneous" uprising led by reactionary, petit bourgeois farmers who were incapable of offering a transformative critique of capitalism. Where Marxists pointed to Populism as a symbol of what was lacking in America's "exceptionalist" history—that is, a viable socialist tradition—Goodwyn reframed the movement as a radical democratic alternative. "No one," he insisted, had yet "regarded the agrarian revolt as a mass democratic movement that was organically shaped by its own internal dynamics and by its own evolving popular culture of democratic thought."[13]

This, in Goodwyn's account, is precisely what Populism was. Beginning with the creation of the Farmers' Alliance in 1877, agrarian Populism built "the largest democratic mass movement in American history."[14] By 1890, the National Farmers' Alliance had organized some forty thousand local alliances across forty-three states and territories. It created a widespread network of cooperative economies and nurtured a mobile system of grassroots education, deliberation, and protest. These "parallel institutions" of political economy and democracy were at the root of Populism's struggle for cultural transformation. When the People's Party forged its way onto the national political scene in the elections of 1892, it was the Alliance cooperative movement—and its tenuous coalitions with black farmers, immigrant laborers, and social reformers—that had laid the tracks. Despite its losses in the electoral arena, Populism's "democratic promise" was its ability to cultivate political subjects capable of challenging received cultures of democracy and aspiring to wield collective power over the fundamental structures of their lives.[15]

Goodwyn's account of nineteenth-century Populism animated "new populists," such as Sheldon Wolin and Harry Boyte, who, like Goodwyn, hoped to cultivate the roots of popular power in an era of neoliberal capitalism. His work rightly remains a touchstone for radical democratic populism today.[16] As such, it contains two key limits. First, Goodwyn reinforces a familiar story of Populism as a movement of white farmers who tried, and ultimately failed, in their "outreach" to black farmers, urban immigrants, and others at the periphery of the movement.[17] The center-periphery narrative of Populism has come into question in recent years. Several studies of Black Populism, in particular, have revealed the independent organizing and vision of blacks in the movement. So too has women's activism become a vital part of the story of Populism.[18] These new revisionist historians do not refute that Populism was, in terms of status and power, a white-led movement. Indeed, most white Populists saw the movement in these terms. Nor do they question the role of the white Farmers' Alliance in mobilizing white farmers as the largest base of the People's Party. But they do avoid the temptation to assimilate marginalized forms of Populist resistance and radical experiments with popular power to the terms of a manly, white Populism. Their work should encourage us to view Populism as a movement without a stable center. Just as the People's Party was the result of an unwieldy coalition, key populist organizations, such as the Farmers' Alliance, Colored Farmers' Alliance, and Knights of Labor, were the product of conflict and negotiation between local, state, and national bodies. Some of these were open to building popular power across lines of race, ethnicity, gender, and class; others became exemplars of white supremacy, nativism, and patriarchy. Viewed in this light, Populism was not only an anticorporate revolt of "the people" against the "money power"; it was also a movement that placed internal contests over race, gender, and national identity at the center of its efforts to enact horizontal popular power.

Second, despite his efforts to the contrary, Goodwyn's account risks reinforcing the widespread belief that Populism was antistatist. By focusing on Populism's "movement culture," of course, he intends to redefine politics. In order to transform the institutions and structures of the state, he insists, Populists first needed to "establish parallel institutions where people could experiment with democratic forms."[19] He thus privileges the role that cooperatives, Alliance schools, and other civil society institutions played in cultivating political actors with democratic aspirations. But what *was* the relationship between Populism's everyday institutions, on the one hand, and its vision for broad structural reform, on the other? Goodwyn's Populists understood that structural reform of government and capitalism would be necessary to protect their experimental spaces of cooperative commonwealth. This understanding led them to form the People's Party. But it has taken more recent scholars to translate Populism's policy ambitions from a set of demands to a positive vision of the democratic state and its role in the structural reform of capitalism. As Elizabeth Sanders argues, Populists sought to expand the powers of the state to "establish public control over a rampaging capitalism" and to "provide certain public goods and services" that would not otherwise flourish in a market economy. A precursor to the Progressive movement, Populism envisioned an interventionist state not as a bureaucratic servant of the people, but as the basis for a broadly participatory citizenry.[20] Absent an active state that could dramatically curb the excesses of corporate capitalism, Populism's rebellious aspirations had little chance of enduring outside the everyday politics of its parallel institutions.

The continued study of nineteenth-century Populism by twenty-first-century scholars has made it possible to pull together the three facets of aspirational democratic populism in the movement. In most studies of Populism, scholars treat either its everyday politics or one or more dimensions of its politics of resistance (against capitalism, white supremacy, nativism, or patriarchy) or, in rare cases, its proposals for structural transformation of capitalism and the state. In reality, Populism was one of a few movements in American history that connected multiform experiments in local politics with polyvocal practices of resistance and concrete proposals for structural change. In these ways, Populism contested not only the horizons of the people and democracy in its time; it also contests the narrowed horizons of the theory and practice of populism in America today.

DEMOCRATIZING ASPIRATIONS
IN THE "BODY OF THE COMMONALITY"

When some ten thousand farmers, laborers, and reformers gathered in St. Louis in 1892 to form a new political party, they met "in the midst of a nation brought to the verge of moral, political, and material ruin." Asserting that "the conditions which surround us justify our cooperation," they drafted a platform that gave collective expression to the hard times endured by countless working people during the Gilded Age: "The fruits of the toil of millions are boldly stolen to build up colossal fortunes for a few, unprecedented in the history of mankind; and the possessors of these, in turn, despise the republic and endanger liberty." In the face of mass dispossession, the People's Party claimed, "This Republic can only endure while built upon the love of the whole people for each other and for the nation."[21] The rhetoric of the Omaha Platform, officially adopted months later at the party's first national nominating convention in Nebraska, gave symbolic voice to the growing social and political cleavage between the "money power" and the "producing classes." Blaming elites for bringing the nation to the edge of ruin, the People's Party promised to redeem the republic by uniting the people under a new democratic commonwealth.

The Omaha Platform is the principal document in the literature on Populism. It is a touchstone for Populism's rhetoric of resistance and popular identification. But it was also a political act. The result of uneasy coalitions and heated debate, the Omaha Platform reflects decades of on-the-ground organizing for economic and social reform. Its central planks drew from twenty years of greenback radicalism and represented the last stand of farmers struggling to keep their ambitious cooperative movement afloat. These include, among others, demands for free and unlimited coinage of silver; government control of the money supply; government loans and debt relief for farmers; nationalization of railroads, telephone,

and telegraph; and government reclamation of unused railroad, corporate, and
foreign-owned lands. Many of the platform's secondary resolutions were born of
years on the picket line, most notably, in calls to demolish the Pinkerton "mer-
cenary armies," enforce the eight-hour workday, and restrict contract labor and
"undesirable immigration." Others reflect the general anticorporate and antielite
sentiment that had crystallized in the trenches of an era of economic and social
reform: a ban on corporate subsidies; a graduated income tax; ballot reform, but
"without federal intervention" to protect blacks in the South; the use of initiative and referendum; direct election of senators; and stricter term limits for the
offices of president and vice president. Finally, the platform indirectly references
temperance, suffrage, and a host of other social issues left out after intense debate.
It declares "the party of reform" to be "upon the side of every proposition which
will tend to make men intelligent, virtuous, and temperate" and promises that the
"forces of reform this day organized will never cease to move forward until every
wrong is remedied, and equal rights and equal privileges securely established for
all the men and women of this country."[22]

Reading the Omaha Platform as a political act highlights the array of struggles
for popular power that joined forces under the umbrella of the People's Party.
These diverse reform movements played a vital role in mobilizing grassroots
energies during the Gilded Age and eventually in generating broad support for
the People's Party. Populism thus developed its rhetorical vision of resistance and
popular identification in tandem with the everyday practices of its myriad "forces
of reform." Populism's coalitional actors had unequal influence on the language
and demands of the national party platform. Some of the democratizing aspirations of blacks, women, socialists, and others didn't make it into the Omaha
Platform (though state and local Populist parties show much wider variation).
What these actors did do, however, is sustain and enliven the rhetoric and practices of horizontality in the movement, that is, ongoing contests over the horizons of the people and democracy. These contests shaped not only Populism's
resistance to the corporate revolution, but also its more rebellious aspirations to
constitute egalitarian, pluralistic forms of popular power. By evaluating Populism
in this way, I want to shift attention from what the movement tells us about the
status of peoplehood, a rather static, bounded concept of collective identity, and
refocus our inquiries on what it can show us about the practices of "peopling,"
that is, the active, negotiated practices of collective identification and constituting popular power. Peopling names the convergence between these ongoing
practices and the moments when new political actors come out of the shadows
to contest the terms of the people and democracy. The active connotation of the
term, "peopling," and its connection to experimental democratic practice, serves
a point of emphasis: Populist actors created their vision of cooperative commonwealth partly by contesting the terms through which Gilded Age Americans

understood themselves as a people, partly by enacting alternative practices of getting into political community with others. Peopling is thus a movement, or many movements, beyond the borders of established peoplehood—including the modes of being and becoming a people.

Populism's Rhetoric of Peopling:
Envisioning Cooperative Commonwealth

As Michael Kazin has observed, Populism's "unstable amalgam of social groups and political organizations" could agree on at least two things: a critique of the cataclysmic tyranny of corporate capitalism and the "urgent need for a messianic awakening to bring about the sweeping changes required" to redeem democracy.[23] In this respect, Populist identification has resonances with the familiar theories of populism associated with Carl Schmitt and Ernesto Laclau. Populists organized around a central cleavage between "the plain people" and "the money power." That cleavage demarcated a political frontier between the status quo, or, "plutocracy," and the Populist vision of a "cooperative commonwealth." A closer look at Populism's rhetoric, however, reveals a more complicated picture. Contra Schmitt, the terrain of Populist rhetoric was internally contested. Thus, we cannot confine the "democratic substance" of Populism to any stable vision of collective or national identity. Populist identification did, however, have substance. Contra Laclau's rarified theory of populist discourse, Populist identification required actors to draw on language that would resonate with the deep strata of the histories and everyday lives of disparate communities of working people. Populists revived and reworked several living traditions of rhetoric contained in America's populist imaginary to articulate both their critique of the corporate revolution and their positive visions of democracy. What we see in Populist discourse, then, is recognition of the social and historically embodied character of language and rhetoric, but not, as many liberals and radical democrats fear, inevitably toward the end of unity. Instead, Populism's rhetoric carried a dual directionality. On the one end, it had the breadth and depth to encourage mass identification with "the plain people" and to mobilize anger and hostility against "the money power." On the other end, marginalized actors within the movement repeatedly appealed to their own substantive traditions to appropriate and redirect the movement's more centralizing rhetoric and vision.

The corporate revolution was at the center of Populist invective. Editorialists and orators cast corporations as "great engines of oppression," as a "gigantic manpower, with soulless existence, moving, acting and dealing in the walks of men." They were like Frankenstein monsters: as "artificial individuals," corporations were the "creation of the law," but in one tale after another, "the creature . . . became greater and larger than the creator."[24] According to Populist rhetoric, the "Reign of the Corporation" had turned courts and judges into "mere tools and vassals and jumping jacks," it had "corrupted legislators and hundreds of thousands [of] sub-servient office-holders," and it had turned the news media into a "Partizan Hireling Press."[25] Such rhetoric was hardly overstated. During the second half of the nine-teenth century, banks, railroads, and manufacturers used a variety of legislative and judicial maneuvers to delineate an autonomous economic sphere; increase the size, mobility, and lifespan of capital power; invent corporate personhood and attach new rights to it; and win policy battles over money and credit, interstate commerce, and labor and land policy.[26] Business interests also tightened their hold over the two major parties and the mainstream press, effectively narrowing the limits of public discourse and political debate.[27] The macro-level organs of politics in America thus began to crowd out opportunities for broad and diverse participa-tion in democratic life. As moneyed elites consolidated power across spheres, they were able to steer the processes of modernization.

Populists also had to contend with a new ideology of progress that justi-fied the corporate revolution and was taking hold of America's burgeoning liberal-capitalist social imaginary. At the heart of this new ideology, classical eco-nomics and social Darwinism amalgamated in the public discourse of the late nineteenth century. The corporate revolution coincided with the growing belief that individual liberty depended on self-regulating markets that could foster pure competition according to the law of supply and demand. While the laws of the market were marshaled to justify economic inequality—"overproduction" and the "iron law of wages" rolled off many elite tongues—it was the rise of social Darwinism in the 1880s that lent modern moral authority to hierarchies of class, race, and gender. In coining the term "survival of the fittest," Herbert Spencer attributed its social beneficence to the fact that "the average vigour of any race would be diminished did the diseased and feeble habitually survive and propa-gate."[28] The new ideology of progress thus established a competitive social terrain in which each individual was deemed master of his own fate and in which human perfectibility mandated letting the weak perish. A major influence on politics, the rules of laissez-faire, Darwinian progress also justified nonintervention in response to the massive social dislocations of capitalist modernization. Elites stoked "the fear of 'paternalism,'" charged the Topeka *Advocate*, whenever the working classes called for government "interference with the system which has caused these conditions."[29]

Not only individual, but also national progress was increasingly understood in economic terms. When the Democratic-Populist fusion candidate William Jennings Bryan lost the presidential election of 1896, he lost to a Republican Party waving the banner of "peace, progress, patriotism, and prosperity." At enor-mous "flag day" rallies across the country, where slogans warned that "1896 is as vitally important as 1861," Republican strategists capitalized on emotionally charged memories of the Civil War to herald William McKinley as the protector of national order and the agent of national prosperity. What McKinley would protect, amid a decade of economic depression and social upheaval, was the gold standard: no less than the basis of "sound money," the "security of contracts," and "the national honor."[30] Lost on many people was the irony that the international gold standard marked the erosion of national authority vis-à-vis international markets and corporate capitalism.[31] Instead, more and more citizens were beginning to believe what US senator and secretary of state William Seward had forecast in 1853: "The nation that draws the most materials and provisions from the earth, and fabricates the most, and sells the most of production and fabrics to foreign nations, must be, and will be, the great power of the earth."[32] On this logic, it was corporate enterprise—which fueled technological advancement and propelled market and territorial expansion—that would inevitably steer America into the future.

Populists countered this dominant social imaginary with their own vision of "cooperative commonwealth." "Common wealers" called for a democracy based on popular ownership of wealth.[33] This would require citizens capable of enacting "the principle of cooperation in every department of life to its fullest extent"— a distant vision, to be sure, for working people trapped on the underside of a laissez-faire, Darwinian ideological universe that declared competition inevitable.[34] In this divided social field, Populists had recourse to the language of producerism, an idiom that had spurred rural and working-class radicalism since early days of the Revolution. Stated succinctly by one Alabama Populist: since labor "produces all the wealth of the country, it should be respected above all things." That was, in great part, because people who engaged in daily toil were said to embody the virtues of discipline, industriousness, and independence that foster economic productivity and republican politics.[35] One *Farmers' Alliance* editorial summed up the grievances of producers during the Gilded Age: "The simple fact that, despite a generation of hard toil, the people are poor today, mortgage-ridden and distressed, is sufficient evidence that the whole system under which they have lived is a lie and an imposture. They have produced but they possess not."[36] This line of critique was not limited to America's bloated economic system, but applied to its political system as a whole. As the Omaha Platform boldly stated, Populists sought to "restore the government of the Republic to the hands of 'the plain people' with whose class it originated."[37] Declaring producers the engines of the nation's economy and the moral backbone of its social and political order, Populists urged working-class people to see themselves as the vital center of American democracy.

As a language of collective identification, producerism had its limits. For one, it constructed the ideal citizen in white, masculine, middle-class terms. Producerism historically celebrated the self-reliance and self-defense of "the middling sort," in opposition not only to wealthy elites but also to a lower class of groups who were seen as undisciplined, servile, or dependent. The latter represented direct economic competition, but also the social depths to which producing classes must not fall.[38] As far back as the pre-Revolutionary era, backwoods farmers insisted that "laboring Men ... support the World of Mankind" and "Farmers in reality uphold the State."[39] They appealed to producer rhetoric to justify violent direct action and demand colonial protection from both aristocratic landlords and indigenous peoples, whom they labeled "lawless banditti."[40] Producer rhetoric's original ties to "settler colonialism" thus associate it with a vicious strain of white working-class ressentiment that deepened as settlers encountered indigenous peoples and Mexicans at the United States' expanding frontiers and as Anglo-Saxon laborers clashed with immigrants and blacks in the nation's industrializing cities.[41] In this vein, white Populists commonly drew on animalistic tropes to dehumanize "filthy, festering" immigrants from Central Europe and Asia, who "degrade[d] labor and aggrandize[d] capital," and to warn against "racial mixing" with blacks, who were said to have "more of the animal and less of the man in [their] nature."[42] Likewise, when Populists called on "the manhood of the nation [to] rise up in defense of liberty," they disavowed the activism of women, who were deemed too "fair" and "weak" for politics, and whose toil signified the poverty of their husbands and fathers.[43]

Yet, as Catherine Stock explains, Populist organizers explicitly relied on the rhetoric of producerism as a "strategy to link the futures of black and white and farmer and laborer together."[44] Despite the dominant white overtones of producer rhetoric, appeals to the "common interests" of the producing classes enabled many blacks, immigrants, and women to make more radical demands for equal economic and political rights.[45] And these were echoed in the claims of white male Populists that "the negro is a man and a citizen," that black men held "the same rights under the law that the white man does," that corrupt labor laws "would [as] soon make a criminal of me" as they did of urban immigrants, and that the reform movement must advocate political rights and economic opportunities for women.[46] If the rhetoric of producerism directed many Populists and their adversaries to imagine the people in myopic terms, that same rhetoric led organizers and actors to look for allies in unexpected places. Thus, the dual directionality of producer rhetoric opened spaces for people to imagine Populism as a coalitional movement that sought "equal rights and equal privileges" for "all the men and women of [the] country."[47]

Producerism also had an uneasy relation to capitalism. Producer rhetoric drew on the familiar Lockean assumption that individual labor was the source of economic value, and the Protestant belief that hard work signified individual moral virtue.[48] As such, producerism at times reinforced the capitalist tenet of private property. Given that small farmers and businessmen comprised the wealthier ranks of Populism, many movement actors appealed to "justice in business for each individual."[49] In its more radical overtones, however, the ideal of producerism resonated with a belief in the social nature of property. Populists rebuked the "use of public powers or public property for private profit."[50] They argued that certain goods, for example, steam, electricity, even land, were "public in nature." Thus, "the government, that is, the people" must assert "rightful dominion" over them.[51] It was common for Populists to contend that "the industrial system of a nation, like its political system, should be a government of and for and by the people alone." They saw "industrial freedom" as the basis for "political freedom" and for a "lasting people's government."[52] For many labor organizations, the Colored Farmers' Alliance, more radical white Alliance leaders and newspapers, and of course, the movement's socialist wing, "industrial democracy" required "collective ownership of all the means of production and distribution."[53] The economic impact of producerism was thus widely contested within Populist rhetoric. These contests bore out in the platform of the People's Party, which envisioned overlapping forms of political economy: greater protection of free enterprise for small farmers, income redistribution, fair loans for cooperatives, state regulation of monetary policy, and even state ownership of public services such as railroads and communication.

Appropriating the popular capitalist trope, Henry D. Lloyd conceded that the "survival of the strongest" is "the whole idea of State and of society." But for Lloyd, it was the "stronger virtues" that must be preserved, along with the contributions of those who aspire to "the self-interest of the community."[54] In this way, Populism's vision of cooperative commonwealth combined the movement's more expansive interpretations of producerism with ideals of radical republicanism. Another idiom through which Americans had long expressed their discontent and aspirations, radical republicanism stressed that freedom, defined as collective self-rule, rested on ensuring that laboring people could "assert a continuous and energetic public power" over the institutions of government. Not strong, self-interested individuals, then, but an egalitarian, cooperative, and politically active citizenry must be the foundation and end of a democratic republic.[55] "I sometimes think," lamented Tom Watson, surveying the "commercial despotism" of his day, "that in the destiny of nations it is not *our* lot to be the *enduring* Republic, but rather the 'terrible example' to show future 'free' Governments that they cannot possibly exist except on the foundation of actual freedom—The ownership of all the nation's wealth by the people."[56] To reverse that course, the mass of producers would need to become citizens. As one editorialist put the issue, "The people who desire to see this republic remain 'the land of the free and the home of the brave' must unite their forces, and devote a reasonable portion of their time to politics."[57]

Populist actors commonly relied on such messianic rhetoric to cast their movement in redemptive terms. "The People's Party," promised one orator, "is the political savior of this country."[58] One of the earliest traditions of radicalism in America, messianism had repeatedly stitched "patterns for radical expression" into the deep linguistic strata of diverse social groups.[59] Messianic rhetoric was manifest in the incipient stages of the Revolution, in multiple Great Awakenings, in secular Enlightenment enthusiasm, in numerous evangelical associations that had formed around issues of charity, abolition, and temperance, and in the everyday spaces of various black and white Protestant denominations. Populism emerged in tandem with the Great Awakening of the 1880s, and shared not only its message of messianic revivalism, but also its associational networks and the infrastructure of thousands of churches. Even labor organizers who had never set foot in a church relied on messianic rhetoric to mobilize people behind Populism.[60] The all-or-nothing quality of messianism is captured in these words by Jacob Coxey to his small army of unemployed workers, during a well-publicized 1894 march on Washington: "This movement will either mark the second coming of Christ or be a total failure."[61] Many movement actors envisioned sweeping popular participation and dramatic governmental response on the side of good, or they expected certain enslavement to the evil forces of monopoly and plutocracy. In this atmosphere, citizens had only two choices: to side with the forces of reform, or to be complicit with the forces of evil. "The columns of the united wealth producers of the nation are preparing for the march and the battle," clarified Tom Watson. "The roster is being made up. Upon the rolls of which army will your name be inscribed?"[62]

Populists thus tapped into an array of rhetoric that mobilized a rag-tag army of poor and working-class people behind the redemptive vision of a cooperative commonwealth. The logic of identification in Populist rhetoric appealed to the shared subordination of the laboring classes, and it offered the hope of collective freedom to those who joined the struggle for a people's economy and a people's democracy. That people, of course, did not yet exist in the social order of the Gilded Age. Crucial to the coalitional character of Populism, then, would be its ability not only to call "the people" together, at times with messianic clarity, but also to find rhetoric that could leave "the people" an open call to be imagined and reworked by disparate and emerging actors. It was here that Populism's rhetoric of peopling, at its best, embodied a commitment to horizontality. To realize their vision of cooperative commonwealth, Populists would need to enact horizontal popular power via their unlikely coalitions. And for that, they would need to open their vision of commonwealth to contests over the horizons of the people and democracy.

According to Harry Boyte, there was a "fiery contest" surrounding the word "commonwealth" during the Populist era: "Whatever people meant when they used it, 'commonwealth' referred to the fact that what was being contested *mattered*, in some deeply communal, supra-individual way. It conveyed passion, even political life or death." Indeed, ideals like "commonwealth" were embedded in "historically and culturally constituted group(s), [their] memories, origins, common territory, and ways of life."[63] Women, blacks, and immigrants drew on distinctive traditions of language and practice to inflect the rhetoric of commonwealth. Despite its own disavowals to the contrary, the commonwealth tradition was indebted to women's activism in a long history of working-class struggle: participating in land and food riots, signing and carrying petitions, supporting and enforcing boycotts, and joining trade unions. In addition, women of different classes and races had repeatedly carved new social and political spaces, forged associational networks, and inserted themselves into leadership roles in movements for religious revivalism, charity, abolition, temperance, and of course, suffrage.[64] For their part, African Americans inherited the hidden transcripts of resistance that emerged during slavery and continued amid the terror of white supremacy.[65] Many could also recount open insurgencies that had brought an end to slavery: everyday acts of defiance, hundreds of uprisings and rebellions, many thousands of escapes, abolitionist speeches and writings, and fighting in the war of emancipation. More immediately, blacks formed local political institutions, won electoral victories, and developed cultures of self-help.[66] Finally, immigrants had access to traditions of working-class struggle, including Catholic social justice theology and strands of socialism, anarchism, and syndicalism. Many immigrants fostered spaces and practices to keep their cultural traditions vital: for example, Finnish hall socialism and Scandinavian folk schools, which combined cultural preservation with economic and political cooperation and agitation.[67]

As a result of the multiple traditions that contested the rhetorical vision of Populism, many populists, including some white male farmers, could imagine a "maternal commonwealth," a commonwealth that was "ripe for socialism," a "Common-Weal army" lead by Jacob Coxey's tramps and vagabonds, and a biracial commonwealth open to the "humblest white or black man" in the country."[68] In these decentering inflections, new actors and visions stretched Populist rhetoric. Take, for example, Henry D. Lloyd's subversive vision of cooperative commonwealth, which would protect the survival of the "strongest virtue." Accented by the cadences of black poet Frances Harper in 1875, Lloyd's declaration would have sounded like this: "The great problem to be solved by the American people is . . . whether or not there is strength enough in democracy, virtue enough in our civilization and power enough in our religion to have mercy and deal justly with four millions of people lately translated from the old oligarchy of slavery to the new commonwealth of freedom."[69] These contrapuntal inflections of commonwealth rhetoric reveal a final aspect of Populism's rhetoric of peopling. Caught up in multiple, sometimes competing modes of becoming a people, Populists at times found that language followed from practice. That is, as Goodwyn argues, Populism had to invent new democratic languages to make sense of its incipient efforts to enact horizontal popular power.[70]

Populism's Practices of Peopling: Constituting the "Body of the Commonality"

Henry Demarest Lloyd's vision of a democracy that would nurture "the body of the commonality" was sharp relief against the exhausted body of the people he chronicled during his day: "The air of our beloved America has been heavy for many years with the weary footfalls of the people—the workingmen tramping about, to find no doors open for them in the palaces of industry they built—the farmer surrendering first the produce of the year, and then his farm itself to market riggers and usurers."[71] A proto-muckraker, Lloyd exposes the undersides of a state-backed corporate revolution that was repatterning the everyday lives and aspirations of working people. Farmers were trapped by a credit system that, in Goodwyn's words, "shap[ed] in demeaning detail the daily options of millions."[72] Under the crop lien system, furnishing merchants lent farmers credit against the anticipated value of their harvests, charging hefty commissions on top of exorbitant interest rates. With their harvests under lien year after year, farmers entered into permanent debt relationships with merchants, on whom they relied for farm supplies, food, and household goods. Many thousands lost their farms.[73] The escalating power of corporations also consigned factory workers, coal miners, and railroad hands to what Lloyd termed "slavery for life."[74] Wage laborers—many having immigrated to the United States with dreams of economic freedom—were shackled to their jobs by an elaborate system of disciplinary measures and intimidation tactics. There was little way out: company stores held workers in perpetual debt, and industries maintained blacklists of employees who tried to leave their companies in search of better wages and conditions. Those who could not find work were subject to so-called tramp laws, which punished unemployed men and women through fines, forced labor, and imprisonment.[75] Situated still more precariously, blacks faced the routine indignities of segregation and disenfranchisement, along with a catalog of daily intimidation and terror that included whipping, shooting, lynching, nightriding, and periodic massacres.[76] In an era that heralded individual mobility, millions of Americans felt little control over their everyday lives.

Denouncing the "competitive system" of capitalism in which workers were "brutalized both morally and physically," Alliance leader Jay Burrows demands, "How can you reach this man, how kindle the divine spark which is torpid in his soul, when he knows that it is greed that enforces the material labor that is . . . abasing and enslaving him?"[77] In other words, how could poor and working-class people aspire to cooperative commonwealth when capitalist modernization was subjecting them to daily routines that habituated them not to see alternatives.[78] Populists knew they could not arouse collective identification around a disembodied vision of cooperative commonwealth. In Goodwyn's account of Populism, people could only "dare to aspire for the kind of society conductive to mass human dignity" once they had the opportunity to " 'see themselves' experimenting in democratic forms."[79] This was the theory of change advanced by the movement's most ambitious grassroots visionaries and organizers. In the words of Henry D. Lloyd, the ideal of cooperative commonwealth would only be "realized and incarnated in the lives of common people" if they had firsthand experiences in economic cooperation and political action.[80] According to Alliance organizers, William Garvin and S. O. Daws, Populism's revolt against plutocracy would depend on "agitation, education, and cooperation, carried on by the means of thorough organization of the masses."[81]

Populism's practices of constituting popular power took place across sites and scales of social and political life, in everyday and extraordinary spaces, and via energetics that ranged from the mundane to the spectacular. On one level, Populism pluralized the everyday spaces and the parallel institutions through which different social groups could learn to enact horizontal popular power. On another level, many Populists came to recognize that they would need to organize popular power on a broader scale to enact a future beyond the mounting collusion of the state and capital. For this, Populists would have to organize across social divides to reshape the horizons of the people and democracy in a movement that was itself beset by white supremacy, nationalism, and patriarchy. As with Populism's rhetoric of peopling, a dynamic of centering and decentering power guided the movement's strategies to organize the rebellious aspirations of its disparate actors. This dynamic was evident in the movement's *dramatic enactments* of popular identification, the *translocal experiments* through which it constituted horizontal power, and the *dynamic institutions* it built to bring about structural change. These strategies centered and decentered power at multiple intersections of bodily dispositions, affective attachments, relational sympathies, collective identification, coalitional action, and institutional structure.

Dramatic Enactments: Performing Popular Identification

Populism's rhetorical practices provide insight into how the movement constituted "the people" who would realize its vision of cooperative commonwealth. During the heyday of the People's Party in the 1890s, Populists staged myriad dramas of popular enactment at mass rallies, parades, and conventions. Farmers, laborers, and other reformers came together regularly for "parades five miles long, meetings lasting days and days, and oratory without end."[82] These frequent rallies and parades as well as larger state and national conventions drew men and women, blacks and whites, Anglo-Saxons and other ethnic groups together in various combinations. People gathered amid floats and banners announcing the presence of suballiances, union locals, temperance crusaders, single-tax advocates, suffragettes, and other reformers; they witnessed pageants in which costumed representatives of Democrats, Republicans, plutocrats, and producers enacted the issues of the day; and they listened to stump speeches by the leaders of various producer and reformer groups. Exemplifying the unparalleled pluralism on display, blacks and whites rode side by side on horseback and stumped at the same podiums in front of interracial crowds.[83] These events enabled Populists, who were downtrodden subjects and unlikely allies, to "see themselves" in the act of building new relationships and getting into community with others across social divides.

Populism's dramatic enactments were sites of performing popular identity for both public audiences and participants. Casting Populists in what Alliance member Fanny Leake called a "death struggle for our liberties," speakers often relied on the symbolic and affective practices of messianic rhetoric to draw lines between friend and enemy.[84] Like Jacob Coxey and Tom Watson, they exhorted disparate actors to put their bodies on the line in an apocalyptic battle of good versus evil. "The people's side in this great battle is the right side," Lorenzo D. Lewelling promised a mixed crowd of farmers and industrial laborers at a Populist meeting in Kansas. "If there is a God in heaven . . . he will hear the cry of his suffering children and the giant Despair will yet be slain by the great uprising of this nation. . . . We are going forth."[85] Calling audiences to action, these iterated performances of collective enmity functioned to produce a bounded people against its enemy. They did not, however, achieve either the substantive unity that characterizes Schmittian theories of populism, or the negative "chains of equivalence" that form Laclau's counterhegemonic people. I want to suggest that overlapping practices of enactment simultaneously decentered lines of collective identification in the movement.

Populist dramas combined the visual and affective practices of symbolic rhetoric with the more Dionysian practices of public enthusiasm. Unlike symbolic politics, public enthusiasm unsettles the line between self and other, body and world. It enables what Slavoj Žižek characterizes as an "open" but "brief, passing moment" in which the people is "not yet hegemonized by any positive ideological project" or any form of cultural or institutional embodiment.[86] Typically associated with narrow forms of religious and popular identification, messianism has also historically been a source of public enthusiasm in America. According to Jason Frank, "ongoing encounters with enthusiasm" were key to the formation of civil subjectivity in pre- and post-Revolutionary America, prevalent in groups ranging from sects of dissenting Protestantism to Enlightenment radicals. Populism inherited this enthusiastic tradition through its ties to the Third Great Awakening and its revival of radical republican rhetoric. As Frank describes it, public enthusiasm momentarily collapses the boundaries between self and other, resulting in both an "undoing of the self" and a "collective fusion" of sympathies. Enthusiastic moments thus rupture the "well-regulated subjectivity" patterned by expected norms and relationships between social groups.[87]

One Kansas reporter described the Alliance Day picnics that later morphed into broad-based rallies for the People's Party during the 1890s: they were like "a religious revival, a crusade, a Pentecost of politics in which a tongue of flame set upon every man [and woman], and each spoke as the spirit gave him utterance."[88] Juxtaposed with the more familiar sound bites of People's Party rhetoric, the "glossolalia" of public enthusiasm opened spaces from which new relationships and ideas could emerge.[89] One of Populism's most enthusiastic moments occurred at the 1892 Industrial Conference in St. Louis. After Ignatius Donnelly, a veteran orator, recited the preamble to what would later become the Omaha Platform, the chairman of the platform committee read out the list of demands. At that point, according to a sympathetic journalist:

> Hats, papers, handkerchiefs, etc. were thrown into the air; wraps, umbrellas and parasols waved; cheer after cheer thundered and reverberated through the vast hall, reaching outside of the building where thousands [who] had been waiting the outcome, joined in the applause till for blocks in every direction the exultation made the din indescribable.[90]

In the words of a less sympathetic observer, who saw the specter of socialism in the crowd, the noise "rose like a tornado" and participants "embraced and kissed their neighbors, locked arms, marched back and forth, and leaped about tables and chairs."[91] The enthusiasm of the gathering ushered forth in a profusion of words and gestures from participants. Their embraces, their reverberations, their leaping and marching: these unruly movements transgressed the lines dividing North, South, Plains, Jewish, Protestant, Catholic, socialist, rural, urban, white, black, men, women, suffragettes, self, other, world. Alliance president Leonidas Polk recognized the subversive quality of Populist enthusiasm: the ruling classes "know that if we get together and shake hands and look each other in the face and feel the touch of kinship, their doom is sealed."[92]

The public enthusiasm of orgiastic bodies proliferated what Michael Warner and Lauren Berlant call "unsystematized lines of acquaintance."[93] These lines temporarily suspend the more routine, disciplinary dialectic between body and world. The corporate revolution had resulted in an unequal and relatively immobile structuring of the routes and barriers of everyday life, and these constraints were reinforced by normalized agitation, social segregation, and widespread dispositions toward deference and fatalism. Polk knew that unexpected "touches of kinship" were subversive because social divides are produced and "stirred up" by the plutocrats and publicists who "try to work upon our passions" to stoke division.[94] By contrast, messianic enthusiasm could incite unpredictable pleasures and generate more elastic relationships between members of competing social groups. Such elasticity between bodies and subjects unsettled social norms and structural relationships—such as classism, racism, and sexual difference—that routinely discipline bodies to support their own existence. The metaphor of "unsystematized lines of acquaintance" explains aspects of Populist identification that Laclau's metaphor of "equivalential chains" cannot. For disparate, marginalized actors to loosen the sediments that kept them bound to hegemonic forms of power and powerlessness, including deep social divisions, they would need to experience the pleasures of "undoing" self and group identity. If Populism's counterhegemonic rhetoric gave voice to the movement's vision, it was through unsystematized lines and unexpected touches that people of disparate backgrounds came to see and feel that their collective action could rupture what one farmer called "the same old Tale of years."[95] As one reporter wrote about the St. Louis convention, "Every man who sat in Exposition Hall as a delegate . . . believed in his soul that he sat there as a history-maker."[96]

Populism's dramatic performances were thus crucial sites for movement leaders to choreograph the forms of popular identity and power they envisioned, while also leaving the lines of popular identification open to be inflected and stretched by different assemblages of actors in different contexts. These dramatic performances, however, faced constraints that limited the participation of the movement's most marginalized members. First, as we have seen, black Populists did not enjoy the same access to public spaces as whites; nor, for that matter, did immigrants or women. Blacks had to contend with the specter of violence and intimidation whenever they mustered the courage to strike, boycott, or even go to the polls. Second, when blacks did occupy Populist stages with whites, their performances adhered to tightly scripted norms of racial hierarchy. If white Populists such as Tom Watson vowed to "wipe out the color line," it was clear that their promise did not extend to "race mixing" and miscegenation in the social realm. "It is best that [blacks and whites] should preserve the race integrity by staying apart," Watson assured white crowds, long before his crusade for political equality for blacks morphed into the open racism of his later years.[97] Immigrants also faced violent crackdowns on the picket line, and these were increasingly sanctioned by the state in the 1880s and 1890s. In other instances, it was striking Knights who enacted public solidarity at the expense of blacks and new immigrants, by hurling racial and ethnic slurs and resorting to violence when these most marginalized workers were brought in as strikebreakers.[98] If women took to the public stage like never before during Populism, they were not always afforded recognition as legitimate speakers. "Do not spend your time in longing for opportunities that will never come, but be contented in the sphere the Lord hath placed you in," one Alliance lecturer chastised his female audience. "If the Lord had intended you for a preacher or a lawyer, He would have given you a pair of pantaloons."[99]

In these different ways, Populism's racialized and gendered scripts acted as interpretive frames that structured Populist vision and affect. They limited how many Populists perceived the events going on in front of their eyes and reinforced white, masculine anxieties. Repeatedly stoked, those anxieties, in turn, led white Populists to cling to racist, patriarchal visions rather than open to new ways of seeing.[100] As such, the symbolic and enthusiastic politics at People's Party rallies could lend itself to narrower forms of collective identification and popular power. Indeed, Populism's dramatic enactments, taken on their own, had key limits for negotiating the tensions between its centering forms of symbolic identification and affective enmity, on the one hand, and its more decentered lines of identification and affective attachment, on the other.

TRANSLOCAL EXPERIMENTS: CONSTITUTING POPULAR POWER

Populism's everyday spaces were ongoing incubators of popular aspirations to power. In the decades leading up to the People's Party, key Populist organizations, such as the Farmers' Alliance, Colored Farmers' Alliance, National Women's Alliance, and Knights of Labor, experimented with grassroots political education and everyday practices of constituting popular power. These experiments took place in countless local spaces, and organizers found ways to connect grassroots actors to each other through an extensive reform press, traveling lecturers, and numerous mass rallies, encampments, and conventions. I develop "translocalism" here as another concept to evaluate Populism's dynamics of centering and decentering collective identification and popular power. Translocalism characterizes the strategies through which Populists connected the everyday politics of different communities to broader mobilizations of power. Translocalism emphasizes the transformative potential of everyday practice to cultivate people's tastes and capacities for power; at the same time, the concept recognizes that everyday practice often generates myopic forms of power if it fails to bring people into relationship across social distances and hierarchies. Through translocal organizing, Populists rerouted the "weary footfalls" of everyday practice, turning ordinary spaces into sites of extraordinary aspiration.

Populism's most thriving and sustained translocal experiments took place in the agrarian and labor movements that were precursors to the People's Party. This is best documented in the white Farmers' Alliance, which understood itself as a vast schoolhouse of democracy.[101] That is what Evan Jones, president of the

Texas Alliance, promised in 1891: elites "dread us because they know that our organization is a school, and through its teachings, the road to liberty will soon be available to the oppressed."[102] On one level, the Alliance aimed to "educate its members upon public questions affecting the welfare of the people in general, and especially the laboring classes."[103] Its pedagogy introduced rank-and-file members to competing theories of political economy, political theory, and practical advances in agricultural production. On a deeper level, the Alliance was a schoolhouse of democracy in the Tocquevillian sense of the term. The organization "labored to improve the condition of [its] members mentally, morally, socially, and financially," that is, "to elevate its members to a higher plane of citizenship."[104] According to the Alliance's "Declaration of Purposes," that meant educating members "in the mutual relations and reciprocal duties between each other, as brethren, as neighbors, as members of society," and cultivating "higher thought, higher aspiration, and higher manhood among the masses."[105]

Alliance publisher Harry Tracy used the term "miseducation" to describe the unquestioned loyalties that had long tied farmers to the status quo. "The condition of things is the result of education, good or bad," he wrote. "Those who labor are educated (in the school of life) to be abject slaves and the rich are educated to be tyrannical, presumptuous, and vicious."[106] Tracy shares this insight with theorists of everyday populism, who recognize that daily routines condition our basic habits of perception and action. In most cases, everyday practice facilitates what Pierre Bourdieu calls "misrecognition," that is, the disposition not to see the ways in which our actions reinforce systems of regulation and subordination.[107] A speech by Texas Populist Thomas Nugent reflects the widespread concern among organizers that the miseducation of farmers and laborers was, at a deeper level, a problem of misrecognition. "Men, from habit, become conservative," he says. "We learn to love what we are accustomed to, and misguided affection makes us cling with death-like tenacity to social and political institutions long after they have ceased to be useful or serviceable to the human race—yes, long after they have become the instruments of injustice and oppression."[108] According to Garvin and Daws, many farmers harbored cruel aspirations to individual prosperity in a rapidly changing economy: they unwittingly propped up commodity agriculture by leading "lonely and secluded lives" and turning "themselves and their families into wheat, corn, and cotton producing machines."[109]

"By our frequent meetings," the Alliance declared, "we confidently believe that we shall be able to break up the isolated habits of farmers, improve their social conditions, increase their social pleasures, and strengthen their confidence and friendship for each other."[110] Organizers thus devised strategies that would both dehabituate farmers from their responsiveness to existing dynamics of power, and rehabituate them toward practices of cooperation and collective action. The suballiance was the central unit of Alliance political education and cooperative organizing. From 1877 to 1892, suballiances proliferated across the South and later the Midwest. Hundreds of thousands participated in weekly or biweekly meetings. White farmers and farm laborers made up most of their numbers, but schoolteachers, local doctors, merchants, mechanics, and ministers also took part. Women filled a quarter of the seats.[111] The lecturing system was the primary organ through which the Alliance connected its suballiances. There were lecturers at the county level, and every suballiance had its own local lecturer. These men, and in some cases, women, traveled through rural America and met with people in churches and schoolhouses. The Alliance also had state and national lecturers, who crisscrossed thousands of miles and forty-three states and territories in the late 1880s and early 1890s, first to build its cooperative movement and then to politicize it on a national scale.[112] In addition, the Alliance circulated over one thousand journals, newspapers, and weeklies across the country. These were home to education materials, reprints of speeches, local and national news, investigative journalism, stories from cooperative movements, and editorials from leaders and rank-and-file members.[113]

Alliance organizers knew that farmers would have to practice cooperation to believe in its transformative potential. That is, as theorists of everyday populism insist, grassroots actors could only repattern their political dispositions and aspirations by engaging in alternative democratic practices. The Alliance thus developed a repertoire of practices aimed at the mutually reinforcing goals of "cultivating that social relationship which should exist among [farmers] as a class" and cultivating farmers' "independence of thought and action."[114] Regular suballiance meetings engaged farmers in debating the lessons of traveling lecturers and deliberating over local, state, and national Alliance policies. The organization's pedagogy used "lessons" from the Alliance paper, the *National Economist*, on issues such as the concentration of wealth, the class structure, and the "financial question." But lecturers tied broad issues to whatever stories filled the pages of a community's local paper, and encouraged rank-and-file members to take turns leading each other in the day's lessons.[115] Suballiance meetings combined this purposeful "public work" with other cultural practices of collective identification, most notably, taking part in meals and other social activities and singing popular hymns from movement songbooks, such as the *Alliance and Labor Songster*. In these spaces, people whose bodies and psyches had been riddled with the normalized agitations of the corporate revolution now gathered to talk about the conditions of their lives and connect their grievances to more systemic patterns of oppression and insurgent stories of hope. The Alliance's repertoire of everyday practices developed relational trust and a widespread sense of political efficacy across locations and across the horizons between everyday experience and farther-reaching visions of social change. By repatterning everyday practices, Alliance translocalism reshaped local spaces as sites of democratic aspiration. As a resolution of the suballiance in Bell County, Texas, declared, the Alliance aimed to enable the "agricultural and laboring people to comprehend their importance in the world of political thought."[116]

Farmers also sharpened their aspirations to power in the day-to-day labor of cooperative buying and selling. In some communities, they established trade committees to negotiate the best prices from competing merchants; in others they ran their own cooperative stores. Through Alliance "exchanges," farmers organized cotton yards to grade, weigh, and store their crops en masse. By "bulking" their cotton in this way, they were able to market it to the highest bidder.[117] Such cooperative practices reconfigured the ritual dynamics of subordination associated with the crop lien system. Farmers no longer came home with empty pockets and an "overproduction" of cotton. Instead, as one newspaper reported after a mass sale in Texas: "Empty wagons returned homeward bearing blue flags and other signs of rejoicing."[118] Repeated successes in the cooperative movement emboldened farmers' aspirations to constitute horizontal power in the name of broader structural change. This was no more evident than in the "joint note" plan of the Texas Exchange. Farmers placed their assets—from mortgages and liens to loose pennies—at the disposal of the group as collateral for bank loans. It was a fight against the credit system, in which landowners risked their property to include poorer tenant farmers in statewide cooperative purchasing. When the joint-note plan was on the verge of collapse, due to reluctance and even obstruction from banks and wholesalers, tens of thousands of farmers gathered at county courthouses across Texas on June 9, 1888, to dig deeper into their pockets. They held "large and enthusiastic mass meeting[s]" and marched by the thousands down main streets. It was not enough to save the ambitious venture, but the day left a lasting impression on farmers and the public alike. Farmers took pride in pledges that "exceeded expectations," and journalists reported that they were "completely astonished by the mammoth proportions" of the initiative.[119]

Although Populism is remembered today for its masculinist discourse of producerism, the political spaces created by the Alliance also acted as "schoolhouses in mixed-gender political culture" and as training grounds for women's collective action.[120] Women in the Alliance spoke and voted in meetings, held office in local and county chapters, and sometimes worked as traveling lecturers.[121] Women typically organized across multiple social and political networks. They combined their work with the Alliance with membership in evangelical societies, the temperance and suffrage movements, and the International and National Councils of Women. In 1891, women from twenty-six states formed the National Women's Alliance (NWA), identifying themselves as "the industrial women of America" and promoting a vision of transclass sisterhood. Their "Declaration of Purposes" became the basis for persistent lobbying in the reform press and at Populist conventions to advance broad improvements in gender equality.[122] Women also edited and wrote for movement circulars and kept up active discussions in the editorial pages of the reform press, where rank-and-file women regularly took up the radical feminist ideas of the day. In these ways, women engaged men in debating the gamut of pressing economic, social, and political issues, including economic and political equality for women.[123]

The role of women in the Alliance exemplifies the radical democratic potential of translocal organizing. Through their multiform networks, women inserted themselves into Populism not just as individuals but as a social group with a radical idea of collective identity and popular power: women organized were a force for social change.[124] "Rule the women out and the reform movement is a dead letter," stated an epigram in the official journal of the NWA. "Put a thousand women lecturers in the field and the revolution is here." The "maternal commonwealth" envisioned in the NWA Declaration of Purposes specified not only full economic and political equality, but also "cooperation in every department of life to its fullest extent," critical analyses of "all questions relating to the structure of human society," and "unity of action among the Sisterhood, in all sections of our country."[125] Indeed, calls for radical change began to echo in daily life: for example, equalizing marriage and divorce laws, striking the word "obey" from marriage vows, winning rights pertaining to family finances, sharing the burden of parenting and housework, and freeing women of the social strictures of household propriety and drudgery.[126] Populism was thus a movement whose struggle for "manly" freedom from the tyranny of capital also succeeded in chipping away at public and everyday forms of patriarchy.

By engaging everyday actors in translocal practices of constituting horizontal popular power, the Alliance mobilized collective identification and political aspiration around a broad, emerging vision of cooperative commonwealth. The Alliance's translocal organizing, however, typically stopped short at the boundaries of race, ethnicity, and rural-urban divides. Though the Alliance eventually played a major role in building the unlikely political coalitions that supported the People's Party, the everyday politics of the cooperative movement largely remained segregated. Until 1889, the Alliance held tightly to an official whites-only policy, and its cooperative efforts largely remained separate from those of the black-led Colored Farmers' Alliance. The white Alliance enforced its segregation policy when it merged with the more inclusive Agricultural Wheel and when it prohibited dual membership in the biracial and multiethnic Knights of Labor. White Alliance translocalism was severely constrained by its refusal to cross racial and ethnic divides, evidence that translocal organizing, narrowly conceived, can itself generate myopic forms of popular power.

The Knights of Labor and black Populists, who developed their own practices of political education and cooperation in the years leading up to the People's Party, fared better at translocal organizing across social divides. Their subsequent

efforts to build coalitions with the Alliance in the electoral arena elucidate both
promising moments and barely traversed limits of Populism's translocal experiments in constituting horizontal popular power.

The Knights of Labor (KOL) was, in the words of Elizabeth Sanders, "a more
diverse and inclusive organization than any other American labor body before
or since."[127] The Knights were active across the North Atlantic and Rust Belt
in the 1870s, before spreading to the South Atlantic, south-central, and western states in the 1880s. Its membership peaked at seven hundred thousand in
1886 and included factory workers, railroad workers, lumber workers, coal
miners, farmers, farmworkers, and domestic servants. Uniting behind the slogan, "An injury to one is the concern of all," the Knights recruited skilled and
unskilled workers, men and women, blacks and whites, native-born citizens and
old and new European immigrants.[128] While not uniformly successful, efforts
to "recognize no line of race, creed, politics, or color" in either labor or citizenship was a point of pride among both leaders and rank-and-file Knights.[129]
Segregated local assemblies were common, but many Knights participated in
multiethnic, mixed-race, or mixed-gender locals. At the union's peak, about half
its local assemblies were organized by trade, the other half across occupational
lines. In contrast to trade unions, which divided and weakened the labor movement, according to leader Terrance Powderly, the Knights believed that organizing across social and trade divides would yield "a radical change in the existing
industrial system."[130]

The Boston *Labor Leader* observed that the success of the KOL lay "in the fact
that the whole life of the community was drawn into it, that all kinds of people
are together . . . and that they all directly sense each other's needs."[131] That "direct
sense" was not born of inherent solidarity or immediate identification among
working-class people who were thrown together by mass demographic shifts and
locked into a competitive wage system. The KOL cultivated working-class solidarity by engaging laborers in everyday practices of moral and political education and cooperation across ranks. "We must get our people to read and think,"
insisted one state-level leader, "and to look for something higher and more
noble in life than working along in that wretched way from day to day and from
week to week and from year to year."[132] Biweekly local assembly meetings were
both "schools of practical economics" and spaces of broad theorizing, where,
as one district leader bragged, "you could hear our members quoting Spencer,
Mill, Ricardo, Walter, Marx, Laselles, Prouddon [*sic*] and other political econo-
mists."[133] To support local education, the Knights developed a widespread network of reform papers, reading rooms, traveling lecturers, and dramatic societies.
KOL leadership also encouraged assemblies to establish producer and consumer
cooperatives. Powderly declared cooperation "the lever of labor's emancipation"
and saw it as a means to working-class solidarity and sustainable economic power

in the face of monopoly capitalism. For several years, until they proved financially unfeasible, grassroots Knights organized cooperative stores, factories, and mines.[134]

In the mid-1880s, local and district assemblies intensified their insurgency in relation to capitalist institutions and the state, often putting grassroots Knights at odds with the national leadership of the KOL. Grassroots insurgents routinely organized boycotts against newspapers, manufacturers, builders, mining companies, hotels, and dealers of household goods. Boycott notices filled the labor press, public halls, union halls, and kitchens, papering the everyday cultural landscape of rank-and-file members. As one Knight grumbled, "To be a sincere and systematic boycotter now requires the carrying about of a catalogue of different boycotted firms or articles."[135] Local assemblies also occupied members with the nitty-gritty work of negotiating better wages and working conditions. Where this failed, grassroots insurgents relied on strikes as a "last resort."[136] The number of strikes doubled each year from 1884 to 1886, with over four hundred thousand workers participating in strikes in 1886. Broad community participation was a "common feature of large strikes during this period," writes Martin Shefter. Crowds marched "from factory to factory in working-class neighborhoods, calling upon all employees to walk off their jobs. . . . The marches and open-air meetings that occurred . . . invited participation of all segments of the population in working-class neighborhoods: unionized workers, non-unionized workers, unemployed men, women, and children."[137] This period of activism correlated with the surge in membership for the KOL.[138] As workers and communities put their bodies on the line in the fight against "the bosses" and experienced success, they gained practical knowledge of the benefits of solidarity.

The Great Southwest Strike was a catalytic moment for cooperation between farmers and laborers. Rank-and-file railroad workers in Texas began walking off the job in March 1886, forcing a reluctant Knights of Labor hierarchy to follow their lead. Bypassing the Texas Alliance, county and local Alliances passed resolutions in support of the workers, organized sympathy boycotts across the state, and provided food and money to striking workers. Cooperation against the railroads and mines led to other practices of translocal organizing between grassroots farmers and laborers. It was common by 1886 for white and black Alliance farmers to share membership in the Knights of Labor (another snub of national policy by white Alliance members). Suballiances and assemblies regularly swapped lecturers, and farmers and laborers attended rallies at which leaders of both the agrarian and labor movements shared the microphone. In some places, farmers and workers established cooperative stores and purchasing ventures. These insurgent movements across social divides informed Populist identification and vision. It was in their joint engagements with the Knights that farmers widely began to take on the identity of industrial laborers, whose struggle for economic and political freedom had the dimensions of a class war.[139] "The line between land lord and tenant," wrote one Nebraska farmer, "is being [as] forcibly put as the line of demarcation ... in the cities between boss and employe [*sic*]." To counter the "monopolists and money changers waxing richer and richer" off their labor, another farmer insisted, the producing classes would need to unite behind a platform that was "broad enough for every farmer, mechanic and laborer; for every Union Labor, United Knight of Labor and Alliance man in the country to stand on and to fight for."[140]

Facing an enthusiastic crowd of thousands of Alliance farmers in central Texas, KOL leader W. E. Farmer stated what was on the minds of many farmers and laborers in 1886: "The laboring classes must either take charge of the ballot box and purify the government or witness one of the most gigantic revolutions known for ages."[141] Once again, it was grassroots farmers and laborers who led Populism into the electoral arena, against the wishes of organizational leaders, who worried that entrenched party loyalties would fracture the cooperative and labor movements. By the mid-1880s, rank-and-file Populists had accumulated firsthand experience with the limits of everyday politics and most deeply felt the need for structural reform. Suballiances played a heavy hand in local and state politics, creating independent tickets and "Alliance tickets" as early as 1886. Grassroots Knights also took to the ballot during that period, as their wave of strikes began to meet brutal resistance from state-backed employers.[142] Farmers and laborers often coordinated local electoral activities. The mass rallies and joint meetings that took place during the Great Southwest Strike, for example, became the basis for many independent tickets in the 1886 elections. Midwestern states such as Kansas and southern states such as Virginia, North Carolina, and Kentucky were also strongholds for local agrarian-labor coalitions.[143] "I have never before seen the people so stirred up in politics & so united as the laboring class are," remarked one supporter in Lampasas, Texas.[144] Eventually, insurgent farmers and laborers brought the leadership of the Alliance and the Knights along with them. By the early 1890s, the Alliance began to transition its organizational energy and even its infrastructure—including traveling lecturers and the reform press—toward building electoral coalitions to back a third-party movement. While the KOL's top brass remained tentative in its support for the People's Party in 1892, local assemblies and rank-and-file workers came out in support of Populism. In 1893, insurgent Knights ousted the more conservative leader Powderly in favor of the Populist James R. Sovereign, and the Knights became ardent organizers for the People's Party.[145]

Despite significant victories at local and state levels, farmer-labor coalitions met steep limits. By the time the Knights became vocal supporters of the People's Party, their membership had declined to fewer than seventy-five thousand. As a result, the voice of labor Populism would have little effect on national politics.[146]

Outside the Knights of Labor and Eugene Debs's American Railroad Union, organized labor was largely uninterested in an electoral coalition between farmers and laborers.[147] The American Federation of Labor (AFL) under Samuel Gompers kept its sights narrowly on trade unionism and never warmed to Populism or to the ideology of a union of the producing classes. Disparaging the notion that farmers were laborers, Gompers called them "woefully ignorant upon the underlying principles and tactics and operations of trade unions."[148] For its part, the Socialist Labor Party (SLP) declared the "misnamed People's Party" merely an attempt to transfer the "plunder" of the "plutocratic class" to "petit bourgeois" farmers.[149] Lacking coalitions with a vibrant labor movement, Populist organizers could do little to loosen the everyday attachments of most urban workers, whose social and political lives were ruled by ethnic factionalism and machine politics. It had taken the Knights and the Alliance years to cultivate the rebellious aspirations of farmers and laborers to form a broad-based movement of the producing classes. Outside the KOL, organized labor did not have comparable spaces of everyday translocal politics.[150] Urban workers of different backgrounds, who came into daily contact on assembly lines and picket lines, thus had few opportunities to discuss the conditions in which they found themselves. Lacking these, the dramatic politics of strikes were not enough to sustain elasticity around the edges of social-group differences. It was quite possible, for example, for Slovak and Anglo workers to fight side by side against the Carnegie Steel Corporation during the Homestead Strike of 1892, but to walk away with divergent interpretations of the epic struggle. Slovak workers shouted the slogan *za chlebom*, which literally meant they were "going for bread." But they would surely have contested Anglo strikers who claimed a monopoly on the values of solidarity and freedom. "We are bound to Homestead by all the ties that men hold dearest and most sacred," one Anglo-American worker told a mass crowd, adding that they would have to decide "if we are going to live like white men in the future."[151]

Racial divisions between whites and blacks proved even more challenging. Analyses of the successes and failures of biracial Populism usually polish the rough edges with one of several glosses. The most prominent sheen among those sympathetic with the movement, especially Goodwyn, portrays white Populists as victims of their age: their attempts at organizing across race were laced with calculations of utility and presumptions of paternalism, but they created significant openings for radically subversive speech and action and by and large stood in contrast to the rampant white supremacy of the Democratic Party.[152] In the hands of those more critical of the movement, white Populists turn into active white supremacists, at best calculating and paternalistic, and at worst agents of institutional segregation, electoral intimidation, and Jim Crow.[153] Others make the compelling argument that Black Populism was a self-organized movement: rather than widely deferring to white Populism, African Americans mobilized around a distinct set of needs and visions, and they chose to build coalitions with whites when it was in their strategic interest to do so.[154] Each of these versions contains an important part of the story of biracial Populism, and yet the partiality of each conveys its strong investments in a certain kind of story: about the political free-dom engendered by social movements, about the exclusions inherent in popu-lar rule, about the self-generated capacities of oppressed groups. What none of them does is wrestle with the fragility of rebellious aspirations to power, which always emerge from spaces that are surrounded by threats of reconsolidation from within and without.

Only recently have scholars revealed Black Populism to be a self-organized movement with its own philosophical traditions and its own social and politi-cal roots and networks. As Gerald Gaither writes, Black Populism was the "culmination of a pattern of agrarian protest that had existed at least since Reconstruction."[155] Populists inherited the philosophy of black self-help that had emerged across the South through the work of churches, beneficial societies, insurance societies, and cooperative enterprises.[156] During the 1880s and 1890s, Black Populism was a "patchwork of mobilization."[157] Like the broader Populist movement, it organized a disparate cast of actors across lines of class and across the different experiences of rural and urban life. Black Populists were members of "overlapping networks" of religious, agrarian, labor, and electoral organizations. At the heart of these organizations were the black Baptist and African Methodist Episcopalian churches, which were "seedbeds for black political activity, and provided much of the organizing and leadership impetus for Populism."[158] Black Populists were also members of the Colored Agricultural Wheel, the Colored Farmers Union, the Cooperative Workers of America, and in their most signifi-cant numbers, the Knights of Labor and the Colored Farmers' Alliance (CFA). Blacks in the Knights of Labor numbered up to sixty thousand at the union's peak in 1886. Black Knights were tenant farmers, day laborers, rail workers, and domestic workers. Some joined biracial local assemblies, though most belonged to one of four hundred all-black locals or sixteen all-black female locals.[159] The CFA, founded in 1886, claimed up to one million members across the South, led by hundreds of mostly black organizers. Sharecroppers, tenants, and farm labor-ers were the black Alliance's base. Landowners and professionals also joined, cre-ating internal class conflicts over insurgent tactics, such as boycotts and strikes.[160]

Relatively little is known about the everyday organizing practices of Black Populism. The climate of intimidation and terror in which black Populists orga-nized meant that they often had to meet secretly, either talking one-on-one or gathering in small groups at night.[161] Political education in the CFA and KOL had broad and holistic aims. Among the main goals of the CFA in Bellevue, Louisiana, for example, were "to elevate our race, to make us better citizens . . . [and] to edu-cate ourselves that we may be able to vote more intelligently on questions that are of vital importance to our people."[162] A black Knight in Philadelphia echoed a similar refrain as the order began to organize in the South: "The Southern negro must be made a self-respecting and respected man through labor organizations. If the Knights of Labor will assume this task, I think they will do a work that no other body has attempted to do, and will forever deserve to be called the saviors and up-builders not only of a race, but of the whole country."[163] At the same time, both organizations "became vehicles to advance locally determined goals and encompass locally inflected patterns of life."[164] Forming coalitions with other local groups, KOL and CFA members took part in multiple, often overlapping initiatives. They published reform papers, organized lecturers, and read the news aloud in meetings and churches before debating the issues affecting their communities. They established cooperatives and farming exchanges; led boycotts and strikes for better wages, rents, and working conditions; raised money for schools; lobbied for political reform to include blacks on juries, enforce federal oversight in voting, and end segregation in public services; and formed independent and fusion parties.[165] In many ways, the KOL and CFA paralleled the white Alliance in their efforts to develop a repertoire of everyday practices that would constitute popular power and cultivate the political aspirations of black farmers and laborers. In other ways, the cross-craft and cross-class makeup of both the KOL and CFA meant that these groups, far more than the white Alliance, oriented the translocal practices of black Populists toward developing "new and shifting sets of social relations."[166]

Experiments in translocal organizing across race did exist at the local level between black and white Populists. In some places, black and white Knights organized joint boycotts, and black delegates participated in district and state assemblies. In other places, however, black and white locals organized separate strikes, and mixed-race locals debated whether black members could even speak in assembly meetings.[167] While both the black and white Alliances remained segregated, grassroots farmers quietly participated in biracial cooperative ventures and boycotts together when it was in their interests. By 1889, some black and white Alliances held their statewide meetings in the same building, sending delegates back and forth between separate meeting rooms. Black and white farmers alike took a calculated rather than a moral approach to cooperation. In many cases, black farmers found it in their best interest to organize away from the paternalistic reach of whites, and refused to merge with the white Alliance in 1891. As a member of the Georgia Colored Alliance explained, "All the Negro wants is protection. You white people attend to your business and let us alone."[168] The calculation of the white Alliance not to support major CFA strikes and boycotts in 1891, however, proved deadly for many black organizers and participants. In 1889, black farmers in Leflore County, Mississippi boycotted local merchants to trade with a white Alliance store in nearby Durant. Whites massacred dozens of

CFA members and their families who demonstrated in support of the boycott. When the CFA called a nationwide cotton-pickers strike in 1891, it led to a wave of firings and a manhunt that ended in the lynching of at least fifteen strike organizers. Neither revolt received official support from the white Alliance. It is no surprise, then, that many black Populists shared the suspicions of a black Knight from North Carolina, who said, "We fear that [the white] Alliance . . . means nothing more than oppression and death to the [black] laborer."[169]

The electoral arena was perhaps the most promising site for black-white cooperation during the Populist era. It was here that black and white workers alike appealed to "common interests" across race, and here that white leaders such as Tom Watson promised to "wipe out the color line," at least when it came to economic and political equality.[170] It was also through direct engagements in coalition building that black Populists succeeded in challenging racial hierarchies within Populism. Black delegates were founding members of the People's Party, and black caucuses participated in state and national party conventions. At the 1891 National Union Conference in Cincinnati, attendees engaged in a heated debate over a proposal by the white southern Alliances to segregate black delegates on the floor of the meeting. Most delegates voted against the resolution, and at successive ad hoc meetings to organize the People's Party, black participants such as CFA member William Warwick of Virginia spoke up to protest the "shoddy treatment" of blacks and demand fair representation.[171] At the founding meeting of the Texas People's Party in 1891, black and white delegates publically debated the issue of black representation on party committees. Melvin Wade, a black trade unionist, exposed the gaps in Populism's language of equality: "When it comes down to the practice such is not the fact. If we are equal, why does not the sheriff summon Negroes on juries? And why hang up the sign, 'Negro,' in passenger cars? I want to tell my people what the People's Party is going to do. I want to tell them if it is going to work a black horse and a white horse in the same field."[172] After a protracted battle—in which another black delegate insisted, "The colored people are part of the people and they must be recognized as such"—the convention agreed to appoint one black representative on each executive and local committee. When the national People's Party was launched in St. Louis in 1892, black and white delegates sat together and shared in the public enthusiasm.[173] Through repeated engagements at local, state, and national levels, Populists debated the tensions between racism and popular power as part of debating the structure and vision of their party. Arguments over seating, committee representation, or party planks were so many micro-level sites of struggle over the boundaries of the "color line" within Populism.

Such spaces of negotiation, previously unthinkable, yielded practical results both within the People's Party and in representative institutions. Beginning with county Alliances as early as 1888 and continuing with the People's Party, Populism supported or nominated black candidates for office in a number of states, including Texas, Kansas, and Oklahoma. Numerous black candidates backed by a tenuous Populist-Republican fusion in North Carolina were elected to local office in 1896.[174] Biracial coalitions influenced People's Party platforms as well. Alabama Populists supported protection of black voting rights in 1892. With eleven black delegates in attendance at its 1892 state convention, the Arkansas Populist Party resolved to support "the downtrodden regardless of race," including "honest pay to equal labor." The Texas Populist platform of 1894 called for reforms in the convict-lease system and free public schools under the control of local citizens of "each race."[175] One of the most successful black-white Populist coalitions lasted from 1892 to 1898 in Grimes County, Texas. The People's Party nominated biracial tickets, elected a black district clerk and a black-friendly sheriff, and won better wages for black schoolteachers. While it outlasted other biracial Populist coalitions, the Grimes County People's Party did not escape the violence that gutted black politics in the South at the end of the nineteenth century. After gaining control of local politics in 1990, members of the White Man's Union terrorized and massacred Populist leaders and supporters in Grimes County.[176]

Appeals to economic and political self-interest were not enough to overcome deeply engrained white supremacy. As W. E. B. Du Bois recognized in his account of the turn toward slavery by another name in the post-Reconstruction era, working-class whites have historically clung to the "psychological wage[s]" of whiteness over forming cross-racial coalitions with impoverished blacks and immigrants. The pleasures and privileges of whiteness, that is, stood in for actual wages and soothed the psychic scars of capitalist exploitation that working-class whites also faced.[177] It did not help Populism's coalitions that, in editorials and stump speeches, white Populists made it uniformly clear that "the question of social equality does not enter into the calculation at all."[178] Even worse, Populists played an active role in stripping the social, economic, and political rights of blacks across the South. The national Alliance lobbied against federal supervision of elections in 1890; county Alliances in North Carolina protested public funds for black schools and sought legal restrictions to protect white landlords against black tenants; beginning in 1890, county Alliances throughout the South worked through the Democratic Party to support railroad segregation measures. When black voters appeared unlikely to ally with the People's Party, white Populists took their cue from white Democrats and resorted to intimidation and violence to disenfranchise black voters. It is little wonder that Georgia black Republican leader William Pledger accused Populists of being "the men who have lynched the colored people in the past; the men who have shot and robbed colored people."[179] His words bring relief to that fact that, for black Populists, the struggle for economic and political freedom was also a struggle against white employers, white officials, white voters, and a pervasive culture of white supremacy. As with rural-urban coalitions, the movements between black and white spaces were too limited and engaged by too few rank-and-file actors—that is, when they were not outright intimidating and violent—to create more than the most fragile, fleeting aspirations toward biracial power.

DYNAMIC INSTITUTIONS:
A POPULIST VISION OF STRUCTURAL CHANGE

The defeat of the People's Party in 1896 marks the final blow to a movement that began in the ambitious cooperative campaigns of agrarian and labor Populism and rallied behind a massive third-party campaign to transform the relationship between democracy, capitalism, and other elite concentrations of power. For many scholars, Populism owes its failure in great part to its reactionary character. This is evident in the movement's slide into ever more rampant forms of racism and nativism after 1896, but also in what is widely perceived as its inability to present a positive alternative to liberal-capitalist democracy. Indeed, Populism has not escaped the familiar populist stamp: it is often branded antistatist or, at least, reactionary in its views of the state.[180] Only recently have scholars begun to appreciate how Populists sought to enlist and transform the state as one key tool for enacting and enhancing popular power. By the time the People's Party was established, an interventionist state was crucial to Populism's vision of democracy. "The grandeur of civilization shall be emphasized by the dawn of a new era in which the people shall reign," announced Kansas's Populist governor Lorenzo Lewelling. "And if found necessary they will 'expand the powers of government to solve the enigmas of the times.'"[181]

For many radical democrats, Populism's move into the electoral arena would represent a move away from democratic politics—defined in terms of enacting egalitarian, pluralistic forms of popular power—and into the disciplinary realm of state regulation and control. They would be partly correct. The People's Party ushered in a transition between the grassroots democratic experiments of agrarian and labor Populism and the administrative centralization that defined Progressive era reform.[182] After decades of struggle, however, millions of insurgent actors recognized that, in order to protect their grassroots spaces and practices of popular power, they would need to transform political economy and government on a national scale. Unlike the Progressive reformers who followed them, however, Populists held enough suspicion of elite consolidations of power that they sought to incorporate their approaches to building horizontal popular power into their visions of large-scale institutions. A familiar dynamic of centralizing and decentering power and vision was at the heart of Populist institutions. Populism's vision of a more dynamic institutionalism is evident, first, in the institutions the movement developed to organize horizontal power across distance and social divides and, second, in the way Populists envisioned the relationship between their own institutions and the institutions of the state.

The popular power of the Alliance in relation to banks, railroads, and merchants expanded with its cooperative selling and buying ventures at county and
state levels. "It may become a great monopoly," observed Alliance supporter Mary
B. Lesesne. "But we predict that it will use its power wisely."[183] Had the Alliance
survived into the twentieth century, it is not difficult to imagine it becoming a
bureaucratic farm trust that excluded black farmers and kept down wages for black
and immigrant farmhands. There were seeds of such a vision already at work in the
cooperative movement. The southern Alliance leader Charles Macune had a centralized vision of business and politics that extended to his vision for the cooperative movement. His plan for the statewide marketing of crops saw business agents
directing the workings of cooperation at a remove from rank-and-file members.
Some local farmers, exasperated at their losses in the cooperative movement,
defended this top-down organization. "Don't you know that one hundred cooperative stores working on an independent basis ... would ruin the Exchange,"
beseeched Texas farmer J. A. McDonald. "Don't you know that a body with out a
head is dead?"[184]

The bureaucratic vision of the Alliance, however, was neither a reality nor a
dominant centralizing force. In significant ways, the Alliance operated as a national
institution by proliferating spaces of local self-help. The organization set policies
at the national and state levels, but proposals were open to vote by rank-and-file
members, and administration was decentered. In this way, the Alliance created
multiple internal spaces for contesting official decisions and experimenting with
alternatives. These were spaces of experimentation, in which "seemingly endless
variants of cooperative arrangements" circulated without inevitably seeking stan-
dardized form. It was a suballiance of Bohemian immigrants in Texas, for example,
whose boycott against local merchants inspired one of the most successful tactics
of the cooperative movement.[185] The Alliance thus thrived, where it did, because
thousands of newly empowered suballiances took it upon themselves to pioneer
innovative forms of cooperation. It prospered on a large scale, that is, because it
was an institution that could not contain its own rebellious aspirations to power.

Like the Alliance, the Knights of Labor had a centralized form of organization on paper. Grand Master Workman Terrance Powderly appointed most of
the committees of the General Assembly, which held "full and final jurisdiction"
over the organization.[186] Yet, the Knights grew from the bottom up, driven by
rank-and-file workers who established local assemblies according to the demographics and needs of their different contexts. The KOL labor movement was
thus an ongoing series of negotiations between the broad vision of Powderly and
the General Assembly, on one side, and on the other, "local and district assemblies [that] were virtually autonomous and did as they pleased."[187] Insurgent
grassroots tactics, such as boycotts, strikes, and local electoral coalitions, flew in
the face of national policies and the budget of the General Assembly. During the

organization's surge of membership in the mid-1880s, grassroots Knights proliferated strikes at a faster clip than the order had finances to support. The General
Assembly adopted a "no strike" policy in 1886, partly due to these organizational
limitations and partly due to Powderly's long-standing belief that strikes were
a diversionary tactic that would do little to address real structural economic
inequalities.[188] What the KOL lost in adopting this policy was a strategy for combining the translocal organizing of its assemblies with a tool for the large-scale
resistance and mass recruitment that could sustain a broader labor movement.
The year 1886 marked the peak of the KOL. Then began the order's precipitous
decline, in the face of brutal losses on the picket line and competition from resurgent trade unions. By the time the Knights threw their weight behind the People's
Party in 1893, under the leadership of J. R. Sovereign, the order had become a
heavily rural organization of fewer than seventy-five thousand workers.[189]

The negotiation between centralizing and decentering forms of power and
vision was also at the heart of the People's Party. To be clear, the purpose of the
People's Party, like the organizations of agrarian and labor Populism before it,
was to organize grassroots power on a large scale and to orient it toward the
shared end of a cooperative commonwealth. Unlike the established Democratic
and Republican parties, which claimed the support of particular social groups,
the People's Party sought to integrate the various social groups that made up the
producing classes.[190] In its efforts to centralize power, it claimed to represent and
enact the power of "the people" as a whole. At the same time, the People's Party
would remain a coalition of autonomous industrial and reform organizations.
In the words of Kazin, the party was an "amalgam of social groups and political
organizations with clashing priorities"—one that, according to Charles Postel,
came together as a "grand national body for political purposes."[191] Even then, the
People's Party took shape locally and regionally in a diverse array of forms: some
with stronger farmer-labor coalitions than others, some with more or less racial
solidarity, some with planks on suffrage or prohibition, but all reflecting the differential makeup of grassroots insurgency and reform in particular contexts.[192]

The People's Party thus gained its power and authority from the array of locally
rooted, parallel institutions that constituted and sustained it. In relation to the
broader Populist movement, the People's Party acted as one among many sites
of popular will-formation. The party and its leaders enjoyed nothing like the
hegemonic influence theorists such as Schmitt and Laclau associate with populism. According to Aziz Rana, the relationship between the People's Party and
Populism "suggested a form of popular politics in which laborers were multiply
organized [and] able to assert control at various local, state, and national sites
of decision making."[193] As a result, farmers, miners, railroad hands, and factory
workers—and the institutions they had organized for decades—sustained an
ambivalent orientation toward the People's Party. Many identified passionately

with the "party of the people"; having cultivated their suspicion of elites, however, they trained a wary eye on party elites who might usurp their power. As Goodwyn describes the vision of one Alliance leader: "The Alliance needed to stand in relation to the People's Party as the Jacobin Clubs of revolutionary France had stood in relation to the new democratic parliamentary government. The self-organized people of the Alliance would serve as 'a mighty base of support' for Populist candidates when they legislated democratically and a strong admonishing force when they did not."[194]

The defeat of the People's Party resulted in part from the inability to sustain a balanced relationship between the institutionally rooted activism of diverse reform organizations and the institutional efforts of the People's Party to organize on a mass scale. If organizations such as the white Alliance, Colored Farmers' Alliance, and Knights of Labor hoped to provide a grassroots base of support and accountability for Populist candidates, rather than transforming into mobilizing engines for third-party politics, the latter is eventually what Populism's agrarian and labor organizations became. By 1886, the Knights and CFA had faced enough losses on the picket lines and in cooperative efforts that rank-and-file members turned their attention to the electoral arena. White Alliance cooperatives followed in their wake from 1890 to 1893. Just as membership in the Knights plummeted when the order abandoned strikes, the decline of cooperatives stole from the Alliance its primary means of recruiting members and cultivating their aspirations for power. At the same time, as the Alliance moved into politics, its traveling lecturer system was replaced by a more traditional lecture circuit, which lacked the robust exchanges and educational practices of agrarian Populism's earlier translocal organizing. Just as Populism was gaining power as a national third-party movement, it was losing the grassroots power at its base. When the People's Party fused with the Democratic Party to nominate William Jennings Bryan for president in 1896, radicals and grassroots insurgents cast the losing votes.[195]

In part, however, the People's Party fell because centralizing dynamics of capitalist and state power had succeeded in diminishing the sites of economic cooperation and popular power.[196] In this context Populism's positive vision of a protective state remains a spark of hope worth saving from obscurity. During the heyday of agrarian and labor Populism in the 1880s and the People's Party in the 1890s, Populists imagined their parallel institutions would create a "permanently mobilized citizenry." They believed they could foster a more direct, immediate relationship between a broadly participatory democracy and the institutions of political economy and the state.[197] For this, active citizens would need recourse to an active, interventionist state. Countering received wisdom about Populism's antistatism, Rana argues that, for the People's Party, "legislative action was not a regrettable necessity." Rather, for democratic freedom to be a reality, the people had to "possess a public power that could continually enact popular laws."[198] As Charles Postel characterizes the "Populist vision" of the state: "The Populists wanted an active government to ensure access to the benefits of modernity."[199] Sanders argues further that Populism initiated a pattern of "radical reformism" that shaped the expansion of state power in the early part of the twentieth century. Populists envisioned a state that governed through strong legislatures and an electoral system democratized by "free and fair" elections, direct election of senators, and the use of initiative and referendums. The People's Party platform, moreover, sought to steer the regulatory and infrastructure-building capacity of the state toward a variety of popular democratic ends: for example, restructuring markets, regulating corporations, reversing concentrations of economic and political power, protecting spaces of local and regional economic innovation, and ensuring the public provision of certain goods and services.[200]

What Populists did not assume, separating them from later reformers, was that the state would hold bureaucratic discretion in policymaking. The movement faced not the seemingly monolithic state bureaucracy we picture today, but a disaggregated complex of rules, organizations, and institutions. And this is how Populists would have kept things. The party's plank for government ownership of railroads, for example, carried explicit language and suggested regulations "to prevent the increase of the power of the national administration" in its new role.[201] More broadly, Populists preferred governance not through bureaucratic programs but through specific statutory mandates, which, when possible, would be carried out through "local, decentralized, ad hoc arrangements in which movement organizations participated."[202] Neither displaying the conservative antistatism of many contemporary populist groups nor calling for sweeping state powers, the movement thus worked on a host of scales and concrete issues both to transform and to use state power to enhance popular democratic capacities. Contemporary populists face circulations and formless forms of power that nineteenth-century Populists could not have fathomed. If this has led everyday populists to disengage from state-level structural reforms and those engaged in populist resistance to reify the state and capital, negotiating centralizing forms of power and decentered sites of contestation is as crucial as ever.

"FANNING THE SPARK OF HOPE" IN NINETEENTH-CENTURY POPULISM

For a brief moment in America's history, nineteenth-century poor and working people vivified America's populist imaginary and cultivated it as a resource to arouse collective identification and organize aspirations to popular power. There is no denying that era's contributions to the cruel and reactionary forms of populism that are most familiar and readily accessible to populist actors today. By aligning with Bryan and the Democratic Party, People's Party elites signaled their support for modest reforms that would enhance state regulation of private economic power; during the first decades of the twentieth century, this same reformist stance ultimately tied the cruel aspirations of farmers and laborers to interest-group leverage and individual mobility within a bureaucratic capitalist state.[203] Grassroots and elite Populists, moreover, popularized rhetorical tropes that continue to tap into deeply held expectations of cultural supremacy; populist actors have since mobilized these tropes to fuel reactionary aspirations to preserve democracy for a nation defined in white, middle-class, masculine, Christian terms. We see this strand of populism in recurring messianic crusades for moral purity from Prohibition to McCarthyism to the Christian Right and in narrow visions of white, male producerism that have inspired reactionary populists from Father Charles Coughlin to George Wallace to Nixon's silent majority to the Tea Party.[204] If these were the only legacies we had inherited from Populism, it would be easy to understand why many democratic theorists and actors might want Populism's vision of democracy to "disappear irretrievably" from historical memory.

I have tried, however, to tell a different story of Populism: one in which a motley crew of actors cultivated an aspirational democratic populist inheritance that has also been vital to America's history. Populism was able to cultivate rebellious aspirations where it succeeded in mobilizing broad-based resistance and identification in tandem with its multiform experiments in constituting horizontal power: for example, in the agrarian cooperative spaces that were the backbone of Alliance radicalism; in acts of solidarity during the Great Southwest Strike that enabled farmers and laborers to envision a union of the producing classes; in the spirited organizing of women who used their Populist activism as a platform to question patriarchy; in myriad efforts by black Populists to cultivate black power in their communities and to bring about social and institutional change by allying with other reformers; and in the dynamic, coalitional institutions of the People's Party. These experiments unsettled the widespread "miseducation" driven by a corporate revolution that had habituated countless working people to accept their lot in life as inevitable. By repatterning everyday practices, Populists cultivated dispositions toward spirited rebellion and horizontal cooperation in grassroots actors. Populism thus enlivened the promise, incarnated in the everyday practices of millions of people, that "the people" could enact popular power beyond the structural horizons that confined them to rituals of subordination. The movement's translocal organizing, moreover, engaged people in more active forms of horizontality that, at their most promising, held the boundaries of

Populist identification and power open to contest and redefinition by the most marginalized Populists.

In telling this story, I have challenged not only public memories of Populism, but also the narrowed horizons of the theory and practice of populism today. I have used the concept of translocalism to explain how Populism's experiments with horizontality built and intensified feedback loops between everyday politics and broader critique and vision, as well as how the movement constituted horizontal power across geographic and social divides. In case after case, Populism's translocal organizing reshaped local spaces as sites of democratic aspiration, while inflecting the centralizing rhetoric of the movement's vision of commonwealth democracy. It is impossible to understand Populism's rebellious aspirations, however, without also talking about its practices of temporal translocalism. It was in great part by reviving and updating inherited visions from past rebels—carried, most notably, in the contested rhetoric of producerism, radical republicanism, and messianism—that Populists were able to rupture the sense of inevitability tied to the liberal-capitalist social imaginary that had taken hold in America during the Gilded Age. Likewise, I have practiced a kind of temporal translocalism in this chapter to "fan the spark of hope" in the traces of Populism that still linger in America's aspirational democratic populist imaginary. The spark of hope in Populism is difficult to identify from the perspective of most theories of populism: my reading of the movement allows neither a dismissal of its reactionary and cruel aspirations, nor a celebration of its rebellious aspirations unbound from habituated bodies and imperfect institutions. Instead, it encourages populists to acknowledge the paradoxical condition of cultivating rebellious aspirations to power: the need to develop visions, practices, and longer-term strategies to engage the world *both* as it is and as it is not yet.

What sparks of hope can populist theorists and actors cultivate by remembering this story of Populism? I want to suggest that rereading Populism offers hope and resources to counter two developments that have limited populist radicalism since the late nineteenth century. The first is what Michael Kazin has called the "conservative capture" of populism. Joe Lowndes traces conservative populism, as we know it, back to the post–World War II Dixiecrat revolt against the New Deal. By stoking white working-class ressentiment against federal support for racial equality, white Dixiecrat elites set in motion a long-term process of social movement organizing, party building, state programs, and rhetorical strategy—one that linked economic conservatism to racism and tied both to antigovernment populism. This process set the stage for Nixon and Reagan to leave their marks on populism in the neoliberal 1970s and 1980s.[205]

Indeed, the conservative capture eventually fueled a separation in mainstream political imagination between populism's economic radicalism and its cultural contests over the people and democracy. During the first half of the twentieth century, white populisms combined the reactionary cultural politics of the People's Party with its rebellious economic legacies. Demagogues from Father Charles Coughlin to Joseph McCarthy exemplify the reactionary brand of twentieth-century populism that mobilized white working-class resentment against "limousine liberals" who were the acolytes of change in America. In a recent genealogy of this term, Steve Fraser traces the development of the people's enemy from Henry Ford's rants about a secret cabal of Jews, bankers, and Bolsheviks to the invective of Republican upstarts, George Wallace and Barry Goldwater, against Ivy League financiers, agents of collectivism, and bureaucratic social engineers (on behalf of racialized social classes). By the Reagan Revolution, however, conservative populisms that once inveighed against Harvard, Washington, *and* Wall Street had dropped their anticorporate rhetoric. Idolizing the "businessman as populist hero"—that is, as the everyman cum successful risk-taking entrepreneur who assured a flourishing, free-market democracy—right-wing populists now aligned their reactionary cultural politics with capitalist ideology.[206] Echoing a common refrain among the religious Right, for example, evangelist Pat Robertson introduced an anti-tax-and-spend message into the Eighth Commandment: "Thou shalt not steal" means that the "God of Jacob forbids a citizen to take what belongs to another citizen . . . to take from the rich and give to the poor."[207] The most powerful fomenter of populist sentiment in America today, as I argue in chapter 1, is the assemblage of think tanks, megachurches, Fox News, and the Republican Party that Bill Connolly has called the "evangelical-capitalist resonance machine." In Connolly's words, its resonances ensure that "the right leg of the evangelical movement today is joined at the hip to the left leg of the capitalist juggernaut."[208]

Center and left populisms *have* mobilized around anticorporate visions of democracy and enacted alternatives ranging from local experiments in social democracy to cooperative efforts and solidarity economies. Until Occupy, however, economic populism lived largely in organizing by everyday populists beneath the radar of the nation-state and antiglobalization activism that was not legible *as* populism in America's national imaginary. With notable exceptions, for example, the Popular Front of the 1930s and the New Left and Civil Rights movements of the 1960s and 1970s, aspirational democratic populisms since the People's Party have been unable to combine broad resistance with effective grassroots organizing to reshape political culture and effect large-scale changes in social, economic, and political institutions. This is the second development that has constrained populist vision and practice since the nineteenth century. If anything, the Right has had more success in this regard. Owing to the successes of the Christian Right, which helped fuel the development of the "evangelical-capitalist resonance machine," the Right has sustained a powerful critique of secular, bureaucratic government, one with both deep roots and intensified resonances in relation to everyday practice and state and national policy arenas.[209] By contrast, since the late 1960s, left populisms have largely exemplified the split between outrageous resistance and everyday populism. On the one hand, the mass antiglobalization protests in Seattle and the more recent uprising in Wisconsin, in support of collective bargaining rights for government workers, share the common belief: "The only way to change [the hegemony of corporate capital] is to shift the power to a culture of resistance."[210] On the other hand, we see steady efforts to regenerate everyday civic culture and bring about incremental institutional reform in the civic renewal movements of the last two decades, in particular the local successes of broad-based community organizing groups on issues spanning schools, jobs, living wages, fair housing, health access, and prison-to-work programs.[211] As a result, left populisms have been unable to fashion rhetoric or organizing strategies to address the social and economic grievances of America's most marginalized groups.

In the context of these developments, Populism offers sparks of hope that might simultaneously enlarge the ambitions of contemporary populists and sharpen their vision of the challenges to constituting horizontal popular power. I have argued that Populism's imagination of the people and democracy was historically constituted and internally contested. This is also true, as I will argue in the next chapter, of America's populist imaginary today. The stakes of recognizing and understanding these contests, then and now, return us to the anxieties about democracy I introduced at the outset of the book. The repeated mobilization of resonant right-wing populisms and the demobilization of radical democratic populisms are not just symptoms of our times: they combine to reinforce the air of inevitability surrounding the de-democratizing trends of today's "second Gilded Age."[212] Rupturing this horizon of inevitability, I argue in chapter 4, will require enlarging the aspirations of everyday populists and yielding the purity of left populist resistance to the unexpected openings and uncertain outcomes of institutional engagement and change. Seeing Populism's past differently, I want to suggest, can open radical democratic populists to new ways of negotiating the centering and decentering dynamics of popular power that are needed to counter contemporary circulations and resonances of power. Finding ways to sustain new intensities of broad-based insurgence with multiform experiments in popular power is vital not only to emboldening the ambitions of radical grassroots democratic movements today, but also to contesting the legacies of white, masculine nationalism that even radical democratic populisms—such as Occupy—inherit in one form or another. In this light, today's populists will need, far more than nineteenth-century Populism, to amplify the aspirations at their margins.

America's Populist Imaginary

Brought to You by Chevrolet and Leonard Cohen

This is our country. This is our truck.

—CHEVROLET

It's coming from the silence
On the dock of the bay,
From the brave, the bold, the battered
Heart of Chevrolet:
Democracy is coming to the USA

—LEONARD COHEN

When Chevrolet released its "An American Revolution" marketing campaign in 2003, it did not predict "revolution" would appear only five years later, in the guise of a global financial tailspin, an automotive industry crisis, and populist uprisings that either assailed corrupt Big Three American auto executives or assaulted citizens who drove foreign cars. Indeed, when Chevrolet unveiled its new Silverado pickup truck to national World Series television audiences in 2006, the car company sought to revive its iconic brand image as "The Heartbeat of America."

The campaign's centerpiece Silverado ad, "Anthem," pairs John Mellencamp's folk song "Our Country" with a montage of images from the United States' past and present: vintage shots of the Statue of Liberty and Wall Street, news footage of Martin Luther King Jr. delivering his "I Have a Dream" speech and Richard Nixon waving from his helicopter after his resignation, video frames capturing the heights of America's feats on the moon and the depths of its natural wonder in Canyonlands National Park. In one sequence, a photograph of Rosa Parks at the front of a bus rests easily next to idyllic, white-1950s leisure scenes, while

Mellencamp sings, "I can stand beside ideals I think are right." He continues, "And I can stand beside the idea to stand and fight," as the ad cuts seamlessly between footage of Muhammad Ali defending his heavyweight title, American soldiers in Vietnam, and hippies dancing back home. Fast-forward to the present and a rousing chorus of "This is our country" carries us through images of disaster and resiliency: forest fires raging out West, Hurricane Katrina flooding the Gulf Coast, volunteers rebuilding homes, the two towers of light beaming above New York's skyline, a team of firefighters, a soldier reunited with his daughter. The ad comes to a close as a Chevy Silverado rolls to a stop in an open wheat field, a young white boy looks up from the driver side window, and a rugged, masculine voice-over provides the tagline: "This is our country. This is our truck."[1]

When I first saw Chevy's ad, I was baffled by its appeal to the unity of the American people and the resilience of American democracy in the midst of scenes that conjure ongoing crisis and conflict. I turn to Chevy's ad here to raise two questions that are central to my concerns in this chapter. First, how do ubiquitous forms of popular culture, such as advertising and music, shape the way political subjects imagine collective identity and popular power? In "Anthem," Chevy commodifies the black freedom movement, anti-Vietnam protests, and the countercultural revolt of the sixties and seventies to sell trucks to its target audience: middle-class, white men. On a symbolic level, the ad's representation of the people and democracy co-opts the aspirational democratic populisms of Civil Rights and the New Left to reproduce a hegemonic vision of "Our Country." On a material level, the ad directs us to the advertising industry's role in shaping social identities and aspirations.[2] Chevrolet is an apt touchpoint for understanding the role of advertising in shaping America's social imaginary. The dominant player in the automotive industry in the 1950s, Chevy's parent company, General Motors, helped fuel America's post–World War II rise as a "consumer republic," that is, a political society in which subjects aspire to individual choice and market action rather than popular power.[3] Viewed in this context, the representations of populism in "Anthem" reinforce anti-democratic dynamics of capitalist political culture.

Given the resonant forces of mass-mediated popular culture, in which the iconoclastic Leonard Cohen also participates, my second question is how rebellious populist aspirations can survive and even flourish. Cohen emerged as part of the countercultural movements of the 1960s and 1970s that rejected the nationalism, commercialism, and social hierarchies of Chevy's post–World War II era. Decades later, the ironic lyrics in his 1992 hit, "Democracy," expose Chevy's complicity in dynamics of capital flight and corporate restructuring that severely weakened the foundations of popular power in the United States. Chevy's master narrative of America skips over the ongoing aftershocks of the neoliberal revolution in the 1980s and 1990s. Cohen envisions grassroots actors enacting democracy from the ruins that Chevy has helped create and, more broadly, from the social and political disorder that characterize contemporary American life. The song's promise, "Democracy is coming to the USA," emerges without any sign that the American people ever have been or ever will be whole. I evaluate "Democracy" in this chapter as one example of the ways in which cultural texts can draw on populism to mobilize rebellious aspirations to power. Cohen's unsettling lyrics and resonant voice have the capacity to stir radical imaginings of collective identity and democracy in the midst of paradox—including his own vocation as a countercultural artist who relies on the mass music industry to reach audiences. By cultivating the paradoxes of democracy in the song and in his career, Cohen emerges as an uncertain prophet of a promise of democratic life sustained by egalitarian, pluralistic aspirations to popular power.

I turn to Chevrolet and Cohen to elucidate competing strands of America's populist imaginary, which coexisted during the nineteenth-century Populist movement and have sharpened since: either narrowing the terms of collective identity and democracy or opening them to contestation by emerging actors. In doing so, I develop a key argument I make at the outset of the book: populist actors who aim to contest the identity of the people and reconstitute popular power do so not only in the narrow field of liberal institutions and procedures, but in a larger cultural context that shapes people's ideas and aspirations related to democracy. Populist rhetoric and images are ubiquitous in contemporary popular culture: the term "populist" describes talk show hosts and shock jocks, rock-and-roll icons (including Mellencamp), automotive brands (including Chevrolet), clothing brands (such as Levi's and Wrangler), and crowds booing everyone from elected officials to wealthy sports stars who let "the people" down.[4] Against the grain of existing scholarship on populism, I want to suggest that populism's ubiquity in popular culture is difficult to bypass when evaluating a style of politics that arouses collective identification and mobilizes popular aspirations.[5] By popular culture, I mean the array of traditions, activities, images, identities, norms, and other expressions of everyday life, whether these reside in the mainstream public sphere or various counterpublic spaces. As scholars of advertising and music have shown, the ever-changing technologies of mass-mediated popular culture have unparalleled influence in their ability to communicate cultural messages and shape people's identities and aspirations.[6] If advertising and music largely reproduce dominant social imaginaries, they can also open spaces for negotiating identities and aspirations in light of changing cultural dynamics.[7] Paired together, Chevy's ad and Cohen's song offer heuristic examples of the kinds of cultural processes that vie to shape America's populist imaginary. I juxtapose them here, but also identify resonances between them that offer insight into both glitches that might disrupt regulated populist aspirations and traps that lure rebellious ones.

CHEVROLET:
REGULATING ASPIRATIONS IN "OUR COUNTRY"

It may seem an unlikely branding strategy for Chevy's ad to conjure the unsettling paradoxes of democratic life in the United States. Companies rely on their brand image—and the "halo of emotions" it inspires—to position themselves in a given market. When consumers identify with a brand, they often seek to gain psychological benefits—for example, to feel young, masculine, or ecologically conscious—or to convey some aspect of their identities.[8] When a company places an ad in the World Series broadcast—a spot that cost $400,000 in 2006—it expects the ad will reinforce its brand image and have a strong resonance with audiences. Chevy believed that its target market would "want to buy an American truck, because they feel Americans still make better pickups than anyone on the market." Adding fantasy to functionality, the ad's producer elaborated, "No other country can build this truck—not Korea, not Japan, not Germany. It is a pure reflection of the American experience."[9] The ad represents "the American experience" in hopes that audiences who want to buy an American truck will say to themselves: that's Chevy.

As the ad reveals, Americans have always contested the "Our" in "Our Country" and struggled to balance the pluralism embodied in the motto, *E pluribus unum*, with the unitary demands of national sovereignty. Chevy, however, does not let its audience linger in that paradox. The twin towers of light are the ultimate symbol of healing in post-9/11 America, and the ad's portrayal of America represents a spatial and temporal wholeness. The scars on our soil have been repaired, the threats to our borders edited out, and the discord of red and blue America replaced by Mellencamp's patriotic chorus circumscribing us "From the East Coast / To the West Coast / Down the Dixie Highway / Back home / This is our country." As "Our Country" shores up its spatial borders, so too does it solidify its master narrative. The ad's glimpse of American history carries viewers from the prosperity of the 1950s, through periods of conflict, crisis, and renewal in the 1960s and 1970s, to the promise of yet another new beginning at the turbulent outset of the twenty-first century. On the precipice of its own bankruptcy in 2009, and presaging its rapid resurgence to the top of the automobile industry in 2011, Chevy stepped up to reassure its audience: "Yeah. These are the bruises and scars that have shaped our nation, and we have rebuilt ourselves spiritually, emotionally, and physically."[10]

The ad's producers want us to remember, too, that Chevrolet has "been standing side by side with all the things America goes through, ups and downs," every step of the way.[11] "Anthem" participates in a rich tradition of associating the automobile with American national identity. Chevrolet's marketing strategies were, historically speaking, at the forefront of that tradition. In the 1950s and 1960s,

Chevrolet's jingle "See the USA in your Chevrolet" headlined the CBS variety show *Inside the U.S.A.* and, later, the popular *Dinah Shore Chevy Show*. Audiences who tuned in every week watched as Shore closed each episode by singing the patriotic verse "See the USA in your Chevrolet / America is asking you to call. / Drive your Chevrolet through the USA / America's the greatest land of all." In the 1970s, Chevrolet ads assured Americans: "Through all the many changes / Some things are for sure." After a turbulent decade, Americans could still count on "baseball, hotdogs, apple pie, and Chevrolet." By the 1980s, Chevrolet had solidified its place as the "Heartbeat of America." When George W. Bush encouraged Americans to keep "continued participations and confidence in the American economy" in the aftermath of the 2001 terrorist attacks, Chevy promised to do its part to "Keep America Rolling."[12] It was in that post-9/11 context—and in the wake of competitor ads touting Toyota's investment and job creation in the United States—that Chevrolet again positioned the Silverado as America's truck. But, of course, Chevrolet and General Motors are multinational corporations, and much of their manufacturing takes place outside the nation's borders. For people living in America, whose work and livelihood depend on the production calculations of multinational firms, Chevy's brand of "revolution" signals the economic and social crises simmering beneath America's continued claims to national sovereignty.[13]

That the production of "Anthem" relies on montage belies the message of spatial and temporal wholeness the ad represents. As a practice of editing in film and media, montages produce narrative and aesthetic effects by juxtaposing selected images and sounds, in deliberate spatial and temporal relationships, oriented or disoriented by choices in duration, tempo, and rhythm. Every montage edits its final take in relation to a multitude of images and sounds. It creates its overall effect by foregrounding what it wants to reveal and backgrounding what it does not. This includes not only imaginative associations, but also its own artifice and techniques of production.[14] General Motor's longtime marketing agency, Campbell-Ewald, waded through a readily accessible archive of stock media footage to produce the ad's feel-good celebration of America.[15] The benefit of stock footage is that it assumes the audience is *already* familiar with that material. We can't interpret the ad without already knowing the iconic highlights of the sixties and seventies, or without having watched the 24/7 news reports from the World Trade Center attacks and Hurricane Katrina. Part of assuming the familiarity of these images is assuming their *legibility* within a select range of common narratives that target audiences are likely to hold. If the images in Chevy's "Anthem" lend themselves to various interpretive narratives, Campbell-Ewald uses continuous and invisible editing techniques to foreground the ad's master narrative of America as a land of freedom, opportunity, and progress. From its establishing shots of the Statue of Liberty and Wall Street, through its seamless cuts of standard duration, easy tempo, and consistent rhythm, to its parting shot of a young white boy at the wheel of a pickup truck, the ad invokes and reinforces the linear futural trajectory of this familiar narrative. Images follow one another in rapid succession, subsumed by the ad's overall narrative without being given time or space to impart any dissonant effects. Potentially divergent and disruptive images are instead woven together by recurrent motifs—hats, crowds, sitting, waving, dancing—and reined in by Mellencamp's foot-stomping backbeat and feel-good, unifying lyrics. The final take is a prepackaged, populist branding of Chevy—and America.

Chevy's populism identifies recent threats to "Our Country" and interpellates its audience as a unified nation that, despite internal conflicts, has always come together to meet the challenges it faces. The producers of "Anthem" invite audiences to identify with the ad's representation of the American people, and it encourages them to align their aspirations to unity and strength with the ad's narrative of progress. What is striking about the ad's populism is its juxtaposition of national unity with a more robust portrayal of cultural pluralism than we usually find in nationalist representations of the people. Like most Silverado commercials, which define what it means to be American in the narrow terms of the nation's white, male heartland, most nationalist populisms portray the people in culturally homogenous terms. I want to suggest that there are two distinct but overlapping readings of "Anthem" as a populist ad. On the one hand, the ad does ultimately overwrite the differences it represents: it energizes reactionary aspirations to shore up the familiar borders of white, masculine nationalism. On the other hand, by incorporating cultural differences, the ad encourages cruel aspirations toward "postracial," individual freedom—aspirations that are impossible for even white men to realize given the structural realities the ad conceals and reinforces. Taking these two readings together, "Anthem" collapses differences of identity and ideology that, if given political power, might counter both white male cultural supremacy and the global capitalist underpinnings of American democracy.

"Anthem" I:
The Reactionary Aspirations of American Nationalism

On the first reading of the ad, Chevy uses populist language and images to reinforce the nation-state as the frontier of American collective identity and democracy. Beneath the ad's taste of Americana, moreover, are unmistakable appeals to a white, masculine brand of nationalism. That ideal, Chevy calculates, will appeal to its target market for the Silverado: white working men.[16] Chevy's integrated marketing campaign kicked off at the 2006 Texas State Fair, where the new 2007 Silverado was first unveiled. From there, a caravan of Silverados embarked on a three-day "Drive for Farm Aid," stopping for street parties in Nashville, Indianapolis, and Pittsburgh and finally reaching the 2006 Farm Aid concert in Camden, New Jersey. To reach male audiences, "Anthem" appeared in heavy rotation during college and professional football games and the 2006 World Series. The campaign also featured print ads in publications such as *Motor Trend, Field & Stream*, and *Popular Science*. Finally, the Silverado campaign sponsored iconic media events, such as the World Series, Sunday Night Football on NBC, and the Country Music Awards.[17] Although Chevrolet ran an entirely separate marketing campaign directed at Latinos—stay tuned for an update on that at our second commercial break—it put most of its budget toward its flagship campaign dedicated to creating brand loyalty among white men.

White men appear as progenitors and inheritors of Chevy's America. Between the ad's opening footage of white soldiers waving their hats in a salute to the Statue of Liberty and its closing shot of a white boy in a cowboy hat gazing out the window of a pickup truck, men are cast in the role of producers and protectors of the nation. They appear as soldiers, firefighters, laborers, farmers, fathers, and neighbors ready to lend a helping hand to those in need. In contrast to the toil and sacrifice of these men, women dance in the background of Chevy's America—with the exception of Parks, whom the ad contains in her seat. For over a decade in the 1990s and early 2000s, Chevrolet dedicated one of the longest-run advertising campaigns in history to creating the reputation that its Silverado is "Like a Rock."[18] Chevy trusted viewers of its new ad campaign to recognize that they, like the Silverado, are the rugged, dependable bedrock of "Our Country." "The research behind this new truck confirmed what we've seen for decades," explains Chevrolet general manager Ed Pepper. "While they would never say so, the people who know Silverado owners see them as 'everyday heroes.' . . . This new marketing campaign celebrates the connection our truck buyers have to their families and their country."[19] As the advertising industry has expanded its images of masculinity—it now markets household products to men, and the "metrosexual" is a consistent money-making market—truck ads offer men the fantasy of more traditional forms of power. They tap into the long-standing producer ethos that celebrates manual laborers as the moral and political backbone of America.[20]

Many viewers would contest the claim that Chevy's America also dreams of white supremacy. After all, advertising critics quickly took exception with the centrality of Parks and King to its portrait of American history: Chevy, they argue, capitalizes on the Civil Rights movement to sell trucks.[21] Joining Parks, King, and Ali from America's past, moreover, are images of black men in the present. A black firefighter poses with three white firefighters in front of a fire engine. A black man stands alone in front of what appears to be his Katrina-ravaged home, his arm resting on his Silverado—perhaps awaiting the rescue squad of white volunteers and Chevy trucks that appear in the very next scene. Although blacks

are present in the ad, racial conflict is largely contained. For one, the stock footage in "Anthem" remembers a wholly sanitized black freedom movement. The
Parks in this narrative is the grandmother who sat down on a bus because her feet
were tired, not the seasoned activist at the forefront of a liberation movement.
Ali's role as a draft resister and outspoken critic of the war in Vietnam is likewise
forgotten. Instead, he assumes the role of so many black men cum all-American
sports heroes: at once a symbol of black power and violence and a reminder that
the spectacle of such strength by black men must always be contained on the field
or in the ring. Finally, Americans appropriate King's image so ubiquitously today
that it already flickers in and out of our daily consciousness as it does in Chevy's
ad, in which the allusion to King's "Dream" is forgotten two frames later with a
wave of Nixon's hand. In the most brazen attempts to whitewash King's legacy
today, conservatives use his wish—that we "not be judged by the color of our
skin, but by the content of our character"—to legitimate their claims that ours is
a postracial America.[22]

Chevy too wants its audience to feel reassured that the era of racial turmoil is
long gone. It is telling that, in Chevy's celebration of American progress, racial
conflict is contained entirely in the past. What would become of Chevy's America,
for example, if its memorials to Parks, King, and Ali as symbols of racial harmony
were supplemented by the bitter narratives of institutional racism and abandonment still surfacing in the Gulf Coast today? What the ad treats as a natural disaster was, in reality, a devastating social disaster. Hurricane Katrina exposed the
enormous structural inequalities and social divisions that exist in America along
lines of race, class, and gender. For many blacks living in New Orleans, the federal
neglect and gross civil rights violations that took place after the hurricane were
the continuation of centuries of oppression. By 2005, that legacy had manifested
in an 84 percent poverty rate among African Americans in the city, the economic
and political isolation of the city's segregated black neighborhoods, and a lack
of transportation that made it difficult for many poor citizens to flee the hurricane.[23] How too would Chevy's montage of "Our Country" be different if it
alluded to the mass immigration reform rallies that erupted in cities and towns
across the country several months before the ad was released? The media footage from those rallies showed millions of brown, black, and white bodies waving diverse flags of the Americas throughout the nation's streets. Chevy detours
around the emotional roadblock of twenty-first-century immigration debates by
editing immigrants out of "Our Country" altogether. The Statue of Liberty may
remind viewers of a bygone era of European immigration that made America the
"nation of immigrants" it is today. No one in the ad, however, is coded as Latino,
Asian, or African.

Nor do the United States' borders with Mexico and Canada figure in the geographical boundaries of "Our Country." On the one hand, what would Chevy's

brand gain from associating itself with the nation's militarized border with Mexico? That border signifies America's military strength, but also the futility of highly trained border guards and sophisticated surveillance technologies in the face of globalization and the mass movement of people across borders. On the other hand, auto ads are historically tied to America's geography and landscape, and this ad appears to feature every other frontier in America's social imagination: "From the East Coast / To the West Coast" to the Colorado River carving its way through the depths of the nation's canyons to the ever-beckoning frontiers of outer space.[24] Indeed, the ad evokes the spirit of settler colonialism that has historically tied American freedom to imperialism (and the violent erasure of Native Americans and Mexicans who stood in the way of the nation's Manifest Destiny from coast to coast). On a closer look, the ad taps into the racialized anxiety that once accompanied America's expansion at its Western frontier and is now directed toward the cosmopolitan pluralism of the nation's two coasts.[25] When Mellencamp's lyrics define the borders of "Our Country," viewers see the sole image of the West Coast in the ad: the wildfires that yearly ravage the coastal ranges. The East Coast fares slightly better: moving on from turbulent images of 1960s protestors and Nixon at the White House, the East Coast renews America's values in the image of a Chesapeake Bay crabber and the twin towers of light dominating the New York skyline. For the most part, however, Chevy's America belongs to those who drive "Down the Dixie Highway / Back home." Back home in America's heartland, Chevy's drivers can rest assured, "This is our country." Indeed, most of the images in Chevy's montage conjure the heartland of the American South and Midwest. This is America's backbone, the home of the middle-class, white workers, soldiers, and neighbors Chevy celebrates with its "Anthem." In doing so, the ad reinforces a populist imaginary in which a racially and geographically homogeneous people no longer has to deal with threats to its survival or its cultural supremacy.

Freed from internal social conflict, middle-American white men can dream of protecting the nation's borders from the threat of terrorism figured in images of the twin towers of light, the team of firefighters, and white soldiers wearing the desert camouflage of the wars in Iraq and Afghanistan. So too can they imagine themselves the backbone of the American economy. In "Anthem," volunteers labor in the wreckage of Hurricane Katrina to repair the single-family homes that symbolize the American dream of economic opportunity and independence. In "Backbone," a companion ad set to Mellencamp's "Our Country," a white, male cast toils as farmers, hunters, loggers, and oil riggers to sustain the manual labor that keeps the economy going. Written copy appears over the images in an unmistakable message to the heartland viewers Chevy intends to reach. "This is our breakfast," the copy reads, as a logger operates his forklift. "This is our chat room," announces the copy in the next frame, depicting two men in cowboy hats catching up over coffee at a rural diner. Back to a logger, now resting on fresh-hewn logs, the ad completes its dig at the latte-sipping liberals on America's two coasts: "This is our coffee break." The remaining frames are more earnest. Several men in hard hats sweat around an oil rig as the moral of the ad becomes explicit: "This is our backbone." A vintage painting of a white Boy Scout confirms, "This is our philosophy." Finally, a young white dad in a clean white T-shirt holds his fair-haired, fair-skinned infant son, as Chevy reminds its target audience: "This is our purpose." What was present as an undercurrent in "Anthem" moves to the forefront of this ad: the reactionary tone of Chevy's marketing to a segment of consumers who, in many cases, feel as if they are clinging to a waning cultural privilege.

In "Anthem," Richard Nixon is the most obvious political symbol of white middle-class ressentiment. Nixon's "Southern Strategy" in the late 1960s and early 1970s spearheaded the Republican campaign to siphon away votes from traditional Democratic Party strongholds. Appealing to the "silent majority," Nixon used racially coded language to tap into the anxieties of white voters in Chevy's southern and Midwestern heartland, as well as working-class white ethnics in the Northeast. Looking backward, Nixon drew from the playbook of populist hero George Wallace to translate the overtly racist rhetoric of earlier reactionary populisms into late twentieth-century terms: for example, "states' rights" (against federal intervention on issues such as desegregation and voting rights), "law and order" (to protect "the great majority . . . the non-shouters, the non-demonstrators" from the disorder of protests for black freedom), and "property rights" (to protect hard-working white men from the racialized and gendered "dependent classes" who now stood to benefit from New Deal policies).[26] Looking forward, Nixon prefigured an echo chamber of right-wing media personalities who have made a living since the 1970s by stoking white men's ressentiment toward liberated women, racialized minorities, and liberal elites. In hiring right-wing talk show host Sean Hannity as the spokesperson for its 2006 "You're a Great American Car Giveaway" promotion, GM shows that it is not above appealing to the same sentiments.[27] Like Hannity and others who foment today's right-wing resonance machines, Chevy plays on and reproduces reactionary rhetoric and affect that resonate in a broad segment of popular culture. To punctuate the ad's intentions, one of its producers responds to criticism that Chevy co-opts images of the Civil Rights movement to sell trucks: "If you want to make a statement that rings true with the majority of people, you are going to piss off some people. . . . So let them get in their Volvo sedans and complain about this spot that they see as exploitative. This is not for them."[28] Translation: Chevy is on the side of real Americans.

But I want to raise the question: what *has* Chevy done for middle-American white men? There is another reason Chevy appeals to a narrow vision of producerism: one in which white men secure their claim to moral and political superiority only by denying similar claims to blacks, immigrants, and women. Consider the more expansive vision of producerism that might emerge, by contrast, if we were to turn the volume down on Mellencamp and up on King. We might hear not only Mellencamp's reassurance, "I do believe there's a dream for everyone," but also King's exhortation that such a dream is impossible unless we first tend to a "deep malady within the American spirit." We might hear that "an edifice which produces beggars needs restructuring," not repackaging in old form.[29] For King, who linked racism and poverty with capitalism, that restructuring would have deep roots in alternative imaginings of political economy. Chevy cannot afford to remember, as it foregrounds King's iconic "I Have a Dream" speech, that he delivered it at the 1963 March on Washington *for Jobs and Freedom*, soon after the crowd heard from Walter Reuther of the United Auto Workers (UAW). During the 1960s, the UAW organized hundreds of thousands of black and white workers in nationwide strikes to win better wages and working conditions from GM.[30] Nor could Chevy's homage to multiculturalism deploy King's favorite analogy for the uniformity of social imagination: America's confusion of social distinction with driving a bigger and better car. "You've seen people riding around in Cadillacs," King admonished, when "they don't earn enough to have a good T-Model Ford."[31] To give airtime to this radical King would expose GM's long-marketed fantasy of social mobility as both conformist and unsustainable. Along with Reuther and the UAW, this King would evoke memories of black-white-brown labor coalitions that GM and Chevy cannot afford. By contrast, Chevy's King remains available for co-option by those who stir ressentiment against "reverse racism" in order to distract white men from the structural causes of their economic insecurity.

Commercial Break I:
General Motors and the Great Recession

There is a "cruel optimism" behind a branding strategy that appeals to America's enduring national promise while rending that promise ever obsolete.[32] By displacing their aspirations to power onto the fantasies marketed by Chevy, consumers have long bolstered political economic dynamics that disempower citizens. In the 1920s, General Motors distinguished itself from Ford by advertising "a car for every purse and purpose" and introducing "planned obsolescence" into the automotive industry—and, in quick succession, into the larger field of industrial design. In contrast to Ford's focus on the durability of its cars, GM offered regular changes in technology and style. Its yearly models boasted new color palettes and, over the next few decades, introduced auto buyers to chrome trim, two-toned paint, tail fins, hardtops, wraparound windshields, and more. GM president Arthur Sloan labeled the approach "dynamic obsolescence," fitting for a production and marketing strategy that built the American dream of social mobility into its brands.[33] The "fantasies" that advertisers produced for Chevy customers, explains Juliann Sivulka, were "visibly and spiritually different from the highest dollar dreams offered to plutocratic Cadillac owners."[34] As Americans expanded their purse strings, they could now convey their social position through "conspicuous consumption," buying the latest model, upgrading models, or even adding a second family car.[35] By 1955, GM was racing to keep up with the insatiable consumer demand it had helped create. "Our job is to hasten obsolescence," vice president and head of styling Harley Earl pronounced. "In 1934, the average ownership span was five years; now it is two years. When it is one year, we will have a perfect score."[36]

By the twenty-first century, GM's perfect score was not so perfect for either the car company or its consumers. Although GM dominated the US market until the mid-1970s, the company had always boasted a bloated and chaotic lineup of brands, and its mismanagement caught up with it. In 1980, GM held 45 percent of the US market; by 1990, its share was down to 35 percent, and the company posted its first-ever net loss. The decade in between saw GM add still more brands—acquiring Saab and founding Saturn—while Asian automakers such as Toyota and Honda broke into the US market with a much leaner manufacturing approach. What followed, in the company's own words, was a period in which GM "needed to continually restructure its business operations to reduce cost and excess capacity." That meant downsizing its workforce, shredding and outsourcing factories, and sacrificing the quality of its automobiles.[37]

By 2009, GM's liabilities outstripped its assets by a ratio of more than two to one—a ratio that had intensified in the midst of a protracted recession, a housing and unemployment crisis, and a credit crunch that slashed auto sales.[38] GM sought a combined bailout of $60.3 billion from the US and Canadian governments and, under close governmental oversight, filed for Chapter 11 bankruptcy on June 1, 2009.[39] President Obama appointed a task force to lead GM and its much smaller American counterpart, Chrysler, through what were coined "quick-rinse" bankruptcies. According to the task force, GM's "restructuring plan must rapidly achieve full competitiveness with foreign transplants and more aggressively implement significant manufacturing, headcount, brand, nameplate, and retail network restructurings."[40] In other words, close more plants, dramatically thin dealership ranks, cut hourly and salaried jobs, and bring labor costs in line with foreign-owned auto plants operating in the United States. The latter requirement meant that GM would have to rework its contract with the United Auto Workers to scale back the generous healthcare and pension plans established through decades of UAW strikes and negotiations. Finally, GM eliminated entire brands to focus its production and marketing energies on its four most successful brands: Chevy, GMC, Buick, and Cadillac.[41] Rapidity was of the essence in the GM's rebirth from "Old GM" to "New GM." All stakeholders agreed that the company would need to emerge from bankruptcy in a matter of months to ensure that its tarnished brand image—during the bailout, GM widely stood for "Government Motors" in financial circles—would rebound in the eyes of consumers.[42]

And it did. In 2011, GM posted its first net profit since 1999, and it returned to the top of the US auto market. The leaner "New GM" has remained profitable and competitive since. In December 2013, the US Treasury Department sold off the last of its shares in the company's stock. Summing up nearly a half decade of government efforts to rescue GM from collapse, President Obama played the part of spokesperson-in-chief: "When things looked darkest for our most iconic industry, we bet on what was true: the ingenuity and resilience of the proud, hard-working men and women who make this country strong."[43] In Obama's rhetoric, GM's renewal becomes yet another iconic flashpoint—alongside Parks, King, and Ali—in the dominant narrative of American progress. Only here, Obama reinforces a neoliberal discourse that puts not active citizens, but the strength of America's workforce and the health of corporate capitalism, at the center of the "American dream."[44] As the president put the issue almost five years earlier, in jus-tifying the government bailout of GM and Chrysler, the auto industry is "a once and future symbol of America's success" and "the pillar of our economy that has held up the dreams of millions of our people."[45] The auto industry crisis resulted not only in the rebirth of American auto companies, but free advertising for their centrality to a neoliberal America.

While GM and Ford are again flourishing—and Chrysler is enjoying a sec-ond chance under the direction of the Italian company, Fiat—people living in America have not fared so well.[46] The condition of the Big Three's hometown Detroit represents the stark contrast between corporate wealth and public depreciation. Detroit is mired in the largest municipal bankruptcy in the nation's history. With no federal bailout coming its way, the city cannot attract industry or even provide basic services. Factories and homes remain abandoned, the city has shut off water access to thousands of residents who are behind on their bills, and nonfunctioning streetlights leave large portions of the city in total dark-ness. About 40 percent of those who live in Detroit after decades of white and middle-class flight (around 80 percent of the city's residents are black, and only 10 percent are white) live below the poverty level. The city's unemployment rate *dropped* to below 15 percent in 2014.[47] While the auto industry once fueled Detroit's growth, providing well-paying jobs and robust tax revenue, corporate restructuring and downsizing is a major part of the story of Detroit's decline. In the 1960s, car companies and their suppliers generated three hundred thousand

jobs in the city. Then came increased automation and a decentralization of production to the white suburban Midwest, the Sunbelt, and overseas. Today, the
auto industry accounts for fewer than thirty thousand jobs in Detroit. Under
pressure from the UAW, the Big Three have recommitted to building jobs in
Detroit. They are also staples of charitable giving to the city—often in the form
of donations and sponsorships that generate publicity and goodwill. By all
accounts, however, the Big Three will not be at the center of any future recovery
in Detroit.[48]

America's grossly uneven "economic recovery" and the longer-term rise of economic inequality that preceded it are evidence of what John Kenneth Galbraith
once called "private opulence amidst public squalor."[49] Galbraith observed this
trend during the heady days of consumer society's emergence in the 1950s.
Those were the years when GM helped create America's "consumer republic,"
a society that equated consumption with not only self-fulfillment and national
prosperity, but also "loftier social and political ambitions for a more equal, free,
and democratic nation." The ideology of the consumer republic, of course, marketed the "American dream" of private consumption at the expense of public
consumption, that is, collective care for schools, hospitals, roads, and other public goods and infrastructure.[50] Today, the supremacy of private over public consumption fuels not only the economy, but also a neoliberal political ideology that
refuses to entertain public solutions to public problems. In the wake of the Great
Recession, the same government that bailed out GM and Chrysler—not to mention financial institutions deemed "too big to fail"—responded to a trillion-dollar
federal deficit not by raising taxes on the richest 2 percent of Americans (those
with incomes above $250,000 a year).[51] Instead, it slashed $37.8 billion in public
spending in 2011 and "sequestered" another $85.3 billion in 2013. This resulted
in a reduction in funding for multiple public sectors: Head Start programs,
afterschool programs, and other educational programs; housing assistance in
the form of subsidies for rent, heating, and plumbing; drug and alcohol addiction treatment; vocational training in prisons; and meals on wheels for sick and
homebound seniors. Cuts in spending for education, defense, national parks, and
social services also resulted in thousands of layoffs or furloughs in the military,
the National Guard, prisons, public defenders offices, schools, parks, hospice
care, police forces, and more. Public spending cuts came on top of the fact that,
by 2012, 99 percent of American families had felt 0 percent of the income growth
that signaled the nation's "economic recovery" from the Great Recession.[52] In
this context, the state's brand loyalty to America's "most iconic industry" reinforces the cruel optimism behind Chevy's marketing campaign. It sends the message that the "proud, hardworking" American people can once again flourish in
GM's America, rather than being subject to the "normalized agitation" of late
capitalism.[53]

"Anthem" II:
The Cruel Aspirations of Neoliberalism in America

Chevy's promise to middle-class white men is difficult to sustain given GM's hand in creating the surplus of instability that threatens the livelihood—not to mention the cultural supremacy—of its target market. Just as Chevy is the bankrolling multinational corporation behind the ad's representation of "Our Country," GM has long been at the forefront of economic and cultural changes that impact "middle America." I want to suggest that Chevy's troubled relationship to its target audience necessitates a second, overlapping reading of "Anthem." Specifically, the ad links the reactionary aspirations of its target audience to the cruel aspiration that individuals can still succeed on their own in America if they work hard and play by the rules of the game. In other words, the ad's nostalgic vision of white, masculine supremacy is tied to a celebration of the unlimited freedom that is supposed to come with it. Whether evoking the extraordinary acts of Horatio Alger's rags-to-riches heroes or the background toil of William Graham Sumner's Forgotten Man, the myth of the self-made man has historically promised that rugged individualism is the key to freedom and success in the laissez-faire, dog-eat-dog world of capitalist America.[54] In 1969, Nixon reincarnated the Forgotten Man in his appeals to the silent majority who had shouldered the burden of the economic and social reforms of the 1960s. By the end of "Anthem," the hero of the silent majority has regained his independence. Footage of Nixon waving to America is paired in the ad's next frame with the mirror image of a young white man dressed in cowboy attire and straddling a tin drum, waving as if from a rodeo in the Wild West. Like the white boy in the pickup truck looking out over an open field, the Forgotten Man's aspirations to individual freedom again know no frontiers. Chevy's populist imaginary thus invests white men in collective identification not in the name of political power—which could be turned against Chevy's brand—but in the name of individual aspirations to experience freedom without limits.

Since the 1970s, that vision has had to coexist with an increasingly celebrated multicultural landscape. Likewise, beneath the promise of white, masculine cultural superiority in "Anthem" is a celebration of the pluralism that has come to define America. For some viewers, it is the ad's feel-good taste of Americana that lingers, not its aggressive, white masculinity. One gets the sense that she is watching American history unfold through the eyes of Forrest Gump: "Life [is] like a box of chocolates. You never know what you're gonna get."[55] You might find Rosa Parks or Martin Luther King at the center, or you might get Richard Nixon; the Vietnam War has a place in the story of American progress, the same as the Civil Rights movement. The wildly popular *Forrest Gump* is an apt parallel for Chevy's ad in American popular imagination. Gump exemplifies popular cultural productions of the innocent white southern male—always good-hearted and well meaning—subjected to the unsettling forces of pluralist rebellions, liberal elites, and federal interventions and wars. While the film is steeped in white masculine ressentiment (most conspicuous in the character of Lieutenant Dan, a bitter Vietnam veteran played by conservative actor and activist Gary Sinise), Gump's slow-witted personality shields him from frustrated aspirations and enables him to make the most of the changing world around him (he ends up founding the successful Bubba Gump Shrimp Company).[56] "Anthem" imitates *Forrest Gump* in substance and style: the ad sustains the ideal of white masculine nationalism by celebrating *and* incorporating the pluralism that threatens it. Like Forest Gump, who ran through the sixties and seventies only to end up back at the tree stump from which he began, viewers can celebrate the varieties of the "American experience" while trusting that the courage and initiative of everyday heroes (coded, like Gump, as white and male) will continue to drive the nation.

This second populist reading of "Anthem" brings Chevy's America up to speed with the cultural and political dynamics of contemporary capitalism. Business buzzwords such as "rapid restructuring" and "flexible labor" signify the accelerated pace of economic and social life; the drive for "paradigm shifts" and "disruptive innovation" exalts the unbridled creativity that speed enables. Critics worry that the winners in today's hyperspeed polity are those who have the social position and marketable skills to keep pace.[57] Enthusiasts are more likely to agree with inventor and futurist Ray Kurzweil. Given the "exponential growth" of digital technologies—think iPhone video cameras, app makers, and 3D printers—Kurzweil gushes, "The means of creativity have been democratized."[58] If the ideology of capitalism celebrates perpetual creativity, capitalism's systemic imperatives have helped mobilize "neoliberal governance." The economic and political vision of neoliberalism endeavors to subject all aspects of life to the domain of the market. Put into practice, neoliberalism relies on discourses, policies, and processes that shift familiar forms of "governing" (which entail hierarchically organized rule) toward ever-adapting processes of "governance" (which entail rule that is networked, integrated, and cooperative). Those invested in neoliberal governance have reconceived politics as a field of management, which operates by entrepreneurializing individuals and facilitating their activities via incentives and norms rather than commands. In this way, neoliberal governance vanishes the vocabularies of power and collective responsibility from political life. In their place, it offers the fantasy of horizontalism without conflict. Neoliberal governance thus "makes individuals responsible for themselves," argues Wendy Brown, while "integrating" subjects—along with their creative energies—into "a common project whose purposes and constraint are given."[59]

Even as "Anthem" sustains an older populist imaginary, then, the ad must also reinvent that vision for a neoliberal era. In other words, Chevy must aim to integrate both the aspirations of white, masculine nationalism *and* a more timely and complicated vision of progress into the same representation of "Our Country." Campbell-Ewald culled from eighty hours of video to create "Anthem."[60] If the ad's producers erased images that would disrupt its narrative, they could have selected dozens of other images in place of the ones that made the final cut. Through seamless and unifying editing techniques, the producers sought to integrate wildly disparate images—along with the affective energies and aspirations they evoke—into Chevy's hegemonic vision of America. The ad does this, in great part, by treating incommensurable differences as equivalences. The montage in "Anthem" suggests equivalence between images of Parks, King, Ali, and peace marchers, for example, and the very things—the white consumer republic, the Vietnam War, and Nixon—they protested. In this way, Chevy's populist incorporation aims to include cultural and political differences while allowing them no impact in contesting the nation.[61]

This technique not only participates in cultural processes that regulate popular visions and aspirations, it enables Chevy to *feed off* the energies of its audiences. Consider Mellencamp's centrality to the performance of "Anthem." On the one hand, Mellencamp fashions himself as "a small-town rowdy from the Midwest," and his image and lyrics are likely to resonate with the reactionary aspirations of Chevy's heartland viewers.[62] On the other, "Our Country's" foot-stomping backbeat and rousing chorus create resonant energetics that may encourage audiences to indulge their unfettered ambitions. Even as the ad taps into anxieties over America's racialized borders, for example, its appeal to manifest destiny and outer space might stir the exhilaration that has historically accompanied the nation's imperialistic efforts. Likewise, by celebrating the energetics of change and the heady days of progress, the ad might generate excitement about Chevy's latest "American Revolution": "the all new Chevy Silverado."

In this second reading of "Anthem" as a populist ad, I want to argue, Chevy incapacitates politics itself—if we understand politics, as I do, to be a collective endeavor between disparate people who must share in the power to shape the world they hold in common. The ad includes, but depoliticizes, many of the cultural differences and conflicts that have shaped the nation in order to propel Chevy's hegemonic vision of America forward. Chevy's ideal of citizenship in today's world aligns, finally, not with the dissident historical figures the ad reins in, nor even primarily with its less disruptive images of voluntarism and heroism, but with its alluring parting message: buy Chevy. Of course, Chevy is not alone in consigning citizens to the role of consumers; Americans have long been told to "vote with our dollars" and to form our judgments in the "marketplace of ideas."[63] As Mellencamp sings in a less reassuring anthem, likening the depreciation of freedom to the sanitized dream of "little pink houses" for everyone, "Ain't that America"?[64] Rather than hopping on the bandwagon of this trend, as we have seen, GM has been behind the steering wheel. From GM's role in popularizing "dynamic obsolescence" to Chevy's "An American Revolution" campaign, the company has helped fuel a consumer America that, to borrow the famous indictment by Alexis de Tocqueville, "love[s] change, but . . . [is] afraid of revolutions."[65]

Just as the ad incorporates disruptive forms of citizenship, it enlists the state that is presumed accountable to "the people." The state cuts a shadowy figure in Chevy's America. It surfaces indirectly as the motor of American expansionism in Vietnam and the space race, in the protective guise of soldiers and firefighters defending the nation's soil, and as the object of insurgent mobilizations for social and political change. It is the absent carrier of a national sovereignty that is both promised in the ad's narrative and undermined in its performance—that is, the act of a transnational corporation imagining "Our Country." It is telling that Richard Nixon is the ad's most obvious symbol of the state. In popular consciousness, we remember Nixon's impeachment and his brazen abuse of executive power. More insidiously, despite his relatively moderate fiscal policies, Nixon initiated the drive to deregulation and downsizing that would define the Reagan era and the decline of the state as a site of collective responsibility.[66] Chevy needs a state that is not only willing to bail it out, but also to write and bend the rules for it. This is why GM spent $8.8 million in lobbying in 2013, in areas spanning transportation, product safety, environmental regulations, workplace safety, labor, taxes, trade, tariffs, budget appropriations, border security, healthcare, and more.[67] "Anthem" promotes an ideology that legitimizes the very deregulated state GM and other multinational corporations seek to create through their lobbying. Nixon's wave is not only lauded in "Our Country." It is universalized in the subsequent frame by its mirror image: the white cowboy waving from his tin drum. The pairing of these iconic images suggests that, from top to bottom, what it means to be an American is to defy all limits on individual—and corporate—aspirations.

Commercial Break II:
Chevy and Segmented Marketing to Latinos

Chevy's aspirations encompass even the Latino audiences whose images and histories it edits out of "Anthem." Latinos are touted as the fastest-growing market in the twenty-first-century United States, and their market share of new automobile purchases has risen faster than the rest of the population. Though outsold by Toyota, Honda, and Nissan, Chevrolet is the top-selling American brand among Latinos in the United States.[68] At a time when GM badly needed revenue to offset its outsized debt, the company could not afford to ignore Latinos all together. Their solution was standard for the marketing industry: they created a separate campaign targeting Latinos.[69] Chevy's marketing directors labeled the campaign "Una Marca que Dura," or "A Mark/Brand That Lasts," and described its feature television ad, "Milestones," as "syngestic" with "Anthem." Created by the Hispanic marketing agency Accentmarketing, the ad highlights the contributions Latinos made to America during the twentieth century. Images include the sports heroes Adolfo Luque, the Cuban-born Major League Baseball pitcher, and Roberto Duran, the Panamanian welterweight boxing champion. Vintage images of Latino laborers building the iconic Hoover Dam are followed by footage of the Mexican engineer Guillermo Camarena showing off his pioneering invention in industrial design: the color television. To ensure audience familiarity with the images, Spanish-language copy appears on the screen. The ad's backing track is the Spanish-language song "Justicia, Tierra, y Libertad," by the Mexican rock band Maná. The song's refrain, "Listen to my song, / Listen to it, listen to it. / Listen to my crying, / Listen to it, listen to it," recall the song's revolutionary title, "Justice, Land, and Freedom," a battle cry made famous by Poncho Villa and Emilio Zapata. At the same time, the refrain's demand for recognition suggests that, for Latinos viewing the ad in the United States, justice and freedom come not with gaining collective power over land—or "the land," that is, America or the Americas—but with living and making their mark on the American dream. The ad ends with images of a farmer in a cowboy hat standing at the gate of his farm; a man poring over his architectural plans on the hood of his Silverado; and a young boy, presumably the man's son, staring in awe at the tree house his father has built him. "Through time we have marked the nation," the voice-over says in Spanish. "Today, our mark is stronger than ever. The new Chevy Silverado 2007. Join us."[70]

Chevy's use of fragmented marketing both reinforces and disrupts a branding strategy that has historically associated the company's image with the American people as a nation. On one level, the ad is indeed synergistic with "Anthem." Yes, the most reactionary white viewers might associate Latinos—especially those who openly speak Spanish—with "illegal" or "unwanted" forms of immigration. In that light, it is perhaps not surprising that the ad appeared only once on English-language television, during game 3 of the 2006 World Series.[71] "Milestones," however, is by and large an assimilationist narrative. Despite its rebellious backing track, the men in this ad are sports heroes, producers, entrepreneurs, and family men. Assuming the role of all-American brand, Chevy invites Latinos to identify with the values and contributions of these men and to aspire to join the nation. This assimilationist narrative is in keeping with broader trends in marketing to Latinos. As Arlene Dávila argues in *Latino, Inc.*, advertising producers commonly represent Latinos using safe tropes—for example, as culturally conservative or family oriented—to make them "easily digestible and marketable within larger cultural structures." Likewise, advertisers typically represent Latinos as a homogeneous group, a "nation within a nation," rather than recognizing values and fantasies that may vary across intersecting lines of nationality, race, gender, and class. Latinos thus remain foreign: their difference is accommodated, but they are not recognized as fully integrated members of American society. In these ways, Latino marketing "reflect[s] the fears and anxiety of mainstream society, reiterating in this manner the demands for an idealized, good, all-American citizenship.'"[72] By enlisting the potentially disruptive cultural differences of Latinos in the United States, "Milestones" increases the visibility of Latinos in the social imagination of the "American people," while largely containing them in safe, sanitized, and depoliticized roles.

On another level, it is baffling to those uninitiated in the marketing industry that "Anthem" and "Milestones" can coexist side by side. Both ads tell a story about what it means to belong to the people-as-nation, and both ads offer the fantasy of individual freedom and mobility to their target audiences. But it is difficult to sustain a populist imaginary in which a celebration of white male cultural supremacy rests easily with demands for recognition by Latinos, even in assimilationist form—unless, that is, media and marketing contribute structurally not to popular unity, but to a fragmenting of American social imagination. Today, consumers with cable, Internet, and mobile devices can access thousands of television channels, websites, personalized social media, and apps. For many people, this means they can tune into content and programming that caters to niche markets along lines of race, ethnicity, class, gender, sexuality, age, lifestyle interests, and so on. Historically, media specialization developed in tandem with market segmentation: as media technologies developed, agencies devoted bigger slices of their budgets to researching niche markets and placing advertisements in niche media.[73] "Milestones" aired primarily on Hispanic television. Complementary ads ran on Hispanic radio, in magazines such as *People en Español, Latino, Hispanic, and Hispanic Business*, and in major Hispanic newspapers in several major cities. Chevy has also sponsored popular Latino music and sporting events and marketed to Latinos via the Internet and mobile devices.[74] With this segmented marketing, Chevy could feed off the countercurrent aspirations of Latinos and the white men who, in the company's calculus, can only imagine individual freedom by denying it to others.

According to media and marketing critics, the increase of this kind of segmentation has helped "feed and maintain particularized social and cultural identities."[75] For Chevy and other brands that ask consumers to identify their aspirations with what it means to belong to America, that means it is possible to market different populisms to different social groups at the same time. Like a Rorschach test, what people take out of the ad depends, in part, on what they bring to them. Communitarian-minded critics worry that segmentation contributes to a fragmenting of society and of the social imaginary that underpins democratic identification and communication. Critical theorists take a more ambivalent approach. On the one hand, they point to the limits of segmented advertising and marketing in pluralizing representations of marginalized groups: disciplinary techniques of representation often increase the visibility of marginalized groups, while containing them in roles that are unlikely to disrupt dominant social imaginaries. On the other hand, some critical theorists argue that the availability of specialized media and marketing has enabled marginalized groups to create and sustain counterpublic spheres in the United States. These emerging public spheres can contribute to transgressive efforts by marginalized groups to articulate alternative interests and aspirations and to claim cultural recognition in America.[76] If Chevy's power to regulate and feed off populist aspirations benefits from effects that fragment and discipline social imagination, it does not seem wary that its marketing strategies may also contribute to more rebellious aspirations among marginalized groups. Company executives appear to believe their all-American brand can sustain the incommensurability between the visions of "the people" it represents. In other words, by regulating disruptive populist aspirations, Chevy tries to conceal with one hand the paradox it aggravates with the other.

By juxtaposing techniques of incorporation with its reactionary representation of the people, Chevy updates Schmittian populism for a neoliberal era. "Anthem" interpellates a white, masculinist, national people against threats to its supremacy. The ad sustains an undercurrent of the existential threat and seething ressentiment that are overt in "Backbone." In contrast to that ad, however, "Anthem" draws equivalence between the reactionary images and emotions of white, masculine, nationalism and a multicultural vision of the nation's past and future. "Anthem" thus neutralizes and feeds off the rebellious aspirations that might contest not only white masculine cultural supremacy, but also the capitalist underpinnings of American democracy. By offering the allure of a populism without oppositional frontiers, Chevy binds the ideology of American imperialism to expanding powers of capitalism that paradoxically undermine America's power as a nation-state. Chevy further weakens the identity of the nation and the power of the state in selling a different populist vision to Latinos (whom Chevy has helped attract to the United States with its jobs and produce as a market segment via its advertising).[77] Whether or not Chevy succeeds in arousing identification with its brand of populism, then, it participates in symbolic and material practices that undercut popular power.

Spoofing "Anthem":
Gaps and Glitches in Aspirational Marketing

This does not, however, mean that corporate-driven popular culture actually enjoys totalizing reach over populist imagination, nor does it succeed in fleecing all aspirations to popular power in its attempts to propel hegemonic visions of American democracy forward. The growth of new media technologies has both intensified the resonant force of advertising and reduced the effect of any given commercial message.[78] Television exemplifies the problem of advertising clutter: "In the mind's eye—and yours—flit hundreds and hundreds of broadcast-advertising images, impinging upon one another in a cluttered mosaic of mediated desire."[79] Even as Americans attune ourselves to the frequencies of mass media, then, we have become highly sophisticated, often cynical consumers of media and advertising. We routinely deconstruct ads and their commercial messages, whether filling the news cycle after every Super Bowl, satirizing ads on the *Daily Show*, analyzing them on blogs, or producing mash-ups via YouTube. Indeed, as the Internet began to enable user-generated content in the early years of the twenty-first century, writes Sivulka, "millions of people no longer passively viewed Internet content, they interacted with it and created it on MySpace, YouTube, Facebook, Wikipedia, and other Web 2.0 sites." In 2006, *Advertising Age* rewarded this consumer creativity by naming "The Consumer" as Ad Agency of the Year, and *Time* named its Person of the Year "You."[80]

Stuart Hall writes that popular culture is inevitably characterized by struggles between containment and resistance.[81] The most cynical critics of popular culture read the emergence of the consumer-as-advertiser as yet another example of the ways in which capitalist culture feeds off the creative aspirations of individuals.[82] Yet this technique is not without its glitches. For example, companies now invite consumers to generate their own advertisements for products, only to have the gimmick backfire. When Chevy released its updated Tahoe in 2006, it created a special website where consumers could arrange video, music, and fonts to produce their own ads for the full-sized SUV. Soon, anti-SUV ads not only filled the site, but also went viral on social media.[83] Spoofs of "Anthem" and "Backbone" on YouTube also exemplify the savvy of today's media users. Over a dozen parodies have appeared since 2006, receiving anywhere from a couple hundred to over one hundred thousand views. These mash-ups pair Mellencamp's lyrics—both his original song and Chevy's abridged version—with their own montage of images and copy. Some appropriate "Anthem" to tout competitor brands and contest America's cultural supremacy. One Toyota spoof depicts images of Japanese culture and products that are popular in the United States; another, called "This is OUR Country," reminds viewers that Toyota boasts the "#1 Selling Car in America," and that it got there by engineering automobiles that win awards for fuel efficiency and retained value.[84] At least two videos repurpose "Anthem" as propaganda for the 2008 elections. A Ron Paul devotee adds back Mellencamp's verse, "There's room enough here / For science to live. / And there's room enough here / For religion to forgive," to celebrate Paul's libertarian pluralism, and the video assures that Paul will deliver on Mellencamp's promise, "The folks who run this land / Help the poor and common man." A spoof that could pass as a campaign commercial for Democrats represents a more robust liberal pluralism: black men replace white volunteers as the heroes of Katrina, World War II replaces Iraq as an honorable war, Kennedy replaces Nixon, American foreign policy looks like the US Agency for International Development instead of the War on Terror, and striking workers take their place as the symbol of the nation's producing classes.[85]

The most scathing (and most viewed) parodies pair Mellencamp's patriotic lyrics with disparaging symbols of America's masculinism, white supremacy, imperialism, and capitalism. One recasts the nation's producers as beer-bellied buffet addicts, and another depicts them as "couch potatoes" who see themselves in the image of John Wayne. Reminders of America's white supremacy run through several parodies of "Anthem." In one, images of Chevy cars and trucks join Native Americans on the "Trail of Tears" and share the auction block with enslaved Africans—a reminder that racism and capitalism have grown hand in hand from the nation's earliest days of colonialism and imperialism. Spoofs also depict state violence against blacks from police-sanctioned lynchings to the use of police dogs and fire hoses against Civil Rights activists to police brutality against Rodney King. One depicts not Martin Luther King Jr.'s "I Have a Dream" speech, but his assassination on a balcony at the Lorraine Motel. Turning the volume up on King again, we might hear a tag line from his speech against the Vietnam War: this is our country, "the greatest purveyor of violence in the world today."[86] Indeed, America's image on the world stage fares no better in parodies of "Anthem." One depicts the nation as Team America: World Police, rampaging through the Middle East in a flag-painted Hummer. Others display images of torture and human rights violations at Guantánamo and Abu Ghraib. That America cannot seem to feel safe in its imperialism is evident in various images of national *in*security: vigilantes at the US/Mexico border, a poster for the Minutemen Border Patrol, and a *Sesame Street* parody of the Homeland Security Advisory System coded by both color and puppet (Red Elmo, Orange Ernie, and so on). A few spoofs, finally, critique the nation's love affair with capitalism. One recalls an ironic Depression-era photo that depicts black folks waiting in line for bread in front of a Chevrolet billboard that boasts, "There's no way like the American Way" and, above a white family in a Chevy sedan, "World's Highest Standard of Living." Another features images of Black Friday crowds ("This is our Christmas spirit"), oil rigs ("This is our addiction"), and—taking a shot at today's consumer citizen—an SUV covered in bumper stickers that advertise candidates, causes, and, of course, "God Bless America" ("This is our activism"). One absurdist parody Photoshops Chevy autos and logos into dozens of images of racism, imperialism, and capitalism—a dissonant branding that makes plain that Chevy is selling not only automobiles, but also an obscene misrepresentation of America.[87]

Because audiences are always coproducers of cultural texts, Chevy cannot entirely obscure the paradoxes at the heart of its representation of "Our
Country." The polysemy of the ad's images, that is, their multiple meanings or
interpretations, triggers a disconnect between some audience responses and
the ad's unified representation of "Our" and "Country." These disconnects create openings for everyday acts of resistance that disrupt and unmask both techniques of branding and hegemonic visions of American democracy in popular
culture.[88] The possibility for gaps and glitches in mass-mediated popular culture necessitates another line of questioning vis-à-vis "Anthem": what can aspirational democratic populism learn from Chevy? The producers of "Anthem"
draw on powerful aural and visual techniques to resonate with America's populist imaginary. Substantively, they tap into traditions of rhetoric and popular
memory both to valorize the "everyday heroes" in the nation's master narrative
and to paint them as white, masculine producers. Aspirational democratic populisms emerge from the undersides of this dominant field of cultural production, that is, from subjugated knowledges and languages and from subterranean
sparks of resistance. Nonetheless, populism's rebellious aspirations must at
times be able to break open, inflect, and even transform dominant social imaginaries. These challenges return us to the impasse between everyday populism
and the outrageous energies of populist resistance. The latter attempts to keep
pace with the dynamics of capitalist culture by disrupting its hegemonic narratives and exposing its social dislocations; the former eschews speed in favor
of the patient work of cultivating popular power. At this impasse, aspirational
democratic populism's everyday heroes risk working at a level of obscurity that
fails to break through or counter large-scale cultural and material dynamics,
while the spirited energetics of populist resistance risk appropriation by the
producers of "hip consumerism": the tactic by which advertisers commodify
revolt by turning it into a marketable lifestyle for new niche markets.[89] How,
then, can populists generate sparks that disrupt and create openings at the
horizons of hegemonic visions of the people and democracy, while also building more durable circuits of desire and capacity that cultivate popular power
in other directions? Which aural and visual repertoires of practice and which
subterranean traditions and images might they mobilize?

LEONARD COHEN:
THE REBELLIOUS ASPIRATIONS
OF "DEMOCRACY"

In the lyrics for "Democracy," Chevy is not the reliable "Heartbeat of America,"
but rather the iconic company that has abandoned America's heartland. Evoking

"the brave, the bold, the battered / heart of Chevrolet," Cohen conjures up a heartland battered by decades of corporate restructuring and silenced into so many ghost towns of closed plants, dried-up docks, and decaying infrastructure.[90] The song promises that democracy will emerge from this wreckage. If we hear an echo of Mellencamp and Obama in Cohen's voice, implying that Chevy's renewal is vital to democracy's future, Cohen does not conceal his ambivalence. "Democracy" begins with the fast-tempo drumbeats of a march, and that rhythm carries what Cohen calls the "anthemic, hymn-like" quality of the song to its conclusion.[91] The song's lyrics, however, appear to mock the genre of the march and, with it, the familiar narrative that heralds the progressive march of American democracy. Cohen's invocation of Chevy reflects his trademark dark humor and irony. He appropriates Chevy's well-known slogan to expose the disrepair at the heart of capitalist America. By the final stanza, the promise of democracy has an uncanny resilience: "But I'm stubborn as those garbage bags / that time cannot decay, / I'm junk but I'm still holding up / this little wild bouquet: / Democracy is coming to the U.S.A."[92] Cohen conjures the disavowed "junk" of America's endless promise of renewal. He depicts scenes from the years Chevy edits out of its montage: the undersides of the neoliberal revolution in the 1980s and early 1990s that challenge Chevy's narrative of progress. His wild promise of democracy is a far cry from Chevy's full-throated "Anthem" to a nation that always overcomes the "bruises and scars" that trouble it.[93]

Cohen's song implicates Chevy in the irreparable gaps at the heart of democracy. Democracy is "coming from a hole in the air" (the ozone layer); it is "coming from a crack in the wall" (the Berlin Wall). Cohen's democracy comes not only from the universalizing promises of modernity, but also from modernity unhinged: from the "creative destruction" of capitalism, from the inevitability of man-made environmental catastrophe, from the collapse of Communist regimes, from a nominally democratic American state that perpetuates "wars against disorder" in its response to drugs, homelessness, and the epidemic spread of HIV/AIDS. In other words, democracy is "coming from" its own incomplete promise, from "the feel / that this ain't exactly real, / or it's real, but it ain't exactly there." In promotional interviews for *The Future*, Cohen describes democracy as the "faith" that sustains modern people whose lives are defined by "intolerable ambiguity." He explains, "When you hear politicians speak, you say to yourself, 'They don't seem to have heard the bad news.' It develops a terrible schizophrenia in society between public utterance and private experience." Cohen channels the feelings of alienation, loneliness, and uncertainty that afflict modern people. We hold faith in democracy, which is "the greatest religion the West has produced." Yet we struggle to connect to others. Cohen asks his listeners to acknowledge that no person or society has yet "surrendered to a democratic heart." We have not truly "affirm[ed] the equality of the white and the black, the poor and the rich";

we have not come to grips with "the notion that we might have to share our room with strangers."[94]

Like the Sermon on the Mount—which the song's narrator doesn't "pretend to understand at all"—democracy is "like a religion in that it's never really been tried." "These words resonate with possibility," Cohen says of Christianity and democracy. "They resonate in our minds, and they create this notion, *this tension*, this direction toward this possibility that we call Christianity, this possibility that we call democracy." Cohen believes we are "on the edge of a democratic experiment . . . it has begun." But he does not offer the fantasy that we will ever be rid of the *tension* at the heart of democracy. "Adam and Eve's expulsion [from the Garden of Eden] is the central myth of our culture," he explains. "Being expelled from paradise sets up the need for utopian theories—socialism, fascism, democracy—to bring us back to paradise. But there is a crack in everything, because this is the realm of the crack, the realm of failure, the realm of death, and unless we affirm failure and death, we're going to be very unhappy."[95] As Cohen sings in *his* "Anthem," the track that precedes "Democracy" on *The Future*, "There is a crack, a crack in everything / That's how the light gets in."[96] For Cohen, it is from "the brokenness of things," not the illusion of wholeness, that the promise of democracy will emerge.[97]

That fundamental brokenness creates a condition of paradox in a song that puts faith not only in the possibility of democracy, but also in the people who must carry forth its promise. The people Cohen calls on to carry democracy's promise are alienated from each other (they live in broken families and face domestic and social conflict on a daily basis) and from public life (they stay home, "getting lost in that hopeless little screen"). In this context, "Democracy" is a different kind of populist anthem: it opens listeners to the possibilities of collective identification behind the promise of democracy and offers a spiritual awakening to popular power among the mass of disavowed people who can carry that promise. Cohen said in interviews about the song, "Democracy is filled with affirmations, with validations for the fragments of society, but unless the fragments of society experience themselves as something other than fragments, then democracy will fail."[98] The paradox of democracy, for Cohen, is that we will always also be fragments. From his early years as a poet and songwriter, Cohen has described the modern human condition as a "constant apocalypse," in which a social and psychic "catastrophe has already taken place, there's no point in waiting for it."[99] In this ongoing state of fragmentation and alienation, the "crack in the wall" of human society is its defining condition. Cohen's populism, then, is not about filling the gap in the flag of a country that was once whole, nor does he dream of any solid foundations of identification between people. Cultivating a populist promise of democracy means learning how to dwell in crisis and loss, to dwell in the brokenness that accompanies the human condition. And it involves cultivating rebellious aspirations to be more than fragments in our myriad collective efforts to enact democracy in our everyday lives.

Contextualizing "Democracy": The Cracks in Chevy's America

By refusing to resolve the paradox of democracy, Cohen fosters the conditions for aspirational democratic populism in the performance and promise of "Democracy." Unlike Chevy's ad, "Democracy" displays Cohen's own ambivalence about the song's rhetorical promise: "Democracy is coming to the USA." That ambivalence is evident in the contrast between the album's opposing tracts, "Democracy" and "The Future." Cohen began writing both songs in the late 1980s. "That was when the Berlin Wall came down and everyone was saying democracy is coming to the East," he explains.[100] "The Future" is Cohen's prophetic witness to the disorder he believed would follow the collapse of Communist regimes in Eastern Europe. "Give me back the Berlin Wall / Give me Stalin and St. Paul," he sings. "I've seen the future brother: / It is murder."[101] "The Future" testifies to Cohen's fears about a condition in which "the populations of the world are no longer content with their previous positions in regard to authority," but in which people remain fundamentally alienated. Lacking a collective psychic orientation, we become "unwilling to deal on the democratic plane." Instead, Cohen fears, "the extremist position . . . is the one that captures hearts."[102] If the future is "murder," Cohen sees democracy as its improbable "flip side." "Democracy" is not only an ironic song, he insists. It is also "a song of deep intimacy and affirmation of the experiment of democracy in this country. This is really where the experiment is unfolding. This is really where the races confront one another, where the classes, where the genders, where even the sexual orientations confront one another."[103] The song affirms, "It's coming to America first, / The cradle of the best and of the worst." Cohen echoes the ambivalent exceptionalism of Walt Whitman, for whom America was destined either to realize its promise as a world-historical experiment in democracy, or else "prove the most tremendous failure of [all] time."[104] Whitman believed that experiment would flourish only if Americans built a political culture that infused the people's materialist inclinations with a spiritual thirst for self-creation in their personal lives, enchantment at the experience of their collective heterogeneity, and "largeness and generosity" in their public attachments.[105] Cohen's lyrics situate us in the everyday experiences of American political culture today, and bring us face to face with its messy psychic landscape of violence, conflict, alienation, desire, and love. He opens the question of *which people* will emerge from this mess—and what kind of people we need *to become*—to carry the promise of democracy toward its most rebellious aspirations.

Cohen knows that the "reefs of greed" and the "squalls of hate" he references in the song are always there to entangle and misdirect people's "best" aspirations to democracy. Indeed, the threat of co-optation circled around the release of "Democracy" itself. Some reviewers suggested that Cohen intended the song as a salute to President Bill Clinton, who returned the Democratic Party to the White House the same year *The Future* was released. For many Americans, Clinton offered hope to a country mired in the very legacies of the Reagan and Bush years that Cohen depicts in "Democracy." The song was played on the radio as a celebration of Clinton's victory, and Don Henley performed a cover of "Democracy" at Clinton's MTV Inaugural Ball.[106] Such appropriation seems fair game in a music industry that relies on mass marketing—during the early 1990s, radio and MTV airplay were primary forms of promotion—to manage which voices resonate with popular audiences.[107] For his part, Cohen denies the interpretation. "I don't want my songs to be slogans for the right, left, or middle," he explains. "There is some kind of moral resurrection that people from all positions on the political spectrum can participate in."[108]

Nonetheless, the mainstream co-optation of "Democracy" raises questions about locating aspirational democratic populism in the songs of a countercultural performer who has made millions recording for a major record label. During the 1960s and 1970s, folk rock was part of a rock-and-roll counterculture that constituted what Michael Kramer calls the "republic of rock." Taking shape in the embodied spaces of rock clubs, folk festivals, and political protests, as well as the underground channels of independent music press and radio, the "republic of rock" became a "crucial cultural form" for grappling with the social and political transformations coming out of Chevy's post–World War II era.[109] An aural populist imaginary emerged as a key strain of rock and roll during the countercultural era. Some songs, such as Don McLean's "American Pie" and Lynyrd Skynyrd's "Sweet Home Alabama," betrayed nostalgia for simpler times and even for a white, southern vision of America. More prominently, political folk singers—such as Bob Dylan, Joan Baez, Phil Ochs, Arlo Guthrie, and Buffy Sainte-Marie—penned irreverent critiques of racism, militarism, and consumerism that offered more radical visions of American democracy.[110] Given the corporate consolidation of the music industry in the middle to late 1960s, however, neither performers nor fans could escape the reality that, in the words of popular music sociologist Simon Frith, "rock, like all twentieth-century pop music, [was] a commercial form, music produced as a commodity, for a profit, distributed through mass media."[111]

In his early years as a poet, Cohen saw himself as a voice for society's outcasts, once describing his readers as "inner-directed adolescents, lovers in all degrees of anguish, disappointed Platonists, pornography-peepers, hair-handed monks and Popists, French-Canadian intellectuals, unpublished writers, curious musicians, etc."[112] By the time he wrote his 1974 song "Field Commander Cohen," he recognized himself as one of many performers who cultivate an outsider status while being implicated in the music industry. He sings of his career: "I never asked but I heard you cast your lot along with the poor. / But then I overheard your prayer / that you be this and nothing more / than just some grateful, faithful woman's favorite singing millionaire, / the patron saint of envy and the grocer of despair, / working for the Yankee dollar."[113] In 1988, when Cohen released "Tower of Song," an ironic tribute to artistic struggle in the commercial music industry, debates over "selling out" still tormented aging countercultural musicians. That year, Neil Young remained defiant in "This Note's for You" (a play on a longstanding Budweiser ad slogan): "Ain't singin' for Pepsi / Ain't singin' for Coke / I don't sing for nobody / Makes me look like a joke." Over the next few decades, the same rock singers who had derided commercialism would become commercial sponsors: among them, Cohen.[114]

Cohen is not Chevy or even Bob Dylan, whose seismic popularity in the sixties and seventies has translated into his profitable second career as a corporate spokesperson in the twenty-first century.[115] Nonetheless, he has wrestled throughout his career to create music that resonates with society's outcasts while also finding a wider audience in the relative mainstream. In his early years, Cohen refused to commercialize his sound to sell albums and did relatively few promotional interviews and tours.[116] His first few albums were certified hits in Europe, but the American market was less favorable. His 1967 debut album, *The Songs of Leonard Cohen*, and his second album, *Songs from a Room*, broke the Top 100 on the Billboard charts, but by his fourth album, he failed to dent the Top 200. Of the years between 1972 and 1985, Cohen has said, "I was effectively shut out of the business and kind of a joke for quite a long time."[117] His second break came with the release of his critically acclaimed 1988 album, *I'm Your Man*, followed four years later by *The Future*. Cohen had reinvented himself as a musician. If his early music possessed, as one critic put it, "a timeless devotional beauty that runs opposite to almost everything that is modern," his new albums were in step with both his own aging and the sounds of a new age of pop music.[118] His once reedy voice had developed into a weathered, often mesmeric baritone. His lyrics, still marked by sexual longing, spiritual yearning, and apocalyptic vision, now gave prominence to the dark, playful humor that had previously been lost on many critics. Most notably, he had modernized his sound: his new albums combined the slick electronics of synthpop with the eclectic orchestration of strings, R & B horns, gospel choirs, and retro pop. By keeping pace with the changing sounds and technologies of the time, Cohen made himself relevant to a new generation in ways that most 1960s musicians never managed.[119] In contrast to Chevy, then, Cohen's populist imagination emerged from the undersides of mainstream popular culture and has straddled the tension that all aspirational democratic populisms face: between cultivating rebellious aspirations and engaging hegemonic culture.

Cohen emerges as an uncertain populist and a reluctant seer. His crisis of faith in the possibilities of social and psychic connection is matched by his uneasy relationship to the corporate and countercultural dynamics that vie over popular culture. Given his promise, "Democracy is coming to the USA," Cohen's Canadian nationality adds another layer of complexity to the claim that "Democracy" exemplifies aspirational democratic populism *in America*. In practice, Cohen has lived a peripatetic life. He has lived in Montreal, the Greek island of Hydra, Manhattan, Tennessee, France, Los Angeles, and at the Mt. Baldy Zen Center near LA. When he talks about "Democracy," he alternates between the role of outsider and intimate. "I'm Canadian and we watch America very carefully. Everybody in the world watches America," he observes in one interview. And yet, the song comes from a "love of America. . . . It's a song of deep intimacy and affirmation" born of years of his experience living in "this country."[120] Cohen's relationship to America suggests the intimacy and affirmation of someone who will always also remain a stranger. He observed in an early interview, "Even though article after article [in the Canadian press] threatens us with the extinction of our identity, I don't think anybody in Canada seriously believes that we're going to become Americans."[121] Cohen's own experiences in the United States included years of rejection by mainstream music reviewers and fans—a far cry from feeling as if he has been incorporated, like Rosa Parks and Martin Luther King, within the "heartbeat of America." Instead, Cohen casts himself in the role of the stranger who, though familiar, does not feel fully welcome in America. Both insider and outsider, Cohen decenters democracy from America's grip, even as he prophesies that it is coming to the USA.

Representing "Democracy": The Paradoxes of Populism

Writing amid these ambiguities, Cohen creates a different kind of montage to represent the people who carry the promise of democracy to the United States. He begins, not unlike Chevy, with a multiplicity of images: he wrote sixty verses for "Democracy." "I addressed almost everything that was going on in America," he reported, before six verses made the final cut. As Cohen notes, the final product is polished, betraying none of the "axe marks" of Cohen's artistic struggle.[122] In contrast to Chevy's ad, however, "Democracy" more nearly recalls the roots of filmic montage as an experimental, politically engaged, artistic movement in Stalinist Russia.[123] Films in this tradition deploy discontinuous editing techniques—for example, disjunctive jump cuts, achronological sequences, and interruptive rhythms—to emphasize the breaks and collisions between images and sounds gathered in relation to each other. Artists seek to represent unsettling ambiguities of space and time, to provoke emotional conflict and critical reflection, and thereby to engage the audience in the collective act of producing film's narrative, aesthetic, and material effects. This more rebellious use of montage offers us a way of understanding how Cohen holds open the paradoxes of populism in the structure and stylistics of "Democracy."

Cohen solicits the dislocated lives and disoriented dreams cast off by the promise of Chevy's America. In the structure of the song, he uses a repetitive form to connect these strangers. The promise, "Democracy is coming to the USA," is iterated at the end of each of six stanzas. Each time, it follows a colon: the promise of democracy is carried by different actors, located in different sites, embodying different affective and performative stances in relation to American society and politics. The people who carry democracy's promise are a motley crew: Chinese dissidents, blacks rebelling in Los Angeles, the police and national guard "waging war" against them, homeless people, queer people, people living and dying with HIV/AIDS, Jesus delivering the Sermon on the Mount, unemployed workers, people living in postindustrial ghost towns, whites and blacks, men and women bitching, men and women making love, women praying for deliverance, broken families, the lonely and the alienated, the masses routinely disregarded by the elites who speak to them through "that hopeless little screen," or in other words, "the people we think are junk, the ideas we think are junk, the television we think is junk."[124] Unlike Chevy's montage, which incorporates visual clichés seamlessly into its vision of the American people, the actors in Cohen's montage are strangers to each other—and many of them strangers to America. The narrative in "Democracy" is not of a people in need of refounding. It is a story of emergence by the disavowed who enact democracy's promise: blacks who refuse to be locked into poverty, gays who refuse to be silenced into death, workers whose collective voices can almost be heard rising from the creative destruction of Chevy's capitalism. These strangers emerge from ordinary and extraordinary spaces to move beyond the borders of established peoplehood in America.

Cohen thus reveals the multitude that always exists within "the people" who carry democracy's promise. In doing so, he also troubles the geographic borders of the people and democracy. In the song's representation of the United States, Cohen relies on generic images. Some images, such as "the sirens night and day" and "the ashes of the gay," conjure the coastal cities of Los Angeles, San Francisco, and New York, with which the race rebellion and HIV/AIDS epidemic were associated. "The heartbeat of Chevrolet," of course, affirms that democracy will also come from the Rust Belt of the Midwest. Beyond these regional associations, the sites of democracy's emergence are all around us, in streets, docks,

dumps, kitchens, bedrooms, dens, churches, mosques, synagogues, deserts, riv-
ers, mountains. These are the everyday spaces in which people encounter each
other and cultivate their individual and collective aspirations. Cohen's use of
generic spatial images adds to a song in which the promise of democracy is not
geographically bound. If democracy comes to America in "amorous array," this
is no patriotic populism bound by love for the nation-state. Democracy may be
"coming *to* America first," but it is coming *from* not only the United States, but
also cross-border spaces and subjects. It is coming from a global warming crisis
that affects everyone on the planet, from spectacles of popular power in China
and Berlin that captured the world's imagination, from the women who pray for
"the deserts here and the deserts far away," from the Canadian Cohen himself.
Cohen's cross-border populism encourages listeners to ask *which* people can
carry democracy's promise in *which* contexts. It opens listeners to the possibility that democracy emerges as people build shifting alliances across borders in
response to needs and challenges that call for a collective response.

Cohen's representation of the state also stands in stark contrast to Chevy's
nationalist populism. "Anthem" celebrates the people as nation, superseding
the limiting functions of a state that gets shifted to the background of the ad.
"Democracy" foregrounds the state in its refrain: "Sail on, sail on / O mighty Ship
of State! / To the Shores of Need / Past the Reefs of Greed / Through the Squalls
of Hate / Sail on, sail on, sail on, sail on." Democracy is "coming to America first,"
in part because "It's here they've got the range / And the machinery for change,"
in part because "it's here they've got the spiritual thirst." The song thus establishes
a close relationship between popular aspirations to democracy and the state that
"cradles" them. Cohen does not mean the machinery of a police state engaged
in "wars against disorder," nor of an administrative state circumscribed by narrow left/right logics that discipline divergent aspirations. Instead, he imagines
the state in a protective and enabling capacity, engaged in unwieldy relationships
with the streets, the kitchen, the workplace, holy places, and even shores beyond
the nation's borders. In place of Chevy's symbolic representation of "the people,"
Cohen depicts what Sheldon Wolin calls the people's "two bodies." As we saw in
Wolin's account of everyday populism in chapter 1, collective identity is not merely
symbolic; it is produced and contested in the relations of power and powerlessness established between the formal constitutional "machinery" of the state and
the everyday cultural constitution of its citizens. Cohen makes us privy to what fellow Canadian James Tully has called the "strange multiplicity" of disparate modes
of becoming a people within and across the formal constitutional borders of the
United States.[125] He orients these strangers to each other in relation both to the
promise of democracy and to the "Ship of State." If Cohen's everyday, cross-border
populism can do without the nation, it cannot flourish unless emerging actors lay
claim to and at times transform the state's "machinery of change."

Detached from the nation, the promise of democracy no longer requires the linear temporality that drives Chevy's familiar master narrative of America. Cohen's cross-border populist imagination does not appeal to a foundational promise of democracy. The refrain does appear to give democracy a telos: "To the Shores of Need." The song ends not with the steady sailing of the refrain, however, but with the "little wild bouquet" of democracy's promise. That promise is uncertain indeed. The "Ship of State" does *not* stop for greed or hate, but its course *is* repeatedly contested and redirected as it encounters democracy's vital sources in everyday culture: "spiritual thirsts," "wells of disappointment," "silences on the dock of the bay," but also "visionary floods of alcohol," lovemaking "so deep / The river's going to weep," tidal floods that come "Imperial, mysterious / In amorous array." Unlike Chevy's seamless master narrative set to the addictive energetics of Mellencamp's feel-good tune, moreover, Cohen's montage situates democracy's promise in relation to competing affective dynamics: love, war, thirst, bitching, prayer, congregation, contagion. These dynamics reflect the divergent temporal rhythms that carry democracy's promise: not toward a hegemonic vision, but toward multiple possibilities for resistance, identification, and collective action. In these uneven waters, Cohen suggests, it is possible, even necessary, to enact the promise of democracy again and again and again, but he leaves his listeners no certainty about where it will lead.

Performing "Democracy":
The Liturgical Practices of Populism

That uncertainty offers Cohen's listeners the opportunity to play an active role in cocreating his song's meaning and its promise of democracy. Cohen takes years to complete a song and often goes through dozens of recording sessions until he feels that his voice and music will connect with his listeners.[126] To find meaning, he believes, his songs must resonate with the lives people live: as "people are doing their courting, people are finding their wives, people are making babies, people are washing dishes, people are getting through the day. . . . Songs don't dignify human activity," he explains. "Human activity dignifies the song."[127] It is with this understanding that Cohen has come to talk about his music in terms of liturgical practice. In one of his earliest interviews, he describes himself as "a priest of a catacomb religion that is underground, just beginning, and I am one of the singers, one of the many, many priests . . . one of the creators of the liturgy that will create the church."[128] Cohen describes this vocation as an extension of his earliest days immersed in a close-knit Jewish community. His grandfathers were rabbis and his family was involved in establishing hospitals, synagogues, businesses, the Hebrew Free Loan Society, and the first Anglo-Jewish newspaper in

North America. What he saw in these practices, going on "all the time, all around me," were people "deeply involved in the organization of a community."[129] To be a *Kohayn* (the Hebrew word for "priest" and the source of the name "Cohen") was to be a leader in carrying out the liturgical practices of building community. Describing the connections between his Judaism and his vocation as a poet and musician, Cohen says he first "lived" poetry "in the songs my mother sang, in the liturgy, in the pop music. There was a certain resonance when something was said in a certain kind of way. It seemed to embrace the cosmos. Not just my heart but every heart was involved."[130]

That Cohen has tried to create a kind of liturgy in his music is evident in the themes he revisits often: a human condition of brokenness, the loneliness of exile (whether from God or the social realm), the abandonment of devotion (whether to sex, love, or a higher spirituality), the possibility of holiness. We can also see it in what observers of his music, including Bob Dylan, have described as the prayerful quality of his lyrics and his regular use of hymn-like melodies.[131] Many of Cohen's songs offer themselves to listeners to play over and over, to sit with in meditation, to *live* in spirit and in flesh. Like the rabbis who hold up the Torah, Cohen holds up a kind of liturgy for those listeners who take hold of it. Many will be only occasional devotees, like religious followers who take to the pews once a week or on major holidays. But Cohen understands liturgical practice in a more abiding sense. In his later life, he brought what he'd learned from decades of regular Zen Buddhist meditation to develop a daily practice of the Shemoneh Esreh. Practicing the eighteen steps of this central prayer of Jewish liturgy was "a way of preparing yourself for the day. . . . While starting from a very low place, you could put your chin up over the windowsill and actually see a world you could affirm."[132] Understood as a regular, iterated, bodily practice, liturgy can habituate people toward certain dispositions and aspirations.[133] These might include strength in the face of injustice, devotion to a vision or cause, receptivity to strangers, or willingness to dwell in the tension between apparently contradictory revelations. For Cohen, who believes "people are a complex of everyday heroes," it might simply mean the courage to "get through the day."[134] In religious communities, as well as in faith-based political organizing, liturgical practice has been crucial to practices of becoming a people. We can see this in the ways devotees talk about enacting Jewish congregation, or the Christian Body of Christ, or the Beloved Community imagined in the writing and practices of black freedom activists.[135] Here, it is through lived liturgical practice, not word or rhetoric alone, that disparate actors become a people—and must often do so again and again across years and generations.

It is in this sense that human activity, conceived as liturgical practice, can dignify a song. In today's mass-mediated public spheres, we are often passive recipients of a rapid succession of images, sounds, and (in the era of the smart phone and surround sound) vibrations of pleasure. These resonant forces attune us to the dynamics of hegemonic cultural power. From within this field, Cohen's music offers those who dwell with it over time a more purposeful liturgical practice. For anyone who experiences the alienation that characterizes the modern human condition, his songs offer a "certain resonance" with a world outside the barricades of our private lives. For those who approach Cohen's music in a liturgical sense, it offers more. His songs are widely covered by an eclectic cast of musicians who enact new interpretations and provide new resonances to a broader liturgical community of listeners. Those who listen to Cohen's music regularly and dwell in the tensions it offers are likely to carry it with them on an emotional and corporeal level. The resonant force of a chord or refrain might surface again and again—like the sayings of a parent, a passage from scripture, or the slogans of a commercial—to help people make sense of daily encounters. Unlike advertising, rote religion, and common sense, however, the resonant force of Cohen's music is likely, more often than not, to draw listeners deeper into an "intolerable ambiguity." Because of their layers of uncertainty, irony, and affirmation, Cohen's songs call listeners to a particular attentiveness to the difficulties and possibilities of wrestling with the brokenness of the human condition and getting into community with others.

"Democracy," in particular, invites listeners to participate in a liturgical practice of getting into community with others. The song's myriad struggles—for recognition, connection, love, power, and grace—resonate directly or indirectly with listeners' experiences. In the final stanza, the narrator speaks directly to the listener for the first time, adopting a familiar tone: "I'm sentimental, if you know what I mean / I love the country but I can't stand the scene." The narrator goes on to express his own alienation from the political scene in America and to affirm his stubborn hope that democracy will instead emerge from the "junked" people and visions "that Time cannot decay." This direct appeal to listeners encourages them to empathize with and feel animated by Cohen's everyday hero, to identify with the call to hold up their own "little wild bouquet" to democracy. In this sense, "Democracy" both parallels and departs from Chevy's "Anthem." Like Chevy, Cohen recognizes the centrality of "everyday heroes" in America's populist imagination, and he elevates the status of common people as carriers of democracy's promise. In contrast to Chevy's ad—which fortifies the individualized, white, male producer as the nation's archetypal hero—Cohen asks listeners to identify solidarities with marginalized heroes who are hardly recognizable as such in mainstream American popular culture.

Again contra Chevy, this moment of identification is neither reified nor overly celebrated. "Democracy" unsettles its listeners, oscillating between affirmation and irony, hope and despair. Combined with the ambivalence of the lyrics, the orchestration of the song cycles listeners through different emotional intensities. The staccato snare drum puts listeners on alert from the outset of the song and grows into a fuller percussive rhythm that sustains a sense of urgency from beginning to end. Cohen's voice, weathered by age and "fifty thousand cigarettes," emerges from what one critic describes as "well-like depths," in what "might pass for the weary voice of God."[136] He begins each stanza alone, hitting a place between recitation and melody that evokes age-old liturgical rituals. As each stanza nears its end, the female backing chorus joins in, picking up intensity until the revelatory declaration: "Democracy is coming to the U.S.A." To this cycle of urgency, incantation, and revelation, the haunting, even melancholic chorus—"Sail on, sail on, sail on, sail on"—adds at once a sense of inevitability and longing. It is as if democracy will always be coming, but we will also always be waiting for it, even wondering if it has passed us by. There is a kind of "cruel optimism" in a vision of democracy that is always incomplete—but for Cohen, it is not unwitting. What he offers in "Democracy" is a searching meditation on the democratic paradox. He refuses to settle his listeners into either cynicism about the irreversible capture of American democracy, or romanticism about the endless possibilities of popular power in the United States. The brokenness of the human condition instead necessitates cultivating "faith" in democracy—that marginalized and emerging actors can still constitute egalitarian, pluralistic forms of power in the face of external and internal limits on democracy.

By situating listeners in "intolerable ambiguity," Cohen holds open the questions that sustain radical democratic practices of becoming a people: Which people carry democracy's promise in *this* moment? Now in *this* moment? How can they connect to each other to enact the promise of democracy in response to *this* crisis or *this* possibility? How can I play a part? Indeed, if we expect the refrain to return at the end of the song, to throw us back into ambivalence, to yield our aspirations to the ship of state, Cohen ends the song on a note of revelation. By the end of the song, many listeners will have traded places with the narrator when they sing along: "I'm junk but I'm still holding up this little wild bouquet: / Democracy is coming to the U.S.A." "Democracy" thus calls listeners to respond to the democratic paradox *and* performs its own practices of bringing a people together. The percussive, incantational revelation—"Democracy is coming to the U.S.A."—acts in the song as both a transgressive threat and an orienting promise. On the one side, the song's disavowed actors emerge to resist established versions of peoplehood and political order that take themselves to be democratic: democracy is coming because it isn't already here. On the other side, democracy is also a promise that calls together and organizes disparate actors, located in different contexts, with a multitude of democratic aspirations.

If "Democracy" foregrounds difference and struggle in ways that render them active and transgressive, it also recognizes in us, no less than Chevy does, a deep affective need to belong. In the unforgiving spaces, amid the unsatisfied hungers of Cohen's America, belonging can seem a scarce good. For "it's here the lonely say / that the heart has got to open / in a fundamental way." Indeed, *belonging to* seems like a precarious fantasy in Cohen's vision of democracy: there is no stable collective identity to which the song's disparate actors can belong. Cohen knows, moreover, that faced with the anxieties of not belonging, many people do often opt out. We opt to "stay home" in a passive cynicism that's more comfortable than risking the wild hope that we might be part of the promise of democracy, that we might *belong with* others in creating it. Belonging with is a crucial practice of radical democratic peopling in the song. As the chorus reminds us, democracy is both fundamentally incomplete and fundamentally revelatory; it will always be coming. Democracy's coming into the world insists that we be active participants, but it also requires receptivity to strangers who iterate the promise of democracy in unfamiliar forms. "Democracy" thus exemplifies practices of radical democratic peopling: it calls disparate actors together around the promise of democracy, while also leavening that promise an open call. In this way, the song might attune listeners to what I call *horizontality*, disposing us to look for those who always emerge at the horizons of collective life to enact new forms of horizontal power.

The Resonances of "Democracy": Between Mainstream and Margins

That most of us are not already attuned to look beyond our peripheral vision or listen for out-of-synch notes attests to the limits of Cohen's aspirational democratic populism. Despite his unusual commercial resilience, Cohen was not exactly Boys II Men or Billy Ray Cyrus when he released "Democracy" in 1992. The R & B group's "The End of the Road" spent thirteen weeks at the top of the Billboard Hot 100, which earned it the number one single of the year; the country artist's debut offering, *Some Gave All*, was the best-selling album of the year, thanks in large part to the hit single "Achy-Breaky Heart." Sharing the Billboard with R & B and country that year were pop, mainstream rock, hard rock, alternative rock, grunge, and hip hop.[137] The last two represent emerging countercultural genres that, to put it mildly, overshadowed the resurgence of an aging folk singer. Grunge went mainstream in the early 1990s, tapping into and fueling a zeitgeist of (largely white) teen alienation, apathy, and rebellion (all three captured in Nirvana's 1992 hit "Smells Like Teen Spirit"). By that time, the recording industry had also turned hip-hop into a commercial success, capitalizing on the popularity of breakthrough artists such as Run-DMC, Public Enemy, and N.W.A. With songs such as "Fight the Power" and "Fuck tha Police," hip-hop gave voice to the anger and aspirations of impoverished black youth, who faced chronic economic degradation, social neglect, and police surveillance in the nation's urban ghettoes.

To rely too heavily on "Democracy" to elucidate aspirational democratic populism in popular culture carries a dual risk: on the one end, it implies that rebellious aspirations cannot carry mainstream appeal; on the other, it limits rebellious aspirations to a white popular culture that rarely appeals to the most marginalized people (as hip-hop did in the late 1980s and early 1990s). I want to suggest, however, that "Democracy" offers a way to conceptualize a broader array of contemporary aspirational democratic populist music. Given the democratic paradox, Cohen reminds us, no populist appeal will reach all audiences—all the more so as market segmentation relentlessly reinforces old social divisions and produces myriad new ones. What remains is the possibility of building resonances across genres and sites of popular culture. The lyrics in "Democracy" not only resonate with themes in rock, hip-hop, and other genres that reached broader subcultural and mainstream audiences in the early 1990s. The song also shifts our attention toward the everyday heroes who went uncelebrated at the time: for example, those who spent their days surviving Reaganomics and the war on drugs, living and dying with HIV/AIDS, or forming ecopopulist groups to fight ozone depletion and other environmental hazards. These everyday struggles and many others became sites of peopling that mobilized cultural and, at times, active political aspirations. Through its resonances, then, "Democracy" orients our attention toward not only mainstream music but also the noise at its margins.

Americans most readily associate contemporary populist music with the heartland rock of artists like Bruce Springsteen, Bob Seger (of "Like a Rock" fame), and Mellencamp. Although this blue-collar brand of rock had its heyday in the 1980s, its icons still produced platinum records and penned chart-topping singles in the early 1990s. In 1992, Springsteen's "Human Touch" and Mellencamp's "Again Tonight" spent time at number one on Billboard's Mainstream Rock Chart. Whereas the rock and roll during Cohen's prime "responded to rising affluence," observes Jon Pareles, "heartland rock reflects the shock of lowered expectations."[138] Using plainspoken lyrics and stripped-down music—three chords and a backbeat—songs sketch the lives of people who have fallen on "hard times." When Cohen evokes "wells of disappointment" and "the brave, the bold, the battered / Heart of Chevrolet," he tunes into a broader aural imaginary dotted with stories of unemployment, limited opportunity, and small-town decline. As early as 1975, Springsteen was "sweat[ing] it out on the streets of a runaway / American dream" in "Born to Run." By 1992's "Better Days," he'd chased that dream for two decades only to find, "It's a sad funny ending to find yourself pretending / a rich man in a poor man's clothes."[139] Facing the decline of an American dream that was promised to them, white male heartland rockers strike the chords of alienation we see in "Democracy." Springsteen finds himself "in a world without pity" and yearns for "Just a little of that Human Touch."[140] In 1991's "Last Chance,"

Mellencamp sings, "I feel nothing I feel no pain / I feel no joy nor hurt inside / I only have myself to blame / If I see that the world's passed me by."[141] In place of mobility and adventure, Mellencamp looks around in "Empty Hands" and sees "Too many people with nothin' planned."[142] Even those who achieve middle-class success can't shake chronic apathy. In "Fifty-seven Channels (and Nothing On)," Springsteen describes a couple who buy a "bourgeois house" only to spend their time, with Cohen's everyday hero, "getting lost in that hopeless little screen."[143]

In a review of Mellencamp's 1987 *Lonesome Jubilee*, Pareles writes, "In heart-land rock, the personal is apolitical." The genre paints an unrelenting picture of the social devastation wrought by large-scale economic changes. Rather than "point[ing] fingers or suggesting action," however, artists like Mellencamp and Springsteen cultivate an air of fatalism and emphasize struggles for individual dignity.[144] This tendency cannot fully obscure the rebellious aspirations that surface in heartland rock. Mellencamp's "Love and Happiness," for example, is an angry rebuke of distorted government priorities. "Well, we're droppin' our bombs / In the southern hemisphere," the song begins, "And people are starving / That live right here." Mellencamp goes on to decry the war in Iraq, gas gouging, mortgage rates, Tipper Gore's campaign to censor music lyrics, and the war on drugs.[145] Springsteen's 1995 album, *The Ghost of Tom Joad*, might pass for the soundtrack to a revamped People's Party of 1996. The album tackles chronic homelessness, the death of a mining town, the dead-end prospects facing (pre-sumably white) ex-cons, and the violent, precarious conditions of undocumented migrants. Springsteen punctuates the album's dark themes and somber tone with fierce populist sentiment. A homeless person waits "for when the last shall be first and the first shall be last." A miner in Youngstown, Ohio, mocks America's capitalist ideology: "Seven-hundred tons of metal a day / Now sir you tell me the world's changed / Once I made you rich enough / Rich enough to forget my name." In the title track, Springsteen alludes to the rebellious character from John Steinbeck's *The Grapes of Wrath* to imagine an ethos of cooperative resistance. "Now Tom said, 'Mom, wherever there's a cop beatin' a guy / Wherever a hungry new born baby cries / Wherever there's a fight 'gainst the blood and hatred in the air / Look for me mom I'll be there. / Wherever somebody's fightin' for a place to stand / Or a decent job or a helpin' hand / Wherever somebody's strugglin' to be free, / Look in their eyes ma you'll see me."[146] That many listeners might *not* see themselves in these insurgent lyrics is evident in the overly patriotic misread-ings of Springsteen's "Born in the U.S.A." and in the shock and outrage by some Mellencamp fans after he rebuked George W. Bush's foreign policy in 2003.[147] Nonetheless, heartland rock's politicized moments offer many mainstream lis-teners the chance to cultivate the rebellious aspirations we find in "Democracy."

Cohen's lyrics also resonate with themes that preoccupied various musical subcultures in the late 1980s and early 1990s. When he cites "the homicidal bitchin' / That goes down in every Kitchen / To Determine who will serve and who will eat," some listeners might recall Tracy Chapman's "Behind the Wall" from her self-titled 1988 album. Chapman grabbed mainstream attention with the album, thanks to the hit songs "Fast Car" and "Talkin 'bout a Revolution." (The latter imagines a poor people's revolution arising from Salvation Army stores and welfare lines.) Those who bought Chapman's multiplatinum album also heard her chilling critique of systemic domestic violence: "Last night I heard the screaming / Loud voices behind the wall / Another sleepless night for me / It won't do no good to call / The police / Always come late / If they come at all."[148] Chapman's music connects to a new wave of feminist and lesbian folk rock acts of the era, including the Indigo Girls and the overtly political singer-songwriters Toshi Reagan and Ani DiFranco. Playing to a devoted fan base at small clubs, colleges, and women's festivals, these performers helped cultivate a new era of feminist consciousness. Claiming "I'm no heroine," DiFranco draws women into a world marked by their *own* everyday heroism—"Self-preservation is a full-time occupation"—and by resistance: "I am not a pretty girl, that is not what I do."[149] Neither were the artists behind the Riot Grrrl movement that exploded in the early 1990s. Feminist punk bands such as Bikini Kill, Bratmobile, Heavens to Betsy, and (a bit later) Sleater-Kinney sang about patriarchy, sexual assault, sexuality, and women's empowerment. In "Blood One," Bikini Kill's Kathleen Hanna screams, "Peace, love and equality / Your terms / I don't fit into those words / Your alphabet is spelled with my blood / Your alphabet is spilled with our blood / Blah, blah, blah, blah, blah / I don't understand / I don't understand."[150] Riot Grrrls revolted against patriarchal culture and refused to speak or act in line with the terms of a male-dominated music industry. Using zines as do-it-yourself media, forming local chapters, and engaging in activism, they developed a subculture dedicated to women's power in music. (Its cultural marks include Rock for Choice, the nonprofit Ladyfest, and Girls Rock Camps.)[151]

Cohen is one of several rock and pop musicians to sing about HIV/AIDS in the early 1990s, as Americans were waking up from the government's reign of silence about the disease. When he evokes "the ashes of the gay," his voice resonates with queer synthpop groups, such as Bronski Beat and the Pet Shop Boys; rock legends Lou Reed and Neil Young; pop stars Elton John, George Michael, Madonna, and Boy George; singer-songwriters Sara McLachlan and DiFranco; the hip-hop group Wu-Tang Clan; and others (including those who performed at the 1990 That's What Friends Are For benefit for HIV/AIDS and the widely televised 1992 Freddy Mercury Tribute Tour to honor the Queen frontman who died of AIDS).[152] It also resonates with a larger popular culture grappling with HIV/AIDS during that time: most dramatically in the HBO docudrama *And the Band Played On*, the blockbuster film *Philadelphia*, and Tony Kushner's Pulitzer Prize–winning "Gay Fantasia on National Themes": *Angels in America*.

In "Dreaming of the Queen," the Pet Shop Boys capture a common theme among these artists, who mourned a generation of lost lovers and friends: "That there are no more lovers left alive / No one has survived / So there are no more lovers left alive / And that's why love has died."[153] Like Cohen, who affirms in "Democracy," "O baby, we'll be making love again," pop music also recovered a sense of love, anger, and hope in the struggle against AIDS. "I won't be ashamed of love," Young insists on the soundtrack for *Philadelphia*. "Can you tell me why?" Bronksi Beat challenges those who add persecution to the list of AIDS symptoms: "You in your false securities tear up my life condemning me. / Name me an illness / you call me a sin—never feel guilty / never give in." An inspirited DiFranco dreams, "I am looking forward / to looking back on these days," but challenges, "Our actions / will define us."[154] Indeed, AIDS activists in the middle to late 1980s accelerated not only research and treatment for HIV/AIDS, but also public confrontation with the disease. Using sophisticated media strategies, groups like ACT UP staged queer kiss-ins in public, secured television coverage of protests, and plastered cities with outrageous posters: for example, "Read My Lips," atop two men kissing; "Silence = Death," underneath ACT UP's now iconic pink triangle; and "Liberty and Justice for All.* *Offer not available to anyone with AIDS." Opening space for queerness and love in public, these early activists played a pivotal role in making AIDS legible in public discourse and popular culture. Amplified resonances between AIDS activism and pop culture then facilitated acts of peopling directed variously at queer people, others at risk of HIV/AIDS, and the American public.[155]

What conclusions can we draw from the resonances between "Democracy" and other genres of popular music—some pulling the song's lyrics into the aural imaginary of middle-class, white, male listeners; others linking its themes (not to mention Cohen's synthpop influences) to the sonic spaces of queer dance parties and the zine-fueled Riot Grrrl subculture? "Democracy" does not resonate with equivalent intensity in relation to the genres I have highlighted. Nor do these genres necessarily resonate with each other. Heartland rock and the Riot Grrrl revolt are dissonant in style and oppositional in gender norms. What I do want to argue is that aspirational democratic populist appeals will always be partial, but they will always also find resonances in expected and unexpected places. The structure and orchestration of "Democracy" offer a kind of organizing lens for understanding how these resonant energies in popular culture might come together and disperse in different combinations. Resonant critiques of an era or issue might become legible as they move toward hegemonic understandings of causes and consequences, or they might radicalize those understandings as Springsteen and Mellencamp do at their most rebellious. Some resonances move toward the margins: for example, from Cohen's reference to domestic violence to

Chapman's unheralded song to the riotous energies of Riot Grrrl subculture. Moving neither simply toward mainstream or margins, artists might gather in unlikely resistance to a common threat: crossing genres, for example, in protest against music censorship, at an AIDS benefit honoring a queer rock icon, or in concerts against George W. Bush's war in Iraq. The notion of liturgies of peopling suggests that resonances find sustained convergence when artists and audiences repeat them through the ongoing practices that build mainstream culture and subcultures: sharing concert rituals, inventing dance moves, following mainstream media, producing alternative radio, circulating zines, inhabiting underground scenes, and so on.

Rather than necessarily pointing to equivalences, resonances can reveal the different inflections given to common themes. Critiques of Reaganomics and the state will diverge, for example, for white men who belong to a declining middle class; single mothers who face state-sanctioned domestic violence on one end and poverty and public dishonor (including from the nation's vice president, Dan Quayle) on the other; and gay men who are abandoned by the government as they confront death and loss. Likewise, Cohen's sense of alienation takes on different inflections in the early 1990s. Middle-class white men lost the economic and social security promised to them by the American dream. Feminists scorned the patriarchal culture that alienated them. Gays and lesbians faced not only deadly social rejection, but also the physical unraveling of their "chosen" families. What surfaces in the song's resonances are cross-currents and tensions that might become the basis of negotiated solidarities in response to systemic wrongs that result in uneven harms. These negotiations have taken place in hip-hop, for example, as feminist and queer artists—Queen Latifah, Missy Elliot, Lauryn Hill, Angel Haze, Lelf, Cakes Da Killa—have pushed the boundaries of a genre overly identified in mainstream media with its misogynist and homophobic lyrics. Overlapping and pluralized sites of peopling are not in themselves populist. Cohen, however, imagines the aspirational democratic populist possibilities of fragmented sites of peopling: "Democracy" both orients us toward these fragmented sites *and* calls their resonant energies together to negotiate the promise of democracy and direct the "machinery [of] change."

The Limits of "Democracy":
Hip-Hop and "America's Nightmare"

The song's resonances with hip-hop stretch Cohen's aspirational democratic populist imagination to its limits and suggest energies and directions for democracy beyond the horizons of any populism. The late 1980s and early 1990s marked hip-hop's commercial crossover from what Michael Jeffries calls its "block party beginnings" as a localized form of cultural resistance and play enacted by DJs, MCs, b-boy dancers, and graffiti artists in America's disavowed urban neighborhoods. Hip-hop's dominant image is that of the gangster rapper obsessed with the exploitative power of drugs, sex, and money. Before white-run record companies and media mass-produced this image in the mid-1990s, hip-hop's early commercial successes combined a scathing critique of America with anger, defiance, and revolt.[156] Cohen—who lived near the Watts neighborhood during the rebellion and saw its fires from his windows—channels Tupac Shakur when he sees democracy arising from the state's "wars against disorder." In one of his early, politically oppositional raps, Tupac offers black urban youth these "Words of Wisdom": "These are the lies that we all accepted / Say no to drugs but the government's kept it / Running through our community, killing the unity / The war on drugs is a war on you and me." Citing a litany of wrongs that include slavery, social neglect, ghettoized poverty, an education system that builds "chains in our brains," police brutality, and more, he continues, "NIGHTMARE that's what I am / America's nightmare / I am what you made me / The hate and evil that you gave me / I shine as a reminder of what you have done to my people / For four hundred plus years / You should be scared / You should be running." Urging blacks to "Fight and die if we must," he prophesies, "Just as you rose you shall fall / By my hands/ America, You reap what you sow."[157]

It is unlikely that most white listeners can sufficiently attune themselves to the ways early hip-hop artists inflect the song's critiques of Reaganomics and state violence or its themes of alienation, apathy, and rebellion.[158] Shakur dramatizes the extreme alienation that hounds urban black youth as they watch America "Killing us one by one." "In one way or another," he writes, "America will find a way to eliminate the problem" of the "troubles" in the ghettos.[159] "Picture me giving a damn, I said never" Chuck D. of Public Enemy concurs. "Here is a land that never gave a damn / About a brother like me and myself."[160] For many hip-hop artists, the appropriate response to catastrophic social neglect and institutionalized state surveillance is not mere apathy, but nihilism. Having abandoned protest lyrics by the mid-1990s, Tupac raps, "I'm a young black male, cursed since birth / Had to turn to crack sales, if worse come to worse / Headed for them packed jails, or maybe it's a hearse."[161] If Shakur "see[s] death around the corner," Dr. Dre celebrates the death wish attached to gangsta rap's reclaimed "thug life": "Fuck it, niggas going wild / Every night they shoot, it's like Beirut / Maybe you should get a Kevlar vest for your chest / Anytime steppin' through my hood / But that'll do you no good."[162] For overtly political groups such as Run-DMC, KRS-One, and Public Enemy, the black radical tradition offered the seeds of revolution. "Elvis was a hero to most," raps Chuck D. "But he never meant shit to me you see / Straight up racist that sucker was / Simple and Plain / Mother fuck him and John Wayne."

Acknowledging with Chuck D. that "Most of my heroes don't appear on no stamps," early hip-hop artists conjure the ghosts of heroes who have been twice murdered by white history: Harriet Tubman, Marcus Garvey, Malcolm X, Eldridge Cleaver, Huey Newton, Bobby Seale, and even an "Ali [who] broke necks."[163] Public Enemy aims to incite a new "Revolutionary Generation" by remembering these heroes and turning up the volume on black radical traditions such as Black Nationalism and Black Power. "This party started right in 66," Chuck D. insists. "With a pro-black radical mix." When Public Enemy demands "Power to the People" and "Fight the Power," then, they envision a revolutionary uprising from the extreme margins of America's populist imaginary: one that is led by "the prophets of rage" and instills "Fear of a Black Planet" in the hearts of white Americans.[164]

Public Enemy joins a long history of black radicals who, like the black Populists of the nineteenth century and W. E. B. Du Bois in the early twentieth century, remain pessimistic about populist visions of democracy in America. Rather than accommodate white anxieties and the terms of an antiblack society, Public Enemy puts its revolutionary critique front and center. In an essay on the limits of populist radicalism, Cornel West writes, "No matter how tired white Americans become hearing critiques of white and American supremacist practices here and around the world, it is the responsibility of black progressives to admonish each emerging wave of American radicalism that racism and ethnocentrism must be resisted in their old as well as new forms."[165] Black activists today are *still* forcing America to confront endemic police violence and the reality that mass incarceration is the nation's "new Jim Crow."[166] Whereas hip-hop artists such as Lauryn Hill have again surfaced "Black Rage," white liberals turn the insurgency of the chant "Black Lives Matter" into the whitewashed universalism of "All Lives Matter."[167] In other words, even many whites who join blacks in opposition to antiblack racism can only do so by incorporating black rage into white populist imagination. What Tricia Rose refers to as the "hidden transcripts" of hip-hop thus remain "black noise" in relation to the "public transcripts" of America's insidious white supremacist social imaginary.[168] Bruce Springsteen, for example, takes note of black social critique in "American Skin," a song about the 1999 police slaying of Guinean immigrant Amadou Diallo, in New York: "Is it a gun, is it a knife / Is it a wallet, this is your life." When he sings the refrain, "You can get killed just for living in your American skin," however, it recalls the contemporary whitewashing of police brutality in the common sentiment: no one is safe when police are not held accountable.[169]

Populist efforts to transform popular culture will undoubtedly require intensive, antiracist practices of peopling: ones that can disrupt the resonant force of whiteness within populism and sustain counterresonant intensities that cultivate rebellious aspirations toward a black-brown planet. At the same time, radical democratic struggles for racial justice (as well as justice along lines of gender,

sexuality, legal status, etc.) will likely also require populists to cede the energetics of everyday populism and populist resistance to other practices of peopling.
Hip-hop's musical style points to one such practice of musical montage from
the extreme margins. In tandem with the verbal play and linguistic innovation
of rap, DJs and producers draw on diverse musical inheritances and recreate the
sounds of the streets in beats, shrieks, sirens, scratches, and other noise. They
use samples to incorporate digitally reproduced sounds—other music, media
sound bites, dialogue from speeches, and so on—in various sequences and loops.
As Michael Eric Dyson has observed, "The practice of sampling expresses the
impulse to collage that characterizes the best of black musical traditions, particularly jazz and gospel."[170] According to Rose, early rap producers "inverted" the
original logic of sampling—which, like Chevy's use of montage, "aimed to mask
the sample and its origin; to bury its identity." Instead, rap producers use samples
to highlight "the process of repetition and recontextualization" of current sounds
as well as musical and cultural inheritances.[171] In "Fight the Power," for example,
Public Enemy and their production team, the Bomb Squad, loop and layer nearly
two dozen samples alongside Chuck D.'s unapologetic raps, Branford Marsalis's
saxophone, and DJ Terminator X's scratches. The song opens with a 1967 speech
by Civil Rights attorney Thomas "TNT" Todd and draws musical samples from
legendary funk singer James Brown, soul groups Guy and the Dramatics, boo-
gie trio West Street Mob, hair metal band Uriah Heep, Afrika Bambaataa ("the
Godfather" of sampling"), and many more. The result is a song whose lyrical
and sonic content resonate to generate a "contained chaos" behind Chuck D.'s
refrain: "We got to fight the powers that be."[172]

The "contained chaos" of insurgent hip-hop can have a sense of both play and
urgency. By privileging marginalized heroes and traditions, splicing together familiar and unfamiliar musical references, and creating disjunctive sounds and rhythms,
hip-hop artists loosen the imaginative shackles of oppressive white cultural scripts
and deadly state surveillance. At the same time, they intensify experiences of tension and fanatic urgency.[173] In these ways, hip-hop's liturgies can cultivate listeners'
attunement toward—and a sense of play and power at—the extreme margins of
history, language, and experience. I do not believe radical democrats can abandon
Cohen's populist impulse to attune listeners as well toward the promise of democracy and the machinery of the state, even as it remains a matter of faith that either
will play a role in creating pluralistic, egalitarian forms of power. Appealing to (in
order to transform) hegemonic visions of the people and democracy remains crucial to radical democratic imagination in an era that is still significantly organized
through nation-states and other institutional sites of accountability. Such appeals
will remain limited, however, without also repeatedly amplifying the disruptive
energetics of strangers. In the words of Chuck D., perhaps riffing on Cohen: "To
revolutionize make a change nothing's strange."[174]

AMERICA'S POPULIST IMAGINARY
AND POPULAR ASPIRATIONS TO POWER

In my discussions of Chevy's "Anthem" and Cohen's "Democracy," I have tried to offer a glimpse of the ways in which ubiquitous cultural processes, such advertising and music, play an inescapable role in shaping how we imagine our collective lives as citizens of a democratic polity. Having done so, I now want to develop an account of America's populist imaginary. Like all social imaginaries, the populist imaginary inhabits and is produced by an array of technologies, institutions, and everyday practices; broad discourses and local idioms; high culture and low culture; media, music, sports, religion, and politics; and sundry emerging counterpublics. As a prominent countercurrent of America's liberal, capitalist imaginary, the populist imaginary harbors both hegemonic and marginalized visions of collective identity, norms of citizenship, and aspirations to power. It resonates in different ways with people in their daily lives and is available to be picked up and reworked by populist actors who hope to engage people in political efforts to contest the terms of collective identity and democracy. Indeed, what we evaluate as populist speech and action in social science can only mobilize popular aspirations *because* it resonates with the broader populist imaginary that exists in the United States.

Since my account of America's populist imaginary borrows heavily from the well-traveled concept of social imaginaries, I want to clarify how I understand that concept. To speak of a social imaginary is to suggest that currents of commonality run between people who live in a political community. This can be a dangerous assumption to make, given the power of cultural forces to discipline norms, identities, and aspirations. As many scholars have shown, however, social imaginaries are multiple, overlapping, and contested. The common appeal to "multiple modernities," for example, recognizes the variety of national imaginaries as well as the subaltern and transnational imaginaries that have emerged in the context of colonialism, imperialism, transnational capital, global media, mass migration, and the quotidian practices of ordinary peoples in every society.[175] While social imaginaries enable people to "fit together with others" in social and political communities, their symbolic ideals and implicit understandings are thus shot through with dissensus from the start.[176] Moreover, social imaginaries shift over time in relation to broad structural dynamics, local cultural inflections, and mobilizations from below. In relation to centralizing forces, such as states, markets, and mass-mediated public spheres, subterranean actors have always emerged to contest and pluralize social imaginaries.

Because social imaginaries shape our sense of reality and possibility and inform our normative visions, they play a crucial role in cultivating our individual and collective aspirations. In his influential essay on the "capacity to aspire,"

Appadurai reminds us that aspirations are social. They are located in what he calls a multilayered "map" of ideas, beliefs, and interactions. Forming the layers of a society's "pathways" of aspiration are myriad feedback loops between broad cultural ideas and norms, locally inflected ideas and norms, and more immediate wants and wishes. The "capacity to aspire," according to Appadurai, grows stronger the more an individual or social group gains "real world" experience identifying a society's many "aspirational nodes" and navigating its "pathways from concrete wants to intermediate contexts to general norms and back again." A key point for Appadurai is that the "capacity to aspire" is unequal. A society's more privileged members have a "bigger stock" of experiences and greater social power to produce the kinds of "justifications, narratives, metaphors, and pathways" that link immediate needs and desires to broader normative visions. As such, they have a "more supple" capacity for navigating a society's aspirational map.[177] This cartographic metaphor, of course, tends to assume a reproductive understanding of social imaginaries and an assimilationist view of aspirations. A person's educational and occupational pathways reflect her aspiration to achieve the American dream, for example, rather than to change it. But subaltern groups have repeatedly contested the terms of recognition and disavowal that shape both local and broad norms and that constrain everyday choice and action. Such mobilization, in Appadurai's account, can "expand" and "enrich" the capacity to aspire.[178] This includes yearning for things that are out of reach: not just beyond the grasp of a social group that cannot yet access available visions of the good life, but beyond the vision of a society that cannot yet imagine them. By creating new repertoires of rhetoric and practice, grassroots movements can "increase the variance, frequency, and density" of aspirational nodes and pathways in a given social context. In this way, the "boundaries of the status quo"—that is, of a social imaginary and its aspirations—"can be pushed and stretched."[179]

Appadurai's account enables us to see how social imaginaries offer unequal aspirations to unevenly situated social groups, as well as how emerging groups can contest and shift social imaginaries over time. A key assumption, here, is that aspirations to this or that form of the good life—for example, to greater personal mobility or economic justice—also imply aspirations to power on the part of individuals or groups. Even if we don't often think of it in these terms, when we yearn for something out of our immediate grasp, we also want for the power to achieve it. This is true even if what we desire is a private space to think and do as we like in frazzled domestic lives that are overwhelmed by economic instability, corporate surveillance and marketing, and for many, the disciplinary arm of the law. It is true no less for social groups on the underside of power and privilege who act collectively to change the conditions of their lives. I use the concept of aspirations, then, to emphasize the ways in which populist actors imagine and reach for visions of democratic life that either reinforce existing modes of power or, with varying success, seek to change them. While I find Appadurai's account of the "capacity to aspire" compelling and helpful, my discussion of Chevy and Cohen suggests that America's populist imaginary harbors a messier array of aspirations than we can understand using a relatively fixed cartographic metaphor. The language of resonance better reflects the way in which aspirations shift in intensity, affinity, and direction as they pass through the political rhetoric and activities of different actors—alternately narrowing or broadening visions of democracy and often doing both at the same time. The resonant quality of aspirations explains too why they so often disperse episodically when rhetoric remains undernourished by practice, but at times take hold more durably through cultural liturgies or repeated experiments in grassroots politics.

Popular culture and political action have historically combined to constitute the populist imaginary in America. It originated as a countercurrent to the norms and practices of popular sovereignty that ultimately took root in American law and politics. Amid the fervor and public enthusiasm of the post-Revolutionary era, the framers of the Constitution adopted an anemic theory of popular sovereignty—one that prefers the order of law over the instability of popular voice and participation.[180] As American politics has come to be defined by extraordinary concentrations of wealth, administrative centralization, and consumer citizenship, popular sovereignty has become even more attenuated in practice—at times taking on the air of a pro forma ritual of legitimacy. And yet populist actors have emerged throughout America's history to contest not only the legitimacy of government as a representative of the people, but also the terms of popular power. From the dramatic invective and parallel institutions of America's insurgent populist revolutionaries, to the cooperative institutions and third-party politics of nineteenth-century Populism, to the grassroots organizing of the Tea Party and the Occupy movement today, populist actors have cultivated a more robust vision and innovative practices of popular sovereignty based on norms of social egalitarianism and radical republicanism.[181]

This more robust vision of popular power has been the basis for ongoing contests over the identity of the people and the terms of democratic culture and politics. From Jacksonian democracy to the Reagan Revolution, from McCarthyism to the Dream Act, from the New Left to the Christian Right, divergent social movements have constituted and reconstituted the populist imaginary in America. In turn, America's populist imaginary has enabled both grassroots and elite actors across the ideological spectrum to mobilize people's aspirations to popular power. The historical development of populism, moreover, has variously reinforced or reconstituted the liberal, capitalist social imaginary that remains hegemonic in the United States. To understand how this is possible, we need to consider the different ways in which a populist imaginary has taken shape in relation to the paradoxes of popular sovereignty. Populist actors have historically exposed the disconnect between the people and political orders that fail to represent them, and at a deeper level, between a given identity of "the people" and those marginalized or emerging subjects it excludes or disavows. What differs is how populists treat these paradoxes in their own visions and practices of politics. Nineteenth-century Populism, as I have argued, sustained key tensions that have since bifurcated in populist imagination. For analytic purposes, I place these differences on a spectrum. At either end, populist actors have mobilized people's aspirations in ways that either close the paradox of popular sovereignty all over again, or hold the identity of the people and the terms of popular power open to question and redefinition.[182] To be clear, this analytic spectrum locates ideal types. In practice, as we see with both "Anthem" and "Democracy," all populist moments contain openings and closures.

On one end of the spectrum, what I call America's regulated populist imaginary harbors visions and aspirations that narrow or reinforce the terms of collective identity and popular power and, in some cases, expand the reach of hegemonic forms of power in the name of the people. This strand of populist imaginary regulates aspirations to power in different ways. Most familiar to liberal critics of populism, regulated populisms mobilize reactionary aspirations to power. The regulated populist imaginary contains a repository of cultural discourse, rhetoric, symbols, dispositions, and affective stances that have been recycled and reworked over time so that reactionary aspirations resonate with people who experience changing cultural dynamics and shifting senses of threat. Exemplified by McCarthyism—and its witch hunts against communists in government, the culture industry, and black and working-class social movements—reactionary aspirations respond to the indeterminacy within a pluralistic society by clamping down on the boundaries of collective identity and popular power. If McCarthyism defines reactionary populism's ideal type, many other populist actors have tapped into America's regulated populist imaginary: for example, the People's Party's exclusionary rhetoric toward Chinese and Eastern European immigrants; Nixon's ominous appeal to the rise of the "silent majority" in the wake of civil rights gains for women, blacks, and Latinos in the 1960s; and Christian Right rhetoric that publically vilified single mothers, women's rights advocates, and gays and lesbians.

The rhetoric of reactionary populisms typically locates popular power in the power of friends over enemies. A group's attachment to a declining social identity or status, for example, may lead those who identify with that group to lash out against perceived threats. Conceived in Schmittian terms, the people's positive aspirations to power—often in the name of national identity or cultural purity—always also expresses itself in the desire to dominate or even annihilate an enemy.[183] Reactionary populisms thus mobilize aspirations to hierarchical and exclusionary forms of power. At the same time, "wounded attachments" to a

140

POPULISM'S POWER

declining social status may cause some populists to engage in a politics of ressentiment.[184] By fomenting cries of "reverse racism" in response to affirmative action,
for example, right-wing pundits have encouraged working and middle-class
whites to adopt stances of victimization and blame. To do so, however, is to
cling to white supremacy at the expense of building cross-racial popular power
to transform political-economic structures that harm working people. In cases
such as these, reactionary populists are jealous of power to the point of devaluing
its role in democratic politics. If this position is often consistent with desiring
power and privilege *over* marginalized groups, reactionary populists rarely aspire
to popular power for the sake of more fundamental change.

Regulated populism's reactionary aspirations to power make sense in the
context of liberal democratic nation-states, which place limits on popular and
governmental power via territorial, administrative, and national borders. As we
saw in my discussion of Chevy, however, scholars who evaluate today's "neoliberal governmentality" identify inclusion as an indispensable tool for regulating
aspirations. As the cultural and economic megacirculations of global capitalism
defy nation-state borders, states have had to invent new legitimating forms of
politics. And they have had to do so in relation to a proliferation of resistance
by national, subnational, and transnational actors. Think, for example, of the
alter-globalization protests that follow Group of Eight (G8) meetings from city
to city across the world or of local movements in India that challenge agricultural corporations in American courts of law. Rather than acknowledge barriers
to inclusion in this context, neoliberal tactics incorporate disruptive forms of dissent within a refashioned vision of "the people." Such populist incorporations
are not inventions of neoliberal democracy. Consider the assimilationist policies
that turned America into a so-called nation of immigrants, as the US government
sought to harness the economic energies of newcomers in the industrialized society of the early nineteenth century. Today, discourses of multiculturalism and
diversity are celebrated everywhere from college campuses to corporate board-
rooms, and Americans celebrate expressions of popular revolt as emblems of the
nation's diversity. In this context, regulated populist discourse not only contains
cultural differences. In a nation of "hip consumerism," it feeds off rebellious
energies to propel hegemonic visions of America.

In this sense, America's regulated populist imaginary also harbors assimila-
tions and cruel aspirations that reinforce existing and ever-expanding modes of
power. A common example of assimilationist populist aspirations are organizing
efforts by middle-class civil rights and immigrant rights groups that seek formal
inclusion within liberal, capitalist institutions at the expense of more rebellious
aspirations to economic and political power by poor and working-class people of
color. Such movements have broadened membership in the American people and
American democracy to include new social groups, while leaving the American

dream unaltered and inaccessible to most people. To the extent that such groups still cling to liberal, capitalist versions of the American dream, those who benefit from such reforms also leave themselves vulnerable to cruel aspirations. What Connolly calls the "aspirational politics of identification" refers to the cruel aspirations of marginalized subjects to be like those in power, rather than to mobilize popular power to revolutionize the status quo. Thus, regulated populisms rarely move beyond aspirational identification. They call working-class people, for example, to identify with the images and social aspirations of wealthy subjects, rather than transform capitalist structures and dynamics that require dramatic disparities in wealth. Such incorporation may expand the symbolic boundaries of the people, by making hegemonic aspirations available to more social groups. To the extent that incorporated populists seek inclusion without fundamentally questioning what it is they are joining, they will do little to disrupt either institutionalized social hierarchies or the expanding reach of neoliberalism. Much like early liberal feminists whose solution to patriarchy often appeared to be "add women and stir," certain claims to inclusion in today's neoliberal context don't do anything to change the structural conditions that oppress marginalized and subjugated groups.

By contrast, I locate America's aspirational democratic populist imaginary in rebellious cultural texts and political activities that enact pluralist, egalitarian alternatives to the status quo. Such populisms are always in danger of being co-opted by the resonances of assimilative or cruel aspirations or of remaining stalled in logics of resistance that, like reactionary populisms, don't mount the durable popular power needed for fundamental social change. Yet actors have repeatedly emerged to revive and reshape the aspirational democratic populist imaginary and cultivate more rebellious aspirations to power. Even as the mainstream Civil Rights movement appealed to a constitutional "promissory note" to demand inclusion within the American dream, for example, coalitional actors pursued more rebellious aspirations to popular power. They cultivated the capacities of sharecroppers and laborers in the South, developed self-help economic institutions in urban neighborhoods, built cross-racial labor coalitions, formed transnational alliances for human rights and decolonization, and in the case of the Mississippi Freedom Democratic Party, organized to transform electoral institutions as part of demanding the right to vote. Some of these initiatives existed at the extreme margins of the movement, much like the insurgent energies of early hip-hop that fanned the spark of hope in the heroes and visions of Black Nationalism and Black Power. From these edges, however, militant and anticapitalist organizers inflected the aspirational democratic vision of Civil Rights activists.[185] The tensions that arose over vision and strategy during the Civil Rights movement exemplify the tensions within and at the edges of all aspirational democratic populisms. They must arouse collective identification around counterhegemonic visions of democracy, while building cross-cutting coalitions among efforts to enact popular power across sites and scales of political life. To do so, aspirational democratic populists must cultivate rhetoric and practices that orient imagination both toward the promise of democracy and toward those making noise at its edges.

At stake in the tensions between collective identification and decentralized experiments with horizontality is the ability to cultivate rebellious aspirations that can endure beyond established horizons of the people and democracy—including those established by any given populist movement. With Cohen, aspirational democratic populism emphasizes not solidity but emergence: that is, belonging with others who engage in ongoing contests to enact the promise of democracy. Rebellious aspirations do not begin in an already articulated—or always publically utterable—vision that constrains identification and power. Like the everyday heroism in "Democracy," efforts to enact popular power often fly beneath the radar of symbolic politics: in the subterranean spaces through which marginalized subjects invent hidden transcripts of resistance or in the subconstitutional spaces in which emerging actors experiment with new forms of power. The song's limits in relation to mainstream popular culture and to hip-hop's hidden transcripts raise key questions for the aspirational democratic populist imaginary that enables contemporary populist movements. How might populist movements invent—and recontextualize—repertoires of rhetoric and practices that can resist the pull of hegemonic visions that dilute and feed off rebellious aspirations? Given America's relentlessly segmented social imaginary, how might populists attend to the partiality of their own visions: a partiality that is both inherent to populist vision and historically constructed? Indeed, how might rebellious aspirations from populism's extreme margins—especially from insurgent people of color, immigrants, foreigners, women, and queers—disrupt and reconfigure the populist imaginary in America? How, finally, might the centering-decentering dynamics of aspirational democratic populisms sustain an organized disorganization that can steer the "machinery [of] change"?

Populist Resonances in the Twenty-First Century

The Tea Party and Occupy

I'm back for the Second Revolution. My weapons this time will be the Constitution, the Internet, and my talk-radio ads.

—*Tea Partier in colonial dress*[1]

From its Latin roots, "to occupy" can, in fact, mean *to seize a space against the status quo and to turn it towards something new.* To occupy is to construct a space in which we can engage in the craft—the occupation—of enacting the world we long for. We need to understand and to enact "occupation" in the widest sense possible . . . to exercise collective power and experiment with new forms of collective life."

—*Occupy activist Ethan Miller*

If the Populist movement responded to America's first corporate revolution, the Tea Party and Occupy Wall Street emerged in the midst of social upheavals brought on by today's neoliberal revolution. A quarter-century of economic liberalization and restructuring in the corporate and financial sectors came to a head with the global financial crisis that hit the United States at the end of 2007. With the collapse of America's housing bubble, years of risky subprime mortgage lending met a logical and devastating conclusion: as homeowners defaulted on their mortgages, the devaluation of mortgage-backed securities sent financial markets reeling. As a result, overleveraged banks approached insolvency and contributed to a credit crunch that dried up both consumer spending and business investment. Government bailouts and surplus spending—to avoid "total economic collapse"—eventually steadied banks and got the economy going. The hemorrhaging, however, continued for working- and middle-class people who now faced mass foreclosure, skyrocketing unemployment, falling incomes, and the evisceration of retirement savings. These experiences shed light on a new reality: American democracy is now based on obscene inequalities of wealth that have reached levels not seen since the Gilded Age.[2]

In this chapter, I evaluate the Tea Party and Occupy as competing populist responses to the crises of neoliberal democracy in the twenty-first century. Both uprisings performed popular outrage at elites who have corrupted democracy, and both garnered widespread grassroots participation and public support.[3] The Tea Party and Occupy were at odds, however, in their diagnoses of what has gone wrong: that is, what is the nature of the crisis facing American democracy, whom or what has been harmed, and by whom. If both uprisings organized the people to take back or transform democracy, moreover, they held dramatically divergent visions of who the people are and how they should enact their power in politics. I argue that the Tea Party enacts a form of regulated populism that narrows the boundaries of the people and the terms of democracy, whereas Occupy reflects the promise of and evolving challenges to aspirational democratic populism.

My interrogations in this chapter stem from a set of debates about democracy that surrounded the Tea Party and Occupy. In the early days of the Tea Party, observers were preoccupied with labeling the movement either "grassroots" or "AstroTurf."[4] Laden in these debates are deep investments in democracy and two erroneous assumptions: first, that grassroots politics is equivalent to democratic politics and, second, that decentralization immediately lends itself to democratic pluralization of populist identity and power. To the contrary, I argue here, the Tea Party's centralizing rhetoric of resistance and its decentered spaces of every-day politics have combined to reinforce hegemonic modes of capitalist, state, and cultural power. As several scholars have concluded, the Tea Party is built on ties between elite and grassroots actors that cannot be disentangled. Returning to Bill Connolly's notion of resonance machines, the Tea Party thrived because think tanks, elected officials, and a powerful right-wing echo chamber were able to contrive resonant assemblages to centralize rhetoric and identification. The Tea Party's centralizing rhetoric of resistance resonated widely with grassroots actors who, in turn, constituted popular power to support neoliberal and reactionary policies. Specifically, the Tea Party's resonance machine tapped into America's regulated populist imaginary to update the familiar narrative brought to us by Chevrolet—one in which "real Americans" must defend unlimited individual freedom for a national people defined as white, male, and Christian. Unlike the People's Party, moreover, the Tea Party's everyday spaces were often the sites of its most reactionary practices. Contestation over vision and strategy in the Tea Party was thus constrained from both above and below. Where rebellious aspirations did emerge—for example, local groups allied with environmentalists to block the corporate-state mergers responsible for the Keystone Pipeline —they were easily circumscribed by the movement's centralizing resonance machine.

Despite the Tea Party's antidemocratic ideology and impact, it was not uncommon to hear radical democratic scholars defend its populist outrage. The answer to the Tea Party, they argued, was not to quiet its anger or its oppositional tactics (though, radical democrats found much to fear in both). To do so would reinforce liberal institutions and procedures that rely on a passive, individualized populace, no matter their ideological position. Instead, some scholars called for a left populism to counter the Tea Party.[5] Behind this exhortation was the belief that the Left needed its own oppositional rhetoric—one that could arouse widespread collective identification to resist global capitalism and the corporate-state mergers that have distorted democracy. For many, Occupy Wall Street embodied that call. Its rhetoric of "the 99 percent" and its dramatic enactments of popular outrage against "the 1 percent" targeted not government overreach into the economy, but rather capitalism's takeover of political life. Unlike the Tea Party's appeals to the "real America," moreover, Occupy's appeal to "the 99 percent" sought broad appeal across lines of class, race, nationality, and even national borders. To understand Occupy's promise and pitfalls, however, it is not enough to distinguish its rhetoric and ideology from the Tea Party. Occupy's rebellious aspirations depended on its ability to build links between its centralizing rhetoric of resistance and its decentered experiments in constituting popular power. In contrast to the everyday politics of the Tea Party, Occupy's experimental spaces were sites in which people enacted egalitarian, pluralistic forms of popular power as alternatives to hegemonic structures and dynamics. Occupy's commitment to what many participants called "horizontalism" was limited, I argue, by its wariness about engaging local groups that had long organized in communities of color and larger-scale institutions that are embedded in the status quo. At its most promising, however, Occupy cultivated rebellious aspirations through experiments with horizontality. In its ties with local and translocal organizing—for example, its coalitions with the local and national organizing of the New Bottom Line campaign and its affinities with populist movements outside the United States—Occupy enacted popular power at the horizons of the people and democracy.

While my aim in this chapter is in part to elucidate the character of regulated and aspirational democratic populisms in our time, my political interests remain allied with radical democracy: in other words, how can aspirational democratic populisms flourish in light of our contemporary condition? Pairing the Tea Party and Occupy, then, is not only an artifact of their proximity in response to the same economic and political moment at the outset of the twenty-first century. If, as I suspect, economic and political neoliberalism create conditions that are ripe for the repeated emergence of regulated populist aspirations, it is all the more crucial to distinguish how aspirational democratic populisms can contribute to democratizing power and politics today.

FORECLOSING ON DEMOCRACY:
THE TEA PARTY'S REGULATED POPULISM

The Tea Party's brand of regulated populism is evident in its catalytic inception. On February 19, 2009—barely a month after the Democratic Party regained control of the White House in the persona of America's first black president—CNBC reporter Rick Santelli issued a call to arms that went viral.[6] Santelli was outraged by President Obama's plan to provide mortgage relief to struggling homeowners after bailing out the nation's elite bankers and auto executives. He accused the government of "promoting bad behavior" and called for a revolution: "President Obama, are you listening? It's time for another tea party!"[7] Libertarians and fiscal conservatives have held fast to postracial talking points to cast the Tea Party as a popular struggle to stave off tyrannical state power over the lives of individuals. The figure of Barack Obama, however, looms large over the history of the Tea Party. With his ambitious governmental response to an economic crisis that disproportionately affected blacks and Latinos, Obama personified the familiar fusion in right-wing discourse between government overreach and a racialized and gendered image of the nation's "dependent classes."[8] From the start, moreover, Tea Party rhetoric and imagery have cast Obama as "un-American": as Hitler, a socialist, a jihadist Muslim, an African "witch doctor," and in the rhetoric of the Tea Party's close cousin, the Birthers, as an "undocumented alien." Such reactionary symbolism adorns a movement that has aroused not only fiscal conservatives, but also an array of cultural crusaders from the Christian Right, various white nationalist groups, and a resurgent John Birch Society.[9] These reactionary ideologies have formed a resonant assemblage with the Tea Party's neoliberal economic ideology. The Tea Party's antistatist populism thus manifests popular anxiety that Americans are losing not only their individual rights, but their American way of life. In the populist imaginary stoked by the Tea Party, Obama—as a symbol of the state—represents an imminent threat to a nation conceived in white, masculinist, Christian, and capitalist terms.[10]

The Tea Party's resonant assemblage of neoliberal and reactionary ideologies echoes Chevy's vision of regulated populism: the Tea Party offers the fantasy of neoliberal individual freedom circumscribed by reactionary cultural norms. While analyses of the Tea Party tend to emphasize either its claims to postracial libertarianism or its various reactionary ideologies, I argue that the resonance between them is key to the Tea Party's ability to mobilize populist aspirations.[11] Like Chevy, Tea Party leaders have tapped into America's regulated populist imaginary to mobilize reactionary and cruel aspirations to power. Moreover, local and national groups have succeeded in combining the centralizing force of Tea Party outrage with everyday practices that constitute narrow forms of popular power. Grassroots Tea Partiers, for example, participate in widespread practices of constitutional fundamentalism, voter suppression, and border policing. The Tea Party's everyday politics have thus cultivated participants' affective stances toward closure and overwhelmingly reinforced the regulated aspirations stoked by the Tea Party resonance machine.

The Libertarian and Reactionary Resonances of Tea Party Peoplehood

The Tea Party's symbolic appeal to the America Revolution marks it as a modern-day revolt against state tyranny. Demanding a return to "constitutional principles" of fiscal conservatism, limited government, and free markets, the Tea Party casts the people as protagonists in a battle to stave off America's "slide into socialism."[12] Seen from this angle, the Tea Party has aroused a fury of collective identification around a neoliberal populist vision. What *the people* demand is the restoration of *individual rights* through ultra-free-market policies—ones that eviscerate the role of government as a representative of popular will. Libertarian and far-right advocacy groups, such as FreedomWorks and Americans for Prosperity, have done the most to articulate this vision and attach it to specific policy battles: for example, extending the Bush-era tax cuts, opposing the Affordable Care Act, impeding its implementation, curbing public sector unions, privatizing public education, and introducing severe austerity measures into the US budget. Echoing earlier conservative populisms from Father Coughlin to George Wallace, the Tea Party's grassroots base does harbor fury at corporate malfeasance. Many Tea Partiers had taken part in grassroots uprisings against George Bush's Troubled Asset Relief Plan, and most opposed the bank bailouts. Libertarians and conservatives saw the specter of socialism in the bailouts. But many also opposed using taxpayer money to clean up after what one protester described as a "culture of recklessness within the financial Investments Industry." Another elaborated, "This bailout could end up breaking the spirit that underlies the true American way. The key word is 'responsibility.' Where is it?"[13] In the lead-up to the 2014 midterm elections, Tea Party elites appeared to catch the grassroots fever; they took to Twitter and the blogosphere to wage the summer 2013 #libertarianpopulism debate. At stake in the libertarian populist rebranding was whether Tea Party Republicans, such as Rand Paul and Paul Ryan, could win support through rhetoric and policies that target "'bigness' in all its forms (corporate as well as governmental)."[14] Such anticorporate sentiment, however, has not yet translated into grassroots or elite campaigns to regulate corporations. Instead, the Tea Party's base has taken to rallies, town hall meetings, social media, and voting booths to back an elite-driven, neoliberal populist vision. Among the 20 percent of adults who sympathize with the Tea Party in national polls, moreover, significant majorities stand to the right of other Republicans in their support for policies that would reduce taxes, cut public spending, and deregulate business.[15]

Tea Partiers insist that their populist vision has universal appeal. In the Tea Party's early days, many grassroots and national leaders tried to marginalize reactionary voices in the movement. They negotiated tirelessly to leave issues such as abortion and immigration off the table and implored unwieldy protesters to leave their racist and evangelical signs at home.[16] Rallies featured token black and Latino speakers, women who took leadership roles spoke of themselves as "conservative feminists," and protesters carried signs such as "Jesus Christ, Libertarian."[17] Like Chevy's hollow celebration of Americana, however, libertarian attempts at multicultural inclusion promise equality to individuals while denying the structural conditions of social group inequality that remain central to America's economic, social, and political life. Indeed, the Tea Party's libertarian populist rhetoric constructs "the-people-as-individuals" against "the state" by disavowing both the need for and legitimacy of group-based claims to justice.[18] Libertarianism's anemic basis for collective identification, moreover, has been bolstered by reactionary cultural ideologies since the Tea Party's inception. Local and national Tea Party groups have been active in the culture wars of the new millennium: for example, protesting the "Ground Zero mosque," opposing "anchor babies," supporting a slew of "papers, please" anti-immigrant bills, organizing voter suppression campaigns, and renewing struggles over guns, abortion, contraception, and gay marriage.[19] Again echoing Chevrolet, when Tea Partiers rally to "take back *our country*," they intend to return it to "the people as nation" defined in hermetic terms. Such reactionary rhetoric has played a powerful role in arousing collective identification with the Tea Party because it crystallizes the friend-versus-enemy distinction that the movement's libertarian populist discourse largely obscures. Setting the people against the state, that is, lacks definition and intensity without discursive frames that clarify whom the state serves and whom it does not.

Race has been the biggest elephant in the Tea Party's not so big tent. The whiteness of the Tea Party is at once obvious to casual observers and difficult to articulate given that the movement largely adheres to postracial discourses and exiles overt racists as "bad seeds." It is not necessary to point to examples of overt racism, however, to tie the Tea Party to a history of racialized populist discourse. Scholars have provided both theoretical frameworks and empirical backing to support the claim: the Tea Party is the latest in a long lineage of racially

motivated backlash by whites who are afraid of losing their social status and economic resources in a period of economic insecurity. When Tea Partiers resur-
rect symbols such as the "Forgotten Man" and the "silent majority," for example,
they tap into nostalgia for what George Lipsitz has described as "racialized social
democracy," that is, social democracy for whites. This vision of democracy pairs
benefits and freedoms for decent, hard-working, taxpaying Americans, with a
denial of resources to those "undeserving classes" who are deemed "dependent"
on the welfare state.[20] Among the first to provide this insight, Theda Skocpol
and Vanessa Williamson show that the Tea Party's base is not as libertarian as its
elites: a significant majority of activists and sympathizers support public funding
for Social Security, Medicare, and Veterans Affairs—programs that typically serve
middle-class Americans or those who have served their country. Many worry that
government is stealing money from those programs and funneling it to programs
that benefit "dependent" classes.[21] Hence, the plethora of Tea Party signs: "You
are not entitled to what I have earned." "Redistribute my work ethic." And "Keep
Working, Millions on Welfare Depend on You."[22] White social democracy is
sustained by a right-wing variant of producerism: one that pits the independent
middle class against both the dependent classes below and the intellectual elites
who engineer policies on their behalf.[23] Both ideologies depend on color-blind
discourses that associate independence with "whiteness," while casting "dependence" as a pathological trait possessed primarily by poor blacks and immigrants.
As Lisa Disch argues, the Tea Party's appeal to white social democracy enables it
to "tap into the ideology of whiteness, whereby programs that selectively benefit
middle-class whites pass as general, race neutral, and universal."[24]

As if to help the Tea Party wipe its dirty laundry under the rug, many analysts
and pundits have highlighted the movement's antisocialist rhetoric as its unifying
force. In other words, despite its reactionary elements, this central "color-blind"
cleavage defines Tea Party populism.[25] Reinforcing this view enables Tea Partiers
to hurl racially veiled epithets while claiming racial innocence. As a popular Tea
Party bumper sticker puts it, extending the charge of socialism from Obama to
the Democratic Party, "I'm not racist. I don't like Biden either."[26] Joe Lowndes
has argued that the cry of "socialism . . . points not away from race, as its defenders would have it, but toward it. The modern conservative movement in the US,
from the late 1940s onward, linked the advance of black civil rights with the
threat of a totalitarian state, and socialism specifically."[27] At once the symbol of
irreligious secularism, un-American political-economic beliefs, and government
on behalf of "undeserving" and "dependent" classes, the rhetoric of socialism is
indeed apt for unifying the disparate forces of the Tea Party—not absent from,
but along with their racist, nationalist, and evangelical overtones. In other words,
socialism becomes the code word for the people's revolt against a state that has
been blackened and rendered un-American.

Against the specter of socialism, the Tea Party promises to return American democracy to its constitutional foundations. The Constitution is central to Tea Party rhetoric and iconography. People often attend protests dressed in colonial attire, and merchandise tables are lined with pocket Constitutions; when the Tea Party Republicans stormed Congress in 2011, the House majority required representatives to cite the constitutional foundations for every law they proposed. A typical sign at rallies concurred, "Find it in the Constitution." What Tea Partiers find in the Constitution is a fundamentalist primer for contemporary politics—one that first obscures the debates in 1787 that resulted in a victor's version of history and then dismisses over two centuries of subsequent struggle to put the Constitution into practice. Many Tea Partiers, moreover, tie their fundamentalist beliefs about the Constitution to God.[28] Much has been made of the Tea Party's "constitutional guru," Cleon Skousen, whose 1981 book, *The 5000 Year Leap*, argues that the framers of the Constitution based the principle of limited government on the ethnic ideals of Anglo-Saxon history and the "divinely inspired" ideals of Christianity.[29] Skousen's ideas likely resonated with Tea Partiers, however, because they were already steeped in the grammars of a Christian Right movement whose rhetoric supported the principles of fiscal conservatism. In the mouth of leaders like Ralph Reed, writes Peter Montgomery, the definition of "family values" came to "embrace Republican's antitax and antigovernment agendas."[30] "It's immoral to take money from people who work and give it to those who don't work," explained one minister. "Our laws were founded on God's word and not on Man's will."[31] This biblical reading of the Constitution also helps explain the Tea Party's insistence on combining fiscal conservatism with conservative stances on gay marriage, reproductive rights, and the role of women in society. Tea Partiers thus appeal to the Constitution to narrow both the reach of government and the categories of rights—and citizenship—that benefit from its protections.

The Tea Party's resonant ideologies have incited both reactionary and cruel aspirations to power among its base. On the one hand, Tea Partiers demand popular power for the hard-working, independent men and women who constitute what Sarah Palin called the "real America." This stance has led Tea Partiers to support reactionary efforts to scale back the institutions that shaped the nation's political economy from the Populist Era through the Great Society—at least insofar as those institutions, already severely weakened, survive only to provide a safety net for people who, by the Tea Party's standards, are not "real Americans." As Charles Postel, the historian of nineteenth-century Populism, asks, "Where is the populism in a movement that demands hard money and to revert to the gold standard. That seeks to repeal the Sixteenth Amendment and the graduated income tax . . . That seeks to remove the funding from public education? That seeks to lift regulations on banks and corporate giants? In short, where is the populism in a movement that seeks to repeal everything the original Populists stood for?"[32] On the other hand, these same themes—long deemed too extreme by mainstream conservatives—point to the Tea Party's radicalism. By returning to the nation's constitutional roots, the Tea Party justifies policies that would accelerate neoliberal trends toward deregulation, privatization, and government of, for, and by the market. In this respect, the Tea Party also encourages the cruel aspirations of a base who still believe that the market is the guarantor of free-dom and that individuals have the agency they need to navigate the vagaries of capitalism—if only the government would leave them alone.[33]

The intensified resonance between libertarian and reactionary ideologies in the Tea Party has already impacted collective identification and public policy and stands to reinforce America's regulated populist imaginary. Like Chevy's montage, the resonant force of Tea Party rhetoric creates equivalences between unlike images, events, and flashpoints. For the Tea Party, this enables ideolo-gies that are often in tension to coalesce around specific actions or policies: this happened, for example, when libertarians and religious activists joined forces to prevent the Obama administration from requiring religious employers to insure contraception.[34] The Tea Party's resonant rhetoric of peoplehood thus obscures the paradox of popular sovereignty. It enables internal conflicts to exist within "the people" while confining those conflicts within ideological boundaries that limit contestation over the terms of the people and democracy.

Practicing Invulnerability in the Tea Party's Everyday Politics

The Tea Party's centralizing rhetoric of resistance has resonated widely with grass-roots actors who, in turn, have constituted widespread popular power to carry the movement and lend it legitimacy. To be sure, elite actors—advocacy orga-nizations, national Tea Party groups, Republican Party officials, and right-wing media—have had a heavy hand in shaping Tea Party vision and strategy. They have provided field coordinators; training sessions for local activists; primers on government institutions and procedures; fact sheets and policy reports; speak-ers for events; and communications support via conference calls, webinars, and new media training. Since the 2010 midterm elections, Tea Party Republicans and advocacy groups have played an even greater role in steering movement strategy and representing the "face" of the Tea Party.[35] Unlike today's profes-sionalized, elite-driven advocacy groups, however, the Tea Party has sustained a grassroots base through bottom-up and largely self-sustaining local organizing. When the movement's base was at its height, some two hundred thousand peo-ple took part in regular, face-to-face community organizing through up to one thousand active groups across the country. Local Tea Parties continue to play an active role in local, state, and national electoral politics; provide loud support for legislative battles over the budget and deficit; and spearhead campaigns to pass voter-suppression laws in many states. Tea Partiers thus negotiate the array of resources, policy initiatives, and national affiliations available to them in a relatively fragmented movement.[36]

The "grassroots versus AstroTurf" debate masks a more important characteristic of the Tea Party: it is impossible to disentangle the movement's bottom-up, everyday politics from the centralizing current of identification and affect generated by the Tea Party resonance machine. The resonant frequencies of the right-wing echo chamber play an unparalleled role in contemporary politics, one that mimics the role of advertising in its ability to reach into the everyday lives of people living in the United States. As rhetoric and information are relayed through feedback loops between Fox News, talk radio, and the blogosphere, they create an echo-chamber effect that both amplifies messages and insulates them from outside critique.[37] Scholars of media and communications have shown that the echo chamber played an important role in the emergence and development of the Tea Party. After lending coherence and legitimacy to the movement in its early stages, right-wing media have repeatedly rallied a conservative base around Tea Party talking points—not to mention paranoid fantasies, such as rumors about Obama's religious and citizenship status, accusations of widespread voter fraud spearheaded by the community organizing group ACORN, the supposed left-wing "Piven-Cloward" strategy to destroy capitalism, and, of course, the infamous provision for "death panels" in the Affordable Care Act.[38] The resonance of these echoing frames and fictions is evident in national opinion polls, but the implications are made vivid in one of Skocpol and Williamson's most intriguing observations about grassroots Tea Partiers: although taking part in the "nitty-gritty" of everyday organizing has given them a "mastery of political processes," many hold "wildly inaccurate" beliefs "about what government does, how it is financed, and what is actually included (or not) in key pieces of legislation."[39]

In addition to centralizing information and vision, the Tea Party resonance machine intensifies emotion. Tea Partiers are notorious, in particular, for their performance of fear and anger. At protests, signs don't just convey messages, they issue battle cries: "Stand your ground. Don't fire unless fired upon. But if they mean to have a war, let it begin here." Critics point to the Tea Party's affective politics to dismiss the movement as reactionary.[40] As feminist theorists and theorists of affect have shown, however, emotions are often productive. They are not merely outward expressions of our inner experiences, but rather practices that, like any other practice, can shape us as subjects. In this sense, we can think of emotions as performative.[41] In social settings, emotional speech and action are usually iterated in relation to discourses and norms that make them legible; in this way, emotions can constitute certain subjects or subject positions with which people can identify. We can also think of emotion as a kind of relational practice that is more or less tightly scripted—at times bound dialectically to the reproduction of social positions, at times loosened through what Lauren Berlant and Michael Warner call "unsystematized lines of acquaintance." In this way, emotional speech and action can reinforce or disrupt the "emotional habitus" of a group, or their "collective and only partly conscious emotional disposition" toward others and the world.[42] While emotions like fear and anger are themselves neutral, Tea Partiers perform them to arouse collective identification and police the boundaries of peoplehood. Indeed, taking a page from Carl Schmitt, Tea Party populism is based on the construction of an existential threat. As we have seen, Tea Partiers fear dispossession: they are afraid of losing their "way of life" and the promise of white, male, Christian privilege—or, independence—that comes with it. Fear then manifests in angry performances that construct and police the lines between friend and enemy.

Tea Party anger is both defensive and aggressive. On one end, Tea Partiers perform resentment at what they perceive as an attack on their economic and cultural status. In national surveys, for example, Tea Partiers have shown markedly higher levels of racial resentment than the general public and even other Republicans.[43] In their public performances, Tea Partiers repeatedly take on a defensive posture to protect their cultural legitimacy. One protest sign read, "It doesn't matter what this sign says, you'll call it racism anyway."[44] As Lisa Disch has argued, such defensiveness does not only reflect hostility toward out-groups. In a culture in which moral status is associated with whiteness, many Tea Partiers cling desperately to their in-group identity to protect all that whiteness has stood for.[45] On the other end, Tea Partiers are notorious for their aggressive anger toward their "enemies." According to national surveys, Tea Party activists and sympathizers are also much more punitive than other Americans, evident in their support for three-strikes drug policies, stricter sentencing, and trying juveniles as adults.[46] At one Republican primary debate in 2011, a crowd full of Tea Partiers erupted in raucous applause when Rick Perry boasted that his administration has executed more death row inmates "than any other governor in modern times." At another, moderator Wolf Blitzer pressed Ron Paul on how to treat someone who chose not to buy healthcare but now needs intensive care, "But Congressman, are you saying the society should let him die?"[47] The crowd cheered, "Yeah!" At times, Tea Party aggression veers toward violence: protestors have held signs that read, "We come unarmed [this time]," amassed in the nation's capital with guns in hand, spit on civil rights hero and Democratic Representative John Lewis, and threatened physical harm toward Democratic candidates.[48] Exemplifying the dual direction of Tea Party anger, one activist reported that reading immigration headlines in *RedState* made her want to "stand on the border with a gun."[49]

The Tea Party's anger itself, as Holloway Sparks has argued, is not what concerns me—at least not in a neoliberal context that pacifies dissent by valuing civility.[50] In the way they perform anger, however, Tea Partiers reinforce a white, masculinist, and Christian nationalism as the privileged site of popular identification in America. What the Tea Party makes legible are dominant norms regarding who can perform anger in America and under what circumstances.

Try to imagine, as Tim Wise did, a rally of black men carrying guns in Washington, DC, or, with Sparks, the likely success of feminist candidates who seek national office by excoriating American militarism and promising to fight patriarchal policies.[51] Beyond policing the borders of collective identity, moreover, anger can produce a sense of agency that moves people from fear to action. For Tea Partiers, that agency means fighting to "take back" the country to restore it to its rightful inheritors: hard-working, independent men and women and their children. By performing anger in the face of fear, Tea Party rhetoric and protests offer participants and sympathizers the promise that they can restore a waning sense of dignity and avoid the anxiety that comes with the vagaries of capitalism.[52] Mobilizing angry indignation and cultivating dignity and hope seem crucial to enacting popular power in an economic and political climate structured to disempower most people. What distinguishes the Tea Party's anger from more rebellious populisms, however, is not only the fact that it reinforces rather than disrupts hegemonic cultural power. In a cultural context that normalizes independence and pathologizes dependence, Tea Party anger is directed at the idea of vulnerability itself. Unwilling to publically acknowledge their own vulnerability, Tea Partiers externalize fear by performing anger at "dependent classes" and at the government that rewards dependence via "favors" and "handouts." The refusal to accept vulnerability—and the resulting failure to imagine responses to neoliberalism that do not entail cultural supremacy—not only implicates Tea Party sympathizers in reactionary aspirations to dominate marginalized groups. It also invests them in cruel aspirations that austerity and deregulation will—finally—enable them to realize independence.

I do not mean to suggest that the Tea Party's resonant rhetoric and affect have had a totalizing impact on the movement. The Tea Party's widespread public performances remind us that its grassroots participants are an active base, not a collection of couch potatoes watching Chevrolet ads in the commercial breaks between yelling along with Fox News. Those who are active in the movement's everyday politics have had opportunities to cultivate the kinds of dispositions and capacities that enable them to contest Tea Party vision and strategy. At their peak, local Tea Party groups met regularly to listen to speakers, watch documentaries, and coordinate activities. Grassroots Tea Partiers took on various tasks: they drew up constitutions and bylaws, planned local rallies, performed education in their communities, organized electoral support for Tea Party candidates, took over local Republican Party committees, lobbied elected officials, and acted as watchdogs (attending local government meetings, monitoring officials, and tracking bills).[53] If first-time activists awaken to politics and come to the Tea Party through its more spectacular events, it is in the everyday politics of local organizing that they cultivated popular power: for example, a keen practical know-how for navigating electoral and legislative processes; the ability to build relationships of trust between libertarians and social conservatives; and the heightened sense of efficacy needed to sustain their aspirations for the long haul.[54] The Tea Party's everyday politics has not only emboldened grassroots insurgents. It has also provided many sites for internal conflict and debate: for example, over the place of social conservative values in its free-market strategies; whether to devote grassroots energies to backing far-right Republican candidates or playing a watchdog role in relation to elected officials in both mainstream parties; and how to maintain grassroots control vis-à-vis elites who speak on behalf of the movement.[55]

In large part, however, the Tea Party's everyday politics has reinforced rather than ruptured its centralizing resonances. As Skocpol and Williamson observe, a "paradox of Tea Party citizenship is the sharp bifurcation between generous, tolerant interaction within the group and an almost total lack of empathy for fellow Americans beyond the group." "We suspect," they add, "Tea Party participants usually find it difficult to stereotype and reject people they actually deal with face-to-face."[56] Indeed, far from being sites of organizing across social divides, the Tea Party's decentered spaces are the sites of its most reactionary aspirations to power. Local Tea Parties have been safe havens for resurgent Birchers, evangelicals, and white nationalist groups. It is also in local Tea Parties that participants have engaged in ongoing, everyday practices of exclusion and domination. Much of the Tea Party's grassroots energy since 2012, for example, has gone into campaigning for "voter identification" laws in counties and states across the country. In many states, local Tea Partiers have organized to support immigration policies that legalize racial profiling and enhance state surveillance. In practice, this means going door to door with messages rooted in fear and anger, organizing poll monitors to prevent people from voting, and standing on the border to keep immigrants out.[57] Like the reactionary nineteenth-century Populists who worked to institutionalize Jim Crow, many of today's grassroots Tea Partiers are foot soldiers in this era's efforts to restrict the franchise and narrow access to full citizenship. In other words, local Tea Partiers routinely take part in everyday practices designed to constitute horizontal-power-for-us. Activities such as these at best reinforce the defensive and aggressive dispositions of Tea Partiers and orient them to police the boundaries of identity and popular power. At worst, local Tea Parties are spaces in which participants can safely cultivate overtly racist sentiments: circulating racist emails and laughing at racist jokes—in other words, not only defending white privilege against collapse, but taking pleasure in white supremacy.

It is also at the local level that Tea Partiers practice the constitutional fundamentalism that underpins their reactionary and radical ideologies. Tea Partiers sell pocket-sized versions of the Constitution as merchandise at rallies and protests, hand them out at their meetings (like "party favors," according to one observer), and give them as gifts or symbols of gratitude. Taking a cue from the Christian Right, many Tea Partiers participate in Constitution study groups, and some attend daylong or even multiday Constitution workshops sponsored by national organizations. In these settings, participants read the Constitution line-by-line, hear lectures on constitutional theory, and engage in debates over the application of key passages to current political issues. Tea Partiers are surrounded by "Constitution talk," as Skocpol and Williamson call it; they can "recite passages by heart," another observer reports, "and refer to it, by article and section, in casual conversation."[58] "It's amazing how quickly the Constitution became a second language," one Tea Party activist reflected. If everyday political spaces are Tocquevillian "schoolhouses of democracy," the Tea Party's disciplinary pedagogy is designed to teach participants how to interpret American history and current events in narrow fashion. By cultivating such fundamentalist interpretive lenses, Tea Partiers profoundly limit their range of memory, perception, and vision in relation to the crises of the day and possible responses. This uncompromising stance backs Tea Party forays into electoral and legislative processes, as seen in the base's support for candidates who call themselves "constitutional conservatives," their demand that all congressional bills reference the Constitution, and their support for obstructionist tactics during negotiations on deficit reduction and public spending.[59]

If the Tea Party's centralizing resonances intensify affective stances of fear and anger that prime participants to police the borders of friend and enemy, its everyday practices largely cultivate narrow dispositions toward popular power. Dispositions toward racism, white supremacy, and fundamentalism, moreover, prime participants to be responsive to, rather than critical of, the Tea Party resonance machine. Against more romantic notions of democratic participation, then, the power of the Tea Party's grassroots participation lies in radical closure. This is not the conclusion I expected to draw when I began studying the Tea Party in 2009. What I found notable about the popular response to the financial collapse and first bank bailout were the pockets of economic populist protest on the both the right and left. These voices were barely discernable through the din of the neoliberal consensus in support of the bank bailouts among Republicans and Democrats in Congress.[60] When the Tea Party brought this outrage to the public's attention—citing corporate-state relationships that encouraged not only government overreach but also corporate irresponsibility—the Right in that moment had a more legible critique of political neoliberalism than a Left that was still awaiting Occupy Wall Street.

Rebellious aspirations have continued to emerge from time to time among the Tea Party's more unruly patriots. Most notably, Tea Partiers in Nebraska, Montana, and Texas teamed up with environmental activists to halt the building of TransCanada's Keystone Pipeline from Alberta to the Gulf of Mexico. Tea Partiers joined grassroots groups, such as Stop Tarsands Oil Pipelines (STOP) and Texas Uniting for Reform and Freedom (TURF), which opposed governmental eminent domain policies that would allow TransCanada to seize private property for corporate profit. In some cases, these groups came to share environmental activists' concerns about the costs of pollution and energy extraction. What most encouraged "lifelong Republicans [to stand] should-to-should with urban tree-huggers," however, was a common critique of outsized corporate influence in politics.[61] In the words of Terri Hall, a Tea Partier with TURF, "You've got Americans for Prosperity out there promoting this and saying we want you to put in comments in favor of the pipeline. . . . Anyone who's done five minutes of research will find out that not only are the Koch brothers involved in this, TransCanada has never made any promises that this is going to be domestic energy."[62] The rebellious aspirations of these unlikely coalitions have fared poorly, however, in proximity to a right-wing resonance machine that supports Keystone. When the Obama administration stepped in to deny Keystone a permit to build, the echo chamber resounded with iterations of climate change denial, false claims linking Keystone to domestic energy independence, and cries of "financial terrorism" against an already troubled economy.[63] In relation to a resonance machine that has unprecedented power to amplify rhetoric and affect, it is exponentially more difficult for grassroots Tea Partiers to deflect the movement's centralizing resonances than it was for the unwieldy coalitions of nineteenth-century Populism.

Rather than dismiss the movement as AstroTurf, we should be concerned with the Tea Party's success in organizing grassroots power to support candidates, policies, and tactics that have shifted the Republican Party and US politics to the right. Indeed, what is striking about the Tea Party is its ability to mobilize popular power by constructing and intensifying feedback loops between a today's right-wing resonance machine and the everyday practices of grassroots organizing. The Tea Party is dangerous to democracy partly because of the antidemocratic impact it has already had on American politics—narrowing citizenship rights, restricting access to social programs, and supporting austerity and tax measures that enhance the ultrarich—but also because it forecasts likely trends in regulated populisms in the coming years. Three points combine to support this claim. First, the Tea Party is the most recent emergence of a strong and latent right-wing base. Looking back, the Christian Right was able to desecularize American political culture because of its ability to form similar feedback loops. The resonances of that battle and many of its foot soldiers survived the movement itself. Indeed, scholars have argued that the Tea Party resulted, in part, from decades of growth and increased conservatism among the activist base of the Republican Party. "By 2009," Abramowitz explains, a large cadre of very conservative Republican activists was available for mobilization by conservative organizations and media outlets."[64] Second, the Tea Party's cruel optimism will necessitate future backlash. In other words, as John Judis has argued, a "Tea Party-like movement will emerge again" precisely because Tea Party–backed austerity measures "will keep inequality and crisis going, and will thrust American politics into perpetual upheaval." Amid ongoing financial crisis, "Middle American radicals will almost certainly reassemble into a new formation."[65] Finally, the Right appears to have figured out the feedback loops between centralizing resistance and everyday politics necessary to move from episodic backlash to more productive forms of popular power. Grassroots regulated populisms, in other words, will continue to be pivotal to the success of the neoliberal project. This is not to say that Sheldon Wolin was wrong when he declared America's oxymoronic neoliberal democracy a form of "inverted totalitarianism": the totalizing reach of today's corporate-state mergers will largely depend on a passive, individualized citizenry. As Wolin himself saw, the success of America's neoliberal project has always and likely will always depend on periodic showings of more robust popular support.[66] When regulated populisms such as the Tea Party can invent and sustain resonances between social conservative and neoliberal rhetoric, and when they can link them to broad affective mobilization and everyday politics, they provide popular power and democratic legitimacy to reinforce the rise of neoliberal democracy.

"FANNING THE SPARK OF HOPE": ASPIRATIONAL DEMOCRATIC POPULISM IN OCCUPY

Like Cohen's "Democracy," Occupy Wall Street originated outside the United States. On July 13, 2011, the Canadian journal *Adbusters* issued a call to action on its website:

> #OccupyWallStreet
> *Are you ready for a Tahrir moment?*
> On Sept 17, flood lower Manhattan, set up tents,
> kitchens, peaceful barricades and occupy Wall Street.[67]

Imagining a "fusion of Tahrir Square with the acampadas of Spain," *Adbusters* hoped to multiply the "people's assemblies" that were gathering in cities across the world to enact "the radical democracy of the future."[68] Thanks to a dedicated group of activists organizing on the ground that summer, about a thousand people marched through Wall Street on September 17. The occupation of Zuccotti Park began that night.[69] In short time, Occupiers erected tent cities in dozens of cities across the United States and Europe. On one weekend in October alone, people took to the streets in fifteen hundred protests in 150 US cities and eighty-two countries, including crowds of two hundred thousand to five hundred thousand in European cities hit hardest by austerity.[70] The Occupy movement undoubtedly revived the antagonistic dimension of politics on the left. From its populist slogan "We are the 99 percent" to its tactics of occupation and direct action, Occupy performed popular outrage against obscene concentrations of corporate and state power. The movement dramatized the people's refusal to accept that the imperatives of global capital must inevitably dictate the priorities of the state or the horizons of democracy. In this respect, many observers saw in Occupy the promise of left populist resistance.[71] The movement's rhetoric of the "99 percent," moreover, had broad appeal. One reporter chronicled among Occupiers in US encampments alone "anarchists and Marxists of a thousand different sects, social democrats, community organizers, immigrants' rights activists, feminists, queers, anti-racist organizers, capitalists who want to save capitalism by restoring the Fordist truce."[72] At its best, then, Occupy offered an egalitarian, pluralistic rhetoric of peopling, opening space for diverse actors to imagine and enact popular power across an array of social and geographic divides.

By many accounts, however, the divide between populist resistance and everyday populism resurfaced with the emergence of Occupy. Although Occupiers experimented with parallel institutions and practices of democracy in their tent cities, the everyday practices of occupation at first failed to connect to the everyday politics of local communities. Two critiques surfaced among everyday populists. First, grassroots actors who had been addressing the same issues for decades—primarily in communities of color—were quick to question the representativeness of a largely white movement that suddenly gave face to their struggles. Organizers in the trenches of these communities questioned what Occupy's bold rhetoric and street theater had to do with the everyday lives of working people, whose daily concerns involved finding and keeping work, affording rent and basic utilities, paying off credit card debt, staying clear of racial profiling and police brutality, and worrying over whether their children can attend decent schools and stay in them.[73] Second, many community organizers questioned the "staying power" of a "quixotic" movement with few ties to the many local institutions—for example, religious congregations, neighborhood associations, and other civil society organizations—that act as "foot soldiers in the daily battle" for democracy and provide "real power to generate lasting change."[74]

Disconnected from everyday experiences and institutions, Occupy's rhetoric of popular power rang hollow.

Occupy was thus confronted with sedimented divisions in an aspirational democratic populist imaginary that was once capacious enough to harbor the tensional relationship between centralizing rhetorics of resistance and decentered experiments in enacting popular power. Evaluating Occupy in relation to America's populist imaginary, I want to argue, offers a sharper understanding of its democratic promise and pitfalls than theories that celebrate or criticize the movement from either side of the divide between resistance and everyday practice—and that includes not only theorists of populism, but those on the left who describe Occupy either as a form of twenty-first-century Marxist class resistance or as exemplary of the antirepresentational politics of anarchism or the "multitude."[75] Aspirational democratic populism is evident in Occupy's flexible, cross-border rhetoric of the 99 percent, which is capable of calling people together to constitute popular power to redress systemic wrongs, while leaving the people an open call to be picked up and reconstituted by marginalized and emerging groups. The concept of aspirational democratic populism also helps us distinguish the limits of Occupy's stance toward existing institutions from its more rebellious experiments in horizontality. Through its direct social media ties to people's movements in Europe and its coalitions with the New Bottom Line campaign in the United States, Occupy combined local and translocal organizing to constitute popular power in everyday practice and at the horizons of the people and democracy.

Though Occupy general assemblies continue to meet in many US cities and the movement has inspired and generated offshoots—for example, Strike Debt and Occupy Central in Hong Kong—I speak about Occupy in the past tense in this chapter. I do so not because I believe the movement has lost its importance for radical democratic politics, but because I am particularly interested in populism's ability to combine everyday politics with the centralizing rhetoric of resistance that was the mark of Occupy's moment on the public stage. I conclude by suggesting ways in which Occupy remains a "spark of hope" that needs to be fanned again and again in the coming years as part of radical democratic mobilizations both in and out of the public eye.

Constituting Horizontalist "People Power" in Occupy

Occupy's slogan—"We are the 99 percent"—aroused broad collective identification with the movement. Pitting the "99 percent" against the "1 percent," Occupy asserted a division in a polity that bases its legitimacy on the principle of "government of the people, by the people, [and] for the people."[76] By exposing an economic and political system that caters to superelites, the rhetoric of the "1 percent" crystallized the tensions—and, for many Occupy activists, the incompatibility—between capitalism and democracy. Occupy thus embodied a moment of rupture in a democratic imaginary circumscribed by what critical theorists have called "capitalist realism": the widespread assumption, voiced by Margaret Thatcher, that "there is no alternative" to liberal, capitalist democracy.[77] That Occupy resonated deeply with many Americans is evident in broad support for the issues it dramatized even after public opinion turned against its tactics. In the brief moment Occupy held public attention, moreover, it succeeded in shifting political discourse by reintroducing economic justice claims into debates about poverty, joblessness, debt, and foreclosure—thus politicizing social issues that were once privatized with little question.[78]

Given the broad identification with Occupy's oppositional rhetoric, would-be supporters of the movement were stymied by its refusal to name concrete demands that could unite people behind large-scale structural change. Indeed, efforts by Occupy Wall Street to present a unified front—a viral *Adbusters* poster, for example, prompted, "What is our one demand?"—ended with a lack of consensus and with insistence on the part of many Occupiers that the absence of demands was part of the solution.[79] With this refusal, Occupy signaled its wariness about representative forms of democracy—and, thus, its departure from theories of populist resistance that aim to displace one hegemonic order only to replace it with a counterhegemonic one. Although Occupy did not escape representation, its centralizing rhetoric of the "99 percent" accompanied two aspects of the movement that aimed at decentralizing popular power. The first, the tactic of occupation, signals both a rebuke of the nation-state's legitimacy as a representative body and the belief that ordinary people can create more viable forms of popular power by recuperating public spaces in their local communities. The second, horizontalism, affirms the principle of radical inclusivity in contrast to the social hierarchies that are always embedded in representative forms of democracy.

Partly, activists described occupation as the antithesis of making demands. Those who were sympathetic with Occupy's vocal anarchist contingent worried that making demands would reinforce the nation-state as the central locus of democratic power and politics. A history of seeing social movements co-opted by the state, moreover, cautioned many Occupiers against seeking reforms that would subordinate popular interests to the narrow dictates of money and bureaucracy.[80] In the act of claiming possession, then, Occupiers staged an act of refusal to recognize the legitimacy of the existing order. Threaded between the disparate grievances of Occupy's motley activists was a rebuke of the wholesale dispossession of popular power by institutions of representative democracy that are more invested in capitalism than in people. "Banks got bailed out, we got sold out," read a sign at one protest. Another clarified, "The System's Not Broken; It's Fixed."[81] The movement's confrontational tactics also allowed the state to reveal its own priorities: in one image that went viral, a police force armed in full riot gear surround Chase Bank to protect it from protestors; in countless others, militarized police use batons, pepper spray, and tear gas to disband tent cities and disperse protests.[82] At the same time that Occupy exposed what Todd Gitlin has called the "moral default of [American] society's chief institutions," the movement decentered the American state's role in both the economic crisis and its solution.[83] By staging its first occupation on Wall Street—a symbol of American capitalism, but also a global financial center—Occupy signaled the global nature of today's devastating economic inequalities and questioned the limits of democratic visions that are confined within America's borders. By erecting a tent city on that stage, Occupiers brought into the open the everyday manifestations of the crisis in local communities that have been left by representative institutions to fend for themselves and to work out solutions on their own.[84]

Partly, occupation enabled people to experiment with new institutions and practices of popular power. In the words of Occupy activist and scholar Ethan Miller, to occupy means "to seize a space against the status quo and turn it toward something new."[85] Yotam Marom, an organizer in New York, uses the concept of a "dual-power struggle" to describe the tactic of occupation: tent cities were not only a "staging ground" for resistance, he explains, but a "home where we get to practice the alternative—by practicing a participatory democracy, by having our radical libraries, by having a medical tent where anybody can get treatment, that kind of thing on a small level."[86] Taking a cue from the M-15 movement in Spain, the alter-globalization movement, and prior American groups ranging from Quakers to the Student Nonviolent Coordinating Committee, Occupiers made decisions through consensus practices in general assemblies. They organized tent cities through working groups, many of which were self-generated as different Occupiers recognized new needs.[87] These included food, sanitation, sustainability, security, medical needs, legal needs, media, libraries, free schools, art stations, children's areas, community gardens, religious communities, and, as social divisions surfaced, working groups for people of color, women, and queer people. Occupied spaces thus became sites of radical democracy and cooperative economy as participants engaged in everyday practices of sharing work, providing public services, engaging in dialogue, and building consensus.[88] Adopting the language of "prefigurative politics," Occupiers believed that only by "embody[ing] the alternative" they desired could they develop the dispositions, capacities, and parallel institutions of self-governance they would need to enact radical democratic forms of "people power."[89]

Occupiers were quick to distinguish "people power" from the vertical, zero-sum logics of power that govern liberal, capitalist social imaginaries. Many

Occupiers used the language of "horizontalism" or *horizontalidad*—adopted from workers' movements in Latin America and two decades of alter-globalization struggles—to describe their experiments in constituting popular power. These concepts, according to activist and writer Marina Sitrin, encapsulate a "dynamic social relationship that represents a break with the logic of representation and vertical ways of organizing . . . [B]ecause social relationships are still deeply marked by capitalism and hierarchy—especially in terms of how people relate to one another over economic resources, gender, race, and access to information—*horizontalidad* has to be understood as an open-ended social process."[90] In other words, horizontal popular power must not be static, but emergent. Occupy's commitment to horizontalism was evident in its consensus practices; in the self-generated working groups that formed in its tent cities; in the efforts of some Occupy groups to build relationships with unions, student groups, and local institutions, eventually including people of color who criticized whiteness in the movement; and in the movement's identification with world-wide popular struggles against state repression and the myriad effects of global capitalism. It also took shape via Twitter, Facebook, and other forms of social media sites that were sources of broader engagement with the movement. In the words of Joe Lowndes and Dorian Warren, "Occupy Wall Street and its model of open-source populism [had] the potential to be as transformative as prior populist movements on the left," while doing more than many of those movements to negotiate issues of white privilege, racism, and nationalism.[91] Unlike the Tea Party, then, Occupy sought not to define the boundaries of *peoplehood*, but to open its rhetoric and practices of *peopling* to emerging actors and groups. Sitrin writes of the experiments with popular power unfolding across the globe: "You can't represent us. You can't even imagine us!" Occupiers' own imagination of "the 99 percent" shifted as disparate actors organized behind the same rhetoric; as activists focused on problems they identified as local, national, or global in scope; and as people of color, various community organizations, and Occupiers in cities across the globe disrupted and inflected a populist vision that never had a center to begin with.

Both lacking and eschewing the centralizing forces of today's right-wing resonance machines, Occupiers experimented with resonant practices of collective voice and identification that had both centering and decentering currents. Occupy's use of the people's microphone during general assemblies and public performances exemplifies these practices on the movement's smallest stages. The "people's mic" describes a call-and-response practice of generating and amplifying collective voice: as one person speaks, the audience repeats her words phrase by phrase until they reach the outer edges of the crowd. Occupiers also turned the people's mic into a tactile practice: as audiences carried a speaker's voice collectively, they used hand signals—for example, four fingers up, four fingers down, hands rolling, crossed wrists—to register varying intensities of agreement or dissent. Observers have noted that the "horizontal acoustics" of the people's mic push back against "the rhythms that saturate our day-to-day affairs" in a digitally mediated world.[92] In contrast to our relatively passive, individualistic relationships to mass-mediated communication, the people's mic was an embodied form of media akin to the music of Leonard Cohen: an active liturgical practice of building community. Embodying the people's mic was, for some participants, a "euphoric" and "personally transformative" experience of refashioning oneself as part of a collective.[93] That collective, however, rarely spoke in unison. Speech went through "generational extensions" as it traveled through large crowds, shifting in rhythm and picking up polyvocal inflections.[94] Using hand signals, moreover, participants added their voices to the collective while embodying the dissensus that always exists in a people. In this way, the resonant vibrations of the people's mic were at once synchronic and asynchronous, allowing Occupiers to experience both centering and decentering currents of identification.

Beyond these face-to-face contexts, activists and sympathizers used social media as a platform for building resonances between everyday aspirations and Occupy's symbolic politics. Occupiers made use of Facebook, Twitter, Tumblr, and YouTube; they ran their own websites, blogs, and wikis; some tent cities used Livestream to offer real-time footage of general assemblies and protests. These media enabled core activists and a broad array of sympathizers to share information and stories, retweet and repost images that circulated widely, recruit people and resources for local actions, and post and edit working group documents.[95] Occupy's social media practices not only enhanced their offline repertoire for organizing tent cities and protests; its "open source" ethos helped build broader horizontalist identification and vision. The widespread resonance of the slogan "We are the 99 percent," for example, was due in great part to a Tumblr site that went viral in the early days of Occupy. Thousands of people posted photos of themselves holding handwritten notes that told stories of hardship—lost jobs, backbreaking labor, obscene medical bills, lifetimes of debt, eviction, foreclosure—and asserted identification with the movement: "I am the 99 percent."[96] As people posted their stories, visited the site, and shared links over Twitter and Facebook, Occupy's rhetoric was translated again and again between the distant spectacles of street theater and the everyday stories and aspirations of people who sympathized with the movement. Initially created by an OWS activist and overpopulated by white youth, the site eventually featured the images and stories of working-class people, union members, people of color, immigrants, and people posting in solidarity from beyond the nation's borders. It thus became a visual archive of grievances that were not exactly alike in the quality or extent of subordination—college loan debt, medical bankruptcy, shut-off utilities, joblessness, labor rights violations, and the precarity of living in America without proper documentation—but that could all be traced to the systemic failures of democracy rooted in global capitalism.

Activists also relied on social media to build resonances between Occupy tent cities and popular struggles in cities across the world. Observers and participants often note that Occupy in the United States was inspired by the Arab Spring and by antiausterity protests in Europe. I want to emphasize, however, the ways in which outside actors used social media like Facebook and Twitter to play a direct role in constituting Occupy. When the Canadian magazine *Adbusters* posted the call to occupy Wall Street, it asked, "Are you ready for another Tahrir?" This was not the first time the magazine had connected the Arab Spring to Wall Street. In February 2011, in the early stages of popular revolutions in the Middle East and North Africa, *Adbusters* published a blog titled "A Million Man March on Wall Street: How to Start a People's Revolt in the West." They created the "#OccupyWallStreet" hashtag in July 2011.[97] Activists in the Spanish M-15 movement, often referred to as the *indignados*, were also pivotal in founding and shaping Occupy. In the summer months before OWS, M-15 activists engaged in conversations in their *encampaderos* and over media with American activists about the need to occupy Wall Street; after Occupiers took over Zuccotti Park, M-15 activists were among the most prolific retweeters of news and developments about the US movement.[98] Scholars have also pointed to the circulation of rhetoric, images, and tactics between Occupy, the Arab Spring, M-15, and other antiausterity protests in Europe.[99] To be sure, some Occupiers and their supporters kept their eyes limited to the horizons of the United States or, narrower still, to the daily administration of tent cities. Many activists, however, made a purposeful effort to build resonances between popular struggles against global capitalism and regimes that do not—and can never fully—represent people. Occupy's "foreign founding" and the cross-border constitution of its vision and tactics are among its key departures from the Tea Party, as well as the People's Party and a tradition of American populisms that have primarily imagined the people and democracy in terms of the nation-state.[100] Occupy's efforts to build virtual horizontalist resonances—resonances that were picked up and circulated by mainstream media—opened activists and a broader public to cross-border visions of the people and popular power that will need to be part of struggles to transform democracy.

Occupy's horizontalism, however, was at times a source of closure. As Kreiss and Tufekci argue, Occupiers often "cast the values and form of the movement itself—how it operates and makes decisions—in terms that are synonymous with its very identity and survival."[101] Gitlin similarly notes Occupy's "intense existential affirmation of its communal self, an insistence that what it stood for was the virtue of encampment itself, assembly as a way of life, a form of being."[102] Many Occupiers, in other words, failed to heed Slavoj Žižek's oft-cited warning to a group assembled at Occupy Wall Street: "Don't fall in love with yourselves."[103] In such instances, Occupiers viewed their experiments with horizontal power in identitarian terms, rather than as practices that were themselves open to competing and emergent forms of power. Where this happened, a movement that was disproportionately white, male, upper middle class, and college-educated proved obtuse at engaging people of color, women, queer and working-class people, and other marginalized actors.[104] It remained unaware, moreover, of the ways in which its rhetoric and strategies reinforced rather than ruptured capitalist rhetoric and dynamics of openness, flexibility, and individual expression.

Occupy's whiteness, in particular, caused intense criticism and debate among participants and observers. Whiteness permeated most Occupiers' presumptions about politics: the belief that they had a stake in American democracy to begin with, the assumption that they could assemble in public without immediate state repression, their shock and outrage at seeing police attack "law-abiding" citizens." Whiteness also permeated Occupy's rhetoric (including its central tropes of "occupation" and "the 99 percent"); their priorities (student loan debt, for example, rather than basic primary education); and even their culturally specific forms of protest (from playfulness and spontaneity to consensus-based politics). Many Occupiers failed to appreciate, moreover, the ways in which their visibility obscured decades of organizing by people of color.[105] Given the habituated limits on Occupy's racial imagination, its unbending commitment to horizontalism left it ill equipped to address racial hierarchies from which the movement was not immune. Many people of color, for example, criticized Occupy's general assemblies: consensus decision-making allowed individuals and minorities to block votes but, at least at first, did little to redress the power imbalances that continue to privilege white voices and discourage marginalized actors from speaking up and being heard in public.[106] Critics also developed deep suspicions of the movement's "leaderless" structure. One group, including jaded former Occupiers, published a "Dis-Occupy" statement: "For People Who Have Considered Occupation But Found It Is Not Enuf." Under the heading "Leaderlessness is the new tyranny," the statement called out the "shadow leadership structure" that formed in most tent cities and documented the experiences of people of color who were intimidated or silenced while trying to speak about racism and other forms of privilege.[107] Occupy's refusal to name demands, finally, proved uncompelling to many people of color whose communities, the "Dis-Occupiers" noted, "have long had demands." Among their demands of Occupy were that their "white allies" own up to the "racial privilege that enables their actions" and that the movement "be clear about its goals, intent, and strategies to ensure that our communities . . . can make informed decisions about our participation."[108] The movement's refusal to name demands, that is, did not offer an unguarded sense of openness and potentiality for people who have historically experienced violent restrictions on their power.

Occupy's horizontalist experiments, moreover, were made possible by an uncompromising tactic—occupation—and a polarizing stance: the 99 percent versus the 1 percent. Claims to horizontal popular power are unconvincing, then, without being willing to draw similar lines when it comes to actively addressing racial and other hierarchies within the 99 percent. By highlighting Occupy's shortcomings, I do not mean to discount the people of color and their allies who disrupted Occupy's racial hierarchies and shifted its vision and practices. Working within Occupy's tent cities and in coalition with them, these insurgents organized people-of-color and antiracist working groups in many tent cities; sought Occupiers out to coordinate marches on affordable housing, foreclosure, workers' rights, immigrant rights, indigenous issues, and more; and organized parallel movements, such as Occupy the Hood, *Ocupemos el Barrio*, and Colorful Mamas of Occupy, to address the pressing issues confronting their communities.[109] These activists also enacted one of the Dis-Occupiers' main demands: "that future encampments be organized and led by those who most need them."[110] Whether reclaiming public space, inventing cooperative institutions at the local level, or organizing to transform larger structures of power, this is one of the key demands aspirational democratic populists must confront. In doing so, they must also accept that populist coalition is one of several strategic tactics available to people organizing from the extreme margins of society. Recall the strategic outlook of black Populists and the strains of nihilism and revolution in late-1980s and early-1990s hip-hop. Wary of accommodating an Occupy movement still invested in colonial structures of white citizenship, Dis-Occupiers made decolonization their "starting point" for an array of radical struggles that link racism with capitalist expropriation of land and resources.[111]

A movement that constituted its identity in part through its opposition to today's capitalist social imaginary, Occupy did not, finally, escape reinforcing and even speaking within its terms. It has not gone undiagnosed that the rhetoric of the 99 percent obscures class divisions.[112] In a satire on Occupy Wall Street, the *Daily Show*'s Samantha Bee interviewed residents of the tent city's divided neighborhoods: "on the one side, the elites with their library, Apple pop-up store, and bike-powered espresso machines; on the other, the downwardly mobile with their drum circles." Bee asks one of the "downtown poors": "What percentage of the 99 percent are those Ivy League assholes up there?"[113] By embracing Bee's satire, I do not mean to deny that the slogan "We are the 99 percent" has the potential to mobilize a broad segment of America's populace in a society that has historically demonized traditional forms of "class warfare." This counterhegemonic line of resistance, however, cannot on its own foster the cross-class coalitions necessary to mobilize a broad-based movement of the 99 percent. An incomplete list of the economic interests of the 99 percent might include elite professionals concerned about their investment portfolios and the specter of an end to the Bush-era tax cuts for those making above $250,000; middle-class people worried about job security, retirement funds, and college savings; college graduates eyeing declining job prospects and student loans; white working- and middle-class people filled with ressentiment toward immigrants and low-income people of color; service workers tripling up on minimum-wage jobs to pay rent and keep utilities on; and a racialized precariat who are chronically underemployed, intermittently homeless, undocumented, and more. No appeal to "the people" could ever encompass these interests. Populist movements have, however, adopted coalitional practices that enable marginalized actors to contest and redirect broad-based appeals (such as nineteenth-century Populism's cooperative commonwealth and the New Deal). Contemporary radical democratic populists can learn from these movements, but also need to move beyond their centralizing images of white, masculine America. At the level of rhetorical vision alone, that is, appeals to the 99 percent cannot remain affixed to images of college students and professionals, or even the unions with whom Occupiers formed tense relationships. The 99 percent would also need to appear in images that update producerism for the twenty-first-century service economy: for example, service workers leading the "Fight for 15," working-class Mamas of Color Rising, domestic workers organizing for the Domestic Workers Bill of Rights, and members of the National Day Laborer Organizing Network.

A pluralistic vision of the 99 percent would require coalitional grassroots organizing among multiple power bases, not simple inclusion. As Jodi Dean has argued, finally, Occupy's celebration of participation, plurality, inclusivity, and individual creative engagement resonates deeply with the rhetoric and ideology of neoliberal capitalism. For those who saw in Occupy an opportunity to resist the structural inequalities of capitalism, the movement's least promising quality was its emphasis on self-expression and what Dean calls equality reduced to "equality of utterance."[114] Take, for example, the response of one Occupy activist when asked about repealing the budget cuts that struck New York's public schools: "I hope there are groups of people who are working on that specific issue ... [I'm] prioritizing what I'm most passionate about ... [which is] figuring out how to make theater that's going to help open people up to this new cultural consciousness. It's what I'm driven to do right now, so I'm following that impulse to see where it leads."[115] Or take Chris Garces's insight that the viral call to "Occupy everything!" is a "naïve reversal of the unconscious neoliberal mantra, 'everything should be privatized.'"[116] To be clear, I believe democratization requires the kinds of theatrics that always accompany the emergence of new ideas and actors, and I am sympathetic with the appeal to "the commons" at work in the desire to "Occupy everything!" Both examples, however, suggest an unwillingness to differentiate strategically between issues, tactics, and sites of politicization that have different stakes and impacts in efforts to democratize power and politics. Treating unlike problems—for example, police aggression against Occupy encampments and police brutality in communities of color—as equivalent waters down those grievances most in need of redress. In Dean's words, it views politics as a "multiple-choice menu of issues" not unlike Chevy's "Forrest Gump" ode to Americana. Occupy's less-considered celebrations of horizontal-ism, then, faced co-optation by a neoliberal ideology that sustains its energy by assimilating desires for individual expression.

Experimenting with Horizontality in Occupy and Beyond

I am sympathetic with those who urged Occupy to connect its experiments with horizontalism to more strategic approaches to prioritizing issues, making demands, and working to transform local and larger-scale institutions. To many Occupiers, this will sound like a voice that echoes the interests of the establish-ment or, at least, the myopic vision of those who can't imagine a world beyond the horizons it polices. What I have called horizontality, however, requires not only rupturing horizons that act as closures on collective identity and democracy, but also negotiating and affirming new horizons that can cultivate and sustain more rebellious aspirations to power. Amid the resonant forces and megacirculations of power that fuel global capitalism, radical democratic horizons need structure. Many Occupiers recognized this when they talked about the need to "scale up" their experimental tent cities, which did try to cultivate dispositions, practices, and institutions that could give structure to emerging aspirations.[117] But "scal-ing up" from such experiments will be impossible without scaling out—which means engaging actors, projects, and institutions that currently reinforce the sta-tus quo. Reflecting on Occupy, Naomi Klein observed, "No movement has ever successfully challenged hyper-mobile global capital at its source. So what we're talking about is so new that it's terrifying . . . [You] end up in a situation where you're saying, 'No, I don't want any structure,' or, 'No, I don't want to be making any kind of policy demands or having anything to do with politics,' when really it's that you're just completely scared shitless of the fact that you have no idea how to do this."[118] What Klein isolates here is left anxiety about the paradox of popular sovereignty. If Occupiers, unlike the Tea Party, celebrate the paradox of popular sovereignty as a source of emergent aspirations, they echo a familiar left paralysis in the face of capitalist dynamics that also mock borders.

Occupy's ambivalence about engaging local institutions and larger-scale struc-tures highlights two key limits on its experiments with horizontality. First, as theorists of everyday populism insist, capitalism and the state are not monolithic entities, but rather more or less coordinated accretions of laws, policies, institutions, agencies, agents, flows, and feedback loops that yield variously to radical experimentation and qualitative transformation. Although building alliances and prioritizing projects may limit energies to act in other directions, engaging strategically in these areas does not translate into thoroughgoing foreclosures on the people or democracy. Nor does it necessarily amount to a zero-sum gain or loss of popular power as if popular power were quantitative, that is, either flourishing from the bottom up or incorporated in "the system." As Bayard Rustin reminded black radicals who were wary of engaging the institutions of white supremacy and capitalism: institutions have tremendous influence in shaping our aspirations. Second, then, long-term strategies to revolutionize institutions are crucial not only to level concentrations of income, wealth, and status, but also to open spaces for people to cultivate aspirations to popular power where they do not yet exist. Evaluating Occupy's promise in its early days, Bill Connolly wrote, "It is when local initiatives, larger social movements, church assemblies, blog activity, university teach-ins, and state policies amplify each other that things will start moving."[119] Occupy amplified these feedback loops momentarily though its rhetorical invective, dramatic performances, and cross-border resonances. It lent visibility and shifted the energetics of ongoing work in these areas. To continue to amplify this work, Occupiers would have needed to scale out to engage the array of everyday populists who are reshaping local institutions and repatterning people's dispositions and aspirations to power. By intensifying the feedback loops between these local experiments and Occupy's centralizing, cross-border resonances, Occupiers could have played a greater role in cultivating rebellious aspirations to enact horizontal popular power toward large-scale structural transformations.

Promising crosscurrents did abound where Occupiers made an effort to build relationships with community groups. It is worth evaluating these to kindle the sparks of hope Occupy ignited in America's aspirational democratic populist imaginary. Even before local governments cracked down on Occupy encampments, the movement began to re-envision its relationship to everyday politics in city after city. Taking their cue from the Spanish M-15 movement, Occupy activists formed affinity groups to address an array of local issues in conjunction with community groups.[120] Occupy Boston was at the forefront these efforts. During its occupation of Dewey Square, Occupy Boston held "movement building" meetings with grassroots organizers in the city; in these meetings, activists addressed the tensions over issues and tactics that surfaced between predominantly white, middle-class Occupiers and low-income people of color in Boston.[121] Occupy Boston's eviction, according to activist Jason Stephany, was a blessing in disguise: "Once folks got out of the tedium . . . of needing to protect that space and maintain that space and the things you need to do to run a small city, you know, keeping people fed, keeping it sanitized. People were able to focus on broader issues."[86] After being evicted, Occupiers formed affinity groups that teamed up with community organizations on a host of issues. For example, Occupy's spirited, sustained protests energized an ongoing campaign for banking reform and a campaign by local groups to block public transportation fare hikes and service cuts. Occupiers also teamed up with City Life / Vida Urbana, a veteran group that organizes people of color locally around issues of fair housing, rent control, and foreclosure evictions. City Life also belongs to networks that organize on a larger scale, including the Right to the City affordable housing alliance and the New Bottom Line campaign to restructure Wall Street.[122]

These links intensified the resonances between populist resistance and everyday efforts to constitute popular power. On one end, Occupiers tied their resistance to more rebellious efforts to transform local institutions. In the words of Antonio Ennis of City Life / Vida Urbana, Occupy Boston is "now hooking up with bona fide agencies that know what they want, that know what they're doing and know how to organize and get legislation passed." In Jason Stephany's words, Occupy Boston is providing "new energy" and "new boots on the ground" for local groups "who have been fighting these economic issues for decades now."[123] On the other end, community groups recognized the ways in which Occupy's outrageous resistance energized local efforts. This was not a foregone conclusion. Ilana Berger of New Bottom Line acknowledges, "A lot of [broad-based community organizers] at first were freaked out by Occupy. They said, 'Who are these people? What are they doing? They don't have demands? We've been organizing for years and where were they?' And I say, 'Yeah, we've been organizing for years and look where we are. So let's open it up. Let's bring in some new blood. Let's open ourselves to looking at different ways of doing things.' "[124] Lew Finfer, the lead organizer of Massachusetts Communities Action Network, an affiliate of the PICO National Network, echoes the sentiment of those who saw Occupy as more than a "quixotic" protest movement: "The facts about our lives and who has power in our country and how they use it could make us feel hopeless. But efforts like Occupy Wall Street and Occupy Boston and the determination that average people everywhere still have for a good life for themselves and their families and neighbors means that we are still a generous and hopeful people."[125] Occupy Boston not only energized the rebellious aspirations of local groups, it also had a concrete impact on discourse and policy in Boston. According to then-city councilor Felix Arroyo, when local groups put forward their city banking bill in 2011, it was dismissed as radical. Backed by new talking points and greater reception in the public arena, the bill was loaded with cosponsors by 2012. In September 2013, two years after Occupy, Boston joined other major cities, such as New York, Los Angeles, and San Diego, in passing the "Invest in Boston" bill, which regulates mortgage and small-business lending and measures banks' commitment to community reinvestment. Of these efforts to rein in banks Arroyo says, "Not only do policy makers listen to it more, but the conversation has become more mainstream."[126]

Among the most ambitious efforts to build resonances across the sites, scales, and energetics of populism were coordinated efforts between Occupy groups and the New Bottom Line campaign. The New Bottom Line launched in the summer of 2011, bringing together several prominent organizing networks and alliances, including the PICO National Network (PICO), Right to the City, National People's Action (NPA), and the Alliance for a Just Society. The coalition develops strategies for local and national reforms aimed at "restructuring Wall Street" by reforming government agencies, private banks, and other corporations. They coordinate their resources in campaigns to abolish predatory lending, end mass foreclosures, win debt relief for families, restructure employment markets, require banks to contribute fairly to public revenue, and invest in community-oriented banks and credit unions.[127] New Bottom Line draws on the different strengths of its member organizations—for example, NPA's militant, strategic direct action and PICO's organizing among low-income communities of color—to build what Berger calls "collective narrative power."[128] In other words, New Bottom Line aims to build resonances between centralizing rhetorics of resistance and myriad local and national efforts to constitute popular power. Early on, New Bottom Line organizers recognized the resonances between their work and Occupy. In a blog linked to PICO's Facebook page, PICO organizer Tim Lilienthal wrote, "The protestors on Wall Street—and now in many other cities as well—are helping expose the pain that so many young people (and others) feel about their shrinking economic opportunities. They are putting the pain where it belongs—directly on the doorsteps of the financial industry. They are joining a long line of struggling homeowners, unemployed and underemployed people, clergy and community leaders who have been standing up and making their voices heard. . . . Now we need to make sure that anger translates into action."[129] Berger adds, "It wasn't pixie dust that started Occupy. There was work that had been happening over the last decade that helped build the moment. Clearly the Occupy crew blew it up—in a good way." They were the "spark we were looking for."[130] She describes the months from the fall of 2011 through the spring of 2012 as a "magical moment of collaboration" in many cities between Occupy, unions, and established community groups that partnered with New Bottom Line. For example, New Bottom Line affiliates brought their skill sets to Occupy Our Homes' successful efforts to block foreclosures and help homeless families reclaim their homes. Occupiers, meanwhile, brought energy and publicity to New Bottom Line's "Move Your Money" campaign, which organizes citizens, churches, and other businesses to divest funds from corporate banks.[131]

Consider the language that activists from Occupy Boston, City Life, and New Bottom Line used to describe their resonant relationships: the "long lines" of struggle and decades of "work" by everyday populists; the "sparks" and "new energy" brought by Occupy's outrageous vision; the "movement building" and "restructuring" needed for large-scale revolutions in power; and, finally, the "magical moments" that "blow it up," that is, intensify resonances and amplify "collective narrative power." This language points to the resonant energetics of aspirational democratic populism: the ambitious experiments in horizontality during Occupy generated feedback loops between the ordinary currents of everyday politics, the outrageous sparks of resistance, and the sustained forces needed for longer-term strategic action. Continuing to build these kinds of feedback loops across sites and scales of political life—and this will mean adding tactics of resistance to the repertoires of everyday organizing that goes on between larger public stagings—will be crucial to preparing for and recognizing the next "magical moment." Berger recalls, Occupy "felt like a rare moment when things happen, and [New Bottom Line was] well situated to ride the wave, or help build the wave. It was a back and forth."[132] In other words, Occupy had a recent populist history: in decades of broad-based organizing, in the prounion occupation in Wisconsin, in the spectacular antiglobalization protests in Seattle and the ongoing alter-globalization movement, in translocal struggles for popular power in Europe, the Middle East, and North Africa. In turn, moments of amplification like Occupy open spaces, (re)introduce rhetoric, and cultivate aspirations and visions to enact ambitious local and large-scale reforms.

Magical moments like Occupy may not surface as repeatedly for radical democratic populists as I suspect they will for right-wing populisms that benefit from proximity to well-oiled resonance machines. Aspirational democratic populisms can emerge with greater frequency and durability, however, if they make persistent efforts to build feedback loops between the shifting energetics of enacting popular power. The resonance of aspirational democratic populisms gains durability as oppositional voices link up with myriad efforts to constitute popular power in everyday lives and with sustained, coalitional strategies to reconstitute large-scale structures that now diminish popular power. The threat of co-optation is real when populists engage administrative logics that narrow aspirations and capitalist logics that assimilate and feed off rebellious energies to sustain capitalism's expansion. Populist movements are more likely to succumb to centralizing and expansive forms of power, however, when they *lack* their own embodied sites of decentered popular power. These myriad sites—community groups, local governmental institutions, unions, cooperatives, anarchist cells, alternative media, regional alliances like the New Bottom Line, and so on—harbor the people and resources that can organize to sustain both resistance and longer-term strategic transformations. They also act as nodes of power and contestation that mitigate the dominance of hegemonic visions within populist movements. The resonance of aspirational democratic populisms not only gains durability, then, but also polyvalence as populists form affinities across many kinds of work and struggle, across local and translocal campaigns, and across geographical borders. This was Occupy's most rebellious contribution to America's aspirational democratic populist imaginary, though such cross-border ties will also need to nourish roots in the everyday politics of diverse groups.[133] By combining magical moments of collective identification with what Ethan Miller calls "the largest explosion of practical experimentation our society has ever seen," a diverse array of grass-roots actors, situated in myriad local communities, can play an ongoing role in negotiating and democratizing the horizons of the people and democracy.[134]

Conclusion

Queering the Borders of Populism

Illegal Faggots for the Destruction of Borders!

—Julio Salgado[1]

Queer orientations might be those that don't line up, which by seeing the world "slantwise" allow other objects to come into view.

—Sara Ahmed, Queer Phenomenology

Weeks after the Supreme Court issued its decision in the *United States vs. Windsor*, paving the way for federal recognition of gay marriage, dozens of queer Latin@ and Asian activists "infiltrated" the San Francisco gay pride parade. They staged a "coming out" party, wearing T-shirts that said, "Love Has No Borders," and carrying signs that read, "We Will No Longer Remain in the Shadows" and "Don't Stop at Marriage. Queers Are Getting Deported." They were coming out as undocumented. Organized by the East Bay Immigrant Youth Coalition (EBIYC), the action was one iteration of a broader movement to come out as "Undocumented, Unafraid, and Unapologetic." That movement is being led by undocumented youth, who have proliferated their "coming out" stories over social media, held sit-ins in the offices of elected officials, chartered UndocuBus rides for justice, and organized public performances at security checkpoints and border fences between the United States and Mexico. In part, UndocuQueer names the intersections between undocumented and queer identities, giving voice to young people who, in the words of one EBIYC activist, are "forging a new identity and new understanding of the power that they have as queer people of color and undocumented migrants in this country."[2] In doing so, they are challenging not only dominant discourses of citizenship and belonging in the United

States but also mainstream movements for immigrant rights and LGBTQ rights. In its broader context, I argue, UndocuQueer reflects a radical orientation toward aspirational democratic populism. Invoking the phrase "Ni de aqui, ni de alla," "neither from here, nor from there," undocumented youth are forming insurgent coalitions that are contesting the horizons of the people and democracy and enacting popular power from the extreme margins of society.[3]

Given common associations of populism with a white, masculine, Christian nation—and the struggles of more rebellious populisms, such as Occupy, with questions of race, gender, and sexuality—American populism may seem anything but undocuqueer. I have argued thus far that America's populist imaginary is a condition of populist politics today: populist actors draw upon an internally contested populist imaginary to narrow or open the horizons of democracy—and often do both at the same time. Must aspirational democratic populisms forever be constrained, then, by national horizons that have historically regulated popular aspirations to power?

By examining populism from the extreme margins of today's society, through a movement whose precarity in and across America's borders stems from intersecting lines of legal, racial, gender, and sexual subordination, I make two kinds of arguments. On the one hand, aspirational democratic populisms have always emerged from the margins of society, balancing the demands of achieving legibility with those of experimenting with alternative modes of becoming a people. Every populism is really many populisms, and what we can learn from populism need not be confined to the victor's version of history. To write blacks, immigrants, women, and socialists out of the history of the People's Party, or people of color, feminists, and queers out of Occupy, is to miss crucial elements of both populism and politics from the extreme margins. As I have argued, it reinforces mainstream discourses that obscure populism's more rebellious aspirations to counter hegemonic forms of nationalist and capitalist democracy. It also smothers sparks of hope lit by the most marginalized actors in the United States, who have repeatedly sought to radicalize populist movements as one strategy for revolutionary change. From nineteenth-century immigrant socialists and black Populists, to black militants in the Popular Front of the New Deal era, to radical student activists in the Civil Rights movement, to queer and people of color affinity groups in Occupy: actors at the extreme margins have taken part in broad-based, counterhegemonic movements to reconstitute the people and democracy.

We fall into a familiar trap if we try to distance immigrants, people of color, feminists, and queers from populism—or, if we discount them *as* populists. We reinforce the tendency in democratic theory to treat the most marginalized actors and theorists as voices of the particular—that is, voices who tell us about democracy's exclusions, such as racism, nationalism, sexism, and homophobia—rather than as democratic subjects who also engage in both exclusionary and universalizing forms of politics. This tendency both romanticizes and obscures politics at the margins. It romanticizes the radicalism of marginalized actors, who have historically organized to open the horizons of the people and democracy at specific sites of contestation, while at the same time reproducing other hierarchies along lines of race, class, gender, and/or sexuality. By distancing politics at the margins from the paradoxical realities that limit democratic politics, moreover, we obscure the visions and practices marginalized actors create to negotiate the challenges of cultivating collective identity and popular power. In other words, scholars and activists risk the temptation to overlook crucial visions for transforming democracy.[4]

On the other hand, then, I want to develop a second line of argument in the concluding pages. If UndocuQueer both inherits and reworks a rebellious tradition of aspirational democratic populisms, its efforts to cultivate popular power across national, racial, gender, and sexual borders raise new challenges to the most pernicious constraints that have historically limited populism's democratizing aspirations. By drawing out UndocuQueer's populist resonances, I treat the movement as a limit case for populism: it enables me to stretch my account of aspirational democratic populism to its edges and identify points at which UndocuQueer strains what any theory of populism can add to radical democracy. What I call an "undocuqueer orientation" toward populism unsettles the centering pull of resistance and identification that overdefine populism and intensifies the marginalized and cross-border practices of peopling I emphasize in my accounts of Leonard Cohen's "Democracy," nineteenth-century Populism, and Occupy. UndocuQueer's unapologetic nonconformity and its (dis)oriented practices of peopling, moreover, often make the movement's energetics more hip-hop than Cohen.

As such, UndocuQueer amplifies what aspirational democratic populisms have only recognized in moments: that the people will always be queer, that is, to use Ahmed's term, "slantwise" from itself. Queering the borders of populism invites us to imagine the people *both* through insurgent counterhegemonic claims and through slantwise lines of collective identification and popular power. Restating the paradox of democracy in these terms not only alerts us to the democratic promise that grassroots constituent moments hold for struggles to reconstitute the people and democracy. It also emphasizes the need for populists to cultivate dispositions and practices of peopling that better recognize and respond to those moments—by orienting actors slantwise to the margins of every counterhegemonic populist movement.

If UndocuQueer adds something to theories of populism, what might populism bring to analyses of UndocuQueer? Some readers will understandably resist a move that risks co-opting the rebellious aspirations of a movement led by undocumented queer youth of color. I share that ambivalence. I want to suggest that populism's centering dynamic—that is, its flair for arousing collective identification against a hegemonic order and around a collective vision of democracy—may help us understand the evolving politics of UndocuQueer. Taken together, the centering-decentering dynamic of aspirational democratic populist identification and power may help theorists and activists evaluate a shift in UndocuQueer's focus: from a politics of recognition and inclusion via the DREAM Act to a cross-border, coalitional politics that aims to disrupt and reconstitute the nation-state. This shift has pulled UndocuQueer activists into fraught negotiations between mainstream DREAMers and immigrant rights activists, on one side, and day laborers, queer and transgender detainees, undocumented immigrants with criminal records, and prison abolitionists, on the other. If UndocuQueer decenters populist immigrant organizing from the narrow horizons of belonging to the nation-state, populist vision and practice may at times enhance UndocuQueer's coalitional efforts to enact large-scale structural transformations.

AN UNDOCUQUEER ORIENTATION TOWARD POPULISM

An insurgent coalition of undocumented youth and their allies, UndocuQueer has been at the forefront of youth immigrant organizing since the late-2000s. It emerged during the struggle to pass the Development, Relief, and Education for Alien Minors Act, otherwise known as the DREAM Act, which would open a path to legal permanent residency for approximately 1.9 million undocumented youth who were brought to the United States before the age of sixteen.[5] Introduced at the federal level in 2001, the Dream Act remained stalled in Congress midway through the decade. By that time, undocumented youth were organizing for similar legislation at the state level, with a strong presence in states like Massachusetts, New York, California, and Texas. After the federal DREAM Act failed to pass in 2007, state and local groups proliferated, and were joined by national organizations, such as United We Dream (UWD), the most recognizable face of the DREAMers, and the more radical groups, DreamActivist. org, the National Immigrant Youth Alliance (NIYA), and the Immigrant Youth Justice League (IYJL). Confronted with a Senate filibuster of the DREAM Act in December 2010 and facing an incoming Tea Party Congress in 2011, DREAM activists saw their window for legislative action close. It took another two years of grassroots organizing and escalated direct action for undocumented youth to secure executive action. In June 2012, the Obama administration announced its policy of Deferred Action for Childhood Arrivals (DACA). Under DACA, unauthorized immigrants who meet certain eligibility requirements—related to their age, date of arrival, period of residency, education and/or military service, and criminal record—can request deferred action on deportation along with employment authorization for a period of two years, subject to renewal.[6]

DREAM activists did not stop there. Today, undocumented youth wear shirts that read "Obama Deports Dreamers" and "Deporter in Chief"; they continue to come out as undocumented; they advocate for the release of detainees and put their bodies in front of vehicles carrying those who are being deported; they advocate for amnesty for all eleven million unauthorized immigrants in the United States; they have formed new groups to address issues at the intersection of immigration status, gender, sexuality, race, and class; and they are forming coalitional ties around issues related to immigrant rights, LGBTQ rights, workers' rights, racial justice, and the carceral state. In response to Obama's November 2014 executive order, extending deferred action to parents of US citizens and legal permanent residents, UndocuQueer activists have kept the pressure on.[7] Since 2001, undocumented youth have developed from an unorganized demographic to a nationwide social movement that is challenging the terms of the people and democracy in America.[8] Along the way, activists have experimented with practices of centering and decentering popular identity and power through their cross-border, coalitional politics.

Queer, undocumented youth have been central to the movement's growth and insurgence since 2009. Most visibly, they introduced the tactic of "coming out of the closet" from the LGBTQ movement of the 1970s and 1980s. Since IYJL organized the first National Coming Out of the Shadows Day in 2010, "coming out" as undocumented has been a pivotal strategy to mobilize collective identification and contest the terms of citizenship and belonging in the United States.[9] Activists have gained mainstream media attention for coming out as "Undocumented, Unafraid, and Unapologetic," and at times, as "Undocumented and Unafraid, Queer and Unashamed." They have told their stories over social media, in activity rooms on college campuses, at UndocuMic nights, through visual art, and in myriad creative writing workshops, such as Dreaming in Ink. They have also occupied public stages, translating the practices of coming out from an art of self-expression to a tactic of political escalation. In protests that range from direct action to civil disobedience, undocumented youth have come out during sit-ins at the offices of elected officials, at security checkpoints, at traffic intersections where they have protested the abuse of transgender detainees, in tandem with undocumented day laborers and domestic workers on a highly publicized UndocuBus ride for justice, and in human chains surrounding Immigration and Customs Enforcement (ICE) busses carrying immigrants to be deported.[10]

Queer activists have disproportionately taken leadership roles in groups such as DreamActivist.org and IYJL, and many DREAM activists publically identify as gay, lesbian, queer, transgender, and/or *jot@*.[11] Since DACA, undocuqueer youth have formed their own organizations, such as the Queer Undocumented Immigration Project (QUIP) of UWD and Queer Undocumented Immigrant Rights Dallas (QUIR Dallas), and raised issues of concern to undocuqueer immigrants to the radar of the immigrant rights and LGBTQ movements. More broadly, undocuqeer youth have helped shift DREAM activism away from strategies that perform model citizenship and seek inclusion within the nation-state and toward structural critique—challenging, for example, the capitalist underpinnings of migration, the racial state, the militarization of the border, and a prison-industrial complex that has identified immigrant detention centers as its latest frontier.[12] Invoking Audre Lorde's insight—"There is no such thing as a single-issue struggle because we do not live single-issue lives"—UndocuQueer's intersectional rhetoric and organizing have enabled DREAMers to cultivate more rebellious aspirations to power that contest the horizons of the aspirational democratic populist imaginary.[13]

I use the proper noun *UndocuQueer* to indicate this shift toward radicalism in today's undocumented youth movement, which is now—thanks to the leadership of undocuqueer youth—inseparable from questions of intersectional identity and organizing. I use the term *undocuqueer* in two distinct ways. First, it refers to an identity that has emerged as part of the UndocuQueer movement. When activists talk about their "undocuqueer identities," they often point not only to the intersections of their legal status, gender, and/or sexuality, but often to their ethnicity, their experiences as people who have been racialized in the United States, or their working-class backgrounds.[14] Second, I draw on the work of queer theorists and queer/migration scholars to develop *undocuqueer* as an approach to populist politics. In one register, as Cristina Beltrán has argued, undocuqueer signifies a queer politics of "non-conformist visibility, voice, and protest."[15] By coming out as undocumented—often tied to direct action and civil disobedience—UndocuQueer activists perform symbolic acts of resistance that aim to destabilize and transform rather than seek inclusion within existing social structures. As a style of oppositional politics, moreover, undocuqueer rhetoric and vision arouse collective identification in ways that attend to intersecting identities and experiences of oppression. In another register, undocuqueer suggests an approach to constituting popular power. UndocuQueer's practices of peopling cultivate what Sara Ahmed calls "queer orientations," that is, orientations toward the extreme margins of social life and toward those who do not or cannot conform to dominant norms of identification. We might also, with Karma Chávez, see "queerness" as a "coalitional term"—one that orients actors toward the "intermeshed horizon" of "identity, subjectivity, power, and politics located on the dirt and concrete where people live, work, and play."[16] Chávez's emphasis on the "dirt and concrete" suggests a queer politics that is both on the ground and underground—that is, a coalitional politics that begins in people's everyday experiences and cultivates attunement toward subterranean actors and spaces. In this sense, an undocuqueer approach to popular power exemplifies aspirational democratic populism: it mixes everyday experiments in constituting popular power with contests over both immediate and broader horizons of the people and democracy. At the same time, an undocuqueer orientation entails cultivating senses for attuning oneself to the dirt: to what offends sensibilities, to whom or what society deems disposable.

To elaborate undocuqueer as an approach to populist politics, I want to begin with Ahmed's account of what she calls queer phenomenology. In her words, "Orientations shape not only how we inhabit space, but how we apprehend this world of shared inhabitance, as well as 'who' or 'what' we direct our energy and attention toward. A queer phenomenology, perhaps, might start by redirecting our attention toward different objects, those that are 'less proximate' or even those that deviate or are deviant."[17] Experiencing oneself as disoriented, Ahmed posits, is a condition of possibility of *experiencing* oneself as *being oriented* at all. In most cases, we are not aware that we are oriented: we simply feel at home in the world. Those who are out of place or out of time—for example, because of their queerness, or their experience of migration, or their experience of being racialized or illegalized—may become more aware of practices of orienting. Experiencing disorientation may enable people to perceive (again and again) the ways in which they do not fit in the world they inhabit or to become aware of the disciplinary ways they have been oriented within existing social structures and dynamics. Ahmed harbors hope, however, that queer orientations might point toward new directions: "Queer orientations might be those that don't line up, which by seeing the world 'slantwise' allow other objects to come into view."[18] To cultivate queer orientations to politics, then, is to orient ourselves toward new objects and different others that offer new grounds for collective identification and organizing power.

Disorientation is the ordinary experience of most undocumented youth: though they may have come to the United States as children, they repeatedly confront the borders between belonging and not belonging in America. Migration scholars today talk about borders in ways that do not solely refer to the territorial and often militarized zones between nation-states. More broadly, borders are "contact zones" in a world characterized by radically uneven circulations of capital, resources, bodies, images, and ideas.[19] For immigrants, these contact zones include a complex array of immigration laws, policies, institutions, administrative practices, and agents; these vary further across federal, state, and municipal contexts and across areas of social life. The norms and barriers associated with nationalism, language, race, gender, sexuality, and class add yet another set of contact zones that immigrants must navigate. As many scholars have noted, undocumented youth, in particular, repeatedly find themselves in positions in which, to use Genevieve Negrón-Gonzales' term, they must "broker illegality." In other words, they must navigate the "tension between their juridical identities as undocumented migrants . . . and their subjective identities as US-raised children (an insiderness constituted by growing up in this country)."[20] Undocumented youth thus confront the ambiguities of at once belonging and not belonging, and their disorientation is multiplied along intersecting lines of recognition and disavowal. Some undocuqueer activists have suggested, with Negrón-Gonzales, that it is their experiences of disorientation that "created a platform for political action" in the movement.[21]

The borders at which undocuqueer youth must daily broker belonging, however, present severe restrictions even as they make possible queer orientations. As Ahmed suggests, how we find ourselves oriented in a given time and place is "shaped by other social orientations, such as gender and class, that affect 'what' comes into view, but also are not simply given, as they are effects of the repetitions of actions over time." As I have discussed in relation to the concept of habitus, orientation "takes shape through repeated and habitual actions" that are themselves the result of disciplinary regimes of the normal. Likewise, "Disorientation is unevenly distributed: some bodies more than others have their involvement in the world thrown into crisis."[22] The experience of repeated disorientation is all too likely to lead to cynicism or even ressentiment rather than to stir rebellious aspirations.[23] I want to suggest that UndocuQueer youth—that is, those who are engaged in the movement—have not weathered their experiences of disorientation passively. Neither have they romanticized it. Rather, their activism politicizes the transformative potentialities—the disorienting and reorienting qualities—of undocuqueer orientation.

Giving voice to myriad experiences of disorientation, UndocuQueer's nonconformist rhetoric of peopling reorients participants *against* the nation-state (insofar as it perpetuates regimes of illegalization and subordination based on gender, sexuality, and race) and *toward* collective identification at multiple intersections of shared critique and vision. The movement's queer, intersectional practices of peopling simultaneously orient participants toward organizing with those who are "least proximate" in America's social imagination. In this way UndocuQueer's rhetoric and practices of peopling generate centering-decentering dynamics that accent the extreme margins and the unstable center of collective identification and popular power. At times, seeing slantwise might facilitate the "unsystematized lines of acquaintance" that have historically stretched populist identification to its limits: for example, in nineteenth-century practices of public enthusiasm that collapsed the boundaries between self and other among rural, urban, Anglo-Saxon, immigrant, and black Populists. This elasticity at Populism's internal borders, in turn, energized the counterhegemonic politics of the People's Party. At times, however, seeing slantwise might strain populist identification and power to the breaking point. Seeing slantwise from Occupy, for example, reinforced pessimism about the movement's whiteness and led many activists to build solidarities in local communities of color or with abolitionist and decolonization struggles. An undocuqueer orientation, then, shifts populism toward practices of belonging-with disparate others who enact the uncertain promise of democracy. It does not, however, ensure that such enactments will always reorient themselves toward the same, or any, counterhegemonic project. Seeing slantwise might instead lead coalitional actors to enact rhizomatic performative disruptions, split off into autonomist communities, practice the arts of "not being governed," or mobilize revolution from the extreme margins.[24] In other words, an undocuqueer orientation might at times shift populist vision and practice to the background of a movement's strategy and action.

"SEEING THE WORLD 'SLANTWISE'": UNDOCUQUEER'S COALITIONAL RHETORIC AND POWER

As a movement from the extreme margins of society, UndocuQueer contests regimes of illegality and deportation that reflect the ties between neoliberal capitalism, America's militarized surveillance state, and the continued policing of national identity along lines of race, gender, sexuality, and class. Illegality is a legal construct that is produced and enforced through shifting laws, policies, and discourses. It marks unauthorized immigrants' absent presence in American life: on one end, to be marked "illegal" is to lack employment authorization, labor rights and protections, access to public services, and mobility; on the other, the discourse of illegality warns citizens that "illegal aliens" (associated with crime waves, terrorism, and disease) pose a national threat that justifies state surveillance and deportation.[25] As Nathalie Peutz and Nicholas De Genova have argued, deportation is a technique through which the state performs—that is, both exerts and makes a spectacle of—its sovereignty over the nation and its subjects. Such shows of state sovereignty are common at a time when capitalist production logics structure global patterns of labor and migration and weaken states' control over their space, resources, and populations. Through deportation laws and policies, the state maintains a degree of control by regulating desirable and undesirable members of the polity. The deportation regime operates via legalized discriminations that define exclusion based on race (priority targets for deportation include racially coded categories of criminals and gang members), class (economic self-sufficiency is a requirement for deferred action and permanent legal residency), and gender and sexuality (queers and women have often been denied admission due to "deviant" status).[26] In the United States, the deportation regime also operates via lucrative contracts to companies that militarize the border, enhance state surveillance, and proliferate and manage immigrant detention centers.[27]

"Undocumented, Unafraid, and Unapologetic": Nonconformist Rhetoric and Visibility

In this context, coming out as undocumented is a rhetorical act of peopling that has the potential to expose the layered paradox of peoplehood and law in America. Through iterations of the phrase "I am an undocumented American," undocumented youth politicize their status as what Mai Ngai refers to as "impossible subjects." To be both "undocumented" and "American" is a contradiction in terms in the legal discourse of citizenship and in the dominant American social imaginary. UndocuQueer youth are thus "person(s) who cannot be and a problem that cannot be solved" without contesting the boundaries of the people and democracy in the United States.[28] By coming out en masse, UndocuQueer activists destabilize the terms of belonging and citizenship in the nation-state and assert their membership in a political community that does not yet exist—one that, moreover, they imagine themselves cocreating through their struggles.[29] Much like prior populist moments, such acts of destabilization and cocreation reflect varying aspirations to popular power: from legal inclusion within a broadened category of liberal citizenship to more fundamental disputes over the constructs of illegality that undergird the deportation regime to pessimism about populism's ability to speak from the extreme margins.

Early DREAM Act advocacy sought recognition and inclusion within the liberal nation-state. DREAMers' rhetoric—including many of their "coming out" stories—hewed closely to the image of the "model immigrant" depicted in the DREAM Act. That model immigrant exemplified the ideals of education and patriotism (as evident in their completion of a two-year college degree or their military service); their respect for the rule of law was evident in the fact that they had crossed the border before the age of consent and had not amassed criminal records. In this way, DREAMers leveraged their relative status and privilege in comparison with other undocumented immigrants. DREAMers and UndocuQueer activists typically speak English and, in some cases, it is their primary language. Having grown up in the United States, they are often fluent in the nation's cultural norms and practices. Many have some experience with higher education or even college degrees. When DREAMers began coming out as undocumented, their tactics reflected their status. They spoke of America as the land of opportunity and sprinkled their narratives with images of how hard they work and study to achieve their dreams. When they came out defiantly in acts of civil disobedience, they wore graduation caps and gowns.[30]

Such tactics certainly challenge which subjects can claim the rights and protections of citizenship in America, as well as how citizens are expected to enact their power vis-à-vis state institutions and procedures. In this respect, DREAM activism resonates with nineteenth-century black Populists and immigrant laborers who relied on strikes to demand state protection from what was often state-sanctioned violence in workplaces and in public. By seeking recognition, however, DREAMers confine their aspirations to the terms of liberal citizenship. This, in turn, is how scholars and policymakers are likely to perceive their movement. One recent study, *Living the Dream*, draws on interviews with one hundred undocumented youth to argue that passing the DREAM Act is necessary for "the United States to stay true to our founding ideals and move toward the goal of becoming a successful ethnoracial democracy." Reinforcing this vision of liberal nationalism, the authors argue that DREAMers' desire "to pursue the American Dream" and "aspire to be fully incorporated into the fabric of the United States . . . economically, socially, and politically."[31] Speaking within the terms of the DREAM Act thus risks reinforcing exclusionary norms of liberal citizenship and leaving the prerogatives of state sovereignty intact. In other words, it closes the paradox laden in the claim "I am an undocumented American," and largely reproduces the image of the model immigrant celebrated in Chevy's "Milestones."

Since 2010 and especially since the implementation of DACA in 2012, UndocuQueer activists have increasingly refused to settle for legal recognition. In the struggle to become "DACAmented," notes organizer and scholar Tania Carrasco, activists recognized that "as advocates and communities emphasize the right of some to remain within, they also define who gets left out, marginalized, criminalized, and deported."[32] As a result, activists began to look "slantwise" toward those whom they were leaving behind: parents who *had* crossed the border by their own reason, friends who could not afford college or who faced the disciplinary arm of the law, and parts of their own identities that deviated from the American dream. In doing so, a segment of the undocumented youth movement has recommitted itself to deepening the paradox of "impossible subjectivity" that remains marked on their bodies at intersecting lines of immigration status, race, gender, sexuality, class, and more. Like the early Populists who kept their eyes attuned to the "cranks, tramps, and vagabonds" of their day, UndocuQueer activists have directed their nonconformist rhetoric toward troubling the line between "good" and "bad" immigrants. In one register, undocumented youth have played a leadership role, along with the National Day Laborer Organizing Network (NDLON), in moving the larger immigrant rights movement toward a shared counterhegemonic line. Behind slogans such as "Not One More Deportation" and "We are ALL 100 percent Deserving," they advocate for deferred action and

amnesty for all undocumented immigrants.³³ In other registers, UndocuQueer
activists have kept *that* line veering slantwise too. They orient their organizing
toward those who are most "deviant" in America's social imaginary, even as their
movement from the margins transforms the center.

A popular poster titled *La Dreamer* exemplifies the ways in which UndocuQueer
youth are beginning to challenge liberal norms of white, bourgeois, gendered
citizenship. Created by artist and musician Nico Shortee, *La Dreamer* depicts a
Latina dressed in the *chola* style associated with urban Latin@ hip-hop culture
and carrying a copy of Gloria Anzaldúa's *Borderlands / La Frontera*.³⁴ Anzaldúa is
a hero for many movement activists. UndocuQueer art and narrative increasingly
mirror her unapologetic approach to asserting citizenship: refusing to whitewash
racial and cultural identity, mixing English with non-English, and showcasing
gender and sexual nonconformity.³⁵ Likewise, many UndocuQueer activists have
dropped their caps and gowns in their public actions. When two NIYA activists
staged and filmed their arrest by an Immigration Customs Enforcement (ICE)
officer in Alabama in 2011, mainstream DREAMers criticized them for not being
"formal" or "articulate." "Why should I try to impress homeland security," one
responded. "I'm trying to get detained not a fucking scholarship . . . why should
I change the way I speak. I'm from [a Latin American country] raised in the . . .
projects in East LA. *I'm a hood and proud of it. . . . I do not believe that I should be
the "good Immigrant.". . . . to get respect and dignity.* We need to be college gradu-
ates with no criminal record to be American."³⁶ The NIYA activists were looking to dramatize skyrocketing rates of deportation and conditions in detention
centers. Their demands for "respect and dignity," however, did not depend on
their willingness to reinforce myths of the "good immigrant" as a "model minority" or "supercitizen." These myths not only stigmatize "bad immigrants," they
also blame other impoverished, nonwhite citizens for their failure to live the
American dream.³⁷ In this respect, UndocuQueer's rhetoric of peopling often
aims at a broader reconstitution of the people, one that also contests the historical limits of America's aspirational democratic populist imaginary.

We might think of *La Dreamer* and the NIYA action as "spoofs" on the American
dream, much like the YouTube videos that parody Chevy's English-language
ad "Anthem." UndocuQueer rhetoric and artistic expression often rely on spirited humor and dissonance to trouble the myth of the American dream. Julio
Salgado's ubiquitous "I am UndocuQueer" posters, for example, celebrated the
deviance and defiance of undocumented youth activists in the lead-up to DACA.
Set against bright colors, the posters depict images of activists and their messages of mobilization. "I am an undocuqueer mujer!" claims Lucina in one poster,
mixing English and Spanish. "Let your light shine. El mundo nos necesita!!" In
another, Alex says, "I am undocuqueer. An inspiring hue of identities. Embracing
my struggle, empowering la joteria, enamoring my passions: Out of the closet(s),

Out of the shadows!"[38] Like the offbeat cast in Cohen's "Democracy," these activists bring their dreams to America in cross-border, "amorous array."[39] In doing so, they defy and disrupt the disciplinary norms of the American dream.

Salgado's art expresses the myriad lines of deviance from the norm in a movement that is multiethnic, multiracial, LGBTQ, straight, and reflective of a range of class and educational backgrounds. One poster depicts immigrant laborers—migrant farmers, construction workers, food service workers, domestic workers, and a seamstress sewing an American flag—who appear to hail from Latin America, Africa, the Middle East, East Asia, and the Pacific Islands. The immigrants are framed by an outline of the map of the United States, which is held up or supported by a brown hand. Text on the hand reads, "Migrant Power," and text outside the map demands, "Who are you calling low-skilled?" The poster challenges the tendency in the United States to associate undocumented immigration with Latin America and to stereotype migrant and undocumented laborers as low skilled or lazy. On his website, Salgado explains, "It takes a lot of skills to work in the fields. To serve entitled people their food. To make your clothes. To take yo' shit. And all the while trying to keep our sanity. That's some skills."[40]

In this light, Salgado's poster updates familiar populist appeals to producerism in the context of today's low-wage labor force, which has expanded into the service economy and involves cross-border, multiethnic, and multiracial workers. The label, "migrant power," paints the producers and servers of today's political society in nonwhite terms, and emphasizes that they provide not only the manual labor but, increasingly, the affective labor—of "tak[ing] yo shit"—that keeps the fantasy of the American dream alive.[41] That this image challenges not only nineteenth-century producerism and today's right-wing variants is evident in another of Salgado's posters: Minhaz, a writer "in an ambiguous state of 'legality," mocks his peers: "You went to an Occupy protest because you have a bachelor's and can't find a job? My parents had masters and worked at gas stations. We are the 0%."[42] That poster is part of Salgado's "Undocumented Apparel" series, in which he takes the popular hipster brand American Apparel to task for its forays into "hip consumerism" with a T-shirt that reads "Legalize LA." Another poster in the series features Luis, who says, "Nice 'Legalize L.A.' t-shirt. But I'd rather walk into an Immigration and Customs Enforcement office and declare my undocumented status."[43] In this series, Salgado conveys the intersecting issues of illegality, unprotected labor, and class that largely remain invisible in the United States—even to the activists behind the 99 percent—and that challenge even the rebellious dreams of Occupy.

UndocuQueer's orientation toward deviance is evident in its organizing at the "contact zones" of intersecting lines of oppression. One youth dramatized the situation of many queer, undocumented people in his coming-out narrative: "My mom often says, 'why stay here, just go back home and we will figure something out?' Of course, she doesn't know that I also happen to be gay and so returning home to a country that has publicly killed people for being gay is just NOT an option."[44] Many campaigns draw attention to the hardships LGBTQ immigrants confront in the United States. Groups such as QUIP and Familia: Trans Queer Liberation Organization, for example, address issues facing transgender immigrants. Transgender people are stigmatized in immigration law if they engage in sex work; they are less likely to qualify for deferred action granted to parents of US citizens or permanent residents; they suffer disproportionately from abuse in detention centers; and they face deadly violence on America's streets. UndocuQueer organizing on these issues has echoed broadly, reaching the larger immigrant rights and LGBTQ communities, racial justice advocates, and even mainstream media.[45] Activists thus challenge not only stigma and oversights in deportation laws tied to gender and sexuality—an issue at the extreme periphery of today's immigration debates. They also challenge the heteronormative assumptions of mainstream immigrant rights and racial justice groups and the vision of a mainstream LGBTQ movement that is largely American and homonormative (that is, oriented toward inclusion in the liberal nation-state).[46] This illustrates the multiform character of UndocuQueer's vision and strategy. In part, groups such as QUIP and Familia play a role akin to black Populists and suffragettes vis-à-vis the People's Party or people of color, feminist, and queer affinity groups vis-à-vis Occupy: they engage strategically in coalition with DREAMers and mainstream immigrant rights activists to radicalize a broader counterhegemonic movement. In part, having emerged slantwise from the undocumented youth movement, queer and trans immigrants of color are creating radical counterpublics that also dream in divergent directions, for example, toward cross-racial genderqueer practices of love.[47]

UndocuQueer activists are radicalizing the broader antideportation movement in ways that extend beyond gender and sexuality, most notably, by organizing against the racist and capitalist underpinnings of mass detention and incarceration.[48] Salgado identifies the capitalist logics that drive both labor and migration patterns and the US deportation regime: "The industrial complex . . . the fact that people who are just trying to feed their families are in detention. It's jail. And people are making money off that. Corporations are benefiting. It's horrible."[49] In his movement art, Salgado increasingly exposes the racist aspects of detention. One poster of three white youth behind bars reads, "Imagine the American outrage if the undocumented kids currently locked up in detention centers looked like this." A poster of Elvira, a woman held in detention, demands, "Stop gang injunctions, police surveillance, racial profiling and Free Elvira Now!"[50] IYJL, which advocates on behalf of individuals facing deportation, has begun to defend youth and adults who carry criminal charges (including identity theft, leaving the scene of an accident, driving under the influence, domestic violence, and gang involvement). In doing so, Carrasco argues, they are "pushing at the boundaries of US citizenship and belonging to include more working class and poor immigrants of color."[51] Paralleling the organizing structure of Cohen's "Democracy," IYJL iterates a central promise of democracy in America—in this case, the presumption of innocence historically reserved for white men—through the voices of undocumented subjects who deviate from the norm.

In April 2012, IYJL joined over two dozen organizations to hold a forum called "Forced Out: A Unity at the Crossroads of Deportation and Incarceration." Partner organizations included immigrant rights groups, prison reformers and abolitionists, antiviolence activists, education advocates, and unions. Activist José Guadalupe Herrera Sota appealed to the audience to "think about the detention and deportation of immigrants as part of the prison industrial complex." In a radical twist on "coming out" as undocumented, he told the forum, "This system was build [sic] for the purpose of profiting out of the criminalization, illegalization, racialization, incarceration, and deportation of human beings. ... I have been labeled a criminal; therefore I stand up and join the struggle of those who are labeled criminals. I join the struggle of fellow human beings who are struggling to survive under the racist capitalist system we live in. I join the struggle of the marginalized, of the poor, of people of color." Herrera Sota directly challenges the limits of DREAM activism: he insists that he wants to be part of a "struggle that fights for all people—not just for a small few who are portrayed as being worthy." He calls for "the abolition of detention centers, prisons, and the capitalist system." By appealing to an audience of both radical and mainstream groups, he hopes to radicalize both prison reform and immigrant rights movements that are contesting the boundaries of citizenship. At the same time, Herrera Sota refuses to affirm "citizenship" as his dream: he aligns himself with "the criminals, the illegal aliens" and indicates that he "will continue to fight and make alliances" with those who see that full abolition, not deferred action or comprehensive immigration reform, is the only way to achieve justice.[52] Looking slantwise thus aligns Herrera Sota with black radicals from W. E. B. Du Bois to Chuck D. He distrusts populist strategies that appeal to normative sensibilities and aim for legibility, and instead imagines revolution against capitalism and the racial state from the extreme margins.

In coming out as undocumented, then, UndocuQueer activists are disrupting normative visions of belonging and orienting their movement toward and around multilayered structural critique and transformation. In doing so, they are troubling the easy lines of center/margins, dominant/deviant, and privilege/precarity that often define politics at the margins and limit the vision of counterhegemonic claims. To be sure, organizers still rely on messages that aim for mainstream legibility.[53] In helping radicalize the immigrant rights movement's current counterhegemonic line—Not One More Deportation—UndocuQueer activists appeal to national values ("Keep Our Families Together") and to Obama as the head of state ("Stop Deportations: Yes You Can").[54] In other iterations, however, UndocuQueer's rhetoric of peopling orients the movement away from the nation-state as the sole or even central locus of collective identification and toward those who deviate from the norm. UndocuQueer's ability to sustain its orientations toward the center and the extreme margins without assimilating to the former or splitting off at the latter is remarkable in contrast to nineteenth-century Populism and Occupy. Part of the contrast is due to the social position of UndocuQueer activists, who organize at the margins of the undocumented youth and mainstream immigrant rights movement, just as blacks, immigrants, and women organized at the margins of Populism and Occupy. As subjects who limn multiple lines of belonging and not belonging in the United States, moreover, UndocuQueer youth are well positioned both to contest and radicalize the horizons of the people and democracy.

In and Out of the Shadows:
Embodied Counterpublics and Undocuqueer Orientations

Proximity to the paradox of democracy, however, does not inevitably translate into democratic vision or action. I want to suggest that the movement's undocuqueer orientation is also due to activists' success in linking their nonconformist rhetoric and visibility to the creation of overlapping radical counterpublics. As Kathy Ferguson has argued, counterpublics are best understood by considering the rhetorical and discursive practices of media and performativity in tandem with the embodied spaces of material and institutional life. In this way, we can see how everyday practices of cultivating alternative habitus—or, in Ahmed's terms, orientations—work together with the world-making practices of narrative, rhetoric, and action to contest social imaginaries.[55] Since 2009, UndocuQueer youth have cultivated counterpublic spaces by building relays between the rhetorical and spectacular politics of collective action I have sketched, the narrative practices of social media, and the institutions and practices of grassroots organizing.

UndocuQueer activists are often tech savvy and leverage their digital literacy in online organizing. Activists rely on social media, as well as print and other media, to communicate information, foster collective identification, and mobilize participation. A variety of social media platforms and open-source sites—including Facebook, Twitter, Tumblr, microblogs, discussion forums, YouTube, and Vimeo—invite a broad base to take part in making media and constructing movement narratives. National and local groups connect to each other regularly over social media by sharing or retweeting images and posts. People with varying levels of participation in the movement rely on these sites to share and view coming out testimonies; circulate information, news, and movement art; and discuss vision and strategy. Users can even participate virtually in actions that are streamed over Livestream.com or recorded and shared.[56]

Scholars have analyzed the undocumented youth movement's sophisticated use of social media, and especially the practice of coming out, or *testimonio*, to explain how movement actors have generated the narrative and affective dimensions of collective identification. They point to the power of stories in fostering feelings of trust, solidarity, and commitment, as well as implicit norms and a shared sense of purpose.[57] We might view coming out as a practice of what Marshall Ganz calls "public narrative." Ganz, who started out as an organizer with the United Farmworkers movement and later led Obama's grassroots ground game in 2008, has worked directly with UndocuQueer youth. They use his ideas at their activist trainings, workshops, conference calls, webinars, and so on.[58] To think of coming-out stories as public narratives is to see them as what Ganz calls stories of "self, us, and now," that is, stories that tie biography to collective identification in the context of concrete actions and imagined futures. While early coming-out stories reinforced the American dream, UndocuQueer activists have since drawn on their diverse cultural backgrounds to fan the spark of hope in less familiar populist and radical inheritances: they find resources in the black freedom movement and the Chican@ movement, among queer feminists of color, and in early LGBTQ and HIV/AIDS activism.[59] Circulating public narratives online (as well as in face-to-face settings) enabled UndocuQueer activists to pluralize their imagination of the movement and to shape movement narratives that contested both DREAM activism and the considerable influence of mainstream immigrant rights groups.[60]

UndocuQueer activists also use social media to negotiate stereotypes and hierarchies within the undocumented youth movement. One of the best-organized examples of such activism is Dreamers Adrift, an online "creative project ABOUT undocumented youth, BY undocumented youth, and FOR undocumented youth."[61] Dreamers Adrift organizers post blogs, share writing, and produce dozens of short videos, ranging from video blogs to skits to documentaries of their officially undocumented lives. Skits in the series "Undocumented and Awkward," for example, are montages that mix mundane scenes from daily life, routine encounters with the challenges of being undocumented, social critique and aspirations, and humor that ranges from playful to ironic to uncomfortable. Aiming, as the title suggests, for dissonance, the videos at times tackle inequalities and assumptions that undocumented youth reinforce within their diverse movement.

In one skit, two college-age undocumented Latin@ friends complain, in Spanish, about the young Chinese man standing next to them at a bus stop. "Since when do *chinitos* ride the bus?" one asks. He adds that he "finds it so annoying that folks here who have proper documentation and a license" choose to ride the bus instead of driving. "I bet he's got a car at home but just doesn't want to pay for gas," the other ads. "Stingy people," the first concludes. When the two friends ask the Chinese man if he has the time, he responds, "Sí, son las doce de la tarde." It turns out that the man not only speaks Spanish but is also undocumented and, as a result, cannot get a license. "You're undocumented and from China," asks one of the two friends? "No, from Peru," the Chinese man responds, challenging assumptions about his nationality in addition to his language, class mobility, and immigration status.[62] Videos also tackle hierarchies of sexuality and gender. In one, several undocumented youth—mostly women—have just spent two hours planning an event when a gay male activist, Julio, arrives and immediately criticizes their ideas. A few minutes later, another male organizer arrives, and Julio updates him on the plans. "Great idea, Julio," he exclaims. "Wow, I am all smiles right now." "I like to think outside the box," Julio responds. As Julio flexes his queer masculinity, the skit ends with the refrain "Awkward," and viewers are left to reflect on the uneven hierarchies of sexuality and gender in organizing.[63]

By dramatizing their own intersecting lines of difference and privilege, UndocuQueer activists help orient the movement's narrative toward what Ahmed calls "bodies that have been made unreachable by the lines of conventional genealogy."[64] In addition to the self-parodies of Dreamers Adrift, recall the art and public narratives that contested and changed the terms of early DREAM activism: Shortee's unapologetic La Dreamer, Herrera Sota's appropriation of "criminality," and Salgado's "I am UndocuQueer" posters, which announced identification variably with "undocuqueer mujer[s]," "undocumented jota[s]," people in and from Mexico, queer Latinas, anyone "coming out of the shadowy closet," and so on.[65] Partly, as I have suggested, such rhetoric and art are directed toward more mainstream audiences: contra Chevy's assimilationist representation of Latinos in "Milestones," for example, UndocuQueer's "spoofs" on the American dream dramatize queer, undocumented youth of color enacting unruly forms of citizenship. Partly, however, such stories and images are directed to other movement activists and help constitute overlapping radical counterpublic sites of identification. By negotiating intersecting experiences and struggles, coming out can thus be what Chávez calls a "coalitional gesture" toward slantwise lines of collective identification and action.[66] Like Cohen's "Democracy," but more strategically, UndocuQueer's rhetoric and practices of peopling might create resonances that reveal rather than obscure differences. As they pluralize history and identity in their public narratives and social media, UndocuQueer activists multiply the contact zones at which they can enact coalitional experiments in constituting popular power.

In contrast to Occupy, UndocuQueer's public performances and social media practices have always coexisted with the movement's extensive grassroots organizing and coalition building. In the lead up to the 2010 congressional vote on the DREAM Act, undocumented youth began to break away from the mainstream immigrant rights movement and build their own insurgent grassroots movement.[67] It was in this period that DreamActivist.org, IYJL, and NIYA drove the campaign to come out over social media and in public. After the DREAM Act failed in 2010, undocumented youth began to build new institutions and radicalize old ones: for example, the DREAM Teams that made up the California Dream Network claimed more autonomy and took more insurgent positions. Walter Nicholls, who chronicles this transition in *The DREAMers*, argues that the post-2010 undocumented youth movement has developed a bottom-up, decentralized infrastructure. The movement now comprises small organizations with a variety of missions situated in cities and on college campuses across the country. They build ties with and draw resources from local immigrant groups, local progressive associations, churches, college administrations, and so on. More prominent undocumented youth groups, such as DREAM Team Los Angeles, act as hubs circulating resources to other groups at local, state, and national scales. Without this infrastructure, Nicholls argues, the radical undocumented youth movement "would have shared the same fate as Occupy: after a series of highly visible and disruptive acts of civil disobedience, they would have dissipated into a political afterthought."[68] Instead, undocumented youth have been able to maintain autonomy from mainstream immigrant rights groups in strategy and message, while coordinating with them and with peripheral groups toward small victories and larger-scale structural changes in America's deportation regime.

While I don't share Nicholls's dismissive view of Occupy, I do share his appreciation for the remarkable grassroots organizing that has enabled the UndocuQueer movement to survive and flourish after defeat and, perhaps more importantly, after the small victory of DACA. The lure of small victories can encourage populist assimilation, and this prospect contributed to Occupiers' anxieties about engaging state institutions and building coalitions with mainstream groups. UndocuQueer activists, however, have radicalized their vision through coalitional engagements around an array of concrete issues. In their organizing with the Not One More campaign for example, UndocuQueer activists joined mainstream groups in celebrating Obama's 2014 executive order extending deferred action to parents of US citizens and permanent residents. This did not stop activists from issuing scathing rebukes of a policy that enhances border securitization and interior surveillance, reinforces discourses of criminalization, and does little to help many of UndocuQueer's coalitional allies: over six million day laborers, domestic workers, queer and trans people, and people with criminal records.[69] Nor did UndocuQueer's counterhegemonic coalitions prevent it from building coalitions in slantwise directions on concrete issues such as the rights of queer and transgender detainees and prison divestment.

UndocuQueer's coalitional politics illustrate Chávez's insight that coalitions form at "horizons" where "two seemingly different things merge and remain separate." In practice, coalitional actors often have difficulty sustaining the intensities of their engagements without either merging or separating. On one end, groups often merge until they "incorporat[e] into one body," as Chevy does by creating equivalence between disparate images in its montage of "Our Country," or as the People's Party did by adopting the image of William Jennings Bryan.[70] This has also historically been a threat for mainstream immigrant rights groups that seek inclusion within the body politic, as well as for radical movements from the margins that obscure their internal differences. On the other end, coalitions may fragment as groups confront the tensions at every contact zone or horizon. As musician and activist Bernice Johnson Reagan insists, "Coalition work is not work done in your home . . . [I]t is some of the most dangerous work you can do. You shouldn't look for comfort."[71] The tenuous coalitions of the black freedom struggle in the sixties, for example, were never comfortable work; as external shocks and differences in organizing philosophy intensified in the late 1960s and early 1970s, a broad-based coalitional movement gave way to fissures between Civil Rights and Black Power and between black radical youth and the largely white base of New Left groups such as Students for a Democratic Society.

UndocuQueer's "bottom-up, decentralized infrastructure" has enabled it to sustain a coalitional politics that more nearly resembles a mash-up of Cohen's "Democracy." Grassroots UndocuQueer groups form coalitions across multiple sites and scales in their effort to promise democracy beyond the deportation regime: coalescing their energies with mainstream groups to resist federal deportation policies, but also with queer, trans, and abolitionist groups to work in different directions. There is a madness to their method. Having sustained their commitment to counterhegemonic organizing for over a decade, undocumented youth activists have come to see that abolishing the deportation regime may also require coalitional work that veers off from and at times takes priority over whatever defines immigration politics in a given moment. At times, UndocuQueer has radicalized the center by moving slantwise, as it did with disruptive coming-out tactics that transformed DREAM activism and with "declaration[s] of independence" from comprehensive immigration reform that helped propel Not One More Deportation to the center of the immigrant rights movement.[72] In other instances, UndocuQueer activists have oriented their coalitional work toward smaller-scale or subterranean contact zones. In these layers of negotiation, undocumented youth transform the qualitative character of the contact zones that condition their everyday lives in the United States and their political organizing. As they organize to lessen the force of contact zones that violently disorient them, they create durable institutions and coalitions for constituting popular power at those contact zones that enable them to flourish. They have reinforced a vital contact zone by creating institutions around issues that confront queer, undocumented youth; they have disaggregated the institutions and laws of the state to advocate for undocuqueer healthcare and the rights of transgender detainees; they have built abolitionist coalitions; and they have introduced deviant images and narratives that become ubiquitous touch points for calling forth new iterations and new participants.[73] Work at these contact zones will not inevitably reorient toward an existing counterhegemonic line, even to radicalize it. Like hip-hop, UndocuQueer activists also celebrate deviance for its own sake. Recalling Chuck D's riff on Cohen: "To revolutionize make a change nothing's strange."[74]

UndocuQueer's relays between rhetorical acts of nonconformist visibility, narrative practices of social media, and everyday practices of grassroots organizing have been key to cultivating the durable dispositions of an undocuqueer orientation toward populism. This orientation has enabled activists to sustain their remarkable intensities of centering and decentering popular identification and power. On one end, movement activists generate dispositions that enable them to amplify nonconformist visibility and voice in a public sphere organized to render undocumented immigrants, people of color, and nonnormative queer people imperceptible and silent. As Carrasco puts it, "Participating in civil disobedience . . . is about owning the risk of deportation with the knowledge that we can challenge deportability."[75] Owning that risk, however, has only been possible for activists on the front lines because of their efforts to cultivate durable, embodied counterpublic spaces and practices: for example, the emboldening experiences of coming out online; collective narratives of resistance that "cast silence as the dangerous choice"; and a decade plus of grassroots organizing through which undocumented youth have built "political clout" and "solid political alliances."[76]

UndocuQueer activists are not only coming out of the shadows. On the other end, they are cultivating dispositions that enable them to inhabit the shadows and navigate the contact zones of the deportation regime. The long-standing and familiar rhetoric that casts undocumented immigrants as a "shadow population" has a dual directionality: it suggests both *living in the shadows* of illegality and America's deportation regime and *being the shadows* (in the sense of racialized images of criminality and "stranger-danger").[77] By reclaiming the aspects of their identities that deviate from the norm and organizing in proximity to the darkest shadows of the deportation regime—that is, undocumented immigrants who are deemed most deportable or who await deportation in the most hidden spaces in America—activists are developing a "slantwise" sixth sense toward people who are "least proximate" in America's social imaginary. Queer feminists of color such as Anzaldúa and Lorde have argued that developing a relationship with the deviant parts within us, or what Anzaldúa calls the "Shadow-Beast," can orient us toward nonsovereign relations with others. Anzaldúa's Shadow-Beast is the "rebel" part of her that "refuses to take orders from [her] conscious will, [that] threatens the sovereignty of [her] rulership."[78] Engaging rebellious movements within us and in our midst might enable us to cultivate dispositions toward familiarity with strangeness, that is, with unexpected and perhaps even unwanted sensations, emotions, and others, which challenge our sovereign identifications. It can also help those working at the contact zones of intersectional identities and desires develop what Anzaldúa calls a "tolerance for ambiguity," that is, a tolerance for the uncertain horizons and unsettling tensions of doing politics in proximity to what we cannot yet see or perceive.[79]

Dispositions toward unapologetic nonconformity, familiarity with strangeness, and tolerance for ambiguity, among others, can develop into a more durable undocuqueer orientation toward populism. Such an orientation can help activists negotiate the disorienting and reorienting paradox of democratic politics and cultivate more egalitarian, pluralistic forms of popular power. We might think of an undocuqueer orientation to populism as one that affirms insurgent claims to popular sovereignty by way of a queer ethos of nonsovereign peopling. I argued at the outset of the book that the paradox of popular sovereignty disrupts the very aspiration to sovereignty at the heart of modern democracy. Throughout, I have highlighted populism's experiments with nonsovereign practices peopling—for example, the public enthusiasm and translocal practices of nineteenth-century Populism, or the people's microphone and practices of *horizontalidad* in Occupy. The decentering dynamics of such experiments, however, have too quickly given way to counterhegemonic rhetoric and strategies that allow participants to cling to their investments in whiteness, heteromasculinity, middle-class security, and the idea of America. Not clinging to these securities will require new dispositions and practices. Undocuqueer orientations, I want to suggest, can help populists attune themselves less to the reactionary and cruel aspirations of individual and collective mastery that are embedded in America's social imaginary—including its populist imaginary. Indeed, a queer ethos of nonsovereign peopling finds an uncanny resilience in the recognition that even the most radical acts of peopling are both rebellious in their aspirations and forever subject to failure. An ethos that affirms the impurity of populism's rebellious aspirations is vital once we see that the "democracies we don't want" always threaten to foreclose—and often remain embedded in—the democracies we desire.[80]

UNDOCUQUEERING AMERICA'S POPULIST IMAGINARY

An undocuqueer orientation situates populism at the intersection of debates in radical democratic theory and practice over the status of popular sovereignty. The de-democratizing trends I outlined at the outset of the book—for example, neoliberal capitalism, corporate-state mergers, and persistent and innovative forms of racism—combine to intensify and obscure the sites and techniques of sovereign power in contemporary times and often implicate "the people" in projects of mastery. In light of this, radical theorists disagree over whether to appeal to popular sovereignty in order to democratize it, or to abandon the ideal of popular sovereignty in the service of enacting popular power at discontinuous sites and scales of collective life.[81] My sense is that finding ways to do politics in the tensions between these approaches is crucial in the midst of heightened anxieties about democracy's future and deepening ambivalence about the emancipatory power of the democratic ideal itself. Democracy may be "fugitive": its rebellious aspirations rarely emerge from today's nominally democratic institutions (which act in the name of a disempowered people), nor can rebellious aspirations avoid reconsolidating in better forms that are themselves exclusionary. In acknowledging the partiality of grassroots democratic movements, however, theorists and activists cannot afford to dream of purity. This dream manifests in disdain for movements that are "not radical enough," for example, reform efforts that merely improve existing institutions or remain invested in many of the hierarchies that structure everyday life. It also manifests in dismissals of activists who are "too radical" or who "misunderstand radicalism"—who, in acting outside the registers of everyday speech, threaten to splinter democracy's carefully tended coalitional roots. What would it mean to regard the varied efforts of others not as foregone conclusions, but as experiments: leaps of faith at the edges of the unknown that, by their very definition, often fail?

An undocuqueer orientation to populism and democracy suggests one answer. In one register, such an orientation affirms insurgent claims to popular sovereignty in the midst of contemporary conditions that both appropriate and undermine it. As I have argued throughout this book, broad-based, counterhegemonic identification, resistance, and movement building have been crucial to populism's emancipatory power and to radical democratic politics more generally. Populists must continue to arouse passionate identification around shared visions of collective life: these intensities can enable grassroots actors to take leaps of faith from our patterns of religiously practiced ambivalence. At times, populists may even need to adopt a kind of Schmittian drag: that is, perform total aversion to the status quo and move in what Cohen calls "amorous array" toward radical visions of the people and democracy.[82] Take Salgado's insurgent epigraph: "Illegal faggots for the destruction of borders!" This take on the promise "Democracy is coming to the U.S.A." headlines a poster that depicts a crowd of multiethnic, cross-racial immigrants protesting at a cracked border wall between the United States and Mexico. They adopt postures of anger and defiance—one holds a hammer in her raised fist, another a sign that says, "Fuck Your Borders!"—as they attempt to break through the artificial barricade. The image suggests total aversion to the sovereignty of the American nation-state: toward the ideal of white, heteromasculine nationalism and the deportation regime it aids and abets. The protestors act as if *they* possess the power and authority to define the terms of popular sovereignty. Their collective reclamation of their identity as "illegal faggots," moreover, suggests a radical affirmation of undocumented, queer people of color. Their insurgent aspirations may never get them "beyond borders," but such dreaming can buoy their efforts to eradicate the most harmful contact zones of America's deportation regime and build alternative contact zones that enable them to flourish.

The slantwise registers of an undocuqueer orientation can enable populists to move back and forth between such insurgent aspirations and the movement building needed to transform the contact zones—or horizons—of the people and democracy. A queer ethos of nonsovereign peopling stresses and inflects populism's more patient efforts to constitute popular power through cross-border, translocal organizing. From the Populist movement to Occupy, such efforts have turned ordinary spaces into spaces of extraordinary aspiration and, in moments, enabled populists to constitute egalitarian, pluralistic forms of popular power across sites and scales of collective life. This kind of coalitional work is often difficult to sustain. Cultivating dispositions and practices of nonsovereignty offers an uncanny insight for those who take up and attempt to radicalize this work today. Slantwise lines of experimentation may disrupt the centering dynamics a movement's counterhegemonic rhetoric and strategies. This is what happened when DREAMers engaged the "deviance" and "criminality" at the edges of their movement. Affirming impurity, however, and thus allowing for the possibility that a movement's own experiments may fail, not only pluralizes populist visions. Against the din of voices prophesying democracy's inevitable failure, it may also help populist actors identify and sustain the unruly coalitions through which rebellious aspirations might endure.

Populism needs many moments when "the people" becomes unrecognizable to itself: as agrarian populism did when it encountered industrial laborers, as Occupy started to do when it negotiated the insurgent claims of its affinity groups, as undocumented youth continue to do in cultivating their deviant dreams. Embracing these moments seems crucial to "fanning the spark of hope" in the populist and radical democratic movements emerging around the world today. The potential for democratizing America's populist imaginary is both promising and urgent. By developing narratives of populism's rebellious aspirations *and their* impurities—and affirming populism's partial successes amid conditions that encourage failure—populists might build relays between the discontinuous spaces and times of populism's most rebellious moments. Such relays might both highlight the larger tradition of aspirational democratic populism in America and orient populist actors toward the cracks in that tradition: as Cohen reminds us, "That's where the light gets in."[83] Seeing slantwise from these cracks might repeatedly open America's populist imaginary to the unruly movements at its edges: the "illegal faggots," prison abolitionists, women of color, socialists, radical environmentalists, transnational actors, and others who organize at democracy's deviant horizons. These movements remain largely unimaginable in America today. Their aspirations, however, are no less vital—indeed, I would argue they need to be more central—to articulating and enacting democracy as an emancipatory ideal in our times. Populism may become unrecognizable to itself as activists tend and intensify engagements at these deviant horizons. But populism's power to transform democracy has always been at its most radical when grassroots actors pluralize and connect their experiments in horizontality.

NOTES

INTRODUCTION

1. Michael Orey and Keith Epstein, "Will Populist Rage Hurt Corporate America?"; Anthony Randazzo, "Populist Rage over Foreclosures Doesn't Justify a Breakdown in the Rule of Law."
2. Lee Conrad, "Populist Outrage Is Back"; David Callahan, "Not So Fast, Sosnik."
3. Charles Cooper, "Got Outrage?"; Barrett Sheridan, "Populist Outrage?"
4. John Cook, "Who Will Be This Depression's Populist Demagogue?," *Gawker* (blog), March 17, 2009, http://gawker.com/5172287/who-will-be-this-depressions-populist-demagogue/; Marty Linsky, "Occupy Wall Street Is Going Nowhere without Leadership."
5. William H. Riker, *Liberalism against Populism*; Koen Abts and Stefan Rummens, "Populism versus Democracy." For other prominent liberal critiques of populism, see, for instance, Nadia Urbinati, "Democracy and Populism"; various essays in Yves Mény and Yves Surel, eds., *Democracies and the Populist Challenge*; various essays in Cas Mudde and Cristóbal Kaltwasser, eds., *Populism in Europe and the Americas*; and Richard Hofstadter, *The Paranoid Style in American Politics*.
6. Pierre Bourdieu, *Pascalian Meditations*, 321.
7. Avi Zenilman, "Obama's Oil Spill Speech"; Jessica Cashmar, "Cornel West"; Conor Friedersdorf, "A Plea to Liberals."
8. Wendy Brown, "We Are All Democrats Now . . .," 55.
9. Michael Kazin chronicles both developments in *The Populist Persuasion*, 245–86.
10. Hofstadter, *The Paranoid Style in American Politics*, 3–8, 25–26, 39–40.
11. As I discuss in chapter 1, Carl Schmitt's theories of politics and democracy have had unparalleled influence on liberal and many radical democratic theories of populism. Schmitt locates politics in the collective identification of friends in opposition to enemies. See Carl Schmitt, *The Concept of the Political*, 26.
12. Between 1979 and 2007, the top 1 percent of American earners took home over half (53.5 percent) of the total income growth in the United States; in the economic recovery after the Great Recession (measured from 2009 to 2012), the top 1 percent captured *all* of the income growth, while the average income of the bottom 99 percent actually fell by 0.4 percent. As a result, income inequality has returned to levels not seen since the 1920s. A similar story can be told for wealth inequality.

Seeing their wealth decline dramatically since the mid-1980s, the bottom 90 percent of families collectively owned 23 percent of US wealth in 2012; the top 0.1 percent's share of wealth neared levels unseen since the late 1920s. See Estelle Sommeiller and Mark Price, "The Increasingly Unequal States of America"; Emmanuel Saez and Gabriel Zucman, "Exploding Wealth Inequality in the United States."

13. For a history and incisive critiques of neoliberalism, see David Harvey, *The Enigma of Capital*; Sheldon S. Wolin, *Politics and Vision*, 557–606; Wendy Brown, *Edgework*, 37–59. On the ways neoliberalism developed in tandem with discourses that reinforce racial, gender, and sexual inequality, see Lisa Duggan, *The Twilight of Equality?* 3–21.

14. Wendy Brown, *Walled States, Waning Sovereignty*, 27.

15. See, for example, James Joyner, "How Perpetual War Became U.S. Ideology"; Jeremy Scahill, *Dirty Wars*; Timothy J. Dunn, *The Militarization of the U.S.-Mexico Border, 1978–1992*; Radley Balko, *Rise of the Warrior Cop*; Shane Harris, *The Watchers*.

16. While I limit my discussion here to state power and racial control, I address additional intersections of state power with the control of gender and sexuality in later chapters. On racialized discourses of criminality, illegality, and terrorism, see Michelle Alexander, *The New Jim Crow*; Cecilia Menjívar and Daniel Kanstroom, eds., *Constructing Immigrant "Illegality"*; Pardis Mahdavi, *From Trafficking to Terror*. On precarity and race, see Judith Butler, *Frames of War*, 3, 25–28; and Lisa L. Miller, "Racialized State Failure and the Violent Death of Michael Brown."

17. Sheldon Wolin describes late capitalist citizenship with particular acuity in *Politics and Vision*, 563–65, 575, 589–94.

18. Bourdieu, for example, cites reactionary backlash and submissiveness as one of the most predictable responses to the perpetual insecurity caused by neoliberal capitalism; Lauren Berlant coined the term "cruel optimism" to explain our abiding faith in ideologies, such as the fantasies of consumer freedom, that reinforce our powerlessness. See my essay "Pierre Bourdieu and Populism," 204–6; Bourdieu, *Acts of Resistance*, 85–86; Lauren Berlant, *Cruel Optimism*, 24–25, 48–49.

19. I develop this argument in depth in the chapter 1.

20. See, e.g., Sheldon Wolin's critiques of contemporary liberalism in *Politics and Vision*; Wendy Brown's essay "Neoliberalism and the End of Liberal Democracy" in *Edgework*; and William Connolly's chapter "Democracy, Equality, and Normality" in *The Ethos Of Pluralization*.

21. Brown, "We Are All Democrats," 44.

22. Jodi Dean, *Democracy and Other Neoliberal Fantasies*, 76.

23. Wendy Brown, "We Are All Democrats," 54.

24. Wolin, *Politics and Vision*, 601–2. Wolin's despair only grows in *Democracy Incorporated*.

25. Wolin scatters these examples and others throughout his writings. See *Politics and Vision*, 603–4; *Democracy Incorporated*, 257–58, 288–89; *The Presence of the Past*, 99; "Contract and Birthright," 285–86.

26. Sheldon Wolin, "Fugitive Democracy," 44.

27. My sketch of the literature on populism in this paragraph is indebted to Jason Frank's characterization of this literature in "Populism and Praxis." For one of the earliest systemic efforts to define populism, see Ghita Ionescu and Ernest Gellner, *Populism*. On populism as a style of rhetoric, see Kazin, *The Populist Persuasion*. As a strategy of electoral mobilization and contentious politics, see the

various essays in Mudde and Kaltwasser, eds., *Populism in Europe and the Americas* and Mény and Surel, eds., *Democracies and the Populist Challenge*. On populism as a syndrome or pathology, see Peter Wiles, "A Syndrome, Not a Doctrine"; Hans-Georg Betz, *Radical Right-Wing Populism in Western Europe*; and Urbinati, "Democracy and Populism." On populism as an ethos or dimension of political culture, see Peter Worsley, "The Concept of Populism"; Lawrence Goodwyn, *Democratic Promise*; and Sheldon Wolin, "Contract and Birthright."

28. Worsley is the earliest to advocate this approach. See Worsley, "The Concept of Populism," 244.

29. See, for instance, Margaret Canovan, "Taking Politics to the People," 32; Cas Mudde, "The Populist Zeitgeist," 544; Koen Abts and Stefan Rummens, "Populism versus Democracy," 408; Ben Stanley, "The Thin Ideology of Populism."

30. Ernesto Laclau, *On Populist Reason*, 69–71, 95–96. For Laclau's earlier writing on popular subjectivity and populism, see *Politics and Ideology in Marxist Theory*.

31. While my interests in this book focus on the relationship between populism and democracy, populism is not exclusive to democratic actors or regimes. Indeed, scholars have tied populist rhetoric and mobilization to fascism and, more broadly, to authoritarian regimes that construct their legitimacy via appeals to the people in the face of enemies. See, for example, Gino Germani, *Authoritarianism, Fascism, and National Populism*; Manochehr Dorraj, *From Zarathustra to Khomeini*; Manochehr Dorraj, "Iranian Populism."

32. For prominent critiques of the very ideal of popular sovereignty, see, for instance, Hannah Arendt's separation of freedom from will in *Between Past and Future*, 151–65; Sara Ahmed's discussion of the "general will" in *Willful Subjects*, 97–132; and Michael Hardt and Antonio Negri's discussion of "the people" in *Empire*, 102–5, 193–95.

33. Jason Frank, *Constituent Moments*, 7. Here, I am also indebted to Frank's essay, "Populism and Praxis," in which he connects populism's emergence to the paradox of democratic peoplehood. On the democratic paradox, see also Bonnie Honig, *Emergency Politics*; Arash Abizadeh, "On the Demos and Its Kin"; Sofia Näsström, "The Legitimacy of the People." Political theorists have taken the impossibility (and, in the view of some, undesirability) of shared popular identity as the basis for evaluating themes as varied as family, constitutionalism, Latino/a politics, and the democratic imaginary of protest marches. See, respectively, Kennan Ferguson, *All in the Family*; Paulina Ochoa Espejo, *The Time of Popular Sovereignty*; Cristina Beltrán, *The Trouble with Unity*; Michaele Ferguson, *Sharing Democracy*.

34. This is a premise of Honig's *Emergency Politics* and Frank's *Constituent Moments*.

35. Honig, *Emergency Politics*, xvii, 15.

36. Danielle Allen, *Talking to Strangers*, 63.

37. Jason Frank elaborates the historical imbrication between these two questions in "Populism and Praxis" and concludes his essay by calling democratic theorists to shift their focus from "who the people are" to "how that people is enacted." I am indebted to his essay and to conversations with him for sharpening my early efforts,

in "Pierre Bourdieu and Populism," to expand populism's dominant focus on resistance to include insights from lesser-known scholars and activists who emphasize populism's practices of constituting popular power. In particular, his work helped me appreciate the ways in which populist antagonism is concerned not only with resisting power but also with creating the symbolic power of popular identification. Analyzing the relationship between identification and enactment, offers a sharper focus to democratic theorists and activists who are interested in the multiple, interrelated practices of constituting popular power.

38. On populism and commonwealth, see Harry C. Boyte, *Commonwealth*; Gar Alperovitz, *America beyond Capitalism*. On cooperative and public work, see John Curl, *For All the People*; Harry C. Boyte, *Everyday Politics*. On populism and broad-based organizing, see Luke Bretherton, "The Political Populism of Saul Alinsky and Broad Based Organizing."

39. Charles Taylor, *Modern Social Imaginaries*, 23–24. I discuss social imaginaries and America's populist imaginary in chapter 3.

40. There are exceptions to these prominent trends by scholars who analyze democratic populisms and left populisms at the grassroots in Europe, Latin America, and South Africa. See, e.g., Yannis Stavrakakis and Giorgos Katsambekis, "Left-Wing Populism in the European Periphery"; George Ciccariello-Maher, *We Created Chávez*; David Howarth, "Populism or Popular Democracy?" In "Why Ernesto Laclau Is the Intellectual Figurehead for Syriza," Dan Hancox makes the controversial claim that Laclau is the "key intellectual figurehead" behind the leftist parties Podemos in Spain and Syriza in Greece.

41. I discuss radical democratic scholarship on American populism in depth in chapter 1.

42. See, for instance, Alexandros Kioupkiolis and Giorgos Katsambekis, eds., *Radical Democracy and Collective Movements Today*; Marina Sitrin and Dario Azzellini, *They Can't Represent Us!*

Chapter 1

1. For the former, see William H. Riker, *Liberalism against Populism*. See also James A. Morone, *The Democratic Wish*. For the latter, see Richard Hofstadter, *The Paranoid Style in American Politics*. See also Hans-Georg Betz and Stefan Immerfall, *The New Politics of the Right*.

2. See Ernesto Laclau, *On Populist Reason*; Chantal Mouffe, "The 'End of Politics' and the Challenge of Right-Wing Populism"; Michael Kazin, *The Populist Persuasion*.

3. See Harry C. Boyte, *Everyday Politics*; Thomas A. Spragens Jr., *Getting the Left Right*; Lawrence Goodwyn, *Democratic Promise*. More recently, Jason Frank has sought to emphasize the imbrications between populism's antagonistic identification and its practices of enactment in "Populism and Praxis."

4. Nadia Urbinati, "Democracy and Populism," 113.

5. See Book II, chapter 7 in Jean-Jacques Rousseau, *On the Social Contract*. Among theorists who link populism to Rousseau are Margaret Canovan, "Taking Politics to the People," 33; Koen Abts and Stefan Rummens, "Populism versus Democracy," 415–17; Donald MacRae, "Populism as an Ideology," 154–56; Bernard Crick,

"Populism, Politics, and Democracy," 626, 628–29; Riker, *Liberalism against Populism*, 11.

6. Bonnie Honig, *Emergency Politics*, 24.
7. See, for example, Peter Wiles, "A Syndrome, Not a Doctrine," 167, 171; Paul Taggart, "Populism and the Pathology of Representative Politics," 62, 79–80; Peter Mair, "Populist Democracy vs. Party Democracy," 82–84; Nadia Urbinati, "Populism and Democracy," 115.
8. Donald MacRae, "Populism as an Ideology," 154–56; Bernard Crick, "Populism, Politics and Democracy," 626–28; Urbinati, "Democracy and Populism," 110, 118
9. Urbinati, "Democracy and Populism," 116. On Schmitt's influence on theories of populism, see Jason Frank, "Populism and Praxis."
10. Carl Schmitt, *The Crisis of Parliamentary Democracy*, 16.
11. Schmitt, *Crisis of Parliamentary Democracy*, 24–29.
12. Schmitt, *Crisis of Parliamentary Democracy*, 17.
13. Carl Schmitt, *The Concept of the Political*, 19–30, 46–47.
14. Schmitt, *Concept of the Political*, 11–12.
15. Riker, *Liberalism Against Populism*, 244, 238.
16. Abts and Rummens, "Populism versus Democracy," 414.
17. See especially Richard Hofstadter, *The Age of Reform*, 23–36, 62–64.
18. MacRae, "Populism as an Ideology," 154–59; Taggart, *Populism*, 91–98.
19. Isaiah Berlin et al., "To Define Populism," 173; Taggart, *Populism*, 96–97; Angus Stewart, "The Social Roots," 183–85.
20. Hofstadter himself went from seeing the "paranoid style" as a fringe feature of American politics to one that was becoming a reoccurring and "acutely felt" feature of his era. Hofstadter, *The Paranoid Style*, xxxvii–xxxviii. See also the essays on right-wing populism in Europe and other established democracies in Betz and Immerfall, *New Politics*.
21. Michael Rogin's provides a critical interpretation of American "political demonology" in *Ronald Reagan the Movie*, 272–300.
22. Urbinati, "Democracy and Populism," 119.
23. Margaret Canovan, "Trust the People!" 3–5, 13–14; Urbinati, "Democracy and Populism," 116–19.
24. Wiles, "A Syndrome," 166; Canovan, "Trust the People!" 3, 114; Abts and Rummens, "Populism versus Democracy," 416; Crick, "Populism, Politics and Democracy," 626; Yannis Papadopoulos, "Populism, the Democratic Question, and Contemporary Governance," 51.
25. On populism as a response to the limits of representative democracy, see Paul Taggart, "Populism," 269–72. On elites and parties, see Jack Hayward, "The Populist Challenge to Elitist Democracy in Europe," 10; Mair, "Populist Democracy," 89–91. On the missing intellectual class, see Urbinati, "Democracy and Populism," 110–11, 114–15. On the limits of constitutionalism, see Yves Mény and Yves Surel, "The Constitutive Ambiguities of Populism," 7–11, 14, 17. Mény and Surel, Mair, and Taggart are among those who see populism's ability to draw attention to the limits of liberal democracy (though Taggart ultimately sees populism as a politics of resistance whose doctrines and institutions are hard to sustain). Joining Urbinati as

critics of populism's apolitical character are Wiles, "A Syndrome," 167; Cas Mudde, "The Populist Zeitgeist," 554.

26. Abts and Rummens, "Populism versus Democracy," 420.
27. Urbinati, "Democracy and Populism," 110.
28. Abts and Rummens, "Populism versus Democracy," 417–18.
29. See Mudde, "The Populist Zeitgeist," 558. Mudde references the influential study of political passivity by John R. Hibbing and Elizabeth Theiss-Morse, *Stealth Democracy*.
30. Urbinati, "Democracy and Populism," 112.
31. Claude Lefort, *The Political Forms of Modern Society*, 279.
32. Lefort, *Political Forms*, 279, 297–98.
33. Riker, *Liberalism against Populism*, 244–45.
34. Rogin describes this dynamic and explains the motivations and investments of consensus liberals such as Hofstadter and Daniel Bell in *Ronald Reagan the Movie*, 275–85.
35. Jürgen Habermas, "Three Normative Models of Democracy," 10. Urbinati, Abts and Rummens, and Papadopoulos all rely on deliberative theory to critique populism.
36. Abts and Rummens, "Populism versus Democracy," 413.
37. See, for instance, Arthur Meier Schlesinger, *The Disuniting of America*; Louis Hartz, *The Liberal Tradition in America*; Seymour Martin Lipset, *American Exceptionalism*; David Miller, *On Nationality*.
38. This is a common critique of John Rawls's notion of a "background culture" in *Political Liberalism*. See, for example, John Tomasi, *Liberalism beyond Justice*; Richard John Neuhaus, *The Naked Public Square*.
39. Charles Taylor, *Modern Social Imaginaries*, 23–24.
40. See, for example, Wendy Brown, *States of Injury*; William Connolly, *The Ethos Of Pluralization* and *Why I Am Not a Secularist*; Sheldon S. Wolin, *Politics and Vision*.
41. Ta-Nehisi Coates, "Blue Lives Matter." On these overlapping trends, see, for instance, Radley Balko, *Rise of the Warrior Cop*; Nicholas De Genova and Nathalie Peutz, eds., *The Deportation Regime*; Cecilia Menjívar and Daniel Kanstroom, eds., *Constructing Immigrant "Illegality"*; Pardis Mahdavi, *From Trafficking to Terror*.
42. A critic of right-wing populisms and what he saw as the authoritarian tendencies of the working class, Lipset writes in *Political Man*, "The belief that a very high level of participation is always good for democracy is not valid," adding that "a stable democracy may rest on the general belief that the outcome of an election will not make too great a difference in society" (14).
43. Canovan, "Taking Politics," 42.
44. Urbinati, "Democracy and Populism," 122.
45. Jason Frank makes this argument in "Populism and Praxis."
46. Laclau, *On Populist Reason*, x.
47. Jason Frank, *Constituent Moments*, 7–8. See also, Frank, "Populism and Praxis"; Lawrence Goodwyn, *The Populist Moment*, vii–xxiv; Sheldon Wolin, "The People's Two Bodies," 12–16.
48. See, for instance, David Harvey, *The Enigma of Capital*; Simon Critchley, *Infinitely Demanding*; the essays by Ernesto Laclau, Chantal Mouffe, Benjamin Arditi, and Francisco Panizza in Panizza et al., *Populism and the Mirror of Democracy*. Scholars

of black political thought in America sound a similar note in relation to liberal nationalism and the color-blind conceits of neoliberalism. See, for instance, George Shulman, *American Prophecy*, xiii–xvii; Joel Olson, "The Freshness of Fanaticism."

49. Chantal Mouffe describes the "neoliberal consensus" and identifies both problems in "The 'End of Politics' and the Challenge of Right-Wing Populism," 50–59.

50. See Laclau, *On Populist Reason*, x, 13, 18–19; Mouffe, "End of Politics," 69–71; and Kazin, *The Populist Persuasion*, 6–7, 289–90. For iterations of this argument in response to contemporary populisms, see Joe Lowndes and Dorian Warren, "Occupy Wall Street"; Chip Berlet, "Taking Tea Parties Seriously"; and George Shulman, "The Politics of the Tea Party," *The Contemporary Condition* (blog), May 3, 2010, http://contemporarycondition.blogspot.com/ 2010/05/politics-of-tea-party.html; Dan Hancox, "Why Ernesto Laclau Is the Intellectual Figurehead for Syriza."

51. Laclau, *On Populist Reason*, 19.

52. Laclau, *On Populist Reason*, 68–72.

53. Ernesto Laclau, "Populism," 37–38.

54. Laclau, *On Populist Reason*, 77–83; Laclau, "Populism," 38–43.

55. Laclau, *On Populist Reason*, xi.

56. Laclau, *On Populist Reason*, 154.

57. Italics added. Benjamin Arditi, *Politics on the Edges of Liberalism*, 74, 77. Arditi does not endorse Laclau's conclusion that this makes populism synonymous with politics, but instead, sees populism as a symptom of democratic politics.

58. Laclau, *On Populist Reason*, 71.

59. Ernesto Laclau, *Politics and Ideology in Marxist Theory*, 142–44.

60. Laclau, *On Populist Reason*, x. The agonistic dimensions of popular subject formation are even more pronounced in Laclau and Mouffe's earlier work, *Hegemony and Socialist Strategy*.

61. Schmitt, *Concept of the Political*, 27, 30–31.

62. Laclau, *On Populist Reason*, 11–12, 71–72.

63. See, for instance, studies by Mouffe, Lowndes, Oscar Reyes, and David Laycock in *Populism and the Mirror of Democracy* and Joe Lowndes, *From the New Deal to the New Right*.

64. Laclau, *On Populist Reason*, 321.

65. Mouffe, "End of Politics," 70–71. On the relationship between resistance and institutional transformation in the World Social Forum, see Boaventura de Sousa Santos, *The Rise of the Global Left*.

66. See Harry C. Boyte and Frank Riessman, eds., *The New Populism*.

67. This is not to say that everyday populists lack a critique of neoliberal capitalism. Wolin, who has spent decades tracking and conceptualizing these developments, outlines their early signs in the inaugural edition of *democracy*. See Sheldon Wolin, "Why Democracy?" 3–5. Scholars such as Boyte and practitioners such as the Industrial Areas Foundation have not been as probing. Moreover, everyday populists, including Wolin, fail to extend their critiques of capital to the production of other socioeconomic inequalities, most notably, race and gender.

68. Questions about the "new populism" propelled the inaugural edition of *democracy*, as well as Boyte and Riessman's *The New Populism*. Goodwyn, Boyte, and Wolin contributed to both projects.
69. Goodwyn elaborates these claims most succinctly in his brief introduction to *The Populist Moment*.
70. Among theorists of the "new populism," Wolin offers the most prescient account of these changes. See "Why Democracy," 3–5.
71. See, e.g., Edward T. Chambers, *Roots for Radicals*, 84.
72. Boyte, *Everyday Politics*, 21, 28, 58; Boyte, *Civic Agency and the Cult of the Expert*, 10.
73. Boyte, *Everyday Politics*, 21.
74. Harry C. Boyte, "Constructive Politics as Public Work," 642.
75. Boyte, "Constructive Politics," 630.
76. Sheldon Wolin, "Contract and Birthright," 285.
77. Wolin, "The People's Two Bodies," 10–11.
78. Here I'm channeling Pierre Bourdieu's concept of habitus, which has been reworked toward freer ends by Saba Mahmood in *Politics of Piety* and Romand Coles in "The Neuropolitical *Habitus* of Resonant Receptive Democracy," xxx. For a longer conversation of Bourdieu and populism, see Laura Grattan, "Pierre Bourdieu and Populism," 203–7.
79. Wolin, "Contract and Birthright," 285–86.
80. Ernesto Cortés, "Education for Citizenship," 125.
81. Craig Calhoun, *The Roots of Radicalism*.
82. I discuss Wolin's account of "fugitive democracy" in the introduction.
83. As we will see in the next chapter, there are exceptions. Some historians of nineteenth-century American Populism chronicle the movement's strategies for reforming state institutions on issues ranging from public control of the economy to platforms on women's suffrage and civil rights. But even these accounts are at the periphery of dominant narratives of Populism, which focus on its nostalgic sentimentality, its rhetoric of resistance, or its tactics of mass mobilization.
84. Inclusion of the Civil Rights Movement as an example of populism is a point of contest in the literature. I want to suggest that populist rhetoric and practices were crucial to mainstream Civil Rights organizations, even as they also pursued other visions and tactics. A significant contingent of activists appealed broadly to transforming the people and democracy, rather than more narrowly to claiming group rights.
85. Bayard Rustin, *Time on Two Crosses*, 128; John D'Emilio, *Lost Prophet*, 379–92.
86. Rustin, *Time on Two Crosses*, 122.
87. Rustin, *Time on Two Crosses*, 124.
88. Rustin, *Time on Two Crosses*, 124.
89. Rustin, *Time on Two Crosses*, 123. Rustin's dismissive stance toward the Nation of Islam and black militancy is outside the scope of my concern here, though I discuss key oversights below.
90. In "Populism and Praxis," Jason Frank situates his account of populist praxis in relation to the call for a new realism in political theory. See, for example, William Galston, "Realism in Political Theory."

91. Rustin, *Time on Two Crosses*, 121. On the organizing tradition Rustin marginalizes, see Charles M. Payne, *I've Got the Light of Freedom*.

92. Rustin, *Time on Two Crosses*, 140, 142–43, 151; quoted in D'Emilio, *Lost Prophet*, 392.

93. D'Emilio, *Lost Prophet*, 392.

94. Gar Alperovitz, *America beyond Capitalism*, 7, 70, 80, 90, 168–70. Alperovitz's crucial account will remain shortsighted without ongoing acts of radical critique and resistance. In particular, many of his schemes entail making capitalist markets more equal and have proven fragile in the face of more powerful market actors. In broader terms, patient, behind-the-scenes work will not survive long without a rhetorical climate that opens space for experimentation.

95. See, for instance, David Barstow, "Tea Party Lights Fuse for Rebellion on Right"; Sarah van Gelder, "This Changes Everything."

96. Quoted in Taggart, "Populism," 71; Crick, "Populism, Politics and Democracy," 625; Wiles, "A Syndrome," 167.

97. Lauren Berlant, *Cruel Optimism*, 24, 48.

98. See Wolin, *Politics and Vision*, 580, 596–97; "Agitated Times," 6.

99. On these trends, see Joseph E. Stiglitz, *Freefall*; Matt Taibbi, "Secrets and Lies of the Bailout"; Rakesh Kochhar, Richard Fry, and Paul Taylor, *Wealth Gaps Rise to Record Highs between Whites, Blacks, Hispanics*.

100. William E. Connolly, *Capitalism and Christianity, American Style*, 42–50.

101. Coles, "Neuropolitical *Habitus*," 281.

102. Richard Cowan and Steve Holland, "Obama Calls Senators in Hopes of Creating 'Common Sense' Caucus on Sequestration"; Brigid Schulte and Paul Duggan, "Obama Urges Nation to Demand a 'Common Sense' Balance on Gun Control, Gun Rights"; "A Common-Sense Immigration Move."

103. On these resonant trends, see Jodi Dean, *Democracy and Other Neoliberal Fantasies*, 17–45.

104. When Chevrolet enlisted John Mellencamp, Martin Luther King Jr., and Rosa Parks to sell its all-new Chevy Silverado in 2006, its ad was part of its "American Revolution" marketing campaign. See David Carr, "American Tragedies, to Sell Trucks."

105. Quoted in Barbara Ransby, *Ella Baker and the Black Freedom Movement*, 188.

106. This is a common liberal critique of populism. See, for example, Urbinati, "Democracy and Populism," 119; Abts and Rummens, "Populism versus Democracy," 418.

107. Jacques Derrida, *Writing and Difference*, 128–29, 133.

108. Derrida, *The Other Heading*, 44, 72, 78.

109. Derrida, *The Other Heading*, 47, 78.

110. Derrida, *Aporias*, 33–34.

111. For a history of cooperative struggles in America, see John Curl, *For All the People*. For analyses of the ways in which they have transformed political dispositions and habits, see Goodwyn, *Democratic Promise*; Coles, "Neuropolitical *Habitus*," including an expanded discussion developed in his forthcoming book, *Visionary Pragmatism*.

112. Connolly, *Capitalism and Christianity*, 15.

113. Gar Alperovitz provides many compelling examples of structural reforms that could be part of "twenty-first century populism" throughout his book, *America beyond Capitalism.*
114. Mark R. Warren, *Dry Bones Rattling,* 32.

CHAPTER 2

1. Ted Nace dates the corporate revolution in the United States from approximately 1850 to 1900 in *Gangs of America,* 68.
2. "Editorials Reprinted from the Farmers' Alliance, 1890–1892," in Norman Pollack, ed., *The Populist Mind,* 18; "Editorial Reprinted from the Topeka Advocate, 1894," in *The Populist Mind,* 343.
3. "National People's Party Platform, July 1892," in Pollack, *The Populist Mind,* 61.
4. See, for example, the articles in the symposium "The Thinking Man's Guide to Populist Rage"; Benjamin Friedman, "Meltdown"; and Howell Raines, "Winning the Populism PR War."
5. Hofstadter's account of People's Party has debts to Oscar Handlin's 1951 analysis of Populist anti-Semitism in "American Views of the Jew at the Opening of the Twentieth Century."
6. Richard Hofstadter, *The Age of Reform,* 94, 4.
7. Hofstadter, *The Age of Reform,* 23–36, 62.
8. For Hofstadter's views on the concept of status anxiety and its fringe character in American society, see *The Paranoid Style in American Politics,* 39–40; *The Age of Reform,* 7–8, 22.
9. Daniel Bell, ed., *The Radical Right*; Seymour Martin Lipset, *The Politics of Unreason.*
10. Saira Anees, "Obama Explains Why Some Small Town Pennsylvanians Are 'Bitter.'"
11. Norman Pollack, *The Populist Response to Industrial America,* 7. See also C. Vann Woodward, *Origins of the New South,* 235–90; and Kazin, *The Populist Persuasion,* 37–42.
12. Lawrence Goodwyn, *The Populist Moment,* xiii.
13. Lawrence Goodwyn, *Democratic Promise,* 601–2. For socialist readings of Populism, see Matthew Josephson, *The Politicos, 1865–1896*; Anna Rochester, *The Populist Movement in the United State*; and James Green, "Populism, Socialism and the Promise of Democracy."
14. Goodwyn, *The Populist Moment,* vii.
15. Goodwyn, *The Populist Moment,* xiii.
16. I discuss Goodwyn's influence on radical democratic theories of populism in chapter 1.
17. While he interrogates the limits of the Farmers' Alliance's "outreach" to black farmers and unionized immigrants, and adds a footnote about the role of women in the movement, the real tragedy of Populism, for Goodwyn, isn't the sedimentations of white supremacy and patriarchy that it carried. It's the fact that Populism's move into electoral politics, necessary as it was, helped weaken the cooperative movement and ended in co-option by the Democratic Party.
18. Following scholars such as Omar Ali, I use the term "Black Populism" as a proper noun to refer to a specific movement that was at once independent and part of the

Populism's broad coalitional base. I use the terms "black Populists" and "white Populists" to indicate the importance of both blacks and whites to the larger Populist movement. On Black Populism, see Ali, *In the Lion's Mouth*; Gerald H. Gaither, *Blacks and the Populist Revolt*; and Steven Hahn, *A Nation under Our Feet*, 412–40. On women in Populism, see Charles Postel, *The Populist Vision*, 69–102; Julie Roy Jeffrey, "Women in the Southern Farmers' Alliance."

19. Goodwyn, *Democratic Promise*, 606.
20. Elizabeth Sanders, *Roots of Reform*, 4. Sanders offers a comprehensive account of Populism's vision of the state and its impact on later state reformers. See also Aziz Rana, *The Two Faces of American Freedom*, 204–9; Postel, *The Populist Vision*, 277–81, 286–89.
21. "National People's Party Platform, July 1892," 60–62.
22. "National People's Party Platform, July 1892," 62–66.
23. Kazin, *The Populist Persuasion*, 10–25, 30.
24. Charles H. Otken, "The Ills of the South or Related Causes Hostile to the General Prosperity of the Southern People," in George Brown Tindall, ed., *A Populist Reader*, 19; N. B. Ashby, "The Riddle of the Sphinx," in *A Populist Reader*, 28; W. Scott Morgan, "History of the Wheel and Alliance and the Impending Revolution," in *A Populist Reader*, 19; Samuel Gompers, "Organized Labor in the Campaign," in *A Populist Reader*, 185.
25. William Allen White, "The Autobiography of William Allen White," in Tindall, *A Populist Reader*, 193; Morgan, "History of the Wheel," 11; Otken, "Ills of the South," 42; Ashby, "Riddle of the Sphinx," 35.
26. Nace, *Gangs of America*, 16–17, 70–86; Sanders, *Roots of Reform*, 17.
27. Goodwyn, *Democratic Promise*, 538.
28. Spencer is quoted in Nace, *Gangs of America*, 118–19. Nace discusses the role of both market ideology and social Darwinism in the corporate revolution. See also William Graham Sumner, *What Social Classes Owe to Each Other*; Robert H. Wiebe, *The Search for Order*, 136; Postel, *The Populist Vision*, 245; Norman Pollack, *The Humane Economy*, 67.
29. "Editorials Reprinted from the Topeka Advocate, 1893," in Pollack, *The Populist Mind*, 335.
30. Quoted in Goodwyn, *Democratic Promise*, 524–29.
31. See Karl Polanyi, *The Great Transformation*, 3.
32. Seward is quoted in Thomas D. Schoonover, *Uncle Sam's War of 1898*, 56.
33. Lorenzo Lewelling, "Speech in Kansas, 1984," in Pollack, *The Populist Mind*, 7; "Editorials Reprinted from the Alliance-Independent, 1892–1894," in *The Populist Mind*, 40. See also Laurence Gronlund, *The Co-operative Commonwealth*; Henry Demarest Lloyd, *Wealth against Commonwealth*.
34. Quoted in Postel, *The Populist Vision*, 106.
35. Quoted in Bruce Palmer, *"Man over Money,"* 14. On producerism and the populist tradition, see also Catherine McNicol Stock, *Rural Radicals*, 15–86; Rana, *Two Faces*, 125–29; Nash, *Unknown American Revolution*, 112–13, 187–88.
36. "Editorials Reprinted from the Farmers' Alliance, 1890–1892," 17.
37. "National People's Party Platform, July 1892," 61.
38. Kazin makes this argument in *The Populist Persuasion*, 13–14, 34–37.

39. Ethan Allen, of the Green Mountain Boys, quoted in Gary B. Nash, *The Unknown American Revolution*, 113.

40. Quoted in Nash, *The Unknown American Revolution*, 132.

41. On producerism's relationships to settler colonialism and ressentiment, see Rana, *Two Faces*, 129–32; Kazin, *The Populist Persuasion*, 35–37; Chip Berlet, *Right-Wing Populism in America*, 6–7, 64–65, 119–20.

42. Quotes taken from Kazin, *The Populist Persuasion*, 36; Postel, *The Populist Vision*, 177.

43. Thomas L. Nugent, "Four Speeches in Texas, 1892–1895," in Pollack, *The Populist Mind*, 283. For a critique of producerism as a gendered rhetoric, see Kazin, *The Populist Persuasion*, 13–14.

44. Stock, *Rural Radicals*, 55.

45. See Ali, *In the Lion's Mouth*, 48–77; Gaither, *Blacks*, 17–25, 55–65; Postel, *The Populist Vision*, 69–101.

46. "Reprinted from Wool Hat (Georgia) as Quoted in People's Party Paper (Atlanta), June 22, 1984," in Pollack, *The Populist Mind*, 390; R. L. Robinson, "Letter to Lorenzo D. Lewelling, December 5, 1983," in *The Populist Mind*, 334; "Editorial from 'Hayseeder' Reprinted from Southern Alliance Farmer (Atlanta), August 2, 1982," in *The Populist Mind*, 387.

47. "National People's Party Platform, July 1892," 63.

48. Lockean interpretations of the labor theory of value have been central to producerism since the pre-Revolutionary era. On this theme in the pre-Revolutionary era, see Nash, *The Unknown American Revolution*, 112–13. In the literary and cultural imagination of the nineteenth century, see Nicholas Bromell, *By the Sweat of the Brow*, 20–22.

49. "Editorials Reprinted from the Farmers' Alliance, 1890–1892," 21.

50. Henry D. Lloyd, "Speech in Chicago 1894," in Pollack, *The Populist Mind*, 70.

51. "Editorial Reprinted from the Topeka Advocate, 1894," in Pollack, *The Populist Mind*, 13.

52. "Editorial Reprinted from the Topeka Advocate, 1894," 13; "Editorials Reprinted from the Farmers' Alliance, 1890–1892," 20–21.

53. Quoted in Palmer, *"Man Over Money,"* 33. See also Ali, *In the Lion's Mouth*, 76; Hahn, *Nation under Our Feet*, 433.

54. Lloyd, "Speech in Chicago 1894," 69.

55. Rana, *Two Faces*, 121, 205. On radical republicanism in America's populist tradition, see also Boyte, *Commonwealth*, 17–25.

56. James H. Davis, "A Political Revelation," in Pollack, *The Populist Mind*, 27.

57. "Editorials Reprinted from the Platte County Argus, 1896," in Pollack, *The Populist Mind*, 42.

58. Quoted in Palmer, *"Man over Money,"* 24.

59. The quote is from David Lovejoy, "Desperate Enthusiasm," 232. My discussion in this paragraph is also informed by Lovejoy, *Religious Enthusiasm in the New World*; and Patricia Bonomi, "'A Just Opposition.'"

60. Kazin, *The Populist Persuasion*, 33.

61. Kazin, *The Populist Persuasion*, 32.

62. Thomas E. Watson, "Reprinted from the People's Party Paper," in Pollack, *The Populist Mind*, 47.

63. Boyte, *Commonwealth*, 31, xii.

64. Nash, *The Unknown American Revolution*, 133–46, 232–37.

65. James C. Scott, *Domination and the Arts of Resistance*, 5–6, 187–92.

66. I discuss Black Populism and its inheritances below.

67. See Dirk Hoerder, *American Labor and Immigration History*, 265–66; Harry C. Boyte and Don Shelby, *The Citizen Solution*, 66.

68. Quoted phrases are from Boyte, *Commonwealth*, 25; "Editorial Reprinted from the Farmers' Alliance, 1892," in Pollack, *The Populist Mind*, 444; and Ali, *In the Lion's Mouth*, 79.

69. Harper is quoted in Boyte, *Commonwealth*, 25.

70. Goodwyn, *Democratic Promise*, xi.

71. Lloyd, "Speech in Chicago 1894," 69.

72. Goodwyn, *The Populist Moment*, 20.

73. Sanders, *Roots of Reform*, 109; Goodwyn, *The Populist Moment*, 20–23.

74. Henry D. Lloyd, "A Strike of Millionaires against Miners," in Pollack, *The Populist Mind*, 423.

75. Lloyd, "A Strike of Millionaires," 119–21; Sanders, *Roots of Reform*, 56; Nace, *Gangs of America*, 125; Philip S. Foner, *History of the Labor Movement*, vol. 2, 20–31.

76. Matthew Frye Jacobson, *Whiteness of a Different Color*, 152–53; Ali, *In the Lion's Mouth*, 38–41; Lawrence Goodwyn, "Populist Dreams and Negro Rights," 1435.

77. Jay Burrows, "Editorial Reprinted from the Farmers Alliance, 1891," in Pollack, *The Populist Mind*, 3–4.

78. For this view of capitalist modernization, see Polanyi, *The Great Transformation*, 171–86.

79. Goodwyn, *Democratic Promise*, 604.

80. Lloyd, "Speech in Chicago 1894," 70.

81. W. L. Garvin and S. O. Daws, *History of the National Farmers' Alliance*, 72–73.

82. Quoted in John D. Hicks, *Populist Revolt*, 261. Dramas of enactment were not new to Populism with the advent of the People's Party. Alliance rallies and encampments, for example, frequently gathered men and women together en mass during the cooperative movement. The same can be said for the millions of workers who participated in strikes from 1877 to 1896, often bypassing injunctions from local officials and newspapers against congregating in the streets. On Alliance encampments, see Goodwyn, *The Populist Moment*, 30–34. On labor strikes and parades, see David O. Stowell, *Streets, Railroads, and the Great Strike of 1877*, 2–3, 8–9, 72–83; Martin Shefter, "Trade Unions and Political Machines," 218–20, 236–37.

83. Hicks, *Populist Revolt*, 661–62.

84. Fanny Leake, "Gillespie County Alliance Minutes, 1895," in Pollack, *The Populist Mind*, 44.

85. Lorenzo D. Lewelling, "Speech at Huron Place, July 26, 1894," in Tindall, *A Populist Reader*, 159.

86. Slavoj Žižek, *Tarrying with the Negative*, 1.

87. Jason Frank, " 'Besides Our Selves,' " 372, 375.

88. Quoted in Michael Lewis Goldberg, *An Army of Women*, 147.

89. Frank, "Besides Our Selves," 390.

90. Quoted in Hicks, *Populist Revolt*, 228.

91. Quoted in Goodwyn, *The Populist Moment*, 173.
92. Quoted in Goodwyn, *The Populist Moment*, 134.
93. Lauren Berlant and Michael Warner, "Sex in Public," 198.
94. Quoted in Goodwyn, *The Populist Moment*, 133–34.
95. J. C. Peoples, "Letter to A.W. Buchanan, December 12, 1890," in Pollack, *The Populist Mind*, 22.
96. Kazin, *The Populist Persuasion*, 28.
97. Thomas Watson, "Speech Reprinted from the People's Party Paper (Atlanta), August 12, 1892," in Pollack, *The Populist Mind*, 380; Watson quoted in Postel, *The Populist Vision*, 196.
98. Shefter, "Trade Unions," 217; Stowell, *Streets, Railroads*, 8.
99. Jeffrey, "Women in the Alliance," 85.
100. My analysis here is indebted to Judith Butler, who traces the mutually reinforcing relationship between racist discourse, racist vision, and white anxiety in "Endangered/Endangering," 15–22.
101. This is due in great part to extensive documentation by the Alliance itself and, according to Theodore Mitchell, to a broader late nineteenth-century interest in educational spaces outside formal institutions of education. Mitchell, *Political Education in the Southern Farmers' Alliance*, 20–22.
102. Quoted in Mitchell, *Political Education*, 47, 95.
103. Garvin and Daws, *National Farmers' Alliance*, viii.
104. Garvin and Daws, *National Farmers' Alliance*, viii.
105. Garvin and Daws, *National Farmers' Alliance*, 76.
106. Quoted in Mitchell, *Political Education*, 70.
107. See Pierre Bourdieu, *Outline of a Theory of Practice*, 159–71.
108. Nugent, "Four Speeches in Texas," 300.
109. Postel, *The Populist Vision*, 77–78.
110. W. Scott Morgan, *History of the Wheel and Alliance and the Impending Revolution*, 135–44.
111. For a concise overview of the Alliance, see Sanders, *Roots of Reform*, 117–33.
112. Goodwyn, *Democratic Promise*, 36–44; Postel, *The Populist Vision*, 49–50.
113. Postel, *The Populist Vision*, 65; Goodwyn, *Democratic Promise*, 368.
114. Garvin and Daws, *National Farmers' Alliance*, 94; Postel, *The Populist Vision*, 66.
115. For an overview of suballiance meetings, see Mitchell, *Political Education*, 47–68. On Alliance pedagogy, see Mitchell, *Political Education*, 111; Sanders, *Roots of Reform*, 123; and Postel, *The Populist Vision*, 168. Postel documents a desire for uniformity of message among the Alliance's top officials: traveling lecturers were recruited by state leaders and were expected to adhere to rules of speech and limit discussion on certain issues (including the structure of the Alliance). As Mitchell and Goodwyn argue, the more radical lecturers often strayed from the organization's message or were challenged by rank-and-file members.
116. Postel, *The Populist Vision*, 66.
117. Michael Schwartz, *Radical Protest and Social Structure*, 201–15; Sanders, *Roots of Reform*, 119, 441.
118. Quoted in Goodwyn, *The Populist Moment*, 30.
119. Quoted in Goodwyn, *The Populist Moment*, 78–80.

120. Goldberg, *An Army of Women*, 141.
121. Sanders, *Roots of Reform*, 40.
122. Mari Jo Buhle, *Women and American Socialism*, 88–89.
123. Postel, *The Populist Vision*, 70–71; Goldberg, *An Army of Women*, 142; Buhle, *Women and American Socialism*, 82–90, 105–6; Jeffrey, "Women in the Alliance," 72–91.
124. Buhle, *Women and American Socialism*, 89.
125. Quoted in Buhle, *Women and American Socialism*, 88–89.
126. Postel, *The Populist Vision*, 72, 85; Buhle, *Women and American Socialism*, 87.
127. Sanders, *Roots of Reform*, 51.
128. Quoted in Foner, *Labor Movement*, 2:56.
129. Quoted in Rana, *Two Faces*, 199.
130. Sanders, *Roots of Reform*, 42.
131. Quoted in Leon Fink, *Workingmen's Democracy*, 14.
132. Quoted in Fink, *Workingmen's Democracy*, 10.
133. Quoted in Foner, *Labor Movement*, 2:76; Fink, *Workingmen's Democracy*, 11.
134. Powderly is quoted in Foner, *Labor Movement*, 2:76. See also Fink, *Workingmen's Democracy*, 11; Postel, *The Populist Vision*, 212.
135. Quoted in Foner, *Labor Movement*, 2:48.
136. Foner, *Labor Movement*, 2:83.
137. Shefter, "Trade Unions," 218.
138. Sanders, *Roots of Reform*, 49–50; Shefter, "Trade Unions," 236.
139. On the Great Southwest Strike as a catalyst for solidarity between the Knights and the Alliance, see Goodwyn, *Democratic Promise*, 51–65.
140. Quotes are from H. H. Haaff, "Letter to the Editor, Farmers' Alliance (Lincoln), June 7, 1890," in Pollack, *The Populist Mind*, 444; "Reprinted from J.M.C. to the Editor, Farmers' Alliance (Lincoln), March 21, 1891," in *The Populist Mind*, 16.
141. Quoted in Goodwyn, *Democratic Promise*, 76.
142. Postel, *The Populist Vision*, 218; Fink, *Workingmen's Democracy*, 18–35.
143. Fink, *Workingmen's Democracy*, 27, 136; Sanders, *Roots of Reform*, 43–45.
144. Quoted in Joseph Gerteis, *Class and the Color Line*, 25.
145. Sanders, *Roots of Reform*, 49–54; Fink, *Workingmen's Democracy*, 19, 26–27.
146. Sanders, *Roots of Reform*, 49–54; Fink, *Workingmen's Democracy*, 27–30.
147. On Debs's involvement in Populism, see Postel, *The Populist Vision*, 222–23. There were local successes in uniting farmers and laborers behind the People's Party. The most promising was a farmer-labor-socialist coalition in Chicago in 1894. See Sanders, *Roots of Reform*, 56–57.
148. Quoted in Sanders, *Roots of Reform*, 84.
149. Quoted in Sanders, *Roots of Reform*, 55, 30.
150. Goodwyn, *Democratic Promise*, 308–10, 418; Sanders, *Roots of Reform*, 4, 411.
151. Kazin, *The Populist Persuasion*, 35; Paul Krause, *The Battle for Homestead*, 220–21.
152. In addition to Goodwyn, see C. Vann Woodward, "The Populist Heritage and the Intellectual"; Walter Nugent, *The Tolerant Populists*.
153. Hofstadter is the chief proponent of this view. Although he offers a measured account of Populism, Postel chronicles the role many local Populist tickets played in the rise of Jim Crow.

154. See Hahn, *Nation under Our Feet*; Ali, *In the Lion's Mouth*; and Gaither, *Blacks*.
155. Ali, *In the Lion's Mouth*, 9.
156. Ali, *In the Lion's Mouth*, 8, 15, 20, 24–25.
157. Hahn, *Nation under Our Feet*, 415–16.
158. Ali, *In the Lion's Mouth*, xv, 24.
159. Foner, *Labor Movement*, 2:67; Ali, *In the Lion's Mouth*, 35. Sanders documents lower membership of black Knights, citing twenty thousand black members in about 120 locals at the union's peak in 1986. See her *Roots of Reform*, 40.
160. Ali, *In the Lion's Mouth*, 18, 27, 34. Estimates of CFA membership range from 250,000 (by Goodwyn) to over a million (by Ali and Postel). For a discussion of these varying estimates, see Ali, *In the Lion's Mouth*, 53. On the conflicting philosophies of black landowners and landless black workers, see Fon Louise Gordon, *Caste and Class: The Black Experience in Arkansas*. Not the primary focus of this chapter, I address the internal hierarchies and tensions that always also trouble the impossible unity of marginalized groups in the book's conclusion.
161. Ali, *In the Lion's Mouth*, 39–41; Hahn, *Nation under Our Feet*, 416.
162. Quoted in Hahn, *Nation under Our Feet*, 417.
163. Quoted in Gerteis, *Class and Color Line*, 61–62.
164. Hahn, *Nation under Our Feet*, 417.
165. Ali, *In the Lion's Mouth*, 8–9.
166. Hahn, *Nation under Our Feet*, 417.
167. Gerteis, *Class and Color Line*, 50–62, 92; Foner, *Labor Movement*, 2:66–74.
168. Quoted in Postel, *The Populist Vision*, 42. On cooperation, joint meetings, and the calculated interests of CFA members see Ali, *In the Lion's Mouth*, 61–65; and Gerteis, *Class and Color Line*, 44–46.
169. Quoted in Ali, *In the Lion's Mouth*, 38. On the CFA strikes and boycotts, see Gaither, *Blacks*, 14–16; Ali, *In the Lion's Mouth*, 67–75; Hahn, *Nation under Our Feet*, 421–23; Postel, *The Populist Vision*, 126, 180.
170. Watson, "Reprinted from the People's Party Paper," 380.
171. Quoted in Ali, *In the Lion's Mouth*, 87, 92.
172. Quoted in Goodwyn, *Democratic Promise*, 288.
173. Quoted in Ali, *In the Lion's Mouth*, 89–90.
174. See Gaither, *Blacks*, 90–93; Ali, *In the Lion's Mouth*, 136–41; Thomas C. Cox, *Blacks in Topeka, Kansas*, 126–32; Anthony Adam and Gerald Gaither, *Black Populism in the United States*, 23–24, 28, 49, 58.
175. Sanders, *Roots of Reform*, 129; Goodwyn, *Democratic Promise*, 295–99.
176. Goodwyn, "Populist Dreams and Negro Rights."
177. W. E. B. Du Bois, *Black Reconstruction in America*, 700; David R. Roediger develops this concept in *The Wages of Whiteness*.
178. Quoted in Rana, *Two Faces*, 198.
179. Quoted in Hahn, *Nation under Our Feet*, 432. For a concise account of Populist voter intimidation and the rise of Jim Crow laws, see Postel, *The Populist Vision*, 177–98.
180. Scholars commonly refer to the People's Party as the "anti-party party," abetted by the attitudes of many Populist organizers themselves. "We call it a party, but it is

not right so," clarified the Kansas Populist Annie Diggs. "It is a great uprising of the people." Quoted in Postel, *The Populist Vision*, 140.

181. Lorenzo Lewelling, "Inaugural Address, 1893," in Pollack, *The Populist Mind*, 53.

182. This is Sanders's argument in *Roots of Reform*.

183. Quoted in Postel, *The Populist Vision*, 118.

184. Quoted in Postel, *The Populist Vision*, 124–25. On the modern, centralizing vision of Alliance leaders, see *The Populist Vision*, 115–25.

185. Goodwyn, *Democratic Promise*, 39. Whereas Postel focuses on Macune's vision of Alliance cooperation, Goodwyn chronicles grassroots contests over national policies and the independent initiatives of suballiances. See *Democratic Promise*, 110–39 (especially 121–24). On the Bohemian boycott, see Postel, *The Populist Vision*, 184.

186. Foner, *History of the Labor Movement*, vol. 1, 508; see also Foner, *Labor Movement*, 2:90–91.

187. Foner, *Labor Movement*, 1:508.

188. Melton McLaurin, *The Knights of Labor in the South*, 52; Foner, *Labor Movement*, 2:82–83.

189. Sanders, *Roots of Reform*, 50–52.

190. Rana, *Two Faces*, 206–8.

191. Kazin, *The Populist Persuasion*, 30; Postel, *The Populist Vision*, 140.

192. Sanders, *Roots of Reform*, 128–31; Kazin, *The Populist Persuasion*, 27.

193. Rana, *Two Faces*, 208.

194. Quoted in Goodwyn, *The Populist Moment*, 306–7.

195. On the KOL's shift from local assembly politics to electoral politics, see Sanders, *Roots of Reform*, 49–55; and Fink, *Workingmen's Democracy*, 19, 27. On the CFA's shift from the cooperative movement to electoral politics, see Ali, *In the Lion's Mouth*, 55, 75. On the decline of the Alliance cooperative movement in tandem with the rise of the People's Party, see Goodwyn, *Democratic Promise*, 483–92, and *Populist Moment*, 298–310.

196. See Goodwyn, *Democratic Promise*, 348; Sanders, *Roots of Reform*, 131.

197. Rana, *Two Faces*, 195, 205–6.

198. Rana, *Two Faces*, 121.

199. Postel, *The Populist Vision*, 288.

200. Sanders, *Roots of Reform*, 1, 4, 128–33.

201. "National People's Party Platform, July 1892," 63.

202. Sanders, *Roots of Reform*, 388. See also *Roots of Reform*, 132, 187–88, 410–17; Postel, *The Populist Vision*, 139–40.

203. See Sanders, *Roots of Reform*, 387–408; Steve Fraser, *The Age of Acquiescence*, 187–95.

204. See Kazin, *The Populist Persuasion*, 109–34, 221–68.

205. Kazin, *The Populist Persuasion*, 245–68; Joseph E. Lowndes, *From the New Deal to the New Right*, 11–44.

206. Steve Fraser, "The Limousine Liberal's Family Tree"; Fraser, *The Age of Acquiescence*, 264–301.

207. Quoted in Linda Kintz, *Between Jesus and the Market*, 43.

208. Connolly, *Capitalism and Christianity, American Style*, 44.

209. See also Paul Apostolidis, *Stations of the Cross*; Kintz, *Between Jesus and Market*.

210. Kevin Zeese, director of Prosperity Agenda, quoted in Allison Kilkenny, "Resistance Has Begun," 191.

211. See, for example, Mark R. Warren, *Dry Bones Rattling*; Jeffrey Stout, *Blessed Are the Organized*; Marion Orr, ed., *Transforming the City*. The Orr volume contains critiques of the limits of community-organizing visions for state and national change.

212. Fraser, *The Age of Acquiescence*, 209–21. Fraser juxtaposes the Populist revolt during the first Gilded Age with the widespread acquiescence in the second. The acquiescence of the Left, he argues, has made way for "the rise of the populist right . . . a resistance on behalf of restoration, one that doesn't pretend to confront the fundamentals our ancestors once did" (221).

Chapter 3

1. To view the ad, see Seth Stevenson, "Can Rosa Parks Sell Pickup Trucks?"

2. I do not mean to suggest that we can determine the effect of "Anthem" on individual or social imagination. Rather than evaluate the impact of specific ads, Roland Marchand explains, advertising critics look for "persistent patterns of verbal and visual expression" that impact social imaginaries over time (xx). In his influential book, *Advertising the American Dream*, Marchand writes that most scholars "acknowledge the power of frequently repeated media images and ideas to establish broad frames of reference [and] define the boundaries of public discussion" (xx). I evaluate "Anthem" as an ad that exemplifies these larger processes.

3. Lizabeth Cohen, *A Consumers' Republic*. I discuss GM's role in the rise of America's consumer society below.

4. Michael Kazin discusses populism's ubiquity in *The Populist Persuasion*, 5–6, 271.

5. As I discuss in chapter 1, some radical democratic scholars attend to the relationship between populism and political culture, understood either as rhetoric (Kazin) or as ethos and practice (Goodwyn, Boyte). By excluding discussions of popular culture, I argue here, they cannot account for its impact on the everyday language and practice of would-be populist actors.

6. The advertising and marketing industry outpaces other forms of communication in its ability to convey cultural messages and shape peoples' perceptions and desires. US companies spent $171 billion on ads in 2013, and that figure does not account for marketing research. By 2007, the typical urban resident saw up to five thousand commercial messages a day, ranging from over one hundred television ads, to Internet pop-ups and sidebars, to magazine and newspaper ads, to direct mailers, to the ads they encounter on billboards, subway walls and trains, the sides of buses and taxis, gas pumps, shopping carts, and on and on. Conceived in this way, advertising and marketing clutter our daily lives with a rapid succession of images and sounds that mediate our perceptions and desires. See "Total US Ad Spending to See Largest Increase Since 2004"; Juliann Sivulka, *Soap, Sex, and Cigarettes*, 335–38, 390–92.

7. As Stuart Hall explains, popular culture is always characterized by a struggle between power and powerlessness, that is, between hegemonic cultural forces and the marginalized groups who variously negotiate, resist, and reconstitute them. Stuart Hall, "Notes on Deconstructing the Popular," 449–50. For examples of such

negotiations, see Arlene Dávila, *Latinos, Inc.*; Anthony J. Cortese, *Provocateur*; Katherine Sender, *Business, Not Politics.*

8. Winston Fletcher, *Advertising*, 12. For a "textbook" guide to brand image and strategy, see Alina Wheeler, *Designing Brand Identity*, 1–27.

9. Quoted in Nick Bunkley, "Aiming to Be the Truck of Patriots." For 2006 playoff advertising costs, see John Vrooman, "Theory of the Big Dance," 72.

10. General Motors press release, quoted in Stevenson, "Rosa Parks." I discuss Chevy's bankruptcy and resurrection later in this chapter.

11. Kim Kosak, Chevy's general director for advertising and sales promotions in 2006, quoted in "Chevy Silverado Ads Go for Reaction."

12. Bush quoted in Amanda Terkel, "With Recession Looming, Bush Tells America to 'Go Shopping More,'" *ThinkProgress* (blog), December 20, 2006, http://thinkprogress.org/politics/ 2006/12/20/9281/bush-shopping/. On previous Chevrolet ad campaigns, see Bradley Johnson, "From 'See the USA in Your Chevrolet' to 'Like a Rock,' Chevy Ads Run Deep." On the history of Chevrolet and the automobile in the marketing of American values, see Sivulka, *Soap, Sex, and Cigarettes*, 94–96, 121–32, 209; and Marchand, *Advertising the American Dream*, 156–61, 220.

13. For the locations of GM's manufacturing, see "General Motors Manufacturing Plants," *GM Authority* (blog), accessed September 24, 2014, http://gmauthority.com/blog/gm/gm-manufacturing/. In their study on US immigration policy toward Mexico, Douglass Massey, Jorge Durand, and Nolan Malone chart what they call the hypocritical equation at its center since the early 1900s. With one hand, government officials enact policies (and leave others unenforced) to appease the demand by businesses for immigrant labor. With the other hand, they appeal to mobilized nativist sentiment by enforcing strict border control (or at least giving the pretense of doing so). The authors argue that the burdens and instabilities of Mexican immigration to the United States, for immigrants and many Americans alike, have heightened since the 1980s as increased economic integration has been met by more rigid border controls. With its appeal to a narrow patriotism in "Anthem," side by side with the lobbying of its parent company, General Motors, to extend the North American Free Trade Agreement to other hemispheric countries, Chevy plays its cards on both sides of the equation. See Douglas S. Massey, Jorge Durand, and Nolan Malone, *Beyond Smoke and Mirrors*. For GM's lobbying activities, which totaled $8.5 million in 2014 and included several trade-related issues, see the Center for Responsive Politics' "General Motors Client Profile: Summary 2014," at OpenSecrets.com, https://www.opensecrets.org/lobby/clientsum.php?id=D000000155&year=2014.

14. David Bordwell and Kristin Thompson, *Film Art*, 456–59.

15. Mary Connelly, "Striking a Nerve"; Paul Farhi, "The Pickup Ad That's Carrying Lots of Baggage."

16. Amanda Hess, "When Did the Rock-Solid Manly Men in Truck Commercials Get So Soft?"

17. Chris Duke, "Our Country, Our Truck: Chevrolet Launches New 2007 Silverado 'Our Country. Our Truck.' Marketing Campaign," *Truckblog*, September 26, 2006, http:// www.truckblog. com/1002-our_country_our_truck. Mellencamp founded Farm Aid.

18. Theresa Howard, " 'Revolution' in Ad Campaign."
19. Quoted in Duke, " 'Our Country.' "
20. Sivulka, *Soap, Sex, and Cigarettes*, 345. I discuss producerism at length in chapter 2.
21. See, for example, Stevenson, "Rosa Parks"; Farhi, "Pickup Ad"; Mary Connelly, "Striking a Nerve"; David Carr, "American Tragedies, to Sell Trucks."
22. Martin Luther King, "I Have a Dream," in *A Testament of Hope*, 219. On the lesser-known Rosa Parks, see Jeanne Theoharis, *The Rebellious Life of Mrs. Rosa Parks*. On white fascination with and disciplining of black heterosexual masculinity—for example, by naturalizing athletic talent and commodifying sports heroes—see Herman Gray, "Black Masculinity and Visual Culture"; Abby L. Ferber, "The Construction of Black Masculinity." On misappropriations of King, see Kevin Bruyneel, "The King's Body." For a prominent example, see Shelby Steele, *The Content of Our Character*.
23. Richelle Swan and Kristin Bates, "Social Justice in the Face of the Storm," 3–14.
24. On the automobile and American geography, see Sivulka, *Soap, Sex, and Cigarettes*, 131.
25. For a history of settler colonialism in the United States, see Walter L. Hixson, *American Settler Colonialism*. On the relationship between American views of freedom and imperial aspirations, see Aziz Rana, *The Two Faces of American Freedom*, 3–14.
26. See Joseph E. Lowndes, *From the New Deal to the New Right*, 106–39.
27. To view "Backbone," see qbnscholar, "Chevy Truck Country 3." On Hannity's GM promotion, see "GM Hires Fox News Mouthpiece Sean Hannity as Spokesman," *ThinkProgress* (blog), September 29, 2006, http://thinkprogress.org/politics/2006/09/29/7772/hannity-gm/.
28. Quoted in Mary Connelly, "Striking a Nerve."
29. Martin Luther King, "A Time to Break Silence," in *A Testament of Hope*, 281.
30. On the UAW's role in the March on Washington and its multiracial organizing against GM, see John Barnard, *American Vanguard*, 388–92, 402, 411, 431, 441, 466–76.
31. Martin Luther King, "The Drum Major Instinct," in *A Testament of Hope*, 261.
32. Lauren Berlant, *Cruel Optimism*.
33. Sivulka, *Soap, Sex, and Cigarettes*, 132. For more on planned obsolescence, see Giles Slade, *Made to Break*. On GM's strategies for shaping social consumption norms, see Tony Tinker, Cheryl Lehman, and Marilyn Neimark, "Bookkeeping for Capitalism," 188–216.
34. Sivulka, *Soap, Sex, and Cigarettes*, 209.
35. GM also helped popularize the ideal of the ideal of the "two-car family." In 1928, Chevrolet ads insisted that "a car for her, too!" was "becoming a necessity." See Marchand, *Advertising the American Dream*, 156, 161. Thorstein Veblen coined the term "conspicuous consumption" in his 1899 book, *The Theory of the Leisure Class*. On consumption as the dominant social relationship in America, see Cohen, *A Consumers' Republic*, 292–344; Stuart Ewen, *Channels of Desire*, 41–80.
36. Sivulka, *Soap, Sex, and Cigarettes*, 209.

37. "This Is the New GM." In GM's first three decades alone, it purchased dozens of car companies in the United States, Britain, and Germany and numerous parts-makers. Its combined shares reached over 50 percent at its height. Unable to forge a unified company, GM allowed its brands to compete with each other for a share of the company's budget and, in some cases, for positioning in the automotive market. The success of foreign automakers in the United States and the economic crisis that hit in the late 1970s precipitated restructuring. Like many firms, GM moved operations from the union-friendly Rust Belt to the Sun Belt and outsourced overseas. That continued in the information age of 1990s, as global competition put American firms under pressure to restructure, consolidate, and simplify. On these trends and the rise and fall of GM, see Seth Worton, "General Motors"; "The Bankruptcy of General Motors"; Ben Austen, "End of the Road"; and Sivulka, *Soap, Sex, and Cigarettes*, 2011, 286, 326.
38. See "Bankruptcy of General Motors"
39. Tim Higgins, "U.S. Lost $11.2 Billion in GM Bailout, TARP Report Says"; Craig Keenan, "Auto Bailouts Won't Be Repaid in Full."
40. Jesse Lee, "GM & Chrysler," *The White House Blog*, March 30, 2009, http://www.whitehouse.gov/blog/09/03/30/GM-and-Chrysler.
41. On GM's bankruptcy restructuring, see Lee, "GM & Chrysler"; "Bankruptcy of General Motors." On UAW victories from the postwar era through the 1960s, see Barnard, *American Vanguard*, 259–313; Francis Donnelly, "UAW's Battles Shape History."
42. "Obama Administration New Path to Viability for GM & Chrysler," *The White House* website, accessed May 31, 2015, https://www.whitehouse.gov/assets/documents/Fact_Sheet_GM_Chrysler_FIN.pdf; Bill Vlasic and Annie Lowrey, "U.S. Ends Bailout of G.M., Selling Last Shares of Stock."
43. Quoted in Vlasic and Lowrey, "U.S. Ends Bailout."
44. There is an irony, of course, when America's first black president is the mouthpiece of neoliberalism: as I will discuss in chapter 4, Obama's election was a lightning rod for populist uprisings on the right and left that alternately decry neoliberalism (as have many black radicals) or attempt to exclude marginalized groups from its benefits (as have many Tea Partiers).
45. Barack Obama, "Remarks by the President on the American Automotive Industry."
46. Douglas McIntyre, "Is GM's Rebound the Real Deal?"; Bill Vlasic, "Annual Sales for American Automakers Reach a 6-Year High." GM's sales continue to despite the most recent hit to its brand image: the manufacturer has had to recall over 1.6 million cars and trucks due to faulty ignition switches that resulted in fatal crashes that claimed the lives of at least thirteen people. See Reuters, "GM Sales Appear Resilient Despite Recalls."
47. On conditions in Detroit, see Susan C. Beachy, "Anatomy of Detroit's Decline"; Elliot Hannon, "Detroit Resumes Cutting Off Water to 150,000 Residents." For unemployment and poverty figures from 2014, see Leonidas Murembya and Eric Guthrie, "Demographic and Labor Market Profile."
48. Under pressure from the UAW, the Big Three have recommitted to building jobs in Detroit. They are also staples of charitable giving to the city. By all accounts,

however, the Big Three will not be at the center of any future recovery in Detroit. See Beachy, "Anatomy of Detroit's Decline"; Bill Vlasic, "Detroit Is Now a Charity Case for Carmakers."

49. Galbraith quoted in Cohen, *A Consumers' Republic*, 10. Galbraith makes this argument in his 1958 book *The Affluent Society*.

50. Cohen, *A Consumers' Republic*, 13.

51. Andrew Ross Sorkin, "Rich and Sort of Rich."

52. On slashed and sequestered public funding, see Andy Sullivan, "Insight"; Suzy Khimm, "The Sequester, Explained"; Tim Murphy, "The United States of Sequestration." On income growth since 2009, see Estelle Sommeiller and Mark Price, "The Increasingly Unequal States of America."

53. Sheldon Wolin, "Agitated Times," 6.

54. William Graham Sumner, *What Social Classes Owe to Each Other*. On the American myth of success from Alger through Sumner's social Darwinism, see Madonna Marsden, "The American Myth of Success," 139–42.

55. Robert Zemeckis, *Forrest Gump*. My reading is indebted to George Shulman and Kevin Bruyneel, who suggested the Forrest Gump metaphor as a way to make sense of the feel-good multiculturalism of Chevy's ad.

56. On *Forrest Gump* as a conservative film and touchstone of conservative mobilization, see Thomas B. Byers, "History Re-membered"; Jennifer Hyland Wang, "A Struggle of Contending Force," 92–96. On the character of Gump as innocent mediator and redeemer of a divided nation, see Peter N. Chomo II, " 'You've Got to Put the Past behind You Before You Can Move On,' " 2–7. On Gary Sinise's conservative activism, see Michael Cieply and Nicholas Confessore, "Leaning Right in Hollywood."

57. See, for instance, David McIvor, "The Politics of Speed"; Rosa Hartmut, "Social Acceleration"; Zygmunt Bauman, *Liquid Times*; Paul Virilio, *Speed and Politics*.

58. Ray Kurzweil, "Frontiers."

59. Wendy Brown, "Governmentality in the Age of Neoliberalism." See also Michel Foucault, *The Birth of Biopolitics*, 117–22, 141–47, 185–213, 291–313; Colin Gordin, "Governmental Rationality," 41–45; Mitchell M. Dean, *Governmentality*, 175–204.

60. Mary Connelly, "Striking a Nerve."

61. On neoliberal multiculturalism, see, for instance, Jodi Melamed, "The Spirit of Neoliberalism."

62. Jon Pareles, "Heartland Rock."

63. Sheldon S. Wolin discusses these features of the "economic polity" in *Politics and Vision*, 575, 589.

64. John Cougar Mellencamp, "Pink Houses," *Uh-huh*.

65. Alexis de Tocqueville, *Democracy in America*, 638.

66. Deregulation began in earnest under Presidents Ford and Carter, and Nixon's fiscal policies typically reflected his famous concession, "We are all Keynesians now." His administration, however, played a major role in initiating the deregulation of the transportation industry. He also helped popularize the racially coded rhetoric that Republicans used to attack the Great Society (which his own policies upheld). As Kazin writes in *The Populist Persuasion*, Nixon "talked like a grassroots conservative while often governing like a liberal" (251). As Lowndes argues in *From the New*

Deal to the New Right, this rhetoric perfected the "discursive shift" that set the stage for government downsizing during the Reagan Revolution (157). Nixon is quoted in David Harvey, *A Brief History of Neoliberalism*, 13. On Nixon's role in deregulating transportation, see Mark H. Rose, Bruce E. Seely, and Paul F. Barrett, *The Best Transportation System*, 151–65.

67. Corporate lobbying plays a major role in framing public and legal discourse in America and, as such, underwrites the expanding influence of corporate capitalism on society and politics. In 1965, for example, Ralph Nader singled out GM in an exposé that alerted Americans to the auto industry's concerted attempts to minimize and sidestep automobile and highway safety standards and environmental regulations. GM has also been influential in judicial decisions, including a noteworthy case that reduced the impact and framing of antidiscrimination laws for black women. On GM's lobbying, see Center for Responsive Politics, "General Motors Client Profile: Summary 2013" and "General Motors Client Profile: Issues, 2013" at OpenSecrets.org, http://www.opensecrets.org/lobby/clientsum.php?id=D000000155&year=2013. See also Ralph Nader, *Unsafe at Any Speed*, 1–51, 306–12; on *DeGraffenreid v. General Motors*, see Kimberle Crenshaw, "Demarginalizing the Intersection of Race and Sex," 141–43.

68. Lindsay Chappell, "Sales to Hispanics Outpacing the Market."

69. Dávila, *Latinos, Inc.*, 49–55; Sivulka, *Soap, Sex, and Cigarettes*, 385–90.

70. "Chevy's 'Subete' Campaign Invites Hispanic Customers to 'Come On Board,'" *The Auto Channel* website, accessed November 1, 2014, http://www.theautochannel. com/news/2004/08/10/ 208254.html; David Shepardson, "Chevy Speaks to Latino Buyers," *GM in the News* (blog), November 6, 2007, http://general-motors. blogspot.com/2006/11/chevy-speaks-to-latino-buyers_06.html.

71. Shepardson, "Chevy Speaks."

72. Dávila, *Latinos, Inc.*, 3, 22.

73. Market segmenting, of course, does not ensure equal access to all social groups. See Sivulka, *Soap, Sex, and Cigarettes*, 2011, 286, 298; Dávila, *Latinos, Inc.*, 7.

74. "Chevy's 'Subete' Campaign"; Karl Greenberg, "Chevy Pitches Fuel Efficiency to Hispanics via Mexican Band."

75. Dávila, *Latinos, Inc.*, 6.

76. Advertising helps define but also pushes the boundaries of norms, identities, and aspirations. For example, advertisers routinely discipline representations of gender, race, sexuality, and nationality to fit acceptable norms; yet advertising has also tested the status quo by bringing working women, metrosexual and gay men, interracial couples, and Spanish-language ads to mainstream living rooms. For a review of this debate, see Dávila, *Latinos, Inc.*, 7.

77. Susan Kim, "The Auto Industry's Forgotten Legacy"; Zaragosa Vargas, *Proletarians of the North*, 5–7, 102–3, 119.

78. In 1995, it took three well-placed ads to reach 80 percent of women. By 2003, it took ninety-seven spots to reach them. Sivulka, *Soap, Sex, and Cigarettes*, 331, 390.

79. Arthur Asa Berger, *Ads, Fads, and Consumer Culture*, 6.

80. Sivulka, *Soap, Sex, and Cigarettes*, 394.

81. Hall, "Deconstructing the Popular," 449–50.

82. For such critiques of user-generated Internet content, see, for instance, Kathleen Mary Kuehn, "There's Got to Be a Review Democracy"; Sarah Banet-Weiser, "Rate Your Knowledge," 307.

83. Sivulka, *Soap, Sex, and Cigarettes*, 394–96. Among the parodies, one showed a sweeping view of the Tahoe on a desert road, with the tagline: "Our planet's oil is almost gone. You don't need a G.P.S. to see where this road leads." See Julie Bosman, "Chevy Tries a Write-Your-Own-Ad Approach, and the Potshots Fly."

84. Jacobsladderfat, "Toyota—This Is Our Country"; PintoPopProductions, "Toyota: This is OUR Country." There are many of these spoofs, ranging from personal, to patriotic, to sports-themed, to several that depict alternative variations of masculine popular culture (e.g., ones by a reader of Every Day Should Be Saturday, College Football, and NationalLampoon.com). See, for instance, Forthoffirth, "This Is Our Country (My Version)"; SpiderRider3, "This Is Our Truck—Chevy Commercial Parody"; Niefga, "NFL Chevy Spoof 1"; CapsNut, "Caps 'Our Country' Commercial'"; Spencer Hall, "EDSBS Presents"; National Lampoon, "Oh Dear God . . . This Is Our Country."

85. Impers1, "This Is Our Country, Ron Paul"; Election06, "Mellencamp Our Country for Real Americans."

86. King, "Time to Break Silence," 233.

87. Election06, "Mellencamp Our Country Red State Satire"; Dvpringle, " 'This Is Our Country' Chevrolet Silverado Ad Parody"; John Paul, "This Is Our Country." John Paul produced a "video of [1,800] unedited randomly ordered images collected by keyword searches such as 'African American,' 'Asian-American,' [and] 'Native American.' " The parody aims to show that "not everyone is a Chevy pickup truck driving white dude." Perhaps unwittingly, its rapid succession of random, unrelated images also parodies Chevy's neoliberal techniques of montage.

88. We now see a complex terrain of political struggle vis-à-vis the advertising industry, ranging from individual acts of appropriation via social media, to the cultural discourse of "opting out" of the digital age, to movements by marginalized groups demanding access and recognition in advertising. See Sivulka, *Soap, Sex, and Cigarettes*, 256, 283, 358, 368, 394; Dávila, *Latinos, Inc.*, 9–15.

89. On hip consumerism, see Thomas Frank, *The Conquest of Cool*, 26–32, 136, 229–31.

90. Picture Flint, Michigan, where Michael More filmed *Roger & Me*, a documentary about the closing of several General Motors plants during the 1980s due to corporate downsizing and outsourcing. These production calculations cost thirty thousand people their jobs and economically devastated the city. See Michael Moore, *Roger & Me*.

91. Cohen quoted in Jeff Burger, *Leonard Cohen on Leonard Cohen*, 272.

92. Leonard Cohen, "Democracy," *The Future*. All Cohen lyrics are from "Democracy" unless otherwise noted.

93. Farhi, "Pickup Ad."

94. Quoted in Burger, *Leonard Cohen*, 300, 320–21.

95. Quoted in Burger, *Leonard Cohen*, 320, 324.

96. Cohen, "Anthem," *The Future*.

97. Cohen is quoted in a 1992 interview by Bob Mackowycz, Doug Thompson, and Alan Lysaght as part of the "The Future Radio Special," a special (and now collector's item) CD released by Sony Music Canada. See the Leonard Cohen Files website, http://www.leonardcohenfiles.com/int-cd.html and the Diamonds in the Lines website, http://www.leonardcohen-prologues.com/anthem.htm, both accessed May 31, 2015.

98. Quoted in Burger, *Leonard Cohen*, 321.

99. Quoted in Burger, *Leonard Cohen*, 75, 300, 313.

100. Quoted in Burger, *Leonard Cohen*, 271

101. Cohen, "The Future," *The Future*.

102. Quoted in Burger, *Leonard Cohen*, 320, 323, 337.

103. Quoted in Burger, *Leonard Cohen*, 271–72.

104. Walt Whitman, "Democratic Vistas," 954.

105. Whitman quoted in Jason Frank, "Promiscuous Citizenship," 155. For this reading of Whitman, see also Cristina Beltrán, "Mestiza Poetics."

106. Philip Nel, *The Avant-Garde and American Postmodernity*, 145. Green Party candidate Ralph Nader later used "Democracy" as a campaign theme song, and a supporter of Libertarian Ron Paul produced a YouTube video set to Cohen reading "Democracy." See Tim De Lisle, "Who Held a Gun to Leonard Cohen's Head?"; Searchin4thesound, "Democracy Coming."

107. The advertising and marketing arm of the music industry plays a big role in constituting the audience for a performer or genre. Record labels also rely on promotional tours and interviews, critical reviews in popular magazines, and airplay on radio, music television, and Internet streaming sites. American industry leaders such as the Billboard charts and the Grammys also influence music trends. By the time audiences hear an album, the image and sounds of a performer have been significantly shaped and framed by these processes. This same mediation serves to interpellate listeners as certain kinds of audiences within the range of popular music styles. In other words, the music industry largely establishes the aesthetic standards—the images, sounds, and styles—of what *counts as popular*. See Simon Frith, "Towards an Aesthetic of Popular Music," 137–40; Geoffrey P. Hull, *The Recording Industry*, 185–86, 245–46; Steve Chapple and Reebee Garofalo, *Rock "n" Roll Is Here to Pay*, xiii, 75–78.

108. Quoted in Burger, *Leonard Cohen*, 254.

109. Michael J. Kramer, *The Republic of Rock*, 5, 9, 12. Kramer's account focuses specifically on connections between the San Francisco Bay Area and Vietnam. Although I do not claim the same empirical grounding, I use the "republic of rock" more broadly here: to conceptualize the myriad virtual and embodied practices through which participants in the rock-and-roll counterculture created and contested shared narratives and terms of identification in the 1960s and 1970s.

110. Don McLean, "American Pie," *American Pie*; Lynyrd Skynyrd, "Sweet Home Alabama," *Second Helping*. Whereas scholars such as Paul Wells credit southern rock with contributing to nostalgic productions of white southern masculinity during the early 1970s, others have noted the genre's more complicated negotiations of race. See Paul Wells, "The Last Rebel," 117; Mike Butler, "Luther King Was a Good Ole Boy," 46–58. On folk rock and other radical themes in rock and roll during the

era, see Richie Unterberger, *Eight Miles High*, 77–132; James E. Perone, *Music of the Counterculture Era*, 33–109.

111. Frith, "Towards an Aesthetic," 137. By the middle to late 1960s, the music industry had become centralized. Independent record companies merged with or gave way to major ones, which were themselves bought out by megamedia conglomerates. At the heart of the relationship between rock and the mass music industry were changing forces of production and new technologies of mass mediation. These were difficult to disentangle from the rapidly developing mergers of capitalist, technological, and state power that had given rise to the very things rock music protested: the military industrial complex and the consumer republic. Indeed, rock musicians weren't just making profits for major record labels; they were making profits for megamedia conglomerates that had hundreds of millions of dollars in annual defense contracts. On these trends, see Chapple and Garofalo, *Rock "n" Roll*, 82–86.

112. Sylvie Simmons, *I'm Your Man*, 77.

113. Leonard Cohen, "Field Commander Cohen," *New Skin for the Old Ceremony*. The tension between vocation and career has contributed to Cohen's long breaks from the public eye. At the height of his success in 1993, Cohen abandoned his career to live in a spare cabin at the Mt. Baldy Zen Center near Los Angeles and participate in monastic life for five years. He did not return to the music scene until 2001's *Ten New Songs*. See Simmons, *I'm Your Man*, 398–426.

114. Neil Young, "This Note's for You," *This Note's for You*. Neil Young did sing for Cadillac in 1983. See John Quinn, "Neil Young 'Big Cadillac Giveaway' 1983 Commercial." On rock-and-roll artists as commercial spokespersons, see Jim Yoakum, "Rock the Cashbox"; Dorian Lynskey, "The Great Rock'n'Roll Sellout." Cohen has licensed his songs for television ads on rare occasion. In 2011, he went so far as to adapt a spoken-word version of his song "A Thousand Kisses Deep" as the voiceover for an ad by his record label Columbia's parent company, Sony. See DrHGuy, "Leonard Cohen's 'That's What I Heard You Say' Featured on Dramatic Sony Two Worlds Ad," *Cohencentric: Leonard Cohen Considered* (blog), May 12, 2015, http://cohencentric.com. On the use of Cohen's songs in other television ads, see the following posts by DrHGuy on *Cohencentric*: "Is 'The Darkness' In Falling Skies Season 3 Trailer the Best Use of a Leonard Cohen Song in an Ad," May 21, 2015; "Old Navy Jeans Ad - Madeleine Peyroux Covers Blue Alert by Leonard Cohen & Anjani Thomas (2007)," May 21, 2015; "Dutch TV Ad for NS International Train to Vienna Features Leonard Cohen's 'Take this Waltz," May 21, 2015; "South Korean Ramen Ad Features Leonard Cohen's 'I'm Your Man," April 14, 2015.

115. Bob Dylan has a history as a "commercial crooner" going at least back to 2006. Jeremy Allen, "The Commercial Crooner."

116. Burger, *Leonard Cohen*, 42, 82.

117. Quoted in Burger, *Leonard Cohen*, 308. By 1984, Cohen's reputation and sales had lagged so much that Columbia refused to release his 1984 album, *Various Positions*, to the US market (though the album contained several of Cohen's eventual greatest hits, including the sensational "Hallelujah"). On Cohen's record sales and reception, see Simmons, *I'm Your Man*, 195, 204, 219, 249, 281–83, 342–43, 367–68.

118. Paul Zollo quoted in Simmons, *I'm Your Man*, 263.

119. See Burger, *Leonard Cohen*, 195, 218, 249, 359–60, 386.

120. Quoted in Burger, *Leonard Cohen*, 303.
121. Quoted in Burger, *Leonard Cohen*, 85.
122. Burger, *Leonard Cohen*, 271, 278.
123. In film theory and practice, montage originated in the 1920s, with an avant-garde school of Soviet filmmakers, such as Lev Kuleshov, Sergei Eisenstein, Vsevolod Pudovkin, and Dziga Vertov. Their movement lasted into the 1930s, when the Soviet government, under Stalin's direction, consolidated its hold on artistic production, promoting readily accessible, realistic forms and censoring experimental, critical ones. See Bordwell and Thompson, *Film Art*, 305, 339–44, 478–81.
124. Quoted in Burger, *Leonard Cohen*, 273.
125. See James Tully, *Strange Multiplicity*, 1–6, 17–29, 92–101, 201–9.
126. On Cohen's perfectionist writing and recording habits and desire to connect with audiences, see Simmons, *I'm Your Man*, 177–78, 187–92, 278–79; Burger, *Leonard Cohen*, 168, 269, 276.
127. Quoted in Burger, *Leonard Cohen*, 264–65.
128. Quoted in Burger, *Leonard Cohen*, 11.
129. Quoted in Burger, *Leonard Cohen*, 377. See also 237, 370–71; Simmons, *I'm Your Man*, 3–14, 37.
130. Quoted in Burger, *Leonard Cohen*, 382. Cohen elaborates his views on Judaism, his idea that "we inhabit a biblical landscape," and his understanding of liturgy in a 1993 interview with Arthur Kurzweil, "I *Am* the Little Jew Who Wrote the Bible," reprinted in Burger, *Leonard Cohen*, 369–87.
131. For the appraisal of Dylan and rock critic Paul Zollo, see Burger, *Leonard Cohen*, 263, 283–84. For remarks by Rabbi Mordecai Finley, who calls Leonard "the greatest liturgist alive today," see Simmons, *I'm Your Man*, 332–33.
132. Quoted in Burger, *Leonard Cohen*, 378.
133. On liturgy as democratic practice, see Rom Coles's discussion in Stanley Hauerwas and Romand Coles, *Christianity, Democracy, and the Radical Ordinary*, 323, 327.
134. Quoted in Burger, *Leonard Cohen*, 77, 264–65. On Cohen's sense that there is "tremendous heroism all around [him]," see also p. 55.
135. On liturgical practice in Christianity and faith-based organizing, see Richard L. Wood, *Faith in Action*, 178–81, 208–13, 253–54; Hauerwas and Coles, *Christianity, Democracy*, 109, 149–50, 162, 209, 235–36, 323–27, 339–40. In the civil rights movement, see Coles in *Christianity, Democracy*, , 48–50, 59–61, 67–68. Charles Marsh explores what he calls the "lived theologies" of Beloved Community in *The Beloved Community*, 6.
136. Cohen quoted in Burger, *Leonard Cohen*, 280; Adrian Chamberlain, "Review."
137. For 1992 singles Billboard rating, see "The Hot 100—1992 Archive," accessed May 31, 2015, https://www.billboard.com/archive/charts/1992/hot-100. Cyrus's album was the top-selling record of the year according to Neilson SoundScan ratings and, until Adele matched his feat in 2013, he held the record for the most consecutive weeks (seventeen) for a debut record atop the Billboard album charts. See Mikael Wood, "Live Review"; Jessica Carter, "Adele's '21' Album Ties Billy Ray Cyrus for Billboard Record," *AXS* website, January 26, 2012, http:// www.axs.com/news/adele-s-21-album-ties-billy-ray-cyrus-for-billboard-record-15470.
138. Pareles, "Heartland Rock."

139. Bruce Springsteen, "Born to Run," *Born to Run*; Springsteen, "Better Days," *Lucky Town*.
140. Springsteen, "Human Touch," *Human Touch*.
141. Mellencamp, "Last Chance," *Whenever We Wanted*.
142. Mellencamp, "Empty Hands," *The Lonesome Jubilee*.
143. Springsteen, "Fifty Seven Channels," *Human Touch*.
144. Pareles, "Heartland Rock."
145. Mellencamp, "Down and Out in Paradise," *The Lonesome Jubilee*; and "Love and Happiness," *Whenever We Wanted*.
146. Springsteen, "The Ghost of Tom Joad" and "Youngstown," *The Ghost of Tom Joad*.
147. On the misunderstood Springsteen and Mellencamp, see David Remnick, "We Are Alive"; Frank Digiacomo, "One from the Heartland."
148. Tracy Chapman, "Behind the Wall," *Tracy Chapman*.
149. Ani DiFranco, "I'm No Heroine," *Imperfectly*; DiFranco, "Talk to Me Now," *Like I Said*; DiFranco, "Not a Pretty Girl," *Not a Pretty Girl*.
150. Bikini Kill, "Blood One," *Pussy Whipped*, recorded 1992, Kill Rock Stars, 1993, compact disc.
151. On the Riot Grrrl movement, see Kristen Schilt and Elke Zobl, "Connecting the Dots." For the movement's impact on music and culture Marisa Meltzer, *Girl Power*.
152. During the 1980s, queer synthpop groups such as Bronski Beat and Pet Shop Boys filled dance clubs with songs whose lyrics addressed antigay violence and HIV. For a sampling of songs addressing HIV/AIDS in the early 1990s, see Sal Cinquemani, "15 Songs about AIDS."
153. Pet Shop Boys, "Dreaming of the Queen," *Very*, recorded 1992–93, Parlaphone, 1993, compact disc.
154. Neil Young, "Philadelphia," *Philadelphia (Music from the Motion Picture)*; Bronski Beat, "Why," *The Age of Consent*; DiFranco, "On Every Corner," *Not So Soft*.
155. My reading of ACT UP is especially indebted to Mark Reinhardt, *The Art of Being*, 166–78. On ACT UP's "intensities" and "transports of enthusiasm," see Deborah B. Gould, *Moving Politics*, 200–212.
156. Michael P. Jeffries, *Thug Life*, 1. On the commercial crossover of R & B and hip-hop, see Mark Anthony Neal, "Rhythm and Bullshit?" For its impact on the content of rap music, see Jennifer Lena, "Social Context and Musical Content of Rap Music."
157. Tupac Shakur, "Words of Wisdom," *2Pacalypse Now*.
158. For an empirical evaluation of similarities and differences in the ways white and black fans interpret hip-hop, see Jeffries, *Thug Life*, 114–88, 191–94.
159. Shakur, "Words of Wisdom."
160. Public Enemy, "Black Steel in the Hour of Chaos," *It Takes a Nation of Millions to Hold Us Back*.
161. Shakur, "Heavy in the Game," *Me Against the World*. Contra Cornel West's argument that nihilism is a threat to black survival, Nicholas De Genova argues persuasively that its presence in literature and hip-hop can be a transgressive act of refusal vis-à-vis the terms of white society. See West, *Race Matters*, 15–32; De Genova, "Gangster Rap and Nihilism in Black America."

162. Tupac, "Death Around the Corner," *Me Against the World*; Dr. Dre, "Lyrical Gangbang," *The Chronic*.

163. Public Enemy, "Fight the Power," *Fear of a Black Planet*. For the lyric "Ali broke necks," see Run-D.M.C, "Proud to Be Black," *Raising Hell*.

164. On the relationship between black radicalism of the 1960s and 1970s and hip-hop (both its potential rebelliousness and its commodification into hip consumerism), see Gwendolyn Pough, "Seeds and Legacies"; Kara Keeling, " 'A Homegrown Revolutionary'?"; S. Craig Watkins, "A Nation of Millions."

165. Cornel West, "Populism," 212.

166. See Michelle Alexander, *The New Jim Crow*.

167. Kory Grow, "Lauryn Hill Dedicates 'Black Rage' Song to Ferguson"; George Yancy and Judith Butler, "What's Wrong with 'All Lives Matter'?"

168. Tricia Rose, *Black Noise*, 99–100. The concept of "hidden transcripts" comes from James C. Scott, *Domination and the Arts of Resistance*, xii–xiii, 4–14.

169. It also assumes that Diallo, who had come to the United States two years before he was murdered, would want to be considered American. Bruce Springsteen, "American Skin (41 Shots)," *The Essential Bruce Springsteen*, Columbia Records, 2003. For the sentiment "No one is safe," see, for instance, Crystal Shepeard, "No One Is Safe from Backlash"; Robert Koehler, "Should the Police Be Armed?"

170. Michael Eric Dyson, "The Culture of Hip Hop," 67. On hip-hop's musical inheritances and techniques, see "Culture of Hip Hop," 62, 66; Rose, *Black Noise*, 62–96; Andrew Bartlett, "Airshafts, Loudspeakers, and the Hip Hop Sample."

171. Rose, *Black Noise*, 73.

172. Public Enemy, "Fight the Power." Dyson uses the term "contained chaos" to describe "the most astute political rappers" (66). On sampling in "Fight the Power," see Mark Katz, *Capturing Sound*, 151–57.

173. Rose discusses the ways in which technology and orality combine to create tension and spaces of improvisation in hip-hop in *Black Noise*, 74–96; Dyson discusses these themes, including rap concerts as sites that loosen "the strictures of the tyrannizing surveillance and demoralizing condemnation of mainstream society," in "Culture of Hip-hop," 61–62, 66–68.

174. Public Enemy, "Fight the Power."

175. Dilip Parameshwar Gaonkar, "Toward New Imaginaries," 4; Michael Warner, *Publics and Counterpublics*, 50–63, 114–24; Craig J. Calhoun, "Imagining Solidarity"; Nilufer Gole, "Islam in Public"; Benjamin Lee and Edward LiPuma, "Cultures of Circulation."

176. Charles Taylor, *Modern Social Imaginaries*, 23.

177. Arjun Appadurai, "The Capacity to Aspire," 67–69.

178. Appadurai, "The Capacity to Aspire," 70.

179. Appadurai, "The Capacity to Aspire," 76.

180. Madison, for example, envisioned representative institutions that would contain the "wicked" factions that now lived on in a "rage for paper money, for an abolition of debts, [and] for an equal division of property." See Alexander Hamilton, James Madison, and John Jay, *The Federalist Papers*, 52. While Federalist constitutional theory based government on popular consent, it did not ensure the people an active role in politics. On the Federalists' diminished vision of popular sovereignty, see

Gordon S. Wood, *The Creation of the American Republic*, 519–23, 444–47; Herbert Storing, *What the Anti-Federalists Were For*, 38-47; Gary B. Nash, *The Unknown American Revolution*, 423–26.

181. See, for example, Nash, *Unknown American Revolution*; Ray Raphael, *A People's History of the American Revolution*; Lawrence Goodwyn, *Democratic Promise*; Harry Boyte, *Commonwealth*; Boyte and Frank Riessman, *The New Populism*; Michael Kazin, *The Populist Persuasion*; Rana, *Two Faces*; John Curl, *For All the People*.

182. It is not my intention to provide a historical tracing here. Kazin provides the best account of the historical split between left and right populisms in US history in *The Populist Persuasion*.

183. Carl Schmitt, *The Concept of the Political*, 26–35.

184. Wendy Brown, *States of Injury*, 52–76.

185. I'm thinking, for example, of the ways in which SNCC and Black Power activists influenced the politics of Martin Luther King Jr. by the time he gave his anti-Vietnam speech, "A Time to Break Silence." On these influences, see David Garrow, *Bearing the Cross*, 475–574.

CHAPTER 4

1. Quoted in Ben McGrath, "The Movement."

2. For a history and account of the economic crisis, see Joseph E. Stiglitz, *Freefall*, 1–57. On America's "second Gilded Age," see Lawrence Mishel et al., *The State of Working America*; David Grusky and Tamar Kricheli-Katz, eds., *The New Gilded Age*.

3. It is not self-evident that the Tea Party and Occupy are concerned primarily with democracy. Devin Burghart and Leonard Zeskind have tracked the presence of white nationalist groups in the Tea Party to argue that some Tea Partiers are more concerned with cultural purity than rule by the people. Jodi Dean has evaluated Occupy in terms of Marxist class struggle and the possibility of a "politics of the commons." See Devin Burghart and Leonard Zeskind, *Tea Party Nationalism*; Jodi Dean, "Occupation as Political Form"; Marco Deseriis and Jodi Dean, "A Movement without Demands?" *Possible Futures* (blog), January 3, 2012, http://www.possible-futures.org/2012/01/03/a-movement-without-demands/.

4. For a scholarly analysis of this debate, see Clarence Lo, "AstroTurf versus Grass Roots." In the media, see Chris Good, "The Tea Party Movement"; Eric Zuesse, "Final Proof the Tea Party Was Founded as a Bogus AstroTurf Movement."

5. See, for instance, Chip Berlet, "Taking Tea Partiers Seriously"; Michael Kazin, "Whatever Happened to the American Left?"

6. For accounts of the Tea Party's rise, see Kate Zernike, *Boiling Mad*, 13–48; Theda Skocpol and Vanessa Williamson, *The Tea Party and Republican Conservatism*, 7–9; Christine Trost and Lawrence Rosenthal, "Introduction," 9–16. I do not mean to discount the fact that early Tea Parties echoed the widespread populist backlash that had first erupted against the Troubled Asset Relief Program (TARP) in the lame-duck days of George W. Bush and had continued to bubble up in grassroots protests prior to Santelli's rant. The rhetorical and affective climate and the nascent grassroots activity is important to understanding the conditions of a movement that

has been far from episodic. But I do agree with those who place Obama's presidency as central to the Tea Party's anxieties and its rhetorical definition of the enemies of the people. On the protests prior to the Tea Party, see Zernike, *Boiling Mad*, 13–20. On Obama's centrality to Tea Party rhetoric, see Joseph Lowndes, "The Past and Future of Race in the Tea Party Movement," 156, 164–67; Christopher Parker and Matt Barreto, *Change They Can't Believe In*, 85–101, 190–217.

7. For Santelli's rant, see Lauren Sher, "CNBC's Santelli Rants about Housing Bailout." Over the next several months, libertarian and fiscally conservative organizations "test-marketed" the Tea Party concept. Leaders from social media sites and advocacy groups such as Top Conservatives on Twitter, American Solutions, and FreedomWorks coordinated with local activists to organize dozens of Tea Party protests during February and March. On April 15, hundreds of thousands of people gathered as part of Tax Day Tea Parties across the country. By that time, the Tea Party had grown into a decentralized movement of several national Tea Party organizations, a cadre of corporate and foundation backers, an echo chamber of right-wing media cheerleaders, and hundreds of local Tea Party groups whose energies exceeded the vision of movement's elites. See Lo, "AstroTurf versus Grass Roots," 98–103.

8. For a recent history of the racialized state in conservative discourse, see Joseph E. Lowndes, *From the New Deal to the New Right.* For its presence in the Tea Party, see Lowndes, "Looking Forward to the History of the Tea Party"; Lisa Disch, "The Tea Party"; Paul Krugman, "That Old-Time Whistle."

9. On makeup of movement, see Skocpol and Williamson, *Tea Party*, 19–44; Devin Burghart, "View from the Top," 68–87.

10. Scholars have provided compelling evidence of the various strands of Tea Party nationalism. See Skocpol and Williamson, *Tea Party*, 59–77; Lowndes, "Past and Future"; Disch, "The Tea Party"; Parker and Barreto, *Change*, 141–89; Alan Abramowitz, "Grand Old Tea Party," 202–8. Abramowitz shows that racial resentment and dislike of Obama fall after ideological conservatism as predictors of Tea Party support.

11. On the Tea Party and neoliberalism, see David Kirby and Emily McClintock Eckins, "Libertarian Roots of the Tea Party"; and Matt Guardino and Dean Snyder, "The Tea Party and the Crisis of Neoliberalism." On the Tea Party as reactionary, see J. M. Bernstein, "The Very Angry Tea Party"; Parker and Barreto, *Change*, 1–6, 21–22, 34–43; Devin Burghart and Leonard Zeskind, "Tea Party Nationalism"; Ruth Rosen, "The Tea Party and Angry White Women." Among those who have been most helpful to me in illuminating the consistencies and resonances between the two faces of the Tea Party are Skocpol and Williamson, *Tea Party*, 54–68, 100–106; Lowndes, "Past and Future," 158–67; Disch, "The Tea Party," 140–42; and Peter Montgomery, "The Tea Party and Religious Right Movements," 242–52.

12. See, for example, the Hartford Tea Party Patriots, "Declaration of Tea Party Independence," *Free Republic* (blog), February 24, 2010, http://www. freerepublic.com/focus/news/2458352/ posts; the "Contract from America" on its website, http://contractfromamerica.org/. Elizabeth Foley concurs that the Tea Party is animated by "enduring fidelity" to constitutional principles of limited government

(to which she adds constitutional originalism and US sovereignty). See Foley, *The Tea Party*.

13. Quoted in Emily Elkins, "Today's Bailout Anniversary." Skocpol and Williamson also report on this anger in *Tea Party*, 56.

14. Ross Douthat provides this widely cited definition of libertarian populism in "Libertarian Populism and Its Limits." See also Ben Domenech, "The Libertarian Populist Agenda"; Jesse Walker, "The Great Libertarian-Populist Roundup"; W. W. Houston, "Libertarian Populism"; Paul Krugman, "Delusions of Populism."

15. On Tea Party activists views toward corporations, see Skocpol and Williamson, *Tea Party*, 56–57. On Tea party sympathizers, see Abramowitz, "Grand Old Tea Party," 202–8.

16. Skocpol and Williamson, *Tea Party*; Parker and Barreto, *Change*; Alan Abramowitz, "Grand Old Tea Party."

17. Skocpol and Williamson, *Tea Party*, 36. Tea Partiers have shown particular vehemence in their efforts to deny racism in the movement. To counter this image, they have mobilized broad support behind Tea Party stars such as Alan West, Marco Rubio, and Nikki Haley. As Joe Lowndes observed, Tea Partiers have at times gone so far as to appropriate black history and culture: Glen Beck's September 2010 "Taxpayer March on Washington," for example, memorialized Martin Luther King and the 1963 March on Washington. See Lowndes, "Past and Future," 158–61.

18. On racism in the era of "color-blind" discourse, see Lowndes, "Past and Future," 158–64; Eduardo Bonilla-Silva, *Racism without Racists*; and Michael K. Brown et al., *Whitewashing Race*.

19. On ground zero, see Laurie Goodstein, "Battles around Nation over Proposed Mosques." On anchor babies and Arizona's SB-1070, see Foley, *The Tea Party*, 144–66. On voter suppression, see Stephanie Saul, "Conservative Groups Focus on Registration in Swing States." On guns, see Mike Harris, "Gun Control Debate Revitalizes Local Tea Party Groups." On gay marriage and women's rights issues, see Montgomery, "Religious Right Movements," 258–65.

20. On "racialized social democracy," see George Lipsitz, "The Possessive Investment in Whiteness." For analyses linking the Tea Party to rhetoric of the "Forgotten Man" and the "silent majority," see Steve Fraser, "The Limousine Liberal's Family Tree," 146; Disch, "The Tea Party," 137–38, 143; Skocpol and Williamson, *Tea Party*, 68–81.

21. Skocpol and Williamson, *Tea Party*, 59–64.

22. Signs cited in Disch, "The Tea Party," 137; Skocpol and Williamson, *Tea Party*, 67.

23. On this variant of producerism in the Tea Party, see Chip Berlet, "Reframing Populist Resentments in the Tea Party Movement," 47–48; George Shulman, "The Politics of the Tea Party," *The Contemporary Condition* (blog), May 3, 2010, http://contemporarycondition.blogspot.com/2010/05/politics-of-tea-party.html.

24. Disch, "The Tea Party," 139.

25. See, for instance, Paul Froese, "The Tea Party's Unifying Bogeyman"; Josh Eidelson, "Tea Party's 'Absurd' Socialism Obsession"; David Paul, "Tea Party Movement Obsession with Socialism."

26. These bumper stickers are available on sites such as Amazon.com and Zazzle.com.

27. Lowndes, "Past and Future," 166. On the Tea Party's anti-statism and race, see also Shulman, "Politics."

28. The sign is quoted in Jill Lepore, "The Commandments." For more on the Tea Party's constitutional zeal, see Lepore's *The Whites of Their Eyes*, 4–16, 43–44, 68–69, 111–12; Jeffrey Rosen, "The Tea Party's Radical Constitutionalism"; and Skocpol and Williamson, *Tea Party*, 49–51.

29. Rosen, "Tea Party's Radical Constitutionalism."

30. Quoted in Montgomery, "Religious Right Movements," 242. Angelia R. Wilson and Cynthia Burack make a similar argument in "Where Liberty Reigns and God Is Supreme," 188–89. This is not to dismiss that the Tea Party's rise renewed long-standing debates between libertarians and religious conservatives over ideology and strategy. See Skocpol and Williamson, *Tea Party*, 35–36, 58.

31. Quoted in Michael Kazin, *The Populist Persuasion*, 247.

32. Charles Postel, "The Tea Parties in Historical Perspective," 28.

33. On the Tea Party's move to the right of decades of mainstream conservatism, see Trost and Rosenthal, "Introduction," 3. Parker and Barreto deploy Richard Hofstadter's notion of "pseudoconservatism" to explain how the Tea Party can be at once reactionary and radical. According to Hofstadter, pseudoconservative movements appeal to conservative rhetoric to pursue nonconservative ends (including ends that defy order and stability). See Parker and Barreto, *Change*, 21–22.

34. See Jane Reitman, "The Stealth War on Abortion."

35. Lo identifies two waves of Tea Party mobilization and outlines the role of elites in facilitating autonomous grassroots Tea Parties from 2009 to 2010. Skocpol and Williamson provide an extensive account of the various players in the Tea Party, in particular elite organizations, the media, and grassroots Tea Parties. See Lo, "AstroTurf versus Grass Roots," 100–108; Skocpol and Williamson, *Tea Party*, 83–120.

36. There are different accounts of the Tea Party's size. Skocpol and Williams identified 804 active Tea Party groups (based on active web presence) as of spring 2011, plus another 164 that appeared to be active in 2009. They estimate 200,000 active Tea Party participants in the movement's early years. Burghart shows an increase in active Tea Party membership from 185,782 in 2010 to 513,712 in 2015. Lo argues persuasively that, rather than being driven by top-down directives, local Tea Parties negotiated their way through the array of resources, policy initiatives, and affiliations offered by elites. See Skocpol and Williamson, *Tea Party*, 22, 90–92; Devin Burghart, *Special Report: Part Two*; Lo, "AstroTurf versus Grass Roots," 99.

37. The right-wing echo chamber has wide reach, as millions of people in America tune into conservative news every day: 25 percent of Americans watch Fox News, and the right-wing talk radio shows of Sean Hannity, Glen Beck, Laura Ingraham, and Michael Savage can each boast ten million viewers. Tea Partiers, in particular, are devoted followers of Fox News. With the support of organizing handbooks produced by national organizations such as FreedomWorks and American Majority, moreover, local groups became increasingly Internet savvy, urging members to communicate and plan events using Meetup, Facebook, Twitter, and even old-fashioned email lists. On the echo chamber, see Kathleen Hall Jamieson and Joseph N. Capella, *Echo Chamber*. On the role of the echo chamber in Tea Party politics, see Guardino and Snyder, "Crisis of Neoliberalism," 535–45; Sébastien Mort, "Tailoring Dissent on the Airwaves," 487, 504. On the Tea Party's use of

social media to communicate and organize, see Corbin Hiar, "How the Tea Party Utilized Digital Media to Gain Power."

38. Looking at the Tea Party's emergence, in particular, Fox News and right-wing radio hosts played a key role in building up to and covering the movement's early nationwide protests and Glen Beck's 9/12 rally. This coverage lent the movement coherence and legitimacy, and it also contributed to generally positive framings of the Tea Party in mainstream media. On the role of Fox News and conservative talk radio in the Tea Party's emergence and in shaping mainstream coverage of the movement, see Skocpol and Williamson, *Tea Party*, 120–40. For more on positive framings of the Tea Party in mainstream media, see Guardino and Snyder, "Crisis of Neoliberalism," 535–39. On misinformation in the Tea Party echo chamber, see Lorraine C. Minnite, "New Challenges in the Study of Right-Wing Propaganda," 508–24; Daniel Skinner, "Keep Your Government Hands Off My Medicare!" 607–18.

39. Skocpol and Williamson, *Tea Party*, 199.

40. See, for instance, Bernstein, "The Very Angry Tea Party"; Zerneke, *Boiling Mad*; John Amato and David A. Neiwert, *Over the Cliff*, 155–75. Image online at John Hockenberry, "A Tea Party Activist Responds to Occupy Wall Street."

41. My discussion of emotion here is indebted to Holloway Sparks, "Mama Grizzlies and Guardians of the Republic," 32–36. On the performativity and publicity of emotions, see Sara Ahmed, *The Cultural Politics of Emotion*; Mary Holmes, "Feeling beyond Rules."

42. On "emotional habitus," see Deborah B. Gould, *Moving Politics*, 32, 10. On the relationship between emotion and cultural scripts, see Catherine A. Lutz and Lila Abu-Lughod, *Language and the Politics of Emotion*. I discuss Warner and Berlant's notion of "unsystematized lines of acquaintance" in relation to the public enthusiasm of Populism in chapter 2.

43. Tea Partiers scored higher than the general public and other Republicans on four questions measuring resentment toward African Americans. They are far more likely to disagree that African Americans are "victims" and have "gotten less," and they are more likely to agree that African Americans need to "try harder" and deserve "no favors." See Abramowitz, "Grand Old Tea Party," 205. Parker and Barreto provide similar data in *Change*, 162–71.

44. The popular sign is quoted in Michelle Malkin, "Tea-Party Saboteurs."

45. Disch, "The Tea Party," 143. Marilynn Brewer analyzes this dynamic in "The Psychology of Prejudice."

46. See Justin T. Pickett, Daniel Tope, and Rose Bellandi, "Taking Back Our Country," 178–82.

47. Wolf Blitzer and audience quoted in ThinkProgress's video, *Crowd Yells Let Him Die*.

48. Sign quoted in Paulo Senra, "We Came Unarmed (This Time)!" See also Tim Wise, "Imagine: Protest, Insurgency and the Workings of White Privilege," *Tim Wise* (blog), April 25, 2010, http://www.timwise.org/2010/04/imagine-protest-insurgency-and-the-workings-of-white-privilege/; Paul Kane, "'Tea Party' Protesters Accused of Spitting on Lawmaker"; Skocpol and Williamson, *Tea Party*, 32–34.

49. Quoted in Skocpol and Williamson, *Tea Party*, 57.

50. Sparks, "Mama Grizzlies," 27, 32–36.

51. Sparks, "Mama Grizzlies," 43; Wise, "Imagine."

52. On Tea Party anger and the promise of "compensatory" or "illusory" agency, see Lauren Langman, "Cycles of Contention," 485–88.

53. Skocpol and Williamson, *Tea Party*, 4–5, 95.

54. Skocpol and Williamson, *Tea Party*, 198–200.

55. Skocpol and Williamson, *Tea Party*, 4–5, 50–52; Trost and Rosenthal, "Introduction," 13.

56. Skocpol and Williamson, *Tea Party*, 200.

57. On the Tea Party's links to True the Vote, see Suevon Lee, "A Reading Guide to True the Vote, the Controversial Voter Fraud Watchdog"; Stephanie Saul, "Conservative Groups Focus on Registration in Swing States." On grassroots Tea Partiers and anti-immigrant activism, see David Holthouse, "Minuteman to Tea Party: A Grassroots Rebranding," *Media Matters for America* (blog), May 24, 2011, http://mediamatters. org/blog/2011/05/24/minuteman-to-tea-party-a-grassroots-rebranding/179373.

58. Skocpol and Williamson, *Tea Party*, 49–51; Rosen, "Tea Party's Radical Constitutionalism."

59. See Abby Brownback and Louis Jacobson, "Require Bills to Include a Clause Citing Its Authority in the Constitution"; Conor Friedersdorf, "The Tea Party."

60. Republicans and Democrats disagreed on the necessity and terms of the bailout, but the Senate passed it with a vote of 75-25 (Republicans, 34-14; Democrats, 41-11), and the House passed it with a vote of 263-171 (Democrats, 172-63; Republicans, 91-108). On the bipartisan rhetoric at the time, see Brian Knowlton and David M. Herszenhorn, "Bipartisan Support for Wall St. Rescue Plan"; Ted Barrett et al., " 'Sobering Moment' Forged Bipartisan Support."

61. Malinda Frevert, a spokeswoman for BOLD Nebraska, quoted in Ambreen Ali, "Keystone Pipeline Finds New Opponents."

62. Quoted in Rachel Weiner, "Keystone XL Pipeline Unites Left and Right." See also Rocky Kistner, "Protesters to Keystone XL Pipeline: Don't Mess with Texas," *Switchboard* (blog), February 19, 2012, http://switchboard.nrdc.org/blogs/ rkistner/protesters_to_keystone_xl_pipe.html; Ali, "Pipeline Finds New Opponents."

63. For a sample of right-wing echoing on Keystone, see "Financial Terrorism: Obama Blocks Vital Oil Pipeline," *Infowars.com*, January 19, 2012, http://www.infowars. com/financial-terrorism-obama-blocks-vital-oil-pipeline-infowars-nightly-news/; "Keystone Pipeline Should Be a No-Brainer"; Gary P. Jackson, "Sarah Palin: Obama Is a LIAR ON ENERGY," *A Time For Choosing* (blog), August 1, 2013, http:// thespeechatimeforchoosing.wordpress.com/2013/08/01/sarah-palin-obama-is-a-l iar-on-energy/; Rachel Marsden, "Environmentalists Do Billionaires' Bidding."

64. Abramowitz, "Grand Old Tea Party," 209.

65. John B. Judis, "Right-Wing Populism Could Hobble America for Decades."

66. Sheldon Wolin, *Democracy Incorporated*, 46–48, 64–65.

67. Culture Jammers HQ, "#OccupyWallStreet."

68. Culture Jammers HQ, "#OccupyWallStreet."

69. Writers for the 99%, *Occupying Wall Street*, 5–23; Manuel Castells, *Networks of Outrage and Hope*, 159–62; Todd Gitlin, *Occupy Nation*, 3–30.

70. Jeffrey S. Juris, "Reflections on #Occupy Everywhere," 259; Castells, *Networks*, 162–71; Nate Silver, "The Geography of Occupying Wall Street."

71. See, for example, Joe Lowndes and Dorian Warren, "Occupy Wall Street"; "Occupy Wall Street Emerges"; Harkinson, "Why Occupy Should Be the Left's Tea Party."

72. Richard Kim, "The Audacity of Occupy Wall Street."

73. Organizers in the trenches of these communities express ambivalence about Occupy, partly aware that the movement's discourse of resistance has opened space to build political will behind more mundane local campaigns around jobs creation or protracted revenue fights, partly wary of a long history of having their energies and efforts co-opted by larger coalitions and movements led by more privileged groups. See, e.g., Joe Garofoli, "Occupy Movement Fails to Connect with Blacks"; "Bridging Community Organizing and #Occupy," *Organizing Upgrade* (online strategy lab), November 1, 2011, http://www.organizingupgrade.com/index.php/strategylabs/occupy-strategylab/item/35-bridging-community-organizing-and-occupy; Joel Olson, "Whiteness and the 99%," *Bring the Ruckus* (blog), October 20, 2011, http://www.bringtheruckus.org/?q=node%2F146.

74. For a textbook account of this view, see Patrick O'Connor and Mike Gecan, "Occupy Wall Street's Anger Isn't Enough."

75. On Occupy as twenty-first century, see Dean, "Occupation as Political Form." On Occupy as an antirepresentational politics of multitude or anarchy, see Michael Hardt and Antonio Negri, "The Fight for 'Real Democracy'"; Marina Sitrin and Dario Azzellini, *They Can't Represent Us!* 151–82.

76. Abraham Lincoln, "The Gettysburg Address," in *Political Writings and Speeches*, 192.

77. Thatcher quoted in David Harvey, *Spaces of Global Capitalism*, 16. On capitalist realism, see Mark Fisher, *Capitalist Realism*, 1–11. In Occupy, see Slavoj Žižek, "Don't Fall in Love with Yourselves," 67.

78. See Wendy Brown, "Occupy Wall Street."

79. Deseriis and Dean, "A Movement without Demands?" See also Eli Schmitt, Astra Taylor, and Mark Greif, "Scenes from an Occupation," 3–4; Kim, "Audacity."

80. Sitrin and Azzellini, *They Can't Represent Us!* 163–70; David Graeber, "Occupy Wall Street's Anarchist Roots," 144–46; Judith Butler, "So, What Are the Demands?" 8–11.

81. Todd Gitlin, "Occupy's Predicament," 9–10.

82. See, for instance, Naomi Wolf, "Revealed"; Frazier Group, *Independent Investigation*. For exemplary images, including Chase Bank, see Curtis Bunn, "Seven Lessons."

83. Gitlin, "Occupy's Predicament," 7.

84. As one activist observed of Occupy Philadelphia's efforts to provide sanitation, food, shelter for homeless residents, medical care, mental health services, and so on, the tent cities "expose[d] everything our society fails to provide, neglects to care about." See Nikil Saval, "Scenes from Occupied Philadephia,"159.

85. Ethan Miller, "OCCUPY! CONNECT! CREATE!"

86. Quoted in Naomi Klein, "Why Now? What's Next?"

87. On Occupy's links to movements that have experimented with similar democratic forms, see, for example, Sitrin and Azzellini, *They Can't Represent Us!* 14–67; Ernesto

Castaneda, "The Indignados of Spain"; Frances Fox Piven, "On the Organizational Question," 191–93.

88. Kim, "Audacity"; Sunaura Taylor, "Scenes from Occupied Oakland," 136, 140.

89. Graeber, "Anarchist Roots," 145; Marina Sitrin, "One No, Many Yesses," 9; Rebecca Solnit, "Throwing Out the Master's Tools," 148–49.

90. Sitrin and Azzellini, *They Can't Represent Us!* 17.

91. Lowndes and Warren, "Occupy Wall Street."

92. Richard Kim uses the term "horizontal acoustics" in "The Audacity of Occupy Wall Street." Chris Garces discusses the contrapuntal rhythms of the people's mic in "People's Mic and Democratic Charisma," 94.

93. Ryan Ruby, "On the People's Mic."

94. Garces, "People's Mic," 96.

95. On Occupy and social media, see Sasha Costanza-Chock, "Mic Check!" 375–85; Neal Caren and Sarah Gaby, "Occupy Online"; Castells, *Networks*, 171–78.

96. See the We Are the 99 Percent website, wearethe99percent.tumblr.com/archive.

97. See Sarah Kerton, "Tahrir, Here?" 302–4.

98. Castaneda, "The Indignados of Spain," 318–19.

99. These scholars are indebted to the social movement theory of Charles Tilly, most recently in his book *Contentious Performances*. See, for instance, Craig Calhoun, "Occupy Wall Street in Perspective"; Castaneda, "The Indignados of Spain"; Juris, "Reflections on #Occupy Everywhere."

100. Here I'm drawing on Bonnie Honig's concept of "foreign founding" and her arguments about subnational and transnational sites of democratic politics in *Democracy and the Foreigner*, 98–106.

101. Daniel Kreiss and Zeynep Tufekci, "Occupying the Political," 163.

102. Gitlin, "Occupy's Predicament," 9.

103. Žižek, "Don't Fall in Love," 68.

104. For a snapshot of Occupy Wall Street's composition, see Ruth Milkman, Stephanie Luce, and Penny Lewis, "Changing the Subject." Two studies analyzing surveys by visitors to the occupywallst.org website show similar demographic makeup. See the unpublished report by Hector R., Cordero-Guzman, "Main Stream Support for a Mainstream Movement: The 99% Comes From and Looks Like the 99%," *OccupyWallSt.org*, October 19, 2011, https://occupywallst.org/media/pdf/OWS-profile1-10-18-11-sent-v2-HRCG.pdf; Sean Captain, "Infographic: Who Is Occupy Wall Street."

105. See Olson, "Whiteness and the 99%"; Kenyon Farrow, "Occupy Wall Street's Race Problem"; Rinku Sen, "Race and Occupy Wall Street"; Jeffrey Juris et al., "Negotiating Power and Difference within the 99%"; "For People Who Have Considered Occupation But Found It Is Not Enuf," *DisOccupy* (blog), accessed November 4, 2014, http://disoccupy.wordpress.com/ 2012/04/24/for-people-who-have-considered-occupation-but-found-it-is-not-enuf/.

106. See, for instance, Manissa McCleave Maharawal, "so real it hurts: Notes on Occupy Wall Street," *Racialicious* (blog), October 3, 2011, http:// www.racialicious.com/2011/10/03/so-real-it-hurts-notes-on-occupy-wall-street/; Darcy K. Leach, "Culture and the Structure of Tyrannylessness," 183–84.

107. "For People Who Have Considered Occupation." Or, perhaps it is the not so new tyranny. See J. Freeman, *The Tyranny of Structurelessness*.

108. "For People Who Have Considered Occupation."

109. On antiracist, feminist, and queer organizing in Occupy encampments, including people of color working groups and the adoption of the "progressive stack" to prioritize the voices of marginalized actors, see Maharawal, "SO REAL IT HURTS." For Occupy offshoots, see Britt Middleton, " 'Occupy the Hood' "; Tanya Pérez-Brennan, "Ocupemos El Barrio"; Julianne Hing, "Mamas of Color."

110. "For People Who Have Considered Occupation."

111. "For People Who Have Considered Occupation."

112. If the rhetoric of the 99 percent strikes many observers as too broad from the analytic standpoint of class power (see *The Daily Show* skit below), others point out that it is also too narrow. In "We Are the 99.9%," an op-ed published during Occupy, Paul Krugman clarified that wealth is concentrated in the top 0.1 percent (whose after-tax income rose by 400 percent from 1979 to 2005 through, among other factors, real income increases and decreased taxes on capital gains).

113. "Occupy Wall Street Divided," *The Daily Show*.

114. While I am persuaded by Dean's critique, I do not share her rejection of Occupy's horizontalist experiments in radical democracy, nor do I agree with her insistence on "locat[ing] the truth of the movement in class struggle." Dean is often polemically unconcerned with the social hierarchies that have always limited Marxist visions of resistance to capitalism; as Occupy's "race problem" confirms, her vision is thus ill equipped to build the collective subjectivity required to enact class struggle. See Dean, "Occupation as Political Form."

115. Kim, "Audacity."

116. Garces, "People's Mic," 91.

117. For the use of this term to describe ambitions ranging from toilets at Occupy Wall Street to the organizing of offshoots "Occupy Our Homes" and "Strike Debt," see Cristian Salazar, "Toilets Bring Relief to Occupy Wall Street"; Amy Dean, "How 'Occupy Our Homes' Can Win," *Occupy Everything!* February 3, 2012, https:// incorporealcommittee.wordpress.com/ 2012/02/03/ how-occupy-our-homes-can-win/; Andrew Ross and Seth Ackerman, "Strike Debt and Rolling Jubilee."

118. Klein, "Why Now?"

119. William Connolly, "What Is to Be Done?"

120. Luis Moreno-Caballud and Marina Sitrin, "Occupy Wall Street, Beyond Encampments."

121. Juris et al., "Negotiating Power," 436–37.

122. Rebecca Oliviera, "City Life Expands to National Activities"; Juris, "Reflections on #Occupy Everywhere," 265.

123. Quoted in Tovia Smith, " 'Occupy Boston' Holds On."

124. Quoted in Amy Dean, "After the 99% Spring."

125. Lew Finfer, "Report from Occupy Boston: We Are Still a Generous and Hopeful People," *PICO National Network* (blog), October 12, 2011, http:// www.piconetwork.org/blog/archive?c= categories&t=affordable-housing.

126. Quoted in Smith, "'Occupy Boston' Holds On." See also Sarah Todd, "Boston Approves Responsible Banking Bill."

127. See the page "Campaign to Hold Banks Accountable to Communities and Families" on PICO's website, www.piconetwork.org/newbottomline; Sean Thomas-Breitfeld and Marnie Brady, "The New Bottom Line."

128. Quoted in Dean, "After the 99% Spring."

129. Tim Lilienthal, "How to Hold Wall Street Accountable," *PICO National Network* (blog), October 5, 2011, http://www.piconetwork.org/blog/archive?c= categorie s&t=affordable-housing.

130. Quoted in Dean, "After the 99% Spring."

131. Quoted in Dean, "After the 99% Spring." See also John D. McKinnon, "Liberal Groups Plan to Protest"; Stephen Lerner and George Goehl, "The New Bottom Line."

132. Quoted in Dean, "After the 99% Spring."

133. Juris contrasts Occupy's "logic of aggregation" (that is, using social media to aggregate individuals in public spaces) from the "networking logic" used in the alter-globalization movement (that is, using digital media to facilitate networks between organized groups and institutions). See Juris, "Reflections on #Occupy Everywhere," 260–61, 266–69.

134. Miller, "OCCUPY! CONNECT! CREATE!"

CONCLUSION

1. See Salgado's website, http://juliosalgado83.tumblr.com/post/74026239907/ fuckyourborders.

2. Yosimar Reyes, quoted in the video clip, New American Media, "For 'Undocuqueers.'" See also Marco Antonio Flores, "Undocuqueer 'Come Out' at S.F. Pride Parade."

3. Kemi, "Undocumented & Queer."

4. The ideas in this paragraph are indebted to Cristina Beltrán, *The Trouble with Unity*, 56–74. For other recent works in political theory that begin with this premise, see, for example, Bonnie Honig, *Democracy and the Foreigner*, 3–4; Paul Apostolidis, *Breaks in the Chain*, xvi, 233.

5. The act would grant a six-year conditional legal status to undocumented youth who entered the United States before the age of sixteen, maintain a continuous presence for five years prior to the bill's enactment, receive a high school diploma or GED, and "demonstrate good moral character." If after six years, they graduate from a two-year college, complete at least two years of a four-year degree, or serve at least two years in the US military, they would qualify to adjust their status from conditional to permanent resident. See the Immigration Policy Center's analysis, "The DREAM Act," May 18, 2011, on its website, http://www.immigrationpolicy. org/just-facts/dream-act#benefit. For estimates of DREAM Act eligibility in 2010 and an analysis of potential benefits, see Jeanne Batalova and Margie McHugh, "DREAM vs. Reality." Eligibility estimates for DACA are 1.2 million in Jeanne Batalova, Sarah Hooker, and Randy Capps, "DACA at the Two-Year Mark."

6. Walter Nicholls provides a thorough history of DREAM Act organizing in *The DREAMers*. On the shifts in UndocuQueer strategies, see also Tania A. Unzueta

Carrasco and Hinda Seif, "Disrupting the Dream," 286–89. On DACA, see "Consideration of Deferred Action for Childhood Arrivals (DACA)" on the US Citizen and Immigration Services' website, http://www.uscis.gov/humanitarian/consideration-deferred-action-childhood-arrivals-daca; Batalova, Hooker, and Capps, "Two-Year Mark."

7. Obama's executive order does not cover all undocumented immigrants; moreover, it enhances surveillance and border security and continues racialized practices of priority targeting for deportations. For UndocuQueer critiques, see Prerna Lal, "Executive Action on Immigration: Good, Bad, and Ugly," *Prerna Lal: Immigration Attorney and Human Rights Advocate* (blog), November 21, 2014, http://prernalal.com/2014/11/ executive-action-on-immigration-good-bad-and-ugly/; "Deporter-in-Chief Fails to Stop All Deportations."

8. Nicholls makes this point in *The DREAMers*, 47.

9. Prerna Lal, "How Queer Undocumented Youth Built the Immigrant Rights Movement."

10. In the "Who We Are" section of its website, IYJL describes coming out as a tactic of self-determination, escalation, and civil disobedience. On major public "coming out" actions, see, for example, Ted Hesson, "9 DREAMer Actions That Advanced Immigration Reform"; Maria Taracena, "Immigration, LGBT Rights Advocates Take the Streets"; "Transgender Protestors Block Traffic," *Voices on the Square* (blog), March 23, 2015, http://www.voicesonthesquare.com/essays/2015/03/23/ transgender-protesters-block-traffic-downtown-la; Jodie Gummow, "Dreamers Put Bodies on the Line"; "Taking Immigration Law into Their Own Hands"; "Breaking: San Francisco Stopping Deportation Buses," *#Not1More* (blog), October 17, 2013, http://www.notonemoredeportation.com/2013/10/17/sfaction/.

11. Lal, "Queer Undocumented Youth." For an introduction to the Spanish concept *jotería*, see the "Association for Jotería Arts, Activism, and Scholarship" website, www.ajaas.com.

12. I will discuss this shift and UndocuQueer coalitions below. On the prison-industrial complex and immigrant detention centers, see, e.g., Lee Fang, "How Private Prisons Game the Immigration System"; Laura Sullivan, "Prison Economics Helped Drive Immigration Law."

13. For uses of Lorde's quote, see Prerna's "I Am Undocuqueer" poster on Julio Salgado's website, http://juliosalgado83.tumblr.com/post/16053458352/i-am-undocuqueer-is-an-art-project-in; and Diana Cardenas' byline in her post, "Long Beach Undocuqueers Take Stage.

14. For use of the term "undocuqueer identities," see Jorge Gutierrez, "I Am Undocuqueer" and the New York State Youth Leadership Council's "UndocuQueer" section, accessed November 24, 2014, http://www.nysylc.org/undocuqueer/.

15. Beltrán, "'No Papers, No Fear,'" 247. On this aspect of queer politics, see also Michael Warner, "Introduction," xxv–xxvii; Diana Fuss, "Inside/Out," 4–6.

16. Sara Ahmed, *Queer Phenomenology*, 171; Karma R. Chávez, *Queer Migration Politics*, 6.

17. Ahmed, *Queer Phenomenology*, 3.

18. Ahmed, *Queer Phenomenology*, 107.

19. Eithne Luibhéid, "Queer/Migration," 174. Mary Louise Pratt introduces the influential concept of the "contact zone" in *Imperial Eyes*, 8. See also Pratt, "Arts of the Contact Zone." Gloria Anzaldúa's *Borderlands / La Frontera* has also been influential in developing this concept of borders.

20. Genevieve Negrón-Gonzales, "Undocumented, Unafraid and Unapologetic," 260, 267. See also Carrasco and Seif, "Disrupting the Dream," 287; Rose Cuison Villazor, "The Undocumented Closet," 51–53.

21. Negrón-Gonzales, "Undocumented, Unafraid and Unapologetic,'" 260–61.

22. Ahmed, *Queer Phenomenology*, 23, 2, 9.

23. I discuss these dynamics in chapter 3 and in "Pierre Bourdieu and Populism," 204–5.

24. I borrow this term from James C. Scott, *The Art of Not Being Governed*.

25. On constructions of "illegality," see Mai M. Ngai, *Impossible Subjects*, 4–5, and the essays in Cecilia Menjívar and Daniel Kanstroom, eds., *Constructing Immigrant "Illegality"*.

26. Nathalie Peutz and Nicholas De Genova, "Introduction," in *The Deportation Regime*, 10–11. On the intersections of the deportation regime with race, gender, and sexuality, see the essays in Eithne Luibhéid and Lionel Cantu Jr., eds., *Queer Migrations* and the essays in the special issue "Queer/Migration" in *GLQ* 14, nos. 2–3 (2008).

27. See Robert M. Morgenthau, "The US Keeps 34,000 Immigrants in Detention Each Day"; Tanya Maria Golash-Boza, *Immigration Nation*, 149–54; Spencer S. Hsu and Andrew Becker, "ICE Officials Set Quotas"; Sullivan, "Prison Economics."

28. Ngai, *Impossible Subjects*, 4–5.

29. On this point, see Villazor, "The Undocumented Closet," 7, 50–54; Nicholls, *The DREAMers*, 125; Chávez, *Queer Migration Politics*, 111.

30. On DREAMers as "exceptional" immigrants, "good" and "bad" immigrants, and early DREAM Act rhetoric, see Nicholls, *The DREAMers*, 49–59; Carrasco and Seif, "Disrupting the Dream," 280–81, 286–89; Beltrán, "No Papers, No Fear," 246, 252–58; Chávez, *Queer Migration Politics*, 93–100.

31. Maria Chávez, Jessica L. Lavariega Monforti, and Melissa R. Michelson, *Living the Dream*, 13, 137. The authors report on similar rationale by policymakers who support the DREAM Act (33–43).

32. Carrasco and Seif, "Disrupting the Dream," 289.

33. In *Documenting DREAMs*, Arely Zimmerman argues that insurgent DREAM activism prior to DACA helped reframe the immigration debate from comprehensive immigration reform toward mass deportation (59–61). See also Nicholls, *The DREAMers*, 143–67. After DACA, UWD shifted its focus to antideportation activism on behalf of all undocumented immigrants. According to the "About" section of the #Not1MoreDeportation website, that campaign grew out of NDLON's UndocuBus ride, DREAMers' coming-out actions, and other antideportation initiatives. After Obama's expansion of deferred action in 2014, #Not1More Deportation transitioned from an NDLON project to a national campaign.

34. Image can be seen in Hatty Lee, "Art and Activism Come Together."

35. Between 2011 and 2012, for example, popular movement artist Julio Salgado shifted gears from images of DREAM activists in caps and gowns with the tagline "I Exist," to his "I Am UndocuQueer" series, which I discuss below. By 2013, he was tackling white supremacy in detention and policing, and in January 2014, he produced

the poster "Illegal Faggots for the Destruction of Borders." See Salgado's archive at
http://juliosalgado83.tumblr.com/archive.

36. Quoted in Nicholls, *The DREAMers*, 125.

37. On the "supercitizen immigrant," see Honig, *Democracy and the Foreigner*, 77–78.

38. Salgado has many "I am UndocuQueer" posters on his website. For the ones quoted
    here, see http://juliosalgado83.tumblr.com/post/15877418282/i-am-undocuqueer-
    is-an-art-project-in.

39. Cohen, "Democracy," *The Future*.

40. See Salgado's website, http://juliosalgado83.tumblr.com/post/52121222633/
    image-inspired-by-something-my-comadre-yosimar.

41. On affective labor, see Michael Hardt, "Affective Labor," and, in the service econ-
    omy, Kathi Weeks, "Life within and against Work," 234–36, 239–41.

42. See Salgado's website, http://juliosalgado83.tumblr.com/post/24053660964/
    in-the-eyes-of-the-haterz-we-are-the-0.

43. See Salgado's website, http://juliosalgado83.tumblr.com/post/26464715380/
    and-here-goes-another-one. American Apparel explains its "Legalize LA" T-shirt
    campaign on its website, http://www.americanapparel.net/contact/legalizela/.

44. Quoted in Michelle Chen, "Queering Immigration."

45. For these echoes, see, for instance, Isa Noyola and Valeria De La Luz, "Obama's
    Order Ices Out Some LGBTQ Immigrants," *Advocate.com* (Op-Ed page), November
    21, 2014, http://www.advocate.com/commentary/2014/11/21/op-ed-obama%E
    2%80%99s-order-ices-out-some-lgbtq-immigrants; Sunnivie Brydum, "HRC and
    Coalition Apologize for Silencing Undocumented, Trans Activists"; Jorge Rodriguez-
    Jimenez, "UndocuQueerActivistsChangingtheImmigrationDebate,"*Mitú*(blog),May
    7, 2015, https://www.mitumix.com/mitu-world/undocuqueer-activist-changing-
    the-immigration-debate/; Julianne Hing, "For Trans Immigrant Detainees"; Emma
    Margolin, "LGBT Immigrants Protest against 'Death Sentence' Deportations."

46. On homonormativity, see Lisa Duggan, Russ Castronovo, and Dana Nelson, "The
    New Homonormativity."

47. For example, UndocuQueer activists helped organize the Association for Jotería
    Arts, Activism, and Scholarship, an organization of Latino/a, Chicana/o, and
    indigenous artists, activists, and scholars who "envision a world that affirms Jotería
    consciousness" and seek to "affirm and (re)create a queer homeland." See their web-
    site, www.ajaas.com, and the poster for their national conference, "We Speak for
    Ourselves," in 2012, ajaas.webs.com.

48. Many UndocuQueer activists cut their teeth at the state level, in the fight against
    a spate of punitive laws profiling undocumented immigrants, most notoriously,
    Arizona's SB 1070.

49. Quoted in Hinda Seif, " 'Layers of Humanity,' " 308.

50. See Salgado's website, http://juliosalgado83.tumblr.com/post/89894680033/
    juliosalgado83-imagine-made-this-image-last; http://juliosalgado83.tumblr.com/
    post/31908487736/please-click-on-the-photo-for-more-information.

51. Carrasco and Seif, "Disrupting the Dream," 281, 293.

52. Herra-Sota quoted in "Forced Out-Jose's Testimony," *Moratorium on Deportations
    Campaign* (website), April 6, 2012. http://moratoriumondeportations.org/
    2012/04/06/forced-out-joses-testimony/. Chávez analyzes José's testimony

in *Queer Migration Politics*, 106–7. For a partial list of attendees at the forum, see the Adler School's website, https://theadlerschool.wordpress.com/2012/03/30/update-new-partners-schedule-announced-for-forced-out-teach-in-and-march-to-end-mass-detention-on-april-5/.

53. For example, when IYJL activists defend immigrants with criminal records, they do emphasize qualities that make them "worthy"; when Obama expanded deferred action, activists praised him while drawing attention to simultaneous executive orders that reinforced his image as "deporter-in-chief." On IYJL, see Carrasco and Seif, "Disrupting the Dream," 292–95. On Obama, see Lal, "Executive Action on Immigration"; "Deporter-in-Chief Fails to Halt All Deportations," *California Immigrant Youth Justice League* (blog), November 20, 2014, http://ciyja.tumblr.com/post/103166326771/deporter-in-chief-fails-to-stop-all-deportations.

54. For dissonant images of insurgent young immigrants staging sit-ins behind signs that appeal to family values, see Laura Meckler, "White House Immigration Protest Has Surprise Ending"; Lauren Pack, "6 Arrested during Protest at Butler County Jail." For the "Yes You Can" tactic, see the #Not1More website, http://www.notonemore-deportation.com/2014/03/07/president-obama-yes-you-can/.

55. Kathy E. Ferguson, "Anarchist Counterpublics," 193, 198.

56. Zimmerman discusses these practices extensively in *Documenting DREAMs*, 6–7, 10–12, 20–32. In *Out of the Shadows*, Costanza-Chock explains, "DREAMers use social media within a broader set of media practices, including print publishing, appearances on Spanish-language commercial radio and television shows, and, most crucially, face-to-face presentations in high schools, at community centers, and in other spaces across the country" (137). These differently embodied sites of virtual, material, and face-to-face communication, along with the political activism I discuss below, are key to understanding undocumented youth counterpublics.

57. See Zimmerman, *Documenting DREAMs*, 39–45; Negrón-Gonzales, "Undocumented, Unafraid and Unapologetic," 272–74.

58. See Marshall Ganz, "Why Stories Matter." I don't mean to suggest that all coming-out stories are "public narratives." Indeed, coming out can be individualized and apolitical when it tends toward therapeutic registers. Coming-out stories *are* often public narratives, however, in the movement-building context of DREAM activism and UndocuQueer. On Ganz's workshops with immigrant youth, see Costanza-Chock, *Out of the Shadows*, 144–49. Laura Corrunker also discusses training in public story-telling in "Coming Out of the Shadows," 146.

59. These inheritances surface in coming-out narratives, movement art, and organizing tools. For example, DreamActivist.org's *Coming Out: A How-to Guide* appealed to Cesar Chávez, Audre Lord, Rosa Parks, and Harvey Milk as inspiration. See Chávez, *Queer Migration Politics*, 97; Claudia Anguiano, "Undocumented, Unapologetic, and Unafraid," 143–44; and Salgado's images from September 2012 on his website, http://juliosalgado83.tumblr.com/archive.

60. For undocumented youth influence on mainstream immigrant rights groups and narratives, see Nicholls, *The DREAMers*, 143–67; Zimmerman, *Documenting DREAMs*, 59–60; Beltrán, "No Papers, No Fear," 252.

61. See the "About" section of the Dreamers Adrift website.

62. Dreamers Adrift, "Undocumented and Awkward: Episode 7."

63. Dreamers Adrift, "Undocumented and Awkward: Episode 13."
64. Ahmed, *Queer Phenomenology*, 107.
65. See the January 2012 archive on Salgado's website, http://juliosalgado83.tumblr.com/archive.
66. See the chapter "Coming Out as a Coalitional Gesture?" in Chávez, *Queer Migration Politics*, 79–111. Chávez critiques the limits of coalitional gestures by DREAMers, as well as some of Salgado's "I Am Undocuqueer" posters. I find her critique of the posters persuasive, especially the concern that "undocuqueer" loses its political power the more activists adopt it as an individual identity, rather than a collective, coalitional ethos. As a moment in movement building that has shaped later radicalism (among Salgado and others), I am less concerned with the fact that the posters "did not mention other issues that are common to social justice struggles, such as power, oppression, or capitalism" (102). As I have discussed in relation to Salgado's art and movement narrative, UndocuQueer activists have since explored those connections.
67. During the previous decade, undocumented youth had played leadership roles in UWD, sponsored by the adult-run National Immigration Law Center, and the California Dream Network, which had DREAM Teams in cities across California. Nicholls documents the organizing of "dissident DREAMers" during this period in *The DREAMers*, 74–98.
68. Nicholls, *The DREAMers*, 117. He documents the undocumented youth movements' post-2010 grassroots movement-building in his chapter "Rebirth from the Grassroots Up," 99–117.
69. On Obama's executive order, see the Immigration Policy Center's "Guide to the Immigrant Accountability Executive Action," on its website, http://www.immigrationpolicy.org/special-reports/guide-immigration-accountability-executive-action. For critiques, see Lal, "Executive Action on Immigration"; "Deporter-in-Chief Fails."
70. Chávez, *Queer Migration Politics*, 7.
71. Bernice Johnson Reagon, "Coalition Politics," 346.
72. See IYJL's "Declaration of Independence from 'Comprehensive Immigration Reform,'" posted on their website, July 17, 2013, http://www.iyjl.org/immigrationstance/.
73. On undocumented youth activism on health access, see the "Undocumented and Uninsured" initiative by the DREAM Resource Center at the UCLA Labor Center at the initiative's website, http://undocumentedanduninsured.org/. For such organizing in action, see Jorge Rivas, "DREAMers Declare Undocumented Youth Mental Health Day," and the YouTube clip posted by the *Sacramento Bee*, "Undocumented Youth Rally for Immigrant Health Care."
74. Public Enemy, "Fight the Power," *Fear of a Black Planet*.
75. Carrasco and Seif, "Disrupting the Dream," 295.
76. Negrón-Gonzales, "Undocumented, Unafraid and Unapologetic,'" 274; Nicholls, *The DREAMers*, 121.
77. Chávez discusses this metaphor, including the idea of "stranger danger," in *Queer Migration Politics*, 88–91. Villazor discusses the legal construction of "the shadow" metaphor in "The Undocumented Closet," 29–31.

78. Gloria Anzaldúa, *Borderlands / La Frontera*, 38.

79. Anzaldúa, *Borderlands / La Frontera*, 101–2. See also Audre Lorde's essay "Poetry Is Not a Luxury," in her book *Sister Outsider*, 36–39.

80. For the quoted material, see the epigraph by Wendy Brown in the introduction. On the ethos of impurity and failure in queer theory, see Michael Warner, *The Trouble with Normal*, and Judith Halberstam, *The Queer Art of Failure*. I am grateful to an anonymous reviewer for suggesting this line of thinking.

81. For an overview of these debates, see Romand Coles, Mark Reinhardt, and George Shulman, "Radical Future Pasts?" 13–16.

82. Cohen, "Democracy," *The Future*.

83. Cohen, "Anthem," *The Future*.

BIBLIOGRAPHY

Abizadeh, Arash. "On the Demos and Its Kin: Nationalism, Democracy, and the Boundary Problem." *American Political Science Review* 106, no. 4 (2012): 867–82.

Abramowitz, Alan. "Grand Old Tea Party: Partisan Polarization and the Rise of the Tea Party Movement." In *Steep: The Precipitous Rise of the Tea Party*, edited by Lawrence Rosenthal and Christine Trost, 195–211. Berkeley: University of California Press, 2012.

Abts, Koen, and Stefan Rummens. "Populism versus Democracy." *Political Studies* 55, no. 2 (June 1, 2007): 405–24.

Adam, Anthony, and Gerald Gaither. *Black Populism in the United States: An Annotated Bibliography*. Westport, CT: Praeger, 2004.

Ahmed, Sara. *The Cultural Politics of Emotion*. New York: Routledge, 2004.

Ahmed, Sara. *Queer Phenomenology: Orientations, Objects, Others*. Durham, NC: Duke University Press, 2006.

Ahmed, Sara. *Willful Subjects*. Durham, NC: Duke University Press, 2014.

Alexander, Michelle. *The New Jim Crow: Mass Incarceration in the Age of Colorblindness*. New York: New Press, 2012.

Ali, Ambreen. "Keystone Pipeline Finds New Opponents." *Roll Call*, February 16, 2012.

Ali, Omar H. *In the Lion's Mouth: Black Populism in the New South, 1886–1900*. Jackson: University Press of Mississippi, 2010.

Allen, Danielle. *Talking to Strangers: Anxieties of Citizenship since* Brown v. Board of Education. Chicago: University of Chicago Press, 2006.

Allen, Jeremy. "The Commercial Crooner: Bob Dylan's Greatest Marketing Hits." *Guardian*, February 4, 2014.

Alperovitz, Gar. *America beyond Capitalism: Reclaiming Our Wealth, Our Liberty, and Our Democracy*. Princeton, NJ: John Wiley & Sons, 2006.

Amato, John, and David A. Neiwert. *Over the Cliff: How Obama's Election Drove the American Right Insane*. Sausalito, CA: Polipoint Press, 2010.

Anees, Saira. "Obama Explains Why Some Small Town Pennsylvanians Are 'Bitter.'" ABCNews.com, April 11, 2008.

Anguiano, Claudia. "Undocumented, Unapologetic, and Unafraid: Discursive Strategies of the Immigrant Youth DREAM Social Movement." Dissertation, University of New Mexico, 2011.

Anzaldúa, Gloria. *Borderlands / La Frontera: The New Mestiza*. 2nd ed. San Francisco: Aunt Lute Books, 1999.

Apostolidis, Paul. *Breaks in the Chain: What Immigrant Workers Can Teach America about Democracy*. Minneapolis: University of Minnesota Press, 2010.

Apostolidis, Paul. *Stations of the Cross: Adorno and Christian Right Radio*. Durham, NC: Duke University Press, 2000.

Appadurai, Arjun. "The Capacity to Aspire: Culture and the Terms of Recognition." In *Culture and Public Action*, edited by Vijayendra Rao and Michael Walton, 59–84. Stanford, CA: Stanford Social Sciences, 2004.

Arditi, Benjamin. *Politics on the Edges of Liberalism: Difference, Populism, Revolution, Agitation*. Edinburgh: Edinburgh University Press, 2008.

Arendt, Hannah. *Between Past and Future*. New York: Penguin Classics, 2006.

Austen, Ben. "End of the Road." *Harper's*, August 2009.

Balko, Radley. *Rise of the Warrior Cop: The Militarization of America's Police Forces*. New York: PublicAffairs, 2013.

Banet-Weiser, Sarah. "Rate Your Knowledge: The Branded University." In *The Routledge Companion to Advertising and Promotional Culture*, edited by Matthew P. McAllister, Emily West, and Sarah Banet-Weiser, 298–312. New York: Routledge, 2013.

"The Bankruptcy of General Motors: A Giant Falls." *Economist*, June 4, 2009.

Barnard, John. *American Vanguard: The United Auto Workers during the Reuther Years, 1935–1970*. Detroit: Wayne State University Press, 2005.

Barrett, Ted, Deirdre Walsh, Lesa Jansen, and Scott Anderson. "'Sobering Moment' Forged Bipartisan Support for Bailout Plan." CNN.com, September 19, 2008.

Barstow, David. "Tea Party Lights Fuse for Rebellion on Right." *New York Times*, February 16, 2010.

Bartlett, Andrew. "Airshafts, Loudspeakers, and the Hip Hop Sample: Contexts and African American Musical Aesthetics." In *That's the Joint! Hip-Hop Studies Reader*, edited by Murray Forman and Mark Anthony Neal, 393–406. New York: Routledge, 2004.

Batalova, Jeanne, Sarah Hooker, and Randy Capps. "DACA at the Two-Year Mark: A National and State Profile of Youth Eligible and Applying for Deferred Action." Washington, DC: Migration Policy Institute, August 2014.

Batalova, Jeanne, and Margie McHugh. "DREAM vs. Reality: An Analysis of Potential DREAM Act Beneficiaries." Washington, DC: Migration Policy Institute, July 2010.

Bauman, Zygmunt. *Liquid Times: Living in an Age of Uncertainty*. Cambridge: Polity, 2006.

Beachy, Susan C. "Anatomy of Detroit's Decline." *New York Times*, December 8, 2013.

Bell, Daniel, ed. *The Radical Right*. 3rd ed. New Brunswick, NJ: Transaction Publishers, 2001.

Beltrán, Cristina. "Mestiza Poetics: Walt Whitman, Barack Obama, and the Question of Union." In *A Political Companion to Walt Whitman*, edited by John E. Seery, 59–95. Lexington: University Press of Kentucky, 2010.

Beltrán, Cristina. "'No Papers, No Fear': DREAM Activism, New Social Media, and Queering Immigrant Rights." In *Contemporary Latina/o Media*, edited by Arlene Dávila and Yeidy M. Rivero, 245–66. New York: New York University Press, 2014.

Beltrán, Cristina. *The Trouble with Unity: Latino Politics and the Creation of Identity*. New York: Oxford University Press, 2010.

Berger, Arthur Asa. *Ads, Fads, and Consumer Culture: Advertising's Impact on American Character and Society*. Lanham, MD: Rowman & Littlefield, 2000.

Berlant, Lauren. *Cruel Optimism*. Durham, NC: Duke University Press, 2011.

Berlant, Lauren, and Michael Warner. "Sex in Public." In *Publics and Counterpublics*, by Michael Warner. New York; Cambridge, MA: Zone Books, 2005.

Berlet, Chip. "Reframing Populist Resentments in the Tea Party Movement." In *Steep: The Precipitous Rise of the Tea Party*, edited by Lawrence Rosenthal and Christine Trost, 47–66. Berkeley: University of California Press, 2012.

Berlet, Chip. *Right-Wing Populism in America: Too Close for Comfort*. New York: Guilford Press, 2000.

Berlet, Chip. "Taking Tea Partiers Seriously." *Progressive*, February 2010.

Berlet, Chip. "Taking Tea Parties Seriously: Corporate Globalization, Populism, and Resentment." *Perspectives on Global Development and Technology* 10, no. 1 (January 2011): 11–29.

Berlin, Isaiah, et al. "To Define Populism." *Government and Opposition* 3, no. 2 (1968): 137–80.

Bernstein, J. M. "The Very Angry Tea Party." *New York Times*, June 13, 2010.

Betz, Hans-Georg. *Radical Right-Wing Populism in Western Europe*. New York: St. Martin's Press, 1994.

Betz, Hans-Georg, and Stefan Immerfall. *The New Politics of the Right: Neo-populist Parties and Movements in Established Democracies*. New York: Palgrave Macmillan, 1998.

Bonilla-Silva, Eduardo. *Racism without Racists: Color-Blind Racism and the Persistence of Racial Inequality in America*. 3rd ed. Lanham, MD: Rowman & Littlefield, 2009.

Bonomi, Patricia. "'A Just Opposition': The Great Awakening as a Radical Model." In *The Origins of Anglo-American Radicalism*, edited by Margaret Jacob and James Jacob, 243–56. Boston: George Allen & Unwin, 1984.

Bordwell, David, and Kristin Thompson. *Film Art: An Introduction*. 5th ed. New York: McGraw-Hill, 1997.

Bosman, Julie. "Chevy Tries a Write-Your-Own-Ad Approach, and the Potshots Fly." *New York Times*, April 4, 2006.

Bourdieu, Pierre. *Acts of Resistance: Against the Tyranny of the Market*. Translated by Richard Nice. New York: New Press, 1999.

Bourdieu, Pierre. *Outline of a Theory of Practice*. Translated by Richard Nice. New York: Cambridge University Press, 1977.

Bourdieu, Pierre. *Pascalian Meditations*. Translated by Richard Nice. Stanford, CA: Stanford University Press, 2000.

Boyte, Harry C. "Civic Agency and the Cult of the Expert." Dayton, OH: Kettering Foundation, 2009.

Boyte, Harry C. *Commonwealth: A Return to Citizen Politics*. New York: Free Press, 1989.

Boyte, Harry C. "Constructive Politics as Public Work: Organizing the Literature." *Political Theory* 39, no. 5 (October 1, 2011): 630–60.

Boyte, Harry C. *Everyday Politics: Reconnecting Citizens and Public Life*. Philadelphia: University of Pennsylvania Press, 2005.

Boyte, Harry C., and Frank Riessman, eds. *The New Populism: The Politics of Empowerment*. Philadelphia: Temple University Press, 1986.

Boyte, Harry C., and Don Shelby. *The Citizen Solution: How You Can Make a Difference.* Saint Paul: Minnesota Historical Society Press, 2008.

Bretherton, Luke. "The Political Populism of Saul Alinsky and Broad Based Organizing." *Good Society* 21, no. 2 (2012): 261–78.

Brewer, Marilynn. "The Psychology of Prejudice: Ingroup Love and Outgroup Hate." *Journal of Social Issues* 55, no. 3 (Fall 1999): 429–44.

Bromell, Nicholas. *By the Sweat of the Brow: Literature and Labor in Antebellum America.* Chicago: University of Chicago Press, 1993.

Brown, Michael K., Martin Carnoy, Elliott Currie, Troy Duster, David B. Oppenheimer, Marjorie Shultz, and David Wellman. *Whitewashing Race: The Myth of a Color-Blind Society.* Berkeley: University of California Press, 2003.

Brown, Wendy. *Edgework: Critical Essays on Knowledge and Politics.* Princeton, NJ: Princeton University Press, 2005.

Brown, Wendy. "Governmentality in the Age of Neoliberalism." Presented at the Pacific Center for Technology and Culture, Victoria, March 18, 2014.

Brown, Wendy. "Occupy Wall Street: Return of a Repressed Res-Publica." *Theory & Event* 14, no. 4 (2011).

Brown, Wendy. *States of Injury.* Princeton, NJ: Princeton University Press, 1995.

Brown, Wendy. *Walled States, Waning Sovereignty.* New York: Zone Books, 2014.

Brown, Wendy. "We Are All Democrats Now ..." In *Democracy in What State?* 44–57. New York: Columbia University Press, 2012.

Brownback, Abby, and Louis Jacobson. "Require Bills to Include a Clause Citing Its Authority in the Constitution." *PolitiFact, Tampa Bay Times,* March 18, 2011.

Bruyneel, Kevin. "The King's Body: The Martin Luther King Jr. Memorial and the Politics of Collective Memory." *History and Memory* 26, no. 1 (Spring–Summer 2014): 75–108.

Brydum, Sunnivie. "HRC and Coalition Apologize for Silencing Undocumented, Trans Activists at Supreme Court Rally." *Advocate,* April 1, 2013.

Buhle, Mari Jo. *Women and American Socialism, 1870–1920.* Urbana: University of Illinois Press, 1981.

Bunkley, Nick. "Aiming to Be the Truck of Patriots." *New York Times,* September 26, 2006.

Bunn, Curtis. "Seven Lessons from How Police Crushed Occupy." *Popular Resistance,* February 4, 2015.

Burger, Jeff. *Leonard Cohen on Leonard Cohen: Interviews and Encounters.* Chicago: Chicago Review Press, 2014.

Burghart, Devin. "Special Report: The Status of the Tea Party Movement—Part Two." Kansas City, MO: Institution for Research and Education on Human Rights, January 21, 2014.

Burghart, Devin. "View from the Top: A Report on Six National Tea Party Organizations." In *Steep: The Precipitous Rise of the Tea Party,* edited by Lawrence Rosenthal and Christine Trost, 67–97. Berkeley: University of California Press, 2012.

Burghart, Devin, and Leonard Zeskind. "Tea Party Nationalism." Kansas City, MO: Institution for Research and Education on Human Rights, Fall 2010.

Butler, Judith. "Endangered/Endangering: Schematic Racism and White Paranoia." In *Reading Rodney King / Reading Urban Uprising,* edited by Robert Gooding-Williams, 15–22. New York: Routledge, 1993.

Butler, Judith. *Frames of War: When Is Life Grievable?* New York: Verso, 2010.

Butler, Judith. "So, What Are the Demands? And Where Do They Go from Here?" *Tidal: A Journal of Theory and Strategy for the Occupy Movement* 2 (March 2012): 8–11.

Butler, Mike. "'Luther King Was a Good Ole Boy': The Southern Rock Movement and White Male Identity in the Post-Civil Rights South." *Popular Music and Society* 23, no. 2 (Summer 1999): 41–61.

Byers, Thomas B. "History Re-membered: Forrest Gump, Postfeminist Masculinity, and the Burial of the Counterculture." *Modern Fiction Studies* 42, no. 2 (Summer 1996): 419–44.

Byrne, Janet, ed. *The Occupy Handbook.* New York: Back Bay Books, 2012.

Calhoun, Craig. "Imagining Solidarity: Cosmopolitanism, Constitutional Patriotism, and the Public Sphere." *Public Culture* 14, no. 1 (2002): 147–71.

Calhoun, Craig. "Occupy Wall Street in Perspective." *British Journal of Sociology* 64, no. 1 (March 1, 2013): 26–38.

Calhoun, Craig. *The Roots of Radicalism: Tradition, the Public Sphere, and Early Nineteenth-Century Social Movements.* Chicago: University of Chicago Press, 2012.

Callahan, David. "Not So Fast, Sosnik: Why Today's Populism May Be Gone Tomorrow." *Demos*, November 26, 2013.

Canovan, Margaret. "Taking Politics to the People: Populism as the Ideology of Democracy." In *Democracies and the Populist Challenge*, edited by Yves Mény and Yves Surel, 25–44. New York: Palgrave Macmillan, 2002.

Canovan, Margaret. "Trust the People! Populism and the Two Faces of Democracy." *Political Studies* 47, no. 1 (March 1, 1999): 2–16.

Captain, Sean. "Infographic: Who Is Occupy Wall Street?" *Fast Company Online*, November 2, 2011.

Cardenas, Diana. "Long Beach Undocuqueers Take Stage at CSU." *Voicewaves Long Beach*, December 16, 2012.

Caren, Neal, and Sarah Gaby. "Occupy Online: Facebook and the Spread of Occupy Wall Street." SSRN Scholarly Paper. Rochester, NY: Social Science Research Network, October 24, 2011.

Carr, David. "American Tragedies, to Sell Trucks." *New York Times*, October 30, 2006.

Carrasco, Tania A. Unzueta, and Hinda Seif. "Disrupting the Dream: Undocumented Youth Reframe Citizenship and Deportability through Anti-deportation Activism." *Latino Studies*, Disrupting the Dream, 12, no. 2 (2014): 279–99.

Cashmar, Jessica. "Cornel West: Obama Just 'Another Neoliberal Opportunist.'" *Washington Times*, August 25, 2014.

Castaneda, Ernesto. "The Indignados of Spain: A Precedent to Occupy Wall Street." *Social Movement Studies* 13, nos. 3–4 (November 2012): 309–19.

Castells, Manuel. *Networks of Outrage and Hope: Social Movements in the Internet Age.* Cambridge: Polity, 2012.

Chamberlain, Adrian. "Review: No Cooler Cat Than Leonard Cohen." *Times Colonist*, March 6, 2013.

Chambers, Edward T. *Roots for Radicals: Organizing for Power, Action, and Justice.* New York: Bloomsbury Academic, 2003.

Chappell, Lindsay. "Sales to Hispanics Outpacing the Market." *Automotive News*, May 18, 2015.

Chapple, Steve, and Reebee Garofalo. *Rock "n" Roll Is Here to Pay: The History and Politics of the Music Industry*. Chicago: Nelson-Hall, 1978.

Chávez, Karma R. *Queer Migration Politics: Activist Rhetoric and Coalitional Possibilities*. Urbana: University of Illinois Press, 2013.

Chávez, Maria, Jessica L. Lavariega Monforti, and Melissa R. Michelson. *Living the Dream: New Immigration Policies and the Lives of Undocumented Latino Youth*. Boulder, CO: Paradigm Publishers, 2015.

Chen, Michelle. "Queering Immigration." *Huffington Post*, July 9, 2012.

Chomo, Peter N., II. " 'You've Got to Put the Past behind You before You Can Move On': *Forrest Gump* and National Reconciliation." *Film and Television* 23, no. 1 (1995): 2–7.

Ciccariello-Maher, George. *We Created Chávez: A People's History of the Venezuelan Revolution*. Durham, NC: Duke University Press, 2013.

Cieply, Michael, and Nicholas Confessore. "Leaning Right in Hollywood, under a Lens." *New York Times*, January 22, 2014.

Cinquemani, Sal. "15 Songs about AIDS." *Slant*, June 5, 2013.

Coates, Ta-Nehisi. "Blue Lives Matter." *Atlantic*, December 22, 2014.

Cohen, Lizabeth. *A Consumers' Republic: The Politics of Mass Consumption in Postwar America*. New York: Vintage Books, 2003.

Coles, Romand. "The Neuropolitical *Habitus* of Resonant Receptive Democracy." *Ethics and Global Politics* 4, no. 4 (December 2011): 273–93.

Coles, Romand. *Visionary Pragmatism: Radical and Ecological Democracy in Neoliberal Times*. Durham, NC: Duke University Press, forthcoming.

Coles, Romand, Mark Reinhardt, and George Shulman. "Radical Future Pasts? An Anti-introduction." In *Radical Future Pasts: Untimely Political Theory*, edited by Romand Coles, Mark Reinhardt, and George Shulman, 1–36. Lexington: University Press of Kentucky, 2015.

"A Common-Sense Immigration Move." *New York Times*, January 6, 2012.

Connelly, Mary. "Striking a Nerve: Silverado Ads Get Strong Reactions from Viewers." *Autoweek*, October 15, 2006.

Connolly, William. *Capitalism and Christianity, American Style*. Durham, NC: Duke University Press, 2008.

Connolly, William. *The Ethos of Pluralization*. Minneapolis: University of Minnesota Press, 1995.

Connolly, William. "What Is to Be Done?" *Theory & Event* 14, no. 4 (2011).

Connolly, William. *Why I Am Not a Secularist*. Minneapolis: University of Minnesota Press, 2000.

Cooper, Charles. "Got Outrage? More Fodder to Feed Your Inner Populist." CBSNews.com, December 8, 2009

Conrad, Lee. "Populist Outrage Is Back—Ready?" *Financial Planning*, November 1, 2011.

Corrunker, Laura. " 'Coming Out of the Shadows': DREAM Act Activism in the Context of Global Anti-deportation Activism." *Indiana Journal of Global Legal Studies* 19, no. 1 (Winter 2012): 143–68.

Cortés, Ernesto. "Education for Citizenship." In *The New Populism: The Politics of Empowerment*. Philadelphia: Temple University Press, 1986.

Cortese, Anthony J. *Provocateur: Images of Women and Minorities in Advertising.* 3rd ed. Lanham, MD: Rowman & Littlefield, 2007.

Costanza-Chock, Sasha. "Mic Check! Media Cultures and the Occupy Movement." *Social Movement Studies* 11, nos. 3–4 (November 2012): 375–85.

Costanza-Chock, Sasha. *Out of the Shadows, into the Streets! Transmedia Organizing and the Immigrant Rights Movement.* Cambridge, MA: MIT Press, 2014.

Cowan, Richard, and Steve Holland. "Obama Calls Senators in Hopes of Creating 'Common Sense' Caucus on Sequestration." *Huffington Post*, March 4, 2013.

Cox, Thomas C. *Blacks in Topeka, Kansas, 1865–1915: A Social History.* Baton Rouge: Louisiana State University Press, 1982.

Crenshaw, Kimberle. "Demarginalizing the Intersection of Race and Sex: A Black Feminist Critique of Antidiscrimination Doctrine, Feminist Theory, and Antiracist Politics." *University of Chicago Legal Forum* 140 (1989): 139–67.

Crick, Bernard. "Populism, Politics and Democracy." *Democratization* 12, no. 5 (December 2005): 625–32.

Critchley, Simon. *Infinitely Demanding: Ethics of Commitment, Politics of Resistance.* London: Verso, 2007.

Culture Jammers HQ. "#OccupyWallStreet." *Adbusters*, July 13, 2011.

Curl, John. *For All the People: Uncovering the Hidden History of Cooperation, Cooperative Movements, and Communalism in America.* Oakland, CA: PM Press, 2009.

Dávila, Arlene. *Latinos, Inc.: The Marketing and Making of a People.* Berkeley: University of California Press, 2001.

Dean, Amy. "After the 99% Spring: What Comes Next." *AlterNet*, July 2, 2012.

Dean, Jodi. *Democracy and Other Neoliberal Fantasies: Communicative Capitalism and Left Politics.* Durham, NC: Duke University Press, 2009.

Dean, Jodi. "Occupation as Political Form." Keynote lecture presented at the Transmediale Festival, Berlin, February 3, 2012.

Dean, Mitchell M. *Governmentality: Power and Rule in Modern Society.* 2nd ed. London: Sage, 2009.

De Genova, Nicholas. "Gangster Rap and Nihilism in Black America: Some Questions of Life and Death." *Social Text* 43 (Autumn 1995): 89–132.

De Genova, Nicholas, and Nathalie Peutz, eds. *The Deportation Regime: Sovereignty, Space, and the Freedom of Movement.* Durham, NC: Duke University Press, 2010.

De Lisle, Tim. "Who Held a Gun to Leonard Cohen's Head?" *Guardian*, September 16, 2004.

D'Emilio, John. *Lost Prophet: The Life and Times of Bayard Rustin.* Chicago: University of Chicago Press, 2004.

Derrida, Jacques. *Aporias.* Translated by Thomas Dutoit. Stanford, CA: Stanford University Press, 1993.

Derrida, Jacques. *The Other Heading: Reflections on Today's Europe.* Translated by Pascale-Anne Brault and Michael B. Naas. Bloomington: Indiana University Press, 1992.

Derrida, Jacques. *Writing and Difference.* Translated by Alan Bass. Chicago: University of Chicago Press, 1978.

Digiacomo, Frank. "One from the Heartland." *Vanity Fair*, February 2007.

Disch, Lisa. "The Tea Party: A 'White Citizenship' Movement?" In *Steep: The Precipitous Rise of the Tea Party*, edited by Lawrence Rosenthal and Christine Trost, 133–51. Berkeley: University of California Press, 2012.

Domenech, Ben. "The Libertarian Populist Agenda." *RealClearPolitics*, June 5, 2013.

Donnelly, Francis. "UAW's Battles Shape History." *Detroit News*, September 16, 2008.

Dorraj, Manochehr. *From Zarathustra to Khomeini: Populism and Dissent in Iran*. Boulder, CO: Lynne Rienner, 1990.

Dorraj, Manochehr. "Iranian Populism: Its Vicissitudes and Political Impact." In *The Many Faces of Populism: Current Perspectives*, edited by Dwayne Woods and Barbara Wejnert, 127–42. Bingley, UK: Emerald Group, 2014.

Douthat, Ross. "Libertarian Populism and Its Limits." *New York Times*, June 4, 2013.

Du Bois, W. E. B. *Black Reconstruction in America, 1860–1880*. New York: Free Press, 1998.

Duggan, Lisa. *The Twilight of Equality? Neoliberalism, Cultural Politics, and the Attack on Democracy*. Boston: Beacon Press, 2004.

Duggan, Lisa, Russ Castronovo, and Dana Nelson. "The New Homonormativity: The Sexual Politics of Neoliberalism." In *Materializing Democracy: Toward a Revitalized Cultural Politics*, edited by Russ Castronovo and Dana D. Nelson, 175–94. Durham, NC: Duke University Press, 2002.

Dunn, Timothy J. *The Militarization of the U.S.-Mexico Border, 1978–1992*. Austin: University of Texas Press, 1996.

Eidelson, Josh. "Tea Party's 'Absurd' Socialism Obsession: An Actual Marxist Sounds Off." *Salon*, March 27, 2014.

Elkins, Emily. "Today's Bailout Anniversary Reminds Us That the Tea Party Is More Than Anti-Obama." *Reason*, October 3, 2014.

Espejo, Paulina Ochoa. *The Time of Popular Sovereignty: Process and the Democratic State*. University Park: Penn State University Press, 2011.

Ewen, Stuart. *Channels of Desire: Mass Images and the Shaping of American Consciousness*. 2nd ed. Minneapolis: University of Minnesota Press, 1992.

Fang, Lee. "How Private Prisons Game the Immigration System." *Nation*, February 27, 2013.

Farhi, Paul. "The Pickup Ad That's Carrying Lots of Baggage." *Washington Post*, October 25, 2006.

Farrow, Kenyon. "Occupy Wall Street's Race Problem." *American Prospect*, October 24, 2011.

Ferber, Abby L. "The Construction of Black Masculinity: White Supremacy Now and Then." *Journal of Sport and Social Issues* 31, no. 1 (February 2007): 11–24.

Ferguson, Kathy E. "Anarchist Counterpublics." *New Political Science* 32, no. 2 (June 2010): 193–214.

Ferguson, Kennan. *All in the Family: On Community and Incommensurability*. Durham, NC: Duke University Press, 2012.

Ferguson, Michaele. *Sharing Democracy*. New York: Oxford University Press, 2012.

Fink, Leon. *Workingmen's Democracy: The Knights of Labor and American Politics*. Urbana: University of Illinois Press, 1983.

Fisher, Mark. *Capitalist Realism: Is There No Alternative?* Washington, DC: Zero Books, 2009.

Fletcher, Winston. *Advertising: A Very Short Introduction*. New York: Oxford University Press, 2010.

Flores, Marco Antonio. "Undocuqueer 'Come Out' at S.F. Pride Parade." *New American Media*, June 26, 2012.

Foley, Elizabeth Price. *The Tea Party*. New York: Cambridge University Press, 2011.

Foner, Philip S. *History of the Labor Movement in the United States*, vol. 1: *From Colonial Times to the Founding of the American Federation of Labor*. New York: International Publishers, 1947.

Foner, Philip S. *History of the Labor Movement in the United States*, vol. 2: *From the Founding of the A. F. of L. to the Emergence of American Imperialism*. New York: International Publishers, 1975.

Foucault, Michel. *The Birth of Biopolitics: Lectures at the Collège de France, 1978–1979*. Edited by Michel Senellart. Translated by Graham Burchell. New York: Picador, 2010.

Frank, Jason. "'Besides Our Selves': An Essay on Enthusiastic Politics and Civil Subjectivity." *Public Culture* 17, no. 3 (October 1, 2005): 371–92.

Frank, Jason. *Constituent Moments: Enacting the People in Postrevolutionary America*. Durham, NC: Duke University Press, 2010.

Frank, Jason. "Populism and Praxis: Between the Electorate and the Multitude." In *Means and Ends: Rethinking Political Realism*, edited by Karuna Mantena. Cambridge University Press, forthcoming.

Frank, Jason. "Promiscuous Citizenship." In *A Political Companion to Walt Whitman*, edited by John E. Seery, 155–84. Lexington: University Press of Kentucky, 2010.

Frank, Thomas. *The Conquest of Cool: Business Culture, Counterculture, and the Rise of Hip Consumerism*. Chicago: University of Chicago Press, 1998.

Fraser, Steve. *The Age of Acquiescence: The Life and Death of American Resistance to Organized Wealth and Power*. New York: Little, Brown, 2015.

Fraser, Steve. "The Limousine Liberal's Family Tree." *Raritan* 31, no. 1 (Summer 2011): 138–55.

Frazier Group. "Independent Investigation: Occupy Oakland Response, October 25, 2011." Commissioned by the City of Oakland, June 14, 2012.

Freeman, J. *The Tyranny of Structurelessness*. Leeds: Leeds Women's Organization for Revolutionary Anarchists, 1972.

Friedersdorf, Conor. "A Plea to Liberals: Stop Marginalizing Peace and Civil Liberties." *Atlantic*, November 7, 2011.

Friedersdorf, Conor. "The Tea Party: 'Constitutional Conservatives' in Name Only." *Atlantic*, November 28, 2011.

Friedman, Benjamin. "Meltdown: A Case Study." *Atlantic*, August 2005.

Frith, Simon. "Towards an Aesthetic of Popular Music." In *Music and Society: The Politics of Composition, Performance and Reception*, edited by Richard Leppert and Susan McClary, 133–50. New York: Cambridge University Press, 1989.

Froese, Paul. "The Tea Party's Unifying Bogeyman: The Socialist." *USA Today*, September 12, 2010.

Fuss, Diana. "Inside/Out." In *Inside/Out: Lesbian Theories, Gay Theories*, edited by Diana Fuss, 1–12. New York: Routledge, 1991.

Gaither, Gerald H. *Blacks and the Populist Revolt: Ballots and Bigotry in the "New South"*. University: University of Alabama Press, 1977.

Galbraith, John Kenneth. *The Affluent Society*. Boston: Mariner Books, 1998.

Galston, William. "Realism in Political Theory." *European Journal of Political Theory* 9, no. 4 (2010): 385–411.

Ganz, Marshall. "Why Stories Matter: The Art Craft of Social Change." *Sojourners* 38, no. 3 (March 2009): 16–21.

Gaonkar, Dilip Parameshwar. "Toward New Imaginaries: An Introduction." *Public Culture* 14, no. 1 (2002): 1–19.

Garces, Chris. "People's Mic and Democratic Charisma: Occupy Wall Street's Frontier Assemblies." *Focaal* 66 (Summer 2013): 88–102.

Garofoli, Joe. "Occupy Movement Fails to Connect with Blacks." *SFGate*, December 13, 2011.

Garrow, David. *Bearing the Cross: Martin Luther King, Jr., and the Southern Christian Leadership Conference*. New York: HarperCollins, 2004.

Garvin, W. L., and S. O. Daws. *History of the National Farmers' Alliance and Cooperative Union of America*. Jacksboro, TX: J.N. Rogers & Co, Steam Printers, 1887.

Gelder, Sarah van. "This Changes Everything: How the 99% Woke Up." *Yes!*, November 18, 2011.

Germani, Gino. *Authoritarianism, Fascism, and National Populism*. New Brunswick, NJ: Transaction Publishers, 1978.

Gerteis, Joseph. *Class and the Color Line: Interracial Class Coalition in the Knights of Labor and the Populist Movement*. Durham, NC: Duke University Press, 2007.

Gitlin, Todd. *Occupy Nation: The Roots, the Spirit, and the Promise of Occupy Wall Street*. New York: It Books, 2012.

Gitlin, Todd. "Occupy's Predicament: The Moment and the Prospects for the Movement." *British Journal of Sociology* 64, no. 1 (March 1, 2013): 3–25.

"GM Sales Appear Resilient Despite Recalls; Dealers Optimistic." *International Business Times*, May 23, 2014.

Golash-Boza, Tanya Maria. *Immigration Nation: Raids, Detentions, and Deportations in Post-9/11 America*. Boulder, CO: Paradigm, 2012.

Goldberg, Michael Lewis. *An Army of Women: Gender and Politics in Gilded Age Kansas*. Baltimore: Johns Hopkins University Press, 1997.

Gole, Nilufer. "Islam in Public: New Visibilities and New Imaginaries." *Public Culture* 14, no. 1 (2002): 173–90.

Good, Chris. "The Tea Party Movement: Who's in Charge?" *Atlantic*, April 13, 2009.

Goodstein, Laurie. "Battles around Nation over Proposed Mosques." *New York Times*, August 7, 2010.

Goodwyn, Lawrence. *Democratic Promise: The Populist Movement in America*. New York: Oxford University Press, 1976.

Goodwyn, Lawrence. "Populist Dreams and Negro Rights: East Texas as a Case Study." *American Historical Review* 76, no. 5 (December 1971): 1435–56.

Goodwyn, Lawrence. *The Populist Moment: A Short History of the Agrarian Revolt in America*. Oxford University Press, 1978.

Gordin, Colin. "Governmental Rationality." In *The Foucault Effect: Studies in Governmentality*, edited by Graham Burchell, Colin Gordon, and Peter Miller, 1–52. Chicago: University of Chicago Press, 1991.

Gordon, Fon Louise. *Caste and Class: The Black Experience in Arkansas, 1880–1920.* Athens: University of Georgia Press, 1995.

Gould, Deborah B. *Moving Politics: Emotion and ACT UP's Fight against AIDS.* Chicago: University of Chicago Press, 2009.

Graeber, David. "Occupy Wall Street's Anarchist Roots." In *The Occupy Handbook,* edited by Janet Byrne, 141–49. New York: Back Bay Books, 2012.

Grattan, Laura. "Pierre Bourdieu and Populism: The Everyday Politics of Outrageous Resistance." *Good Society* 21, no. 2 (2012): 194–218.

Gray, Herman. "Black Masculinity and Visual Culture." *Callaloo* 18, no. 2 (Spring 1995): 401–5.

Green, James. "Populism, Socialism and the Promise of Democracy." *Radical History Review* 1980, no. 24 (1980): 7–40.

Greenberg, Karl. "Chevy Pitches Fuel Efficiency to Hispanics via Mexican Band." *Marketing Daily,* May 16, 2007.

Gronlund, Laurence. *The Co-operative Commonwealth: An Exposition of Modern Socialism.* New York: Cosimo Classics, 2008.

Grow, Kory. "Lauryn Hill Dedicates 'Black Rage' Song to Ferguson." *Rolling Stone,* August 21, 2014.

Grusky, David, and Tamar Kricheli-Katz, eds. *The New Gilded Age: The Critical Inequality Debates of Our Time.* Stanford, CA: Stanford University Press, 2012.

Guardino, Matt, and Dean Snyder. "The Tea Party and the Crisis of Neoliberalism: Mainstreaming New Right Populism in the Corporate News Media." *New Political Science* 34, no. 4 (December 2012): 527–48.

Gummow, Jodie. "Dreamers Put Bodies on the Line to Stop Bus from Deporting Dozens of People." *AlterNet,* August 23, 2013.

Gutierrez, Jorge. "I Am Undocuqueer: New Strategies for Alliance Building for the LGBTQ and Immigrant Rights Movements." *Huffington Post,* January 21, 2013.

Habermas, Jürgen. "Three Normative Models of Democracy." *Constellations* 1, no. 1 (1994): 1–10.

Hahn, Steven. *A Nation under Our Feet: Black Political Struggles in the Rural South from Slavery to the Great Migration.* Cambridge, MA: Belknap Press of Harvard University Press, 2005.

Halberstam, Judith. *The Queer Art of Failure.* Durham, NC: Duke University Press, 2011.

Hall, Stuart. "Notes on Deconstructing the Popular." In *People's History and Socialist Theory,* edited by Raphael Samuel, 442–53. London: Routledge & Kegan Paul, 1981.

Hamilton, Alexander, James Madison, and John Jay. *The Federalist Papers.* Edited by Clinton Rossiter. New York: Signet, 2003.

Hancox, Dan. "Why Ernesto Laclau Is the Intellectual Figurehead for Syriza and Podemos." *Guardian,* February 9, 2015.

Handlin, Oscar. "American Views of the Jew at the Opening of the Twentieth Century." *Publications of the American Jewish Historical Society* 40, no. 4 (June 1951): 323–44.

Hannon, Elliot. "Detroit Resumes Cutting Off Water to 150,000 Residents, Prompting Appeal to United Nations for Help." *Slate,* June 23, 2014.

Hardt, Michael. "Affective Labor." *Boundary 2* 26, no. 2 (Summer 1999): 89–100.

Hardt, Michael, and Antonio Negri. *Empire*. Cambridge, MA: Harvard University Press, 2001.

Hardt, Michael, and Antonio Negri. "The Fight for 'Real Democracy' at the Heart of Occupy Wall Street." *Foreign Affairs*, October 11, 2011.

Harkinson, Josh. "Why Occupy Should Be the Left's Tea Party." *Mother Jones*, May 2, 2012.

Harris, Mike. "Gun Control Debate Revitalizes Local Tea Party Groups." *Huffington Post*, April 22, 2013.

Harris, Shane. *The Watchers: The Rise of America's Surveillance State*. New York: Penguin, 2011.

Hartmut, Rosa. "Social Acceleration: Ethical and Political Consequences of a Desynchronized High-Speed Society." *Constellations* 10 (2010): 3–33.

Hartz, Louis. *The Liberal Tradition in America*. 2nd ed. San Diego: Mariner Books, 1991.

Harvey, David. *The Enigma of Capital and the Crises of Capitalism*. 2nd ed. New York: Oxford University Press, 2011.

Harvey, David. *Spaces of Global Capitalism*. London: Verso, 2006.

Hauerwas, Stanley, and Romand Coles. *Christianity, Democracy, and the Radical Ordinary: Conversations between a Radical Democrat and a Christian*. Eugene, OR: Cascade Books, 2008.

Hayward, Jack. "The Populist Challenge to Elitist Democracy in Europe." In *Elitism, Populism, and European Politics*, edited by Jack Hayward, 10–32. Oxford: Clarendon Press, 1996.

Hess, Amanda. "When Did the Rock-Solid Manly Men in Truck Commercials Get So Soft?" *Slate*, December 26, 2013.

Hesson, Ted. "9 DREAMer Actions That Advanced Immigration Reform." ABCNews. com, August 10, 2013.

Hiar, Corbin. "How the Tea Party Utilized Digital Media to Gain Power." MediaShift.org, October 28, 2010.

Hibbing, John R., and Elizabeth Theiss-Morse. *Stealth Democracy: Americans' Beliefs about How Government Should Work*. New York: Cambridge University Press, 2002.

Hicks, John D. *Populist Revolt: A History of the Farmers' Alliance and the People's Party*. Minnesota Archive ed. Minneapolis: University of Minnesota Press, 1931.

Higgins, Tim. "U.S. Lost $11.2 Billion in GM Bailout, TARP Report Says." *Bloomberg Business*, May 1, 2014.

Hing, Julianne. "For Trans Immigrant Detainees, Deportation Is Sometimes the Better Option." *Colorlines*, November 17, 2014.

Hing, Julianne. "Mamas of Color and Their Kids Tell Greedy Banks: It's Time to Share." *Colorlines*, November 7, 2011.

Hixson, Walter L. *American Settler Colonialism: A History*. New York: Palgrave Macmillan, 2013.

Hockenberry, John. "A Tea Party Activist Responds to Occupy Wall Street." *The Take Away Online*, WNYC Radio and Public Radio International, October 10, 2011.

Hoerder, Dirk. *American Labor and Immigration History, 1877–1920s: Recent European Research*. Urbana: University of Illinois Press, 1983.

Hofstadter, Richard. *The Age of Reform*. New York: Vintage, 1960.

Hofstadter, Richard. *The Paranoid Style in American Politics*. New York: Vintage, 2008.

Holmes, Mary. "Feeling beyond Rules: Politicizing the Sociology of Emotion and Anger in Feminist Politics." *European Journal of Social Theory* 7, no. 2 (2004): 209–27.

Honig, Bonnie. *Democracy and the Foreigner*. Princeton, NJ: Princeton University Press, 2001.

Honig, Bonnie. *Emergency Politics: Paradox, Law, Democracy*. Princeton, NJ: Princeton University Press, 2009.

Houston, W. W. "Libertarian Populism: Unpopular and Impolitic." *Economist*, July 20, 2013.

Howard, Theresa. "'Revolution' in Ad Campaign." *USA Today*, October 17, 2004.

Howarth, David. "Populism or Popular Democracy? The UDF, Workerism and the Struggle for Radical Democracy in South Africa." In *Populism and the Mirror of Democracy*, edited by Francisco Panizza, 202–23. London: Verso, 2005.

Hsu, Spencer S., and Andrew Becker. "ICE Officials Set Quotas to Deport More Illegal Immigrants." *Washington Post*, March 27, 2010.

Hull, Geoffrey P. *The Recording Industry*. 2nd ed. New York: Routledge, 2004.

Ionescu, Ghita, and Ernest Gellner, eds. *Populism; Its Meaning and National Characteristics*. New York: Macmillan, 1969.

Jacobson, Matthew Frye. *Whiteness of a Different Color: European Immigrants and the Alchemy of Race*. Cambridge, MA: Harvard University Press, 1999.

Jamieson, Kathleen Hall, and Joseph N. Capella. *Echo Chamber: Rush Limbaugh and the Conservative Media Establishment*. New York: Oxford University Press, 2010.

Jeffrey, Julie Roy. "Women in the Southern Farmers' Alliance: A Reconsideration of the Role and Status of Women in the Late Nineteenth-Century South." *Feminist Studies* 3, nos. 1–2 (Autumn 1975): 72–91.

Jeffries, Michael P. *Thug Life: Race, Gender, and the Meaning of Hip-Hop*. Chicago: University of Chicago Press, 2011.

Johnson, Bradley. "From 'See the USA in Your Chevrolet' to 'Like a Rock,' Chevy Ads Run Deep." *Advertising Age*, October 31, 2011.

Josephson, Matthew. *The Politicos, 1865–1896*. New York: Harcourt, Brace, 1938.

Joyner, James. "How Perpetual War Became U.S. Ideology." *Atlantic*, May 11, 2011.

Judis, John B. "Right-Wing Populism Could Hobble America for Decades." *New Republic*, October 27, 2013.

Juris, Jeffrey S. "Reflections on #Occupy Everywhere: Social Media, Public Space, and Emerging Logics of Aggregation." *American Ethnologist* 39, no. 2 (May 1, 2012): 259–79.

Juris, Jeffrey S., Michelle Ronayne, Firuzeh Shokooh-Valle, and Robert Wengrownowitz. "Negotiating Power and Difference within the 99%." *Social Movement Studies* 11, nos. 3–4 (November 2012): 434–40.

Kane, Paul. "'Tea Party' Protesters Accused of Spitting on Lawmaker, Using Slurs." *Washington Post*, March 21, 2010.

Katz, Mark. *Capturing Sound: How Technology Has Changed Music*. Revised ed. Berkeley: University of California Press, 2010.

Kazin, Michael. *The Populist Persuasion: An American History*. Ithaca, NY: Cornell University Press, 1998.

Kazin, Michael. "Whatever Happened to the American Left?" *New York Times*, September 24, 2011.

Keeling, Kara. "'A Homegrown Revolutionary'?" Tupac Shakur and the Legacy of the Black Panther Party." *Black Scholar* 29, nos. 2–3 (Summer–Fall 1999): 59–63.

Keenan, Craig. "Auto Bailouts Won't Be Repaid in Full." *Globe and Mail*, May 30, 2011.

Kemi. "Undocumented & Queer: How Lulú Martinez Is Melting Borders." *Autostraddle*, July 25, 2013.

Kerton, Sarah. "Tahrir, Here? The Influence of the Arab Uprisings on the Emergence of Occupy." *Social Movement Studies* 11, nos. 3–4 (November 2012): 302–8.

"Keystone Pipeline Should Be a No-Brainer." *Rush Limbaugh Show*, March 5, 2013.

Khimm, Suzy. "The Sequester, Explained." *Washington Post*, September 14, 2012.

Kilkenny, Allison. "Resistance Has Begun." In *We Are Wisconsin: The Wisconsin Uprising in the Words of the Activists, Writers, and Everyday Wisconsinites Who Made It Happen*, edited by Erica Sagrans, 191–93. Minneapolis, MN: Tasora Books, 2011.

Kim, Richard. "The Audacity of Occupy Wall Street." *Nation*, November 21, 2011.

Kim, Susan. "The Auto Industry's Forgotten Legacy: Diversity." *Time*, December 11, 2008.

King, Martin Luther, Jr. *A Testament of Hope: The Essential Writings of Martin Luther King, Jr.* Edited by James M. Washington. San Francisco: Harper San Francisco, 1991.

Kintz, Linda. *Between Jesus and the Market: The Emotions That Matter in Right-Wing America*. Durham, NC: Duke University Press, 1997.

Kioupkiolis, Alexandros, and Giorgos Katsambekis, eds. *Radical Democracy and Collective Movements Today: The Biopolitics of the Multitude versus the Hegemony of the People*. Burlington, VT: Ashgate, 2014.

Kirby, David, and Emily McClintock Eckins. "Libertarian Roots of the Tea Party." *Policy Analysis* 705 (August 6, 2012): 1–52.

Klein, Naomi. "Why Now? What's Next? Naomi Klein and Yotam Marom in Conversation about Occupy Wall Street." *Nation*, January 9, 2012.

Knowles, Eric D., Brian S. Lowery, Elizabeth P. Shulman, and Rebecca L. Schaumberg. "Race, Ideology, and the Tea Party: A Longitudinal Study." *PLoS ONE* 8, no. 6 (June 2013): 1–11.

Knowlton, Brian, and David M. Herszenhorn. "Bipartisan Support for Wall St. Rescue Plan Emerges." *New York Times*, September 22, 2008.

Kochhar, Rakesh, Richard Fry, and Paul Taylor. "Wealth Gaps Rise to Record Highs between Whites, Blacks, Hispanics." Washington, DC: Pew Research Center, July 26, 2011.

Koehler, Robert. "Should the Police Be Armed?" *Common Dreams*, April 16, 2015.

Kramer, Michael J. *The Republic of Rock: Music and Citizenship in the Sixties Counterculture*. New York: Oxford University Press, 2013.

Krause, Paul. *The Battle for Homestead, 1880–1892: Politics, Culture, and Steel*. Pittsburgh: University of Pittsburgh Press, 1992.

Kreiss, Daniel, and Zeynep Tufekci. "Occupying the Political: Occupy Wall Street, Collective Action, and the Rediscovery of Pragmatic Politics." *Cultural Studies / Critical Methodologies* 13, no. 3 (June 2013): 163–67.

Krugman, Paul. "Delusions of Populism." *New York Times*, July 11, 2013.

Krugman, Paul. "That Old-Time Whistle." *New York Times*, March 16, 2014.

Krugman, Paul. "We Are the 99.9%." *New York Times*, November 24, 2011.

Kuehn, Kathleen Mary. "'There's Got to Be a Review Democracy': Communicative Capitalism, Neoliberal Citizenship, and the Politics of Participation on the

Consumer Evaluation Website Yelp.com." *International Journal of Communication* 7 (2013): 607–25.

Kurzweil, Ray. "Frontiers." *Atlantic*, November 2007.

Laclau, Ernesto. *On Populist Reason*. London: Verso, 2007.

Laclau, Ernesto. *Politics and Ideology in Marxist Theory: Capitalism, Fascism, Populism.* New York: Verso, 2012.

Laclau, Ernesto. "Populism: What's in a Name?" In *Populism and the Mirror of Democracy*, edited by Francisco Panizza, 32–49. New York: Verso, 2005.

Laclau, Ernesto, and Chantal Mouffe. *Hegemony and Socialist Strategy: Towards a Radical Democratic Politics*. 2nd ed. New York: Verso, 2001.

Lal, Prerna. "How Queer Undocumented Youth Built the Immigrant Rights Movement." *Huffington Post*, March 28, 2013.

Langman, Lauren. "Cycles of Contention: The Rise and Fall of the Tea Party." *Critical Sociology* 38, no. 4 (July 2012): 469–94.

Leach, Darcy K. "Culture and the Structure of Tyrannylessness." *Sociological Quarterly* 54, no. 2 (Spring 2013): 181–91.

Lee, Benjamin, and Edward LiPuma. "Cultures of Circulation: The Imaginations of Modernity." *Public Culture* 14, no. 1 (2002): 191–213.

Lee, Hatty. "Art and Activism Come Together to Make DREAM a Reality." *Colorlines*, November 30, 2010.

Lee, Suevon. "A Reading Guide to True the Vote, the Controversial Voter Fraud Watchdog." *ProPublica*, September 27, 2012.

Lefort, Claude. *The Political Forms of Modern Society: Bureaucracy, Democracy, Totalitarianism*. Cambridge, MA: MIT Press, 1986.

Lena, Jennifer. "Social Context and Musical Content of Rap Music." *Social Forces* 85, no. 1 (2006): 479–95.

Lepore, Jill. "The Commandments." *New Yorker*, January 10, 2011.

Lepore, Jill. *The Whites of Their Eyes: The Tea Party's Revolution and the Battle over American History*. Princeton, NJ: Princeton University Press, 2010.

Lerner, Stephen, and George Goehl. "The New Bottom Line: Fighting Organized Money Takes Organized People." *Shelterforce*, Fall 2011.

Lincoln, Abraham. *Political Writings and Speeches*. Edited by Terence Ball. New York: Cambridge University Press, 2012.

Linsky, Marty. "Occupy Wall Street Is Going Nowhere without Leadership." CNN.com, October 28, 2011.

Lipset, Seymour Martin. *American Exceptionalism: A Double-Edged Sword*. New York: W. W. Norton, 1997.

Lipset, Seymour Martin. *Political Man: The Social Bases of Politics*. Exp. ed. Baltimore: Johns Hopkins University Press, 1981.

Lipset, Seymour Martin. *The Politics of Unreason: Right Wing Extremism in America, 1790–1970*. New York: Harper & Row, 1970.

Lipsitz, George. "The Possessive Investment in Whiteness: Racialized Social Democracy and the 'White' Problem in American Studies." *American Quarterly* 47, no. 3 (September 1995): 369–87.

Lloyd, Henry Demarest. *Wealth against Commonwealth*. New York: Harper & Brothers, 1894.

Lo, Clarence. "AstroTurf versus Grass Roots: Scenes from Early Tea Party Mobilization." In *Steep: The Precipitous Rise of the Tea Party*, edited by Lawrence Rosenthal and Christine Trost, 98–130. Berkeley: University of California Press, 2012.

Lorde, Audre. *Sister Outsider: Essays and Speeches*. Berkeley, CA: Crossing Press, 2007.

Lovejoy, David S. "'Desperate Enthusiasm': Early Signs of American Radicalism." In *The Origins of Anglo-American Radicalism*, edited by Margaret Jacob and James Jacob, 231–42. Boston: George Allen & Unwin, 1984.

Lovejoy, David S. *Religious Enthusiasm in the New World: Heresy to Revolution*. Cambridge, MA: Harvard University Press, 1985.

Lowndes, Joseph. *From the New Deal to the New Right: Race and the Southern Origins of Modern Conservatism*. New Haven, CT: Yale University Press, 2009.

Lowndes, Joseph. "Looking Forward to the History of the Tea Party." *Logos* 10, no. 3 (2011).

Lowndes, Joseph. "The Past and Future of Race in the Tea Party Movement." In *Steep: The Precipitous Rise of the Tea Party*, edited by Lawrence Rosenthal and Christine Trost, 152–70. Berkeley: University of California Press, 2012.

Lowndes, Joseph, and Dorian Warren. "Occupy Wall Street: A Twenty-First Century Populist Movement?" *Dissent*, October 21, 2011.

Luibhéid, Eithne. "Queer/Migration: An Unruly Body of Scholarship." *GLQ: A Journal of Lesbian and Gay Studies* 14, nos. 2–3 (2008): 169–90.

Luibhéid, Eithne, and Lionel Cantu Jr., eds. *Queer Migrations: Sexuality, U.S. Citizenship, and Border Crossings*. Minneapolis: University of Minnesota Press, 2005.

Lutz, Catherine A., and Lila Abu-Lughod, eds. *Language and the Politics of Emotion*. Cambridge: Cambridge University Press, 1990.

Lynskey, Dorian. "The Great Rock'n'Roll Sellout." *Guardian*, June 30, 2011.

MacRae, Donald. "Populism as an Ideology." In *Populism: Its Meanings and National Characteristics*, edited by Ghita Ionescu and Ernest Gellner, 153–65. London: Weidenfeld and Nicolson, 1969.

Mahdavi, Pardis. *From Trafficking to Terror: Constructing a Global Social Problem*. New York: Routledge, 2013.

Mahmood, Saba. *Politics of Piety: The Islamic Revival and the Feminist Subject*. Princeton, NJ: Princeton University Press, 2005.

Mair, Peter. "Populist Democracy vs. Party Democracy." In *Democracies and the Populist Challenge*, edited by Yves Mény and Yves Surel, 81–98. New York: Palgrave Macmillan, 2002.

Malkin, Michelle. "Tea-Party Saboteurs." *National Review Online*, April 14, 2010.

Marchand, Roland. *Advertising the American Dream: Making Way for Modernity, 1920–1940*. Berkeley: University of California Press, 1986.

Margolin, Emma. "LGBT Immigrants Protest against 'Death Sentence' Deportations." MSNBC.com, September 9, 2014.

Marsden, Madonna. "The American Myth of Success: Visions and Revisions." In *Popular Culture: An Introductory Text*, edited by Kevin Lausé, 134–48. Madison: University of Wisconsin Press, 1992.

Marsden, Rachel. "Environmentalists Do Billionaires' Bidding in Fight against Keystone Pipeline." *Town Hall*, February 5, 2014.

Marsh, Charles. *The Beloved Community: How Faith Shapes Social Justice from the Civil Rights Movement to Today*. New York: Basic Books, 2006.

Massey, Douglas S., Jorge Durand, and Nolan Malone. *Beyond Smoke and Mirrors: Mexican Immigration in an Era of Economic Integration*. New York: Russell Sage Foundation, 2003.

McGrath, Ben. "The Movement: The Rise of Tea Party Activism." *New Yorker*, February 1, 2010.

McIntyre, Douglas. "Is GM's Rebound the Real Deal?" *DailyFinance*, May 3, 2011.

McIvor, David. "The Politics of Speed: Connolly, Wolin, and the Prospects for Democratic Citizenship in an Accelerated Polity." *Polity* 43, no. 1 (January 2011): 58–83.

McKinnon, John D. "Liberal Groups Plan to Protest at Shareholder Meetings." *Wall Street Journal*, April 24, 2012.

McLaurin, Melton. *The Knights of Labor in the South*. Westport, CT: Praeger, 1978.

Meckler, Laura. "White House Immigration Protest Has Surprise Ending." *Wall Street Journal*, June 5, 2014.

Melamed, Jodi. "The Spirit of Neoliberalism: From Racial Liberalism to Neoliberal Multiculturalism." *Social Text* 24, no. 4 (December 21, 2006): 1–24.

Meltzer, Marisa. *Girl Power: The Nineties Revolution in Music*. New York: Faber & Faber, 2010.

Menjívar, Cecilia, and Daniel Kanstroom, eds. *Constructing Immigrant "Illegality": Critiques, Experiences, and Responses*. New York: Cambridge University Press, 2015.

Mény, Yves, and Yves Surel. "The Constitutive Ambiguities of Populism." In *Democracies and the Populist Challenge*, edited by Yves Mény and Yves Surel, 1–24. New York: Palgrave Macmillan, 2002.

Mény, Yves, and Yves Surel, eds. *Democracies and the Populist Challenge*. New York: Palgrave Macmillan, 2002.

Middleton, Britt. "'Occupy the Hood' Joins Wall Street Protests." BET.com, October 9, 2011.

Milkman, Ruth, Stephanie Luce, and Penny Lewis. "Changing the Subject: A Bottom-Up Account of Occupy Wall Street in New York City." New York: Murphy Institute, City University of New York, n.d.

Miller, David. *On Nationality*. Oxford: Oxford University Press, 1997.

Miller, Ethan. "OCCUPY! CONNECT! CREATE!—Imagining Life beyond 'the Economy.'" *Grassroots Economic Organizing*, October 2011, http://www.geo.coop/node/718.

Miller, Lisa L. "Racialized State Failure and the Violent Death of Michael Brown." *Theory & Event* 17, no. 3 (2014).

Miller, Worth Robert. *Oklahoma Populism: A History of the People's Party in the Oklahoma Territory*. Norman: University of Oklahoma Press, 1987.

Minnite, Lorraine C. "New Challenges in the Study of Right-Wing Propaganda: Priming the Populist Backlash to 'Hope and Change.'" *New Political Science* 34, no. 4 (December 2012): 506–26.

Mishel, Lawrence, Josh Bivens, Elise Gould, and Heidi Shierholz. *The State of Working America*. 12th ed. Ithaca, NY: Cornell University Press, 2012.

Mitchell, Theodore R. *Political Education in the Southern Farmers' Alliance, 1887–1900*. Madison: University of Wisconsin Press, 1987.

Montgomery, Peter. "The Tea Party and Religious Right Movements: Frenemies with Benefits." In *Steep: The Precipitous Rise of the Tea Party*, edited by Lawrence Rosenthal and Christine Trost, 242–74. Berkeley: University of California Press, 2012.

Moreno-Caballud, Luis, and Marina Sitrin. "Occupy Wall Street, beyond Encampments." *Yes!*, November 2011.

Morgan, W. Scott. *History of the Wheel and Alliance and the Impending Revolution.* J.H. Rice & Sons, 1891.

Morgenthau, Robert M. "The US Keeps 34,000 Immigrants in Detention Each Day Simply to Meet a Quota." *Nation*, August 13, 2014.

Morone, James A. *The Democratic Wish: Popular Participation and the Limits of American Government.* Rev. ed. New Haven, CT: Yale University Press, 1998.

Mort, Sébastien. "Tailoring Dissent on the Airwaves: The Role of Conservative Talk Radio in the Right-Wing Resurgence of 2010." *New Political Science* 34, no. 4 (December 2012): 485–505.

Mouffe, Chantal. "The 'End of Politics' and the Challenge of Right-Wing Populism." In *Populism and the Mirror of Democracy*, edited by Francisco Panizza, 50–71. London: Verso, 2005.

Mudde, Cas. "The Populist Zeitgeist." *Government and Opposition* 39, no. 4 (Fall 2004): 541–63.

Mudde, Cas, and Cristóbal Rovira Kaltwasser, eds. *Populism in Europe and the Americas: Threat or Corrective for Democracy?* New York: Cambridge University Press, 2012.

Murembya, Leonidas, and Eric Guthrie. "Demographic and Labor Market Profile: Detroit City." Lansing: Michigan Department of Technology, Management, and Budget, April 2015.

Murphy, Tim. "The United States of Sequestration." *Mother Jones*, April 30, 2013.

Nace, Ted. *Gangs of America: The Rise of Corporate Power and the Disabling of Democracy.* San Francisco: Berrett-Koehler.

Nader, Ralph. *Unsafe at Any Speed.* New York: Grossman, 1965.

Nash, Gary B. *The Unknown American Revolution: The Unruly Birth of Democracy and the Struggle to Create America.* New York: Penguin, 2006.

Näsström, Sofia. "The Legitimacy of the People." *Political Theory* 35, no. 5 (October 1, 2007): 624–58.

Neal, Mark Anthony. "Rhythm and Bullshit?" *PopMatters*, June 3, 2005.

Negrón-Gonzales, Genevieve. "Undocumented, Unafraid and Unapologetic: Re-articulatory Practices and Migrant Youth 'Illegality.'" *Latino Studies* 12, no. 2 (2014): 259–78.

Nel, Philip. *The Avant-Garde and American Postmodernity: Small Incisive Shocks.* Jackson: University Press of Mississippi, 2002.

Neuhaus, Richard John. *The Naked Public Square: Religion and Democracy in America.* 2nd ed. Grand Rapids, MI: Wm. B. Eerdmans, 1988.

Ngai, Mai M. *Impossible Subjects: Illegal Aliens and the Making of Modern America.* Princeton, NJ: Princeton University Press, 2004.

Nicholls, Walter. *The DREAMers: How the Undocumented Youth Movement Transformed the Immigrant Rights Debate.* Stanford, CA: Stanford University Press, 2013.

Nugent, Walter. *The Tolerant Populists: Kansas, Populism and Nativism*. Chicago: University of Chicago Press, 1963.

Obama, Barack. "Remarks by the President on the American Automotive Industry." Speech given at the White House, March 30, 2009.

O'Connor, Patrick, and Mike Gecan. "Occupy Wall Street's Anger Isn't Enough: How the Push for Change Can Be Sustained." *NY Daily News*, October 16, 2011.

Oliviera, Rebecca. "City Life Expands to National Activities." *Jamaica Plain Gazette*, March 30,

Olson, Joel. "The Freshness of Fanaticism: The Abolitionist Defense of Zealotry." *Perspectives on Politics* 5, no. 4 (2007): 685–701.

Orey, Michael, and Keith Epstein. "Will Populist Rage Hurt Corporate America?" *BusinessWeek*, March 24, 2009.

Orr, Marion, ed. *Transforming the City: Community Organizing and the Challenge of Political Change*. Lawrence: University Press of Kansas, 2007.

Pack, Lauren. "6 Arrested during Protest at Butler County Jail." *Dayton Daily News*, December 19, 2013.

Palmer, Bruce. *"Man over Money": The Southern Populist Critique of American Capitalism*. Chapel Hill: University of North Carolina Press, 2010.

Panizza, Francisco, Benjamin Arditi, Sebastian Barros, Glenn Bowman, and David Howarth. *Populism and the Mirror of Democracy*. London: Verso, 2005.

Papadopoulos, Yannis. "Populism, the Democratic Question, and Contemporary Governance." In *Democracies and the Populist Challenge*, edited by Yves Mény and Yves Surel, 45–61. New York: Palgrave Macmillan, 2002.

Pareles, Jon. "Heartland Rock: Bruce's Children." *New York Times*, August 30, 1987.

Parker, Christopher, and Matt Barreto. *Change They Can't Believe In: The Tea Party and Reactionary Politics in America*. Princeton, NJ: Princeton University Press, 2013.

Paul, David. "Tea Party Movement Obsession with Socialism Misses the Cause of Middle Class Plight." *Huffington Post*, October 10, 2010.

Payne, Charles M. *I've Got the Light of Freedom: The Organizing Tradition and the Mississippi Freedom Struggle*. 2nd ed. Berkeley: University of California Press, 2007.

Pérez-Brennan, Tanya. "Ocupemos El Barrio: A Growing Voice within the 99 Percent." *Fox News Latino*, December 21, 2011.

Perone, James E. *Music of the Counterculture Era*. Westport, CT: Greenwood, 2004.

Peutz, Nathalie, and Nicholas De Genova. "Introduction." In *The Deportation Regime: Sovereignty, Space, and the Freedom of Movement*, edited by Nicholas De Genova and Nathalie Peutz, 1–29. Durham, NC: Duke University Press, 2010.

Pickett, Justin T., Daniel Tope, and Rose Bellandi. "'Taking Back Our Country': Tea Party Membership and Support for Punitive Crime Control Policies." *Sociological Inquiry* 84, no. 2 (May 2014): 167–90.

Piven, Frances Fox. "On the Organizational Question." *Sociological Quarterly* 54 (2013): 191–93.

Polanyi, Karl. *The Great Transformation: The Political and Economic Origins of Our Time*. 2nd ed. Boston: Beacon Press, 2001.

Pollack, Norman, ed. *The Populist Mind*. Indianapolis: Macmillan, 1967.

Postel, Charles. *The Populist Vision*. New York: Oxford University Press, 2007.

Postel, Charles. "The Tea Parties in Historical Perspective: A Conservative Response to a Crisis of Political Economy." In *Steep: The Precipitous Rise of the Tea Party*, edited by Lawrence Rosenthal and Christine Trost, 25–46. Berkeley: University of California Press, 2012.

Pough, Gwendolyn. "Seeds and Legacies: Tapping the Potential in Hip-Hop." In *That's the Joint! Hip-Hop Studies Reader*, edited by Murray Forman and Mark Anthony Neal, 283–90. New York: Routledge, 2004.

Pratt, Mary Louise. "Arts of the Contact Zone." *Profession*, 1991, 33–40.

Pratt, Mary Louise. *Imperial Eyes: Travel Writing and Transculturation*. 2nd ed. New York: Routledge, 2007.

Raines, Howell. "Winning the Populism PR War." *Washington Post*, July 27, 2004.

Rana, Aziz. *The Two Faces of American Freedom*. Cambridge, MA: Harvard University Press, 2010.

Randazzo, Anthony. "Populist Rage Over Foreclosures Doesn't Justify a Breakdown in the Rule of Law." *National Review Online*, November 1, 2010.

Ransby, Barbara. *Ella Baker and the Black Freedom Movement: A Radical Democratic Vision*. Chapel Hill: University of North Carolina Press, 2005.

Raphael, Ray. *A People's History of the American Revolution: How Common People Shaped the Fight for Independence*. New York: Harper Perennial, 2002.

Rawls, John. *Political Liberalism*. 2nd ed. New York: Columbia University Press, 2005.

Reagon, Bernice Johnson. "Coalition Politics: Turning the Century." In *Home Girls: A Black Feminist Anthology*, edited by Barbara Smith, 343–56. New Brunswick, NJ: Rutgers University Press, 1983.

Reinhardt, Mark. *The Art of Being Free: Taking Liberties with Tocqueville, Marx, and Arendt*. Ithaca, NY: Cornell University Press, 1997.

Reitman, Jane. "The Stealth War on Abortion." *Rolling Stone*, January 15, 2014.

Remnick, David. "We Are Alive: Bruce Springsteen at Sixty-Two." *New Yorker*, July 30, 2012.

Riker, William H. *Liberalism against Populism: A Confrontation between the Theory of Democracy and the Theory of Social Choice*. Prospect Heights, IL: Waveland Press, 1988.

Rivas, Jorge. "DREAMers Declare Undocumented Youth Mental Health Day." *Colorlines*, January 31, 2012.

Rochester, Anna. *The Populist Movement in the United States*. New York: International Publishers, 1943.

Roediger, David R. *The Wages of Whiteness: Race and the Making of the American Working Class*. London: Verso, 2007.

Rogin, Michael. *Ronald Reagan the Movie and Other Episodes in Political Demonology*. Berkeley: University of California Press, 1988.

Rose, Mark H., Bruce E. Seely, and Paul F. Barrett. *The Best Transportation System in the World: Railroads, Trucks, Airlines, and American Public Policy in the Twentieth Century*. Philadelphia: University of Pennsylvania Press, 2010.

Rosen, Jeffrey. "The Tea Party's Radical Constitutionalism." *New York Times*, November 26, 2010.

Rosen, Ruth. "The Tea Party and Angry White Women." *Dissent* 59, no. 1 (Winter 2012): 61–65.

Rose, Tricia. *Black Noise: Rap Music and Black Culture in Contemporary America*. Hanover, NH: Wesleyan University Press, 1994.

Ross, Andrew, and Seth Ackerman. "Strike Debt and Rolling Jubilee: The Debate." *Dissent*, November 13, 2012.

Rousseau, Jean-Jacques. *On the Social Contract*. Translated by Donald A. Cress. Indianapolis: Hackett, 1988.

Ruby, Ryan. "On the People's Mic: Politics in a Post-literate Age." *Journal for Occupied Studies*, February 2012.

Rustin, Bayard. *Time on Two Crosses: The Collected Writings of Bayard Rustin*. San Francisco: Cleis Press, 2003.

Saez, Emmanuel, and Gabriel Zucman. "Exploding Wealth Inequality in the United States." Washington, DC: Washington Center for Equitable Growth, October 20, 2014.

Salazar, Cristian. "Toilets Bring Relief to Occupy Wall Street." *Huffington Post*, November 5, 2011.

Sanders, Elizabeth. *Roots of Reform: Farmers, Workers, and the American State, 1877–1917*. Chicago: University of Chicago Press, 1999.

Santos, Boaventura de Sousa. *The Rise of the Global Left: The World Social Forum and Beyond*. London: Zed Books, 2006.

Saul, Stephanie. "Conservative Groups Focus on Registration in Swing States." *New York Times*, September 16, 2012.

Saval, Nikil. "Scenes from Occupied Philadelphia." In *Occupy! Scenes from Occupied America*, edited by Astra Taylor, Keith Gessen, et al., 157–62. London: Verso, 2011.

Scahill, Jeremy. *Dirty Wars: The World Is a Battlefield*. New York: Nation Books, 2014.

Schilt, Kristen, and Elke Zobl. "Connecting the Dots: Riot Grrrls, Ladyfests, and the International Grrl Zine Network." In *Next Wave Cultures: Feminism, Subcultures, Activism*, edited by Anita Harris, 171–92. New York: Routledge, 2007.

Schlesinger, Arthur Meier. *The Disuniting of America: Reflections on a Multicultural Society*. Rev. ed. New York: W. W. Norton, 1998.

Schmitt, Carl. *The Concept of the Political*. Chicago: University of Chicago Press, 2008.

Schmitt, Carl. *The Crisis of Parliamentary Democracy*. Cambridge, MA: MIT Press, 1988.

Schmitt, Eli, Astra Taylor, and Mark Greif. "Scenes from an Occupation." In *Occupy! Scenes from Occupied America*, edited by Astra Taylor, Keith Gessen, et al., 1–6. London: Verso, 2011.

Schoonover, Thomas D. *Uncle Sam's War of 1898 and the Origins of Globalization*. Lexington: University Press of Kentucky, 2003.

Schulte, Brigid, and Paul Duggan. "Obama Urges Nation to Demand a 'Common Sense' Balance on Gun Control, Gun Rights." *Washington Post*, September 22, 2013.

Schwartz, Michael. *Radical Protest and Social Structure: The Southern Farmers' Alliance and Cotton Tenancy, 1880–1890*. Chicago: University of Chicago Press, 1976.

Scott, James C. *The Art of Not Being Governed: An Anarchist History of Upland Southeast Asia*. New Haven, CT: Yale University Press, 2010.

Scott, James C. *Domination and the Arts of Resistance: Hidden Transcripts*. New Haven, CT: Yale University Press, 1992.

Seif, Hinda. " 'Layers of Humanity': Interview with Undocuqueer Artivist Julio Salgado." *Latino Studies* 12, no. 2 (June 2014): 300–309.

Sen, Rinku. "Race and Occupy Wall Street." *Nation*, October 26, 2011.

Sender, Katherine. *Business, Not Politics: The Making of the Gay Market*. New York: Columbia University Press, 2005.

Senra, Paulo. "We Came Unarmed (This Time)!" *CNN iReport*, January 10, 2011.

Shefter, Martin. "Trade Unions and Political Machines: The Organization and Disorganization of the American Working Class in the Late Nineteenth Century." In *Working-Class Formation: Nineteenth-Century Patterns in Western Europe and the United States*, edited by Aristide R. Zolberg and Ira Katznelson, 197–276. Princeton, NJ: Princeton University Press, 1986.

Shepeard, Crystal. "No One Is Safe from Backlash When Criticizing the Police, Even the Police." *Truthout*, January 11, 2015.

Sher, Lauren. "CNBC's Santelli Rants about Housing Bailout." ABCNews.com, February 19, 2009.

Sheridan, Barrett. "Populist Outrage? There's an App for That." *Newsweek*, July 21, 2009.

Shulman, George M. *American Prophecy: Race and Redemption in American Political Culture*. Minneapolis: University of Minnesota Press, 2008.

Silver, Nate. "The Geography of Occupying Wall Street (and Everywhere Else)." *FiveThirtyEight, New York Times*, October 17, 2011.

Simmons, Sylvie. *I'm Your Man: The Life of Leonard Cohen*. New York: Ecco, 2013.

Sitrin, Marina. "One No, Many Yesses." In *Occupy! Scenes from Occupied America*, edited by Astra Taylor, Keith Gessen, et al., 7–11. London: Verso, 2011.

Sitrin, Marina, and Dario Azzellini. *They Can't Represent Us! Reinventing Democracy from Greece to Occupy*. London: Verso, 2014.

Sivulka, Juliann. *Soap, Sex, and Cigarettes: A Cultural History of American Advertising*. 2nd ed. Boston: Cengage Learning, 2011.

Skinner, Daniel. "'Keep Your Government Hands Off My Medicare!': An Analysis of Media Effects on Tea Party Health Care Politics." *New Political Science* 34, no. 4 (December 2012): 605–19.

Skocpol, Theda, and Vanessa Williamson. *The Tea Party and the Remaking of Republican Conservatism*. New York: Oxford University Press, 2013.

Slade, Giles. *Made to Break: Technology and Obsolescence in America*. Cambridge, MA: Harvard University Press, 2007.

Smith, Tovia. "'Occupy Boston' Holds On as Other Camps Close." NPR.com, February 9, 2012.

Solnit, Rebecca. "Throwing Out the Master's Tools." In *Occupy! Scenes from Occupied America*, edited by Astra Taylor, Keith Gessen, et al., 146–56. London: Verso, 2011.

Sommeiller, Estelle, and Mark Price. "The Increasingly Unequal States of America: Income Inequality by State, 1917 to 2012." Washington, DC: Economic Policy Institute, January 26, 2015.

Sorkin, Andrew Ross. "Rich and Sort of Rich." *New York Times*, May 14, 2011.

Sparks, Holloway. "Mama Grizzlies and Guardians of the Republic: The Democratic and Intersectional Politics of Anger in the Tea Party Movement." *New Political Science* 37, no. 1 (2015): 24–47.

Spragens. Thomas A. *Getting the Left Right: The Transformation, Decline, and Reformation of American Liberalism*. Lawrence: University Press of Kansas, 2009.

Stanley, Ben. "The Thin Ideology of Populism." *Journal of Political Ideologies* 13, no. 1 (February 2008): 95–110.

Stavrakakis, Yannis, and Giorgos Katsambekis. "Left-Wing Populism in the European Periphery: The Case of Syriza." *Journal of Political Ideologies* 19, no. 2 (2014): 119–42.

Steele, Shelby. *The Content of Our Character: A New Vision of Race in America.* New York: Harper Perennial, 1998.

Stevenson, Seth. "Can Rosa Parks Sell Pickup Trucks?" *Slate*, October 9, 2006.

Stewart, Angus. "The Social Roots." In *Populism: Its Meanings and National Characteristics*, edited by Ghita Ionescu and Ernest Gellner, 180–96. London: Weidenfeld and Nicolson, 1969.

Stiglitz, Joseph E. *Freefall: America, Free Markets, and the Sinking of the World Economy.* New York: Norton, 2010.

Stock, Catherine McNicol. *Rural Radicals: From Bacon's Rebellion to the Oklahoma City Bombing.* New York: Penguin, 1997.

Storing, Herbert. *What the Anti-Federalists Were For: The Political Thought of the Opponents.* Chicago: University of Chicago Press, 1981.

Stout, Jeffrey. *Blessed Are the Organized: Grassroots Democracy in America.* Princeton, NJ: Princeton University Press, 2012.

Stowell, David O. *Streets, Railroads, and the Great Strike of 1877.* Chicago: University of Chicago Press, 1999.

Stringer, Kortney. "Chevy Silverado Ads Go for Reaction: Some Viewers Offended, Others Feel Patriotic about Images." *Detroit Free Press*, October 23, 2006.

Sullivan, Andy. "Insight: Largely out of Sight, U.S. Budget Sequester Still Cuts Deep." Reuters. September 28, 2013.

Sullivan, Laura. "Prison Economics Helped Drive Immigration Law." NPR.com, October 28, 2010.

Sumner, William Graham. *What Social Classes Owe to Each Other.* Champaign, IL: Book Jungle, 2008.

Swan, Richelle, and Kristin Bates. "Social Justice in the Face of the Storm: When Natural Disasters Become Social Disasters." In *Through the Eye of Katrina: Social Justice in the United States*, edited by Kristin A. Bates and Richelle Swan, 3–14. 2nd ed. Durham, NC: Carolina Academic Press, 2010.

Taggart, Paul. *Populism*. Buckingham, UK: Open University Press, 2000.

Taggart, Paul. "Populism and Representative Politics in Contemporary Europe." *Journal of Political Ideologies* 9, no. 3 (2004): 241–52.

Taggart, Paul. "Populism and the Pathology of Representative Politics." In *Democracies and the Populist Challenge*, edited by Yves Mény and Yves Surel, 62–80. New York: Palgrave Macmillan, 2002.

Taibbi, Matt. "Secrets and Lies of the Bailout." *Rolling Stone*, January 4, 2013.

"Taking Immigration Law into Their Own Hands: Protesters Form Human Chain to Stop Deportation Bus." *Fox News Latino*, October 11, 2013.

Taracena, Maria. "Immigration, LGBT Rights Advocates Take the Streets of Phoenix to Demand Release of Transgender Asylum Seeker in Detention." *Tucson Weekly*, January 28, 2015.

Taylor, Charles. *Modern Social Imaginaries.* Durham, NC: Duke University Press, 2003.

Taylor, Sunaura. "Scenes from Occupied Oakland." In *Occupy! Scenes from Occupied America*, edited by Astra Taylor, Keith Gessen, et al., 134–45. London: Verso, 2011.

Theoharis, Jeanne. *The Rebellious Life of Mrs. Rosa Parks.* Boston: Beacon Press, 2014.

"The Thinking Man's Guide to Populist Rage." *Newsweek*, March 30, 2009.

"This Is the New GM: General Motors Company 2010 Annual Report." Detroit: General Motors Company, 2010.

Thomas-Breitfeld, Sean, and Marnie Brady. "The New Bottom Line: Building Alignment and Scale to Confront the Economic Crisis." New York: Building Movement Project, 2014.

Tilly, Charles. *Contentious Performances*. New York: Cambridge University Press, 2008.

Tindall, George Brown, ed. *A Populist Reader: Selections from the Works of American Populist Leaders*. Gloucester, MA: Peter Smith, 1966.

Tinker, Tony, Cheryl Lehman, and Marilyn Neimark. "Bookkeeping for Capitalism: The Mystery of Accounting for Unequal Exchange." In *Political Economy of Information*, edited by Vincent Mosco and Janet Wasko, 188–216. Madison: University of Wisconsin Press, 1988.

Tocqueville, Alexis de. *Democracy in America*. Edited by J. P. Mayer. Translated by George Lawrence. New York: Harper Perennial Modern Classics, 2006.

Todd, Sarah. "Boston Approves Responsible Banking Bill." *National Mortgage News*, September 20, 2013.

Tomasi, John. *Liberalism beyond Justice: Citizens, Society, and the Boundaries of Political Theory*. Princeton, NJ: Princeton University Press, 2001.

"Total US Ad Spending to See Largest Increase since 2004." *eMarketer*, July 2, 2014.

Trost, Christine, and Lawrence Rosenthal. "Introduction: The Rise of the Tea Party." In *Steep: The Precipitous Rise of the Tea Party*, edited by Lawrence Rosenthal and Christine Trost, 1–22. Berkeley: University of California Press, 2012.

Tully, James. *Strange Multiplicity: Constitutionalism in an Age of Diversity*. New York: Cambridge University Press, 1995.

Unterberger, Richie. *Eight Miles High: Folk-Rock's Flight from Haight-Ashbury to Woodstock*. San Francisco: Backbeat Books, 2003.

Urbinati, Nadia. "Democracy and Populism." *Constellations* 5, no. 1 (1998): 110–24.

Vargas, Zaragosa. *Proletarians of the North: Mexican Industrial Workers in Detroit and the Midwest, 1917–1933*. Berkeley: University of California Press, 1999.

Veblen, Thorstein. *The Theory of the Leisure Class*. Edited by Martha Banta. Oxford: Oxford University Press, 2009.

Villazor, Rose Cuison. "The Undocumented Closet." *North Carolina Law Review* 92 (2013): 1–74.

Virilio, Paul. *Speed and Politics*. Translated by Mark Polizzotti. Los Angeles: Semiotext(e), 2006.

Vlasic, Bill. "Annual Sales for American Automakers Reach a 6-Year High." *New York Times*, January 3, 2014.

Vlasic, Bill. "Detroit Is Now a Charity Case for Carmakers." *New York Times*, September 22, 2013.

Vlasic, Bill, and Annie Lowrey. "U.S. Ends Bailout of G.M., Selling Last Shares of Stock." *DealBook, New York Times*, December 9, 2013.

Vrooman, John. "Theory of the Big Dance: The Playoff Pay-off in Pro Sports Leagues." In *The Oxford Handbook of Sports Economics*, vol. 1: *The Economics of Sports*, edited by Leo H. Kahane and Stephen Shmanske, 51–75. New York: Oxford University Press, 2012.

Walker, Jesse. "The Great Libertarian-Populist Roundup: Hit & Run." *Reason*, July 29, 2013.

Wang, Jennifer Hyland. "'A Struggle of Contending Forces': Race, Gender, and Political Memory in *Forrest Gump*." *Cinema Journal* 39, no. 3 (Spring 2000): 92–96.

Warner, Michael. "Introduction." In *Fear of a Queer Planet: Queer Politics and Social Theory*, edited by Michael Warner, vii–xxxi. Minneapolis: University of Minnesota Press, 1993.

Warner, Michael. *Publics and Counterpublics*. New York: Zone Books, 2005.

Warner, Michael. *The Trouble with Normal*. New York: Free Press, 1995.

Warren, Dorian. "Occupy Wall Street Emerges as 'First Populist Movement' on the Left since the 1930s." Interview by Amy Goodman. *Democracy Now!* October 10, 2011.

Warren, Mark R. *Dry Bones Rattling: Community Building to Revitalize American Democracy*. Princeton, NJ: Princeton University Press, 2001.

Watkins, S. Craig. "A Nation of Millions: Hip-Hop Culture and the Legacy of Black Nationalism." *Communication Review* 4, no. 3 (January 1, 2001): 373–98.

Weeks, Kathi. "Life within and against Work: Affective Labor, Feminist Critique, and Post-Fordist Politics." *Ephemera: Theory and Politics in Organization* 7, no. 1 (2007): 233–49.

Weiner, Rachel. "Keystone XL Pipeline Unites Left and Right." *Washington Post*, November 14, 2011.

Wells, Paul. "The Last Rebel: Southern Rock and Nostalgic Continuities." In *Dixie Debates: Perspectives on Southern Culture*, edited by Richard King and Helen Taylor, 115–29. New York: New York University Press, 1996.

West, Cornel. *Race Matters*. New York: Vintage, 1994.

West, Cornel. "Populism: A Black Socialist Critique." In *The New Populism: The Politics of Empowerment*, edited by Harry C. Boyte and Frank Riessman, 207–12. Philadelphia: Temple University Press, 1986.

Wheeler, Alina. *Designing Brand Identity: An Essential Guide for the Whole Branding Team*. 4th ed. Hoboken, NJ: John Wiley and Sons, 2012.

Whitman, Walt. "Democratic Vistas." In *Walt Whitman: Poetry and Prose*. New York: Library of America, 1982.

Wiebe, Robert H. *The Search for Order, 1877–1920*. New York: Hill and Wang, 1966.

Wiles, Peter. "A Syndrome, Not a Doctrine." In *Populism: Its Meanings and National Characteristics*, edited by Ghita Ionescu and Ernest Gellner, 166–79. London: Weidenfeld and Nicolson, 1969.

Wilson, Angelia R., and Cynthia Burack. "'Where Liberty Reigns and God Is Supreme': The Christian Right and the Tea Party Movement." *New Political Science* 34, no. 2 (June 2012): 172–90.

Wolf, Naomi. "Revealed: How the FBI Coordinated the Crackdown on Occupy." *Guardian*, December 29, 2012.

Wolin, Sheldon. "Agitated Times." *Parallax* 11, no. 4 (2005): 2–11.

Wolin, Sheldon. "Contract and Birthright." In *The New Populism: The Politics of Empowerment*, edited by Harry C. Boyte and Frank Riessman, 305–18. Philadelphia: Temple University Press, 1986.

Wolin, Sheldon. *Democracy Incorporated: Managed Democracy and the Specter of Inverted Totalitarianism*. Princeton, NJ: Princeton University Press, 2010.

Wolin, Sheldon. "Fugitive Democracy." In *Democracy and Difference: Contesting the Boundaries of the Political*, edited by Seyla Benhabib, 31–45. Princeton, NJ: Princeton University Press, 1996.

Wolin, Sheldon. "The People's Two Bodies." *Democracy: A Journal of Political Renewal and Radical Change* 1, no. 1 (1981): 9–24.

Wolin, Sheldon. *Politics and Vision: Continuity and Innovation in Western Political Thought*. Princeton, NJ: Princeton University Press, 2004.

Wolin, Sheldon. *The Presence of the Past: Essays on the State and the Constitution*. Baltimore: Johns Hopkins University Press, 1990.

Wolin, Sheldon. "Why Democracy?" *Democracy: A Journal of Political Renewal and Radical Change* 1, no. 1 (1981): 3–5.

Wood, Gordon S. *The Creation of the American Republic, 1776–1787*. Chapel Hill: University of North Carolina Press, 1998.

Wood, Mikael. "Billy Ray Cyrus Plays L.A.'s Bootleg Bar." *Los Angeles Times*, September 1, 2012.

Wood, Richard L. *Faith in Action: Religion, Race, and Democratic Organizing in America*. Chicago: University of Chicago Press, 2002.

Woodward, C. Vann. *Origins of the New South, 1877–1913: A History of the South*. Revised ed. Baton Rouge: Louisiana State University Press, 1981.

Woodward, C. Vann. "The Populist Heritage and the Intellectual." *American Scholar* 29, no. 1 (Winter 1959): 55–72.

Worsley, Peter. "The Concept of Populism." In *Populism: Its Meanings and National Characteristics*, edited by Ghiṭa Ionescu and Ernest Gellner, 212–50. London: Weidenfeld and Nicolson, 1969.

Worton, Seth. "General Motors: Lost Dominance." In *Industry and Firm Studies*, edited by Victor J. Tremblay and Carol Horton Tremblay, 269–92. Armonk, NY: M.E. Sharpe, 2007.

Writers for the 99%. *Occupying Wall Street: The Inside Story of an Action That Changed America*. Chicago: Haymarket Books, 2012.

Yancy, George, and Judith Butler. "What's Wrong with 'All Lives Matter'?" *New York Times*, January 12, 2015.

Yoakum, Jim. "Rock the Cashbox: The Great Rock n Roll Sellout." *PopMatters*, April 14, 2014.

Zenilman, Avi. "Obama's Oil Spill Speech: Will the Technocrat Take Action?" *Huffington Post*, June 16, 2010.

Zernike, Kate. *Boiling Mad: Inside Tea Party America*. New York: Times Books, 2010.

Zimmerman, Arely. "Documenting DREAMs: New Media, Undocumented Youth and the Immigrant Rights Movement." Los Angeles: Media, Activism and Participatory Politics Project at the Annenberg School for Communications and Journalism, University of Southern California, June 6, 2012.

Zimmerman, Arely. "A Dream Detained: Undocumented Latino Youth and the Dream Movement." *NACLA Report on the Americas*, November–December 2011.

Žižek, Slavoj. "Don't Fall in Love with Yourselves: Remarks at Zuccotti Park, October 9." In *Occupy! Scenes from Occupied America*, edited by Astra Taylor, Keith Gessen, et al., 66–69. London: Verso, 2011.

Žižek, Slavoj. *Tarrying with the Negative: Kant, Hegel, and the Critique of Ideology.* Durham, NC: Duke University Press, 1993.

Zuesse, Eric. "Final Proof the Tea Party Was Founded as a Bogus AstroTurf Movement." *Huffington Post*, October 22, 2013.

DISCOGRAPHY

Bikini Kill. *Pussy Whipped.* Kill Rock Stars, 1993.
Chapman, Tracy. *Tracy Chapman.* Elektra, 1988.
Cohen, Leonard. *New Skin for the Old Ceremony.* Columbia, 1974.
Cohen, Leonard. *The Future.* Columbia, 1992.
DiFranco, Ani. *Imperfectly.* Righteous Babe, 1992.
DiFranco, Ani. *Like I Said: Songs 1990–1991.* Righteous Babe, 1993.
DiFranco, Ani. *Not a Pretty Girl.* Columbia, 1995.
Dr. Dre. *The Chronic.* Death Row, 1992.
Lynyrd Skynyrd, *Second Helping.* MCA, 1974.
McLean, Don. *American Pie.* United Artists, 1971.
Mellencamp, John. *The Lonesome Jubilee.* Mercury, 1987.
Mellencamp, John. *Uh-huh.* Mercury, 2005.
Mellencamp, John. *Whenever We Wanted.* Mercury, 1991.
N.W.A. *Straight Outta Compton.* Ruthless Records, 1988.
Pet Shop Boys. *Very.* Parlaphone, 1993.
Philadelphia (Music from the Motion Picture). Epic Soundtrax, 1993.
Public Enemy. *Fear of a Black Planet.* Def Jam, 1990
Public Enemy. *It Takes a Nation of Millions to Hold Us Back.* Def Jam, 1995
Run-D.M.C. *Raising Hell.* Profile, 1986.
Shakur, Tupac. *2Pacalypse Now.* Interscope, 1991.
Shakur, Tupac. *Me against the World.* Interscope, 1995.
Springsteen, Bruce. *Born to Run.* Columbia, 1975.
Springsteen, Bruce. *The Essential Bruce Springsteen.* Columbia, 2003.
Springsteen, Bruce. *The Ghost of Tom Joad.* Columbia, 1995.
Springsteen, Bruce. *Human Touch.* Columbia, 1992.
Springsteen, Bruce. *Lucky Town.* Columbia, 1992.
Young, Neil. *This Note's for You.* Reprise Records, 1988.

VIDEOGRAPHY

Albright, David. "This Is Our Country." *YouTube* video, 1:01. January 13, 2007. https://youtu.be/nv1vZG0zdhg.
CapsNut. "Caps 'Our Country' Commercial." *YouTube* video, 0:30. December 14, 2006. https://youtu.be/YIZunthwQO8.
Dreamers Adrift. "Undocumented and Awkward: Episode 7." *YouTube* video, 1:23. December 21, 2011. https://youtu.be/II7AfS2iAb4.
Dreamers Adrift. "Undocumented and Awkward: Episode 13." *YouTube* video, 2:33. June 4, 2012. https://youtu.be/CkdonvXGt5U.

Dvpringle. " 'This Is Our Country' Chevrolet Silverado Ad Parody." *YouTube* video, 1:07. October 10, 2006. https://youtu.be/SPNMERRPuHw.

Election06. "Mellencamp Our Country for Real Americans." *YouTube* video, 0:43. November 19, 2006. https://youtu.be/gHvXaOLO3Bg.

Election06. "Mellencamp Our Country Red State Satire." *YouTube* video, 0:32. November 19, 2006. https://youtu.be/wJ70Fe0WeKY.

Forthoffirth. "This Is Our Country (My Version)." *YouTube* video, 0:41. October 13, 2007. https://youtu.be/vbfk5aDhpwI.

Gooberman, Russ. "This Is Our Country." *YouTube* video, 2:47. July 3, 2007. https://youtu.be/tM9PGB65STg.

Hall, Spencer. "EDSBS Presents: This Is Our Country." *YouTube* video, 3:37, July 2, 2008. https://youtu.be/wly-F6NWXv4.

Impers1. "This Is Our Country, Ron Paul." *YouTube* video, 3:46. December 8, 2007. https://youtu.be/NTiubLO0X5A.

Jacobsladderfat. "Toyota: This Is Our Country." *YouTube* video, 0:59. March 9, 2011, https://youtu.be/YQxC58naORc.

Moore, Michael. *Roger & Me*. Warner Home Video. 1990.

National Lampoon. "Oh Dear God . . . This Is Our Country." *YouTube* video, 0:40. May 23, 2007. https://youtu.be/ANguu1WJ8jw.

New American Media. "For 'Undocuqueers,' SCOTUS Rulings Only Half the Battle." *Vimeo* video, 2:49. http://vimeo.com/71148667.

Niefga. "NFL Chevy Spoof 1." *YouTube* video, 3:38. December 5, 2006. https://youtu.be/GKwIEzx1AVw.

"Occupy Wall Street Divided." *Daily Show* video, 5:52. November 16, 2011. http://thedailyshow.cc.com/videos/5510me/occupy-wall-street-divided.

Paul, John. "This Is Our Country." *YouTube* video, 3:17. November 14, 2006. https://youtu.be/i9GAqzbwfWM.

PintoPopProductions. "Toyota: This Is OUR Country." *YouTube* video, 0:52, December 7, 2006. https://youtu.be/gnF0-J5V7qk.

Qbnscholar, "Chevy Truck Country 3." *YouTube* video, 0:29. October 31, 2006. https://youtu.be/xVd5Ut-R_lE.

Quinn, John. "Neil Young 'Big Cadillac Giveaway' 1983 Commercial." *YouTube* video, 0:59. January 15, 2012. https://youtu.be/Hu_0X0dLkPs.

Searchin4thesound. "Democracy Coming." *YouTube* video, 2:21. November 25, 2007. https://youtu.be/Q0qlpHRycEc.

SpiderRider3. "This Is Our Truck: Chevy Commercial Parody." *YouTube* video, 1:08. August 11, 2010, https://youtu.be/yEYPLek6EF8

ThinkProgress6's channel. "Crowd Yells Let Him Die." *YouTube* video, 1:04. September 12, 2011. https://youtu.be/PepQF7G-It0.

Zemeckis, Robert. *Forrest Gump*. Paramount, 1994.